GREENLAND

GILL & ALISTAIR CAMPBELL

www.bradtguides.com

Bradt Guides Ltd, UK
The Globe Pequot Press Inc, USA

Bradt GUIDES

TRAVEL TAKEN SERIOUSLY

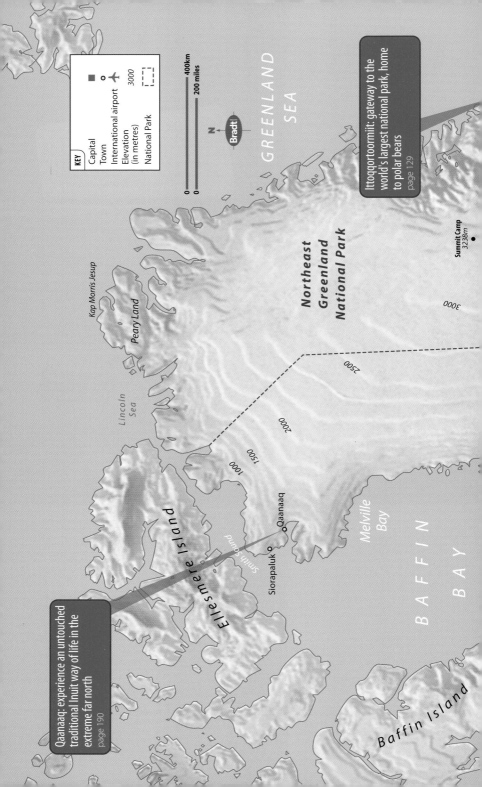

Qaanaaq: experience an untouched traditional Inuit way of life in the extreme far north
page 190

Ittoqqortoormiit: gateway to the world's largest national park, home to polar bears
page 129

KEY

■ Capital
○ Town
✈ International airport
3000 Elevation (in metres)
⌐ ⌐ National Park

400km
200 miles
0
0

N

Bradt

GREENLAND SEA

Kap Morris Jesup

Peary Land

Lincoln Sea

Northeast Greenland National Park

Summit Camp
3238m

3000

2500

2000

1500

1000

Ellesmere Island

Smith Sound

Qaanaaq

Siorapaluk

Melville Bay

BAFFIN BAY

Baffin Island

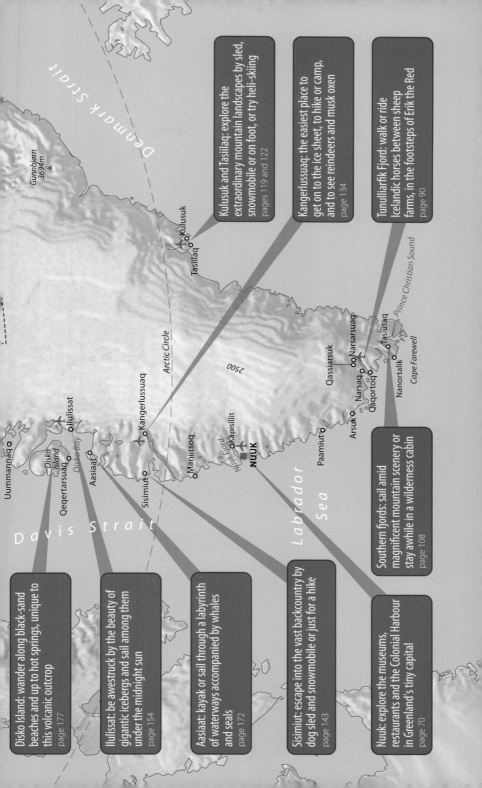

Kulusuk and Tasiilaq: explore the extraordinary mountain landscapes by sled, snowmobile or on foot, or try heli-skiing
pages 119 and 122

Kangerlussuaq: the easiest place to get on to the ice sheet, to hike or camp, and to see reindeers and musk oxen
page 134

Tunulliarfik Fjord: walk or ride Icelandic horses between sheep farms, in the footsteps of Erik the Red
page 90

Denmark Strait

Gunnbjørn 3694m

Arctic Circle

Kulusuk
Tasiilaq

2500

Narsarsuaq
Tasiusaq
Qassiarsuk
Narsaq
Qaqortoq
Nanortalik
Cape Farewell

Prince Christian Sound

Kangerlussuaq

Maniitsoq

Kapisillit
NUUK

Paamiut
Arsuk

Nuuk Fjord

Uummannaq
Disko Island
Qeqertarsuaq
Disko Bay
Ilulissat
Aasiaat
Sisimiut

Davis Strait

Labrador Sea

Southern fjords: sail amid magnificent mountain scenery or stay awhile in a wilderness cabin
page 108

Disko Island: wander along black-sand beaches and up to hot springs, unique to this volcanic outcrop
page 177

Ilulissat: be awestruck by the beauty of gigantic icebergs and sail among them under the midnight sun
page 154

Aasiaat: kayak or sail through a labyrinth of waterways accompanied by whales and seals
page 172

Sisimiut: escape into the vast backcountry by dog sled and snowmobile or just for a hike
page 143

Nuuk: explore the museums, restaurants and the Colonial Harbour in Greenland's tiny capital
page 70

GREENLAND
DON'T MISS...

ICEBERGS
Some jagged, some totally smooth, icebergs can be the size of a car or larger than a high-rise building; they are all beautiful and spell-binding PAGES 4 & 31
(M/D)

WHALES
Thirteen species of whale swim off the coast in summer; humpbacks (pictured) are the most impressive until you see the mythical narwhal PAGE 9
(LL/S)

DOG SLEDDING
Always a magical way to travel and, at times, it may be the only way PAGE 31
(MP/VG)

NORTHERN LIGHTS
Beautiful dancing waves of light; with little light pollution, Greenland is surely the best place in the world to watch the aurora borealis and be mesmerised PAGE 31
(RG/VG)

INUIT CULTURE
Isolated for thousands of years, the Inuit have the purest hunting culture that survives today PAGE 20
(DD/S)

GREENLAND
IN COLOUR

above
(VN/D)

Traditional houses overlook the fjord on the outskirts of Nuuk, Greenland's tiny
capital city PAGE 70

below
(BT/S)

Tiny Qassiarsuk Church sits above the Brattahlíð farmstead – a UNESCO World
Heritage Site – where Erik the Red settled in AD982 PAGE 96

Some 1,400 Inuit live in Uummannaq, a gateway to Greenland's vast uncompromising wilderness 600km north of the Arctic Circle PAGE 181

above
(DD/S)

In winter, pack ice can prevent ships from reaching port and the fjords become roadways for dog sleds and snowmobiles PAGE 4

right
(L/D)

A centuries-old whale-watching hut near Qeqertarsuaq – one of the best places to spot humpbacks and bowheads PAGE 181

below
(OF/D)

AUTHORS

In 1971, **Gill Campbell** joined an exploratory expedition which spent four months establishing a new overland route from London to Singapore. After two years teaching in New Zealand, she returned to the UK, spending several months backpacking across the Pacific, South America and the Caribbean. With few guidebooks and no internet, local people and fellow travellers were the only source of information.

Alistair Campbell's early travels were often business related; he spent months, sometimes years, working in cities all over Europe and Asia. Whenever not at work, he was walking, talking, eating and drinking with local people. The differences between countries, between peoples, has constantly fascinated him.

Gill and Alistair continue to travel, both in the UK and across the world. With over 148 countries visited, they are always looking for that new place to visit; that new person who has stories to tell. Now living in Exmoor National Park, they volunteer for the National Trust, restoring ancient dry-stone walls. As keen walkers, they have covered all the UK's national trails and written two walking guidebooks. They are also co-authors of two other guidebooks for Bradt.

First edition published July 2024
Bradt Travel Guides Ltd
31a High Street, Chesham, Buckinghamshire, HP5 1BW, England
www.bradtguides.com
Print edition published in the USA by The Globe Pequot Press Inc,
PO Box 480, Guilford, Connecticut 06437-0480

ISBN: 9781784770617

British Library Cataloguing in Publication Data
A catalogue record for this book is available from the British Library

Photographs Alamy Stock Photo: Paul Harris (PH/AWL); Dreamstime.com:
Checco (C/D), Frederik Mathiassen (FM/D), Jiri Vondrous (JV/D), Lochstampfer
(L/D), Mathiasrhode (M/D), Oliver Foerstner (OF/D), Smallredgirl (S/D), Vadim
Nefedov (VN/D), Wirestock (W/D); Shutterstock.com: Anders Peter Photography
(APP/S), Beata Tabak (BT/S), BMJ (BMJ/S), Casper Zuidwijk (CZ/S), Danita
Delimont (DD/S), LouieLea (LL/S), Mathias Berlin (MB/S), Nicolaj Larsen
(NL/S), RavenEyePhoto (REP/S), Tomas Zavadil (TZ/S), Vadim Petrakov (VP/S);
Visit Greenland: Aningaaq Rosing Carlsen (ARC/VG), Mads Pihl (MP/VG),
Rebecca Gustafsson (RG/VG)

Front cover Fishing trawler passing through the Ilulissat Icefjord (PH/AWL)
Back cover, clockwise from top Walking on the ice sheet, Kangerlussuaq (W/D);
carved faces, part of the Stone and Rock sculpture trail, Qaqortoq (JV/D); the
aurora borealis over Nuuk (FM/D)
Title page, clockwise from left Itilleq Church (DD/S); hiking the Arctic Circle Trail
(TZ/S); sled dogs (DD/S)

Maps David McCutcheon FBCart.S. FRGS. Made with Natural Earth. Free vector
and raster map data @ naturalearthdata.com

Typeset by Ian Spick, Bradt Travel Guides Ltd; and Dataworks
Production managed by Jellyfish Print Solutions; printed in India
Digital conversion by www.dataworks.co.in

KEY TO SYMBOLS

════════ Main road	† Church
════════ Minor road	👤 Statue
---------- Footpath	🏛 Cemetery
– –⛴– – Passenger ferry	⊞ Hospital
🚢 Cruise ship berth	🏺 Museum/gallery
⌐=====¬ Airport runway	🎭 Theatre/cinema
➤ Water taxi/small boat	❋ Viewpoint
✈ Airport	🏃 Walking
🚁 Heliport	⛷ Skiing/cross-country skiing
🛈 Tourist information	□––○––□ Ski lift
$ Bank	∴ Historic (archaeological) site
✉ Post office	• Other place of interest
🚗 Car rental/taxis	▲ Summit (height in metres)
🚌 Bus station	National park
	Glacier/ice cap

Acknowledgements

We couldn't have written this book without help from so many people. First among those whom we wish to thank are Hilary Bradt, who so wanted the book to be published, and Tanny Por of Visit Greenland, who looked us in the eye and said, 'We can make this happen.'

The support from friends in Greenland has been huge. Laali Berthelsen and Mirjam Johannesen at Visit Greenland and all the regional destination managers who gave us their time, introduced us to their friends and took us to places we would never have discovered alone – Anna Burdenski, Sara Nissen, Sarah Woodall, Tupaarnaq Kreutzmann Kleist and Asbjørn Dissing Bargsteen – we thank you all.

Our travels in Greenland were not without their challenges but we had a guardian angel in Arnatsiaq Lynge Martens at Greenland Travel who always found a way to get us to our destination. Thanks, too, to Air Greenland whose planes and helicopters not only transported us but also gave us unforgettable views, and to Erna Møller, who organised our travels on the Arctic Umiaq Line coastal ferry, and to the staff on board who made us laugh so often.

Our experiences in Greenland have been enhanced by those who have guided us, more people than we could possibly name, but we especially thank Naasunnguaq Lund of Riding Greenland, Julia Lings at Greenland Dog Adventure, Daniel Mouritsen from Aasiaat Tours, Niels Arkaluk Heilmann of Nuuk Water Taxi, and Ane Kriegbaum Ottens at Albatros Arctic Circle; thank you all for showing us your beautiful country.

We are grateful to three writers who have contributed boxes to our book. Edward Cooper and Matt Spenceley, who have described their lives with the Inuit in northern Greenland and east Greenland respectively, and Oscar Scott Carl for his portrait of a young Greenlandic musician.

Thank you to all the fellow travellers who have told us of their Greenland travels at *kaffemiks*, in airport lounges, over dinner and on boats – your contributions to our book have been invaluable. One fellow traveller we have to name, Ajay Singh, whose generosity got us out of a rather windy east Greenland.

Finally, thank you to Bradt, to Claire Strange, Anna Moores and Susannah Lord, who have been by our side the whole way. We have been Bradt readers for many, many years and we always feel honoured to be Bradt writers, part of an organisation with such a strong commitment to independent travel; reaching the parts of the world that others never venture to.

Contents

LIST OF MAPS

Introduction

Greenland is unlike anywhere else in the world. An island of snow and ice where people have lived for thousands of years; with a culture of hunting and fishing along a coastline of deep, unexplored fjords and sheer, unclimbed mountains. With an adventurous spirit and an inquisitive mind, the opportunities for exploration are endless.

You can camp on the ice sheet with nothing but ice around for hundreds of kilometres and no sound except your breathing. Icebergs larger than tower blocks may float past your hotel window and glaciers calve with thunderous cracks, the shock waves rolling under your small boat. Out to sea, a pod of narwhal may swim past, their tusks breaking above the water, or you might spot a seal or walrus resting on a slab of sea ice. A wilderness walk may end at a remote hut where you can fish for your dinner, watched by a musk ox that's come down to drink. This is the world of the Inuit, and through these experiences you start to appreciate their country and the power of nature here. The sheer size and majesty of this land is almost overwhelming: the biggest icebergs, the largest national park, the largest fjord system, the largest ice sheet and coldest temperatures in the northern hemisphere.

But Greenland is embracing modern technology. Mobile phones have replaced landlines, the airline has more helicopters than planes, electric cars are the new norm and you'll get Wi-Fi and satellite TV in your hotel room. Some things don't change, though. There are still no roads between towns and, in winter, a dog sled is more useful than a boat or car. Some settlements still rely on just two or three supply ships a year and then only when the sea ice allows.

Tourism is developing in Greenland and all the towns have good hotels, as well as budget-friendly hostels. Being a tourist here is relatively expensive, but we have been able to include a wide range of accommodation in most places plus ideas on how to keep your costs down. Small tour operators offer specialist local knowledge and excellent local guides – whether you want to spend a day understanding the Inuit art and culture in Nuuk or two weeks heli-skiing in the mountains, these are the people to make it happen.

The traditional strengths of the Inuit are still evident today. Their communities are close-knit but always welcoming. A change in the weather may mean that their plans become impossible. So the plans change, coffee is drunk, new friends are made and everyone gets to do what they need to do…eventually. The relaxed way the Inuit greet adversity is initially strange, but it is born from their respect for nature.

To immerse yourself in the culture, put on a sealskin suit to ride a traditional dog sled across the frozen wilderness pulled by 12 pure-bred Greenlandic dogs, walk Inuit hunting trails among herds of reindeer, ride Icelandic horses on tracks used by Erik the Red, kayak in a labyrinth of waterways among the icebergs and whales, put on crampons and walk on to the ice sheet, or sit on a sunlit terrace, enjoying a local beer while watching icebergs slowly drifting past. Only then will you appreciate the beauty and grandeur and be lost for words to describe this country and wonder why you had never visited before.

HOW TO USE THIS GUIDE

PRICE CODES Throughout this guide we have used price codes to indicate the cost of those places to stay and eat listed in the guide.

Accommodation price codes Accommodation price codes are based on a standard double room in high season.

$$$$	Luxury	over 1,800kr
$$$	Upmarket	1,301–1,800kr
$$	Mid-range	1,001–1,300kr
$	Budget	under 1,000kr

Restaurant price codes Meal price codes are based on the average cost of a main course.

$$$$	Expensive	over 300kr
$$$	Upmarket	225–300kr
$$	Reasonable	151–224kr
$	Budget	up to 150kr

MAPS
Keys and symbols Maps include alphabetical keys covering the locations of those places to stay, eat or drink that are featured in the book. Note that regional maps may not show all hotels and restaurants in the area: other establishments may be located in towns shown on the map.

Grids and grid references The map on page 76 uses gridlines to allow easy location of sites. Map grid references are listed in square brackets after the name of the place or site of interest in the text, with page number followed by grid number, eg: [76 C3].

x

Part One

GENERAL INFORMATION

Location Northeast of Canada and northwest of Iceland, straddling the Arctic Circle.

Size 2,166,086km^2. About nine times the area of the UK or three times the area of the state of Texas.

Population 56,609 (2023)

Population density 0.026/km^2 – probably the least densely populated area in the world.

Life expectancy 70 years for men; 76 years for women

Climate Arctic. Around the coast, the climate is sub-Arctic but nowhere has a mean temperature of more than 10°C.

Status Greenland is a self-governing autonomous territory within the Kingdom of Denmark.

Capital Nuuk (population 19,604)

Other main towns Sisimiut (5,436), Ilulissat (4,848), Qaqortoq (3,005), Aasiaat (2,903), Maniitsoq (2,519), Tasiilaq (1,904)

Languages The main language is West Greenlandic Inuit or Kalaallisut; Greenlanders also learn Danish and English at school. In east Greenland a different Inuit language, Tunumiit oraasiat, is spoken; it has no written form.

Religion The Church of Greenland is the official Lutheran church.

Currency Danish krone (DKK or kr) which is linked to the euro

Exchange rate £1 = 8.7kr; $1 = 7.0kr; €1 = 7.5kr (April 2024)

National airline Air Greenland

International airports Ilulissat, Ittoqqortoormiit, Kangerlussuaq, Kulusuk, Narsarsuaq, Nuuk

International telephone code +299

Time Most of Greenland is on GMT −2 all year. Three small areas have their own time zones: the Thule air base in the extreme northwest uses GMT −4 in winter and GMT −3 in summer; Ittoqqortoormiit, on the east coast, uses GMT −1 in winter and GMT in summer; and Danmarkshavn, in the far northeast, uses GMT all year round.

Electrical voltage 220V, 50Hz

Weights and measures Metric

Flag Two equal-sized horizontal bands, the top half white and the bottom half red. To the left of centre is a large disk that is coloured in the opposite way, top half red and bottom half white.

National anthem Greenland adopted the national anthem 'Nunarput, utoqqarsuanngoravit' (You, our ancient land) in 1916, but since 1979 'Nuna asiilasooq' (The land of great length) is also recognised and it is particularly used by pro-self-government Inuit people.

Public holidays 1 January (New Year's Day), 6 January (Epiphany), Maundy Thursday, Good Friday, Easter Monday, Prayer Day (fourth Friday after Easter Sunday), Ascension Day (6 weeks after Maundy Thursday), Whit Monday (7 weeks after Easter Monday), 21 June (Ullortuneq or National Day), 24–26 December (Christmas), 31 December (New Year's Eve)

1

Background Information

GEOGRAPHY AND GEOLOGY

Covering an area of 2.16 million square kilometres, Greenland is the world's largest non-continental island; two-thirds of this area is north of the Arctic Circle. Greenland's southernmost point, Cape Farewell or Nunap Isua, is on the same latitude as Anchorage in Alaska, Oslo in Norway and the UK's Shetland Islands. Its northern tip, Cape Morris Jesup, at latitude 83°N, is only 740km from the North Pole. From north to south the island is 2,670km long, and 1,050km from east to west at its widest point.

Canada's Ellesmere Island is only 26km from northwest Greenland across the Nares Strait. Despite this proximity, there is no easy way to cross the strait – it is hazardous for navigation and shipping as icebergs are present all year. Iceland lies 290km off Greenland's southeastern coast across the Denmark Strait (also called the Greenland Strait or Grænlandssund) – there is no ferry connecting these countries.

Many of the geographical statistics for Greenland are astounding. Eighty per cent of the island is virtually flat and covered with an ice sheet that gradually slopes down to the sea. The rocks beneath the ice sheet are ancient; in fact some are the oldest rocks ever to be discovered on earth, dating back 3.8 billion years. The 44,087km-long coast is mountainous and rocky, the highest point being Gunnbjørn Fjeld (3,694m) on the east coast located in the Watkins mountain range.

The ice sheet covers an area of 1.71 million square kilometres. In some parts of Greenland, the ice sheet ends more than 200km from the coast, while in other areas it extends all the way to the sea. In places the ice sheet is 3km thick, and the ice is so heavy that it has pushed the land in the centre of the island below sea level. As the ice sheet continues to thaw, due to climate change (page 5), scientists expect that the land in the centre will slowly rise again. It is a sobering thought that, if Greenland's ice sheet did melt completely, it would increase the water level in all the oceans of the world by 7m.

There are hundreds of glaciers in Greenland flowing from the ice sheet: the three largest are Jakobshavn Isbræ near the town of Ilulissat on the west coast, and Kangerlussuaq and Helhelm on the east coast. These glaciers move down to the ocean at up to 40m per day; on reaching the sea, huge chunks of ice break off the glaciers creating icebergs, a process known as calving.

With a population of just 56,609, Greenland has the lowest population density in the world – there is nearly 40km² of land for every Greenlander – but there is only a narrow coastal strip that supports all of the settlements. There are no roads or railways between settlements, so all travel is by boat, plane, helicopter, snowmobile or dog sled. The dramatic coastline is heavily indented with the largest fjords in the world; glacial water flowing out of the ice sheet plunges into the Arctic waters down these steep-sided inlets. North of the Arctic Circle, the sub-soil remains frozen for

ICE

It is said that there are 50 words for snow and ice in Greenlandic. About 20 of them describe what is falling from the sky – snow, hail, icy mist... – and the remaining 30 describe ice and snow on the ground. This seems an awful lot of words but, if you are Inuit, knowing the difference between *siku* (sea ice) and *qinuq* (slush laying on water) might save your life.

Snow and ice have created the landscape of Greenland and they are something the Inuit live with every day. Describing ice as just 'ice' is useless to them. Do you mean sea ice, pack ice, glacial ice, an ice floe, ridged ice, smooth ice, an iceberg, an icicle, calved ice?

Sea ice is saltwater ice that extends from the shore out to sea. It is up to 5m thick and, when it is formed, is fairly flat. Out to sea, the sea ice is periodically broken up by wave action and this becomes **drift ice**. Single pieces of drift ice can float off alone, looking like giant flat icebergs but actually called **ice floes**. Drift ice pieces tend to move together, driven by wind and currents until they get blocked. When this happens, the drift ice piles into itself and ridges are made as one sheet is pushed into or on to another, forming **pack ice**.

The sea ice that forms in fjords seldom gets very thick because it melts or floats out to sea during the summer. The water at the top end of a fjord is much less saline than seawater due to the fresh water flowing down from the mountains. Fresh water freezes more easily than salt seawater. This can result in the very top of fjords being the last areas to thaw in spring and the first to freeze in autumn.

Glaciers repeatedly calve lumps of ice from their face and, if the glacier reaches the waterline, the calved ice becomes an **iceberg** as it floats away. Because icebergs come from glaciers and glaciers are formed from snow, icebergs are made of fresh water. Since nine-tenths of every iceberg is under water, they often ground on the fjord bed. In winter, icebergs get trapped as sea ice forms around them.

much of the year; most vegetation is stunted and dominated by dwarf trees and shrubs, mosses, lichens and herbs.

The world's largest national park covers 972,000km² of northeastern Greenland – an area more than twice the size of Germany or California – and is a UNESCO Biosphere Reserve. There is no permanent human population in the park, apart from those manning the meteorological and research stations and the Danish Armed Forces Surveillance Unit (Sirius Patrol; page 132). This wild and pristine wilderness is home to abundant wildlife including polar bears, musk oxen, Arctic foxes and snowy owls.

CLIMATE

Owing to its northerly latitude (59° to 83°N), Greenland experiences an Arctic climate. In general, the winters are long and cold and the summers are short and cool, but there are huge variations between the regions. Greenland's remote location and sparse population mean that its air quality is among the best in the world.

COASTAL REGION More than 90% of the population live on the coast, where Greenland's ice-free land is limited to a coastal strip less than 200km wide.

In winter, the temperatures on the west coast are moderated by the warming influence of the Gulf Stream and average about –10°C; the east coast is a little cooler as a cold current from the north carries floating ice into the coastal waters. In the summer months, as the daylight hours increase, temperatures climb, rising to above freezing but still staying mostly below 10°C. In recent years, however, with the effect of climate change, coastal temperatures have, on occasion, exceeded 20°C in July and August.

Precipitation is more abundant along the coasts than on the ice sheet, especially below the Arctic Circle. There can be up to 800mm a year, mostly falling as snow in the winter months. Humidity here is very low, which does make the cold weather feel a little warmer.

Many coastal settlements are found in sheltered bays and fjords, protected from the full force of the winds, which can be strong and cold especially in winter when they blow from the ice sheet and are funnelled down the glaciated valleys. Due to the proximity of the ice sheet, some areas occasionally experience katabatic winds, locally called *piteraqs*. These sweep down under the force of gravity; wind speeds can exceed 300km/h and temperatures can drop below –20°C.

FAR NORTH AND CENTRAL REGION Few people live in this vast northern, inland region permanently covered with snow and ice, and where temperatures remain at or below freezing all year. In December 1991, near the summit of the ice sheet, scientists measured the lowest temperature ever recorded in the northern hemisphere at –69.6°C.

Precipitation is usually light and mainly falls as snow; humidity is very low. Peary Land (the northernmost peninsula) is classified as a polar desert – the air is so dry that no snow falls and the rocks are bare. At any time of year, strong winds blowing down from the North Pole can cause further, significant, drops in temperature.

HOURS OF SUNLIGHT In the very south, the sun will set every day but, in midsummer, there will be daylight for at least 20 hours a day. The further north one goes, so the summer days lengthen and once north of the Arctic Circle between early June and mid-July, there are days of midnight sun. In the south in winter, the hours of daylight are short but the sun will always rise; once you are above the Arctic Circle there are days when the sun will not appear. In the far north, there are four months in the summer when the sun never sets, and in winter, the sun sets in late October and does not return again until February.

CLIMATE CHANGE As summer temperatures in Greenland rise, increasingly large lakes of water have been observed forming on the surface of Greenland's ice sheet. These lakes can exist for weeks or months until the ice fractures, when they can drain in a matter of hours down large vertical holes called moulins. Vast amounts of water and heat percolate down to the bottom of the ice sheet which then accelerates the melting process. The white ice sheet has always acted as a mirror, reflecting heat, but as sea and rocks are exposed as a result of this accelerated melting, their darker surfaces absorb the heat, further increasing the melt. Each year the amount of sea ice around the shores of Greenland is reduced.

Most scientists have agreed for many years that the ice sheet and glaciers are melting; the question is how fast? NASA can now measure the volume of ice using satellites and radar, and they have discovered that, since the early 2000s, 5 trillion

AVERAGE CLIMATE CONDITIONS 1991–2020

	Jan	Feb	Mar	Apr	May	Jun	Jul	Aug	Sep	Oct	Nov	Dec
Nuuk												
High °C	−5.3	−5.8	−5.5	−1	3.7	8.0	10.5	9.7	6.3	2.0	−1.3	−3.1
Low °C	−9.8	−10.5	−10	−5.3	−1.1	2.0	4.2	4.4	2.1	−1.6	−5.1	−7.3
Rainfall (mm)	72.8	55.4	59.2	53.0	60.5	61.7	75.5	92.7	106.0	79.7	82.6	74.9
Aasiaat (Disko Bay)												
High °C	−9.2	−12	−11.7	−5	1.5	6.5	9.6	8.4	4.7	0.2	−3.2	−5.3
Low °C	−14.8	−18	−17.6	−10.9	−3.2	1.5	4.2	4.1	1.4	−3.2	−7.3	−10.2
Rainfall (mm)	28.1	17.6	17.8	19.6	18.6	21.7	25.7	45.8	33.7	36.5	33.8	31.7
Narsarsuaq												
High °C	−2.1	−2.6	−0.7	4.9	10.0	14.0	15.7	14.1	9.9	5.1	0.4	−1.6
Low °C	−10.5	−11.1	−9.1	−2.6	1.6	5.1	6.7	5.8	2.3	−2	−7.3	−9.8
Rainfall (mm)	40.0	52.3	37.1	44.7	32.8	44.8	49.8	66.3	80.2	56.7	68.2	39.5
Tasiilaq												
High °C	−3.3	−3.1	−2.6	1.3	4.5	8.4	10.9	10.3	6.9	2.5	−0.4	−2.3
Low °C	−8.9	−9.2	−9.2	−5.7	−1.8	1.3	3.5	3.8	1.7	−2.2	−5.2	−7.6
Rainfall (mm)	113.2	99.3	93.6	75.4	58.3	34.9	39.4	58.8	89.8	71.0	91.4	90.0

Source: Danish Meteorological Institute

tonnes of ice have been lost from the Greenland ice sheet, with 2022 the 26th year in a row that Greenland lost ice overall. The last year the island saw an annual net gain of ice was in 1996.

As the ice recedes, life on Greenland changes; new shipping routes are opened up and harbours remain ice free for longer, extending the sea fishing season. However, the traditional Inuit way of life is threatened as melting ice floes restrict the movement of dog-sled teams that travel across the sea ice to hunt for seals.

The melting ice is also revealing potential mineral deposits; scientists believe there may be vast amounts of rare minerals buried under the ice sheet. Extraction would bring wealth and jobs to Greenland, but this would be at the cost of pollution and increasing CO^2 emissions. A warming climate would, of course, attract many more tourists, too.

Greenland is now home to many research teams who are trying to understand the effects of climate change here – Greenland is 'the canary in the coal mine', we were told. Supporting these research teams has become an industry in its own right and you may well meet scientists and technicians during your travels. The changes to the glaciers and ice sheets of the Arctic and Antarctic regions, caused by the warming of our climate, are a warning to the rest of the world that all of our lives are about to be changed.

NATURAL HISTORY AND CONSERVATION

FAUNA Greenland and its surrounding waters are home to a diverse range of wildlife. Large areas of the island, such as the Northeast Greenland National Park, are rarely visited by humans, and the wildlife is left undisturbed.

Land animals To survive the extreme cold of an Arctic winter, warm-blooded animals need extra protection. There are nine species in Greenland that live on land and each has developed its own survival strategy.

Polar bear (Ursus maritimus) Most polar bears live in the remote north and northeast of Greenland or on ice drifting down the east coast. They can grow up to 3m long and weigh as much as 500kg. A calorie-rich diet of seals and small whales helps build up a thick layer of fat which keeps them warm and they have two layers of hair which also insulate them from the cold: the outer layer contains long, hollow hairs that trap the air and protect the shorter, denser inner hairs. A second, inner, eyelid helps to protect the bear's eyes from snow blindness; and their large hairy feet and claws help them to run on the slippery ice.

Polar bears do not hibernate; in fact winter is their favourite time to hunt. Travelling across the frozen sea ice, they wait for a seal to appear in a breathing hole and then pounce; they are much faster than a seal on land.

Polar bears do build dens, but primarily these are a place to rest and give birth; in the spring, the female will emerge with one or two cubs. In the summer, as the sea ice breaks up, the bears travel south on the ice down the east coast. When the sea ice starts to disappear and hunting becomes more difficult, they retreat to the mainland to find birds and berries to eat, and then slowly walk back north.

As the climate warms, it is becoming more difficult for polar bears to find ice to hunt from. In 2022, NASA scientists located, in southeast Greenland between Tasiilaq and Prince William Sound, a previously unknown group of about 200 polar bears that were hunting from chunks of ice which had calved off the end of a glacier. The bears were travelling between fjords by crossing inland ice and hiking over mountains. This research gives hope that the bears can adapt to the changing conditions in a warming world. This small population clearly possesses genes and knowledge that should be passed on to future generations. It has been suggested that a nature reserve should be created to protect the bears from both hunters and tourists.

Specialist tour operators offer trips (pages 109 and 123) specifically to see polar bears but there are never any guarantees. Being on a boat or cruise ship may offer the best chance of spotting a bear, probably when it is hunting from the sea ice.

Musk ox (Ovibos moschatus) Musk oxen are, surprisingly, related to goats and are well adapted to extreme Arctic conditions. They live in herds on unsheltered tundra where they survive all year, even when temperatures drop to below −50°C. They have very long shaggy hair, nearly down to the ground and a thick layer of underfur; the only parts of their body not wrapped in fur are their lips and nostrils. Having short legs also helps minimise surface heat loss.

Feeding on a diet of tundra plants, musk oxen have a good sense of smell and use their hooves to dig through the snow for food. When the Arctic winds blow, the herd will stand with their backs to the weather and huddle together for warmth. If threatened by wolves, the herd will form a circle facing outwards, with their young in the centre, and, if necessary, adults will use their large, curved horns to fight. An adult musk ox can grow up to 1.5m tall (at the shoulder) and can weigh 300kg.

It is difficult to estimate Greenland's musk ox population as many of them live in the northeast, but nowadays drones are being used to calculate their numbers. Hunting by the Inuit over the years decimated the musk ox population on the west coast but, in the 1960s, 27 musk oxen were transported from east to west Greenland where they have thrived and multiplied ever since. You can now take a safari trip from Kangerlussuaq to view them (page 137).

Reindeer (Rangifer tarandus groenlandicus) Reindeer, also known as caribou, live mostly in herds giving them greater safety from predators. An average reindeer grows to about 1.6m in length and weighs 100–300kg; their coats are very dense with two layers of hair, an ultra-fine under layer and a shaggy outer layer. They live on tundra plants and, like the musk ox, use their hooves to dig through the snow; in winter there is only lichen, moss and fungi to eat. Reindeer have poor eyesight but they have a keen sense of smell, and are able to sniff out food through the snow.

Reindeer antlers are made of dead tissue so are not affected by freezing temperatures and, in the spring, the antlers are shed and new ones grow. Antlers are also useful for clearing snow and as a weapon to protect themselves and members of the herd. A reindeer's eyes are sensitive to ultraviolet light which is very useful during the long, dark nights of winter. A furry nose full of blood vessels warms the air before it reaches the animal's lungs, thus protecting them from the Arctic cold. Reindeer's feet are large with two weight-bearing toes and two toes higher up which only touch the ground on soft surfaces like snow, helping to spread their weight and provide extra grip. As they walk, the tendons in their feet click, a noise that helps the herd stay together in poor visibility.

Reindeer can be spotted all over Greenland – popular locations are Inglefield Land, north of Qaanaaq, and in the area from Ilulissat to Kangerlussuaq and all the way down to Neria Fjord, south of Paamiut. Take a walk or trip into the countryside and you should be rewarded with a sighting, or you can stay for a few days on a reindeer farm (page 92). Reindeer hunting is subject to quotas which keeps their numbers sustainable.

Arctic fox (Vulpes lagopus groenlandicus) Arctic foxes weigh only 2–5kg but their super-thick furry winter coat protects them from the freezing Arctic conditions. In summer, their coats are brown-grey but, as winter approaches, they thicken and turn white, providing excellent camouflage against the snow. Typically, an Arctic fox grows to 50cm–1m long including its long tail. This thick furry tail is vital to survival, providing extra insulation: when the fox lies down, it can curl its tail right around its body. An Arctic fox even has furry foot pads. When the biting winds start to blow, a fox will tunnel beneath the snow and gain extra insulation from it. Although they do not hibernate, they do build dens for shelter and to raise their young; a litter can contain anywhere between five and twenty pups.

An Arctic fox's diet consists mostly of lemmings and other small mammals. Acute hearing enables them to detect lemmings moving through their tunnels in the snow; the fox then pounces and digs the lemming out of its tunnel. If food is scarce, foxes will also eat seabirds and their eggs. Arctic foxes can be spotted all over Greenland.

Arctic hare (Lepus arcticus) Compared with hares that live in warmer climates, Arctic hares have shorter limbs and ears: this means they have less surface area from which to lose heat. In summer, their hair is grey-brown but in winter they are a fluffy ball of thick white hair with black ear tips. Weighing 2–7kg, they grow to 40–60cm long. Large, fur-padded back feet act like snowshoes and enable them to reach an amazing top speed of 60km/h. A keen sense of smell helps them locate food such as grasses, herbs and roots; they use their strong claws to dig. Females give birth to between two and eight leverets in the spring. Arctic hares can be spotted anywhere in Greenland and are easier to see in the spring, when they are still partially white even though the snow has already melted.

Arctic wolf (Canis lupus arctos) Arctic wolves are a subspecies of the grey wolf and live in the north and east of Greenland, so you would be very lucky to see one. In 2020, the Greenland Wolf Research Centre estimated that there were about 50 wolves living in the country; and because of their isolation, they are not threatened by hunting or habitat destruction. Weighing about 30–70kg, these wolves grow to about 1–1.8m long. They feed on musk oxen, lemmings and Arctic hares. Frozen ground prevents them from digging a den so they find shelter mostly in rocky outcrops or caves, where the females give birth to two or three pups each year.

Other land mammals Stoats (*Mustela erminea*) are Greenland's smallest carnivores (23–50cm long including the tail) and, like hares and foxes, they turn white in winter except for the very tip of their tail which stays black. Their white fur, or ermine, is used for ceremonial robes for the UK's House of Lords. Even smaller, **lemmings** (*Dicrostonyx groenlandicus*) are the size of a small rat (12cm) and they live on grass and the leaves of Arctic willow. Their population varies dramatically from year to year but it is a myth that they jump off clifftops. Lemmings do not hibernate but live in tunnels beneath the snow. You may be lucky enough to spot stoats or lemmings anywhere in Greenland. The rare **wolverine** (*Gulo gulo*) lives mostly in the unpopulated north of Greenland, so you are unlikely to see one.

Marine mammals
With Greenland boasting over 44,000km of coastline, it's not surprising that there are as many as 13 species of whale that swim in its waters. Several locations offer whale-watching trips that enable a close encounter. The best time to take a trip is May to September, when the waters are relatively ice free. Three whale species – narwhal, bowhead and beluga whales – live year-round in Greenland's waters. All the other whales and sea mammals are seasonal visitors.

In the summer months on a whale-watching trip you may also see **harbour porpoise** (*Phoecena phoecena*) and **white-beaked dolphins** (*Lagenorthynchus albirostris*).

Whales Narwhals (*Monodon monoceros*) are sometimes called 'unicorns of the sea' because of the spiral tusk that protrudes from their head. This tusk is found only on males and is really a distended tooth, which can grow up to 3m long. Scientists have discovered that this tusk is packed with nerves which makes it very sensitive to any changes in the environment and, probably, helps it locate food by sensing the temperature and salt content of the water. The males also use the tusk as a sword when battling over rights to mate with a female. Travelling in groups, this toothed whale – with black-and-white mottled skin and a white underbelly – feeds mainly on fish, squid and crustaceans. They can grow to over 5m long and weigh 1.6 tonnes and are one of the deepest-diving whales in the world – they will typically dive to a depth of 800m but can go to twice that depth. A female narwhal will usually produce one calf every three years. In summer, narwhals can be seen in the fjords all around the coast of Greenland. Narwhals have been hunted for centuries for their ivory tusks; now there is a strict quota on how many can be killed.

Bowhead whales (*Balaena mysticetus*) are enormous, weighing between 50 and 100 tonnes and growing up to 18m long. Their body is entirely black apart from a white chin, and an incredibly thick layer of blubber prevents them from freezing in the depths of winter. Using their large heads, they can break up the ice to find food. It is quite a sight to see them blow out a 3m spout before diving deep underwater with just a final flick of their V-shaped tail, or fluke. Incredibly, despite their huge weight, bowhead whales can jump entirely out of the water. The bowhead is a baleen whale, which means it doesn't have teeth; instead filtering food by straining ocean water through baleen plates – akin to the teeth of a comb which capture large quantities of plankton, krill and small marine creatures. A bowhead whale can live up to 200 years and is among the longest-living animals in the world. Typically, a female gives birth to one calf every three to four years. Bowheads may be seen off the west Greenland coast between Sisimiut and Qaanaaq; there is also a small population off the coast of east Greenland.

Beluga whales (*Delphinapterus leucas*) are very distinctive on account of their white skin. They are relatively small, reaching 3m in length, but are quite solid, weighing in at 1.7 tonnes. They have an unusually flexible neck which can turn in different directions and a prominent round lump on the top of their head called a melon. Beluga whales are very sociable and travel in large groups called pods. They communicate by a series of clicks, squeaks and whistles; scientists now believe that the melon helps create these sounds. Belugas eat mostly fish and females produce a single calf every two to three years. A good place to spot them is in the waters between Maniitsoq and Disko Bay, where they swim among the icebergs.

Named for the distinctive hump in front of their small dorsal fins, **humpback whales** (*Megaptera novaeangliae*) can be up to 16m long and weigh 48 tonnes, so when they breach in the water they make quite a splash. Their tails, or flukes, are white on the underside, and when they lift them vertically before diving you get a good view of their markings and scars. Each tail pattern is unique, like a fingerprint, and if you take a photo of a humpback's tail you can send it to Happy Whale (w happywhale. com), where they catalogue humpback and other whale sightings; you will discover whether your whale has been logged before. They will also email you if there are any further sightings of your whale. The humpback is one of the largest baleen whales and feeds on krill and small fish; they can communicate with each other over many kilometres and have a very distinctive whale song. In October, these whales leave the fjords of Greenland and swim 6,000km to the Caribbean, returning the following May. They are mostly seen off Greenland's west coast near Nuuk, Aasiaat, Ilulissat and Disko Island.

The second-largest whales in the world after the blue whale, **fin whales** (*Balaenoptera physalus*), are up to 27m long and weigh 90 tonnes. They are dark grey in colour with a pale underside; the left jaw is black and, strangely, the right jaw is white – no-one knows why. Despite their size, their long slender bodies are graceful and sleek. Fin whales are quite solitary and like to swim alone or in small groups. They are quite difficult to spot as they don't breach the water, though their 8m spout is impressive. In winter, they migrate south and can travel up to 300km a day; they are believed to be the fastest swimming of all the whales. As with other baleen whales, they feed on krill and small fish but they have to sift through a lot of water to find enough food to survive. You may spot fin whales off Greenland's west coast north of Upernavik or off the east coast. Adult whales can live up to 120 years.

Minke whales (*Balaenoptera acutorostrata*) are among the smallest baleen whales, growing up to 10m in length and weighing about 8 tonnes. Dark grey with lighter bellies and white bands on their fins, they have long pointy snouts. They swim rather like a dolphin, breaching and diving as they travel at speed, and will often surface two or three times before they dive to feed on krill and fish. Minkes are inquisitive and will sometimes follow a boat. They can be spotted in summer in the fjords along the coast of southwest Greenland up to Disko Bay.

Also occasionally swimming around the shores are **orca** or **killer whales** (*Orcinus orca*), **blue whales** (*Balaenoptera musculus*), **sperm whales** (*Physeter macrocephalus*), **long-finned pilot whales** (*Globicephala melas*), **North Atlantic right whales**

(*Eubalaena glacialis*), **northern bottlenose whales** (*Hyperoodon ampullatus*) and **Sei whales** (*Balaenoptera borealis*).

Whales are still hunted in Greenland, but all hunting is subject to strict quotas. To prove that catches are sustainable, the Greenland Institute of Natural Resources regularly makes an aerial count of the whale populations. Four Greenland whales – the blue, fin, North Atlantic right and Sei – are now classified by the World Wildlife Trust as Endangered.

Seals Seals can be sighted all around the coast of Greenland. They may be lounging on a rock or ice floe or they may swim out to your boat to check you out. In areas where they are heavily hunted, they may be a little shy. There are five main species to watch out for.

The **harp seal** (*Pagaphilus groenlandicus*) is easy to identify – the young are very cute with a silvery coat and black nose and eyes. When mature their coat is darker with a curved black patch on their back which resembles a harp. The harp seal likes to spend most of its time in the water rather than on land. The **ringed seal** (*Pusa hispida*) is quite small with a grey back and dark spots surrounded by light-grey rings. It is quite shy when approached, which is not surprising as it is the favourite prey of polar bears. The **hooded seal** (*Cystophora cristata*) has a silver-grey body with black markings – the male attracts females by inflating a large bladder on his head. The **bearded seal** (*Erignathus barbatus*) is the largest seal in the northern waters, up to 3m long with an extremely long set of distinctive drooping whiskers. The **harbour seal** (*Phoca vitulina*) or common seal can be various shades of brown and grey with a speckled pattern on its back. Harbour seals like to congregate together and spend a large part of the day basking on rocks.

Seals are still hunted for their meat and skins in Greenland. In the summer, hunters go out in boats and kayaks; in the dark winters they use dog sleds and dogs experienced in sniffing out seal breathing holes. Seal hunting was banned by the EU in 2009 but the Inuit hunters were given an exemption provided the hunt is conducted for, and contributes to, the subsistence of the community and is not conducted primarily for commercial reasons.

Walrus (*Odobenus rosmarus*) are the largest member of the seal family. These elephant-like mammals can be up to 3m long and weigh 1.4 tonnes and are found mostly on the north coast, though they do migrate south with the ice in the autumn. Walrus live most of their life at sea, but you might be lucky enough to spot one on an ice floe or resting on shore. They have been hunted over time for their ivory tusks, which can grow up to 1m long, but their numbers have started to recover since Greenland enacted laws to regulate hunting in 2000 and 2006.

Fish The deep cold Arctic waters that surround Greenland and the countless fjords and rivers are home to more than 200 species of fish. Over recent years, warming waters due to climate change have caused more fish to migrate north to Greenland, affecting the dominance of certain species. The species that you are most likely to see are described below.

Atlantic cod (*Gadus morhua*) is the most common fish caught and exported. It has a long dark body with a paler underside and a distinctive barbel (long whisker) that hangs from its chin. **Greenland halibut** (*Reinhardtius hippoglossoides*) is found in the seas north of Qaanaaq and Ittoqqortoormiit and in some fjords. It is a large flat fish which can grow up to 4m long. One side has an eye and is brown while the other side is lighter in colour and the second eye sits on top of the head. **Atlantic salmon** (*Salmo salar*) and **Arctic char** (*Salvelinus alpinus*) are found in the

1

fjords and rivers; several lodges provide fishing trips (pages 104, 146, 152 and 182). The silvery salmon migrate from North America and Europe in late summer and autumn and spawn in Nuuk Fjord. Arctic char are generally smaller than Atlantic salmon and have distinctive pink, white or red spots. Other common fish are the distinctive blue **wolffish** (*Anarhichas lupus*) and **golden redfish** (*Sebastes marinus*) with a red body and large mouth and eyes; both can be found in the fjords and waters along the west coast and north of Tasiilaq. **Capelin** (*Mallotus villosa*) are a tiny silver fish, food for many larger marine species. They are often eaten dried and the roe is used for sushi. You may see all these species of fish served in restaurants.

The **Greenland shark** (*Somniosus microcephalus*) is the most northerly shark and can grow up to 6.5m in length. Its flesh is dried and used for dog food. Two popular shellfish (crustaceans) found in restaurants are the **Greenlandic deep-water shrimp** (*Pandalus montagui*) and the **snow crab** (*Chionoecetes opilio*). The shrimps are not farmed but grow slowly on the seabed at a depth of 500m. It takes four to six years for them to develop and this slow growth enhances their flavour. Snow crabs have an orange-red shell and long, thin legs. They live in mud and sand at the bottom of fjords and are caught in crab pots. Sweet and slightly salty, they are considered a delicacy, particularly their legs. Both shrimps and crabs are found along the west coast.

Birds There are believed to be more than 200 different species of birds in Greenland; however, only about 30 remain here all year. In summer, their numbers increase with the arrival of summer migratory visitors. While most birds live on the coastal cliffs and in the fjords, there are a few birds that enjoy the milder summers inland.

When you are out hiking one of the many trails, watch out for grey and black **northern wheatears** (*Oenanthe oenanthe*), which you may see hopping around on the rocks, looking for insects and berries; in autumn they migrate to Africa. Pretty black-and-white **snow buntings** (*Plectrophenax nivalis*), also known as Arctic sparrows, are often seen around the shoreline; they are seed and insect feeders. In winter they migrate to North America or Russia. A bird that is difficult to miss is the noisy, jet-black **raven** (*Corvus corax*) which is seen throughout the year. **Rock ptarmigan** (*Lagopus mutus*) breed all over Greenland and change colour, from brown with dark stripes in the summer to white in the winter. These birds are a favourite prey for foxes, falcons and eagles.

There are three common birds of prey. The **white-tailed eagle** (*haliaeetus albicilla*) is a sea eagle and the largest breeding bird in Greenland with a wingspan of over 2m and 20cm talons. It can be recognised by its deeply fingered wings and white wedge-shaped tail. The eagles nest in south Greenland and the west coast south of Nuuk where they feed mostly on fish. It is estimated by the Greenland Institute of Natural Resources that there are 150 to 170 breeding pairs. **Peregrine falcons** (*Falco peregrinus*) and **gyrfalcons** (*Falco rusticolus*) are both much smaller and may be spotted in the mountains. Peregrines have a blue-grey back, white barred underparts and a black head; they are generally thought to be the fastest birds in the world. Gyrfalcons are larger and may be off-white through to dark brown; they often feed on ptarmigan which they may take in flight. Eagles and falcons are often seen in south Greenland and around Nuuk Fjord.

Numerous seabirds nest on the coastal cliffs and the sides of fjords. There are more than ten species of gull including the **Iceland gull** (*Larus glaucoides*) which has a white head and yellow bill. It breeds on the west coast and overwinters in Iceland. The large solid **glaucous gull** (*Larus hyperboreus*) has white wing tips and a rather fierce expression. They are to be avoided in the breeding season when they mainly feed on the eggs and chicks of other birds and can be aggressive if you approach their nests. One of the smallest seabirds are **little auks** (*Alle alle*); they are even smaller than a puffin and have black heads and backs and short tails and wings. Little auks live in large colonies; Greenland is home to 80% of the world's population. They only come ashore to breed and it is thought there are well over a million breeding pairs in Greenland. Good places to spot them are Qaanaaq, Nuuk Fjord and Ittoqqortoormiit.

You may spot **kittiwakes** (*Rissa tridactyla*), with their black-tipped wings, building their nests on the edge of cliffs or even on glacier ledges. They fly out to sea in flocks to hunt for fish and stay in western Greenland all winter. Black-backed **fulmars** (*Fulmarus glacialis*), which breed in colonies on mountainsides close to the sea, will chase fishing boats looking for scraps of fish thrown overboard. The **black guillemot** (*Cepphus grylle*), with their red legs and white patches on their wings, fish close to shore. They stay all year as long as they can find open water for fishing. Finally, there are the graceful **Arctic terns** (*Sterna paradisaea*), white or light grey with a black cap and living in large colonies on the coast, especially around Disko Bay and Tasiilaq. This slender bird migrates in winter to the Antarctic, an average annual round trip of 70,000km.

Two sea ducks, the **common eider** (*Somateria mollissima*) and **king eider ducks** (*Somateria spectabilis*), are found all around the coasts of Greenland with large colonies of common eider in Upernavik and Tasiilaq. King eider are predominantly seen in Sisimiut and the Nuuk Fjord but may also be found in the far north. The black-and-white male king eider has spectacular head plumage; the red-and-orange bill is set below a blue-grey forehead and pale green cheeks. The female is just brown. These birds were traditionally hunted by the Inuit for their eggs, meat and soft, warm fluffy down. Small colonies of **puffins** (*Fratercula arctica*) nest in crevices or earthy burrows along the west coast. Outside the breeding season the puffins fly south and live out at sea. There are 'Puffin Express' boat trips from Nuuk to visit a nearby colony (May–Sep; page 75). Don't forget your binoculars.

FLORA Nothing grows on the ice sheet, not even in summer, but as the warmth returns to the coastal tundra that landscape comes alive again. Hillsides are covered with a carpet of low-growing **bilberry** (*Vaccinium uliginosum*), **crowberry** (*Empetrum nigrum*) and **juniper** (*Juniperus communis*) bushes. In boggy areas, **mosses** and **lichen** cover the rocks and tufty-headed **cotton grasses** (*Eriophorum* spp.) warn walkers of the squelchy ground ahead. Meadows in the south are covered with yellow **Arctic poppies** (*Papaver radicatum*), **snow buttercups** (*Ranunculus nivalis*) and **Arctic dandelions** (*Taraxacum arcticum*) which create a sea of golden flowers. Blue **harebells** (*Campanula ritundifolia*) and **snow** and **purple saxifrage** (*Saxifraga nivalis* and *S. oppositifolia*) cover the slopes of sheltered valleys.

On mossy heaths you might spot **narrow-leaf Labrador tea** (*Ledum palustre*), a small, aromatic evergreen shrub with clusters of white flowers, or the **blue** or **mountain heath** (*Phyllodoce caerulea*) with its bell-like purple flowers.

The national flower, purple **dwarf fireweed** (*Chamerion latifolium*), grows in the flooded gravel beds where winter snow has melted. There are even thought to be five species of **orchid**, but these are very rare. **Dwarf willow** (*Salix herbacea*) and **dwarf birch** (*Betula nana*) grow into shrubs and stunted trees wherever they can find enough soil for their roots. The return of flowers to the coastal lands lifts the spirit of the people in the spring and heralds the return of long summer days.

Over the last decade, as temperatures have risen, the growing season has been extended by about three weeks. Satellite imagery indicates that the treeline has expanded northwards, and a greater area is now covered with shrubs. Trees are now growing to a greater height in some areas.

In 1966, American scientists in northwest Greenland drilled down through a mile of ice and found, at the bottom of this sample, well-preserved remains of twigs and leaves, which implies that Greenland was not always covered in ice (w scitechdaily.com).

CONSERVATION The Greenland government is committed to the conservation of the flora and fauna of the island. Since self-government in 1999, laws have been passed protecting nature in many ways, including controlling and, in some instances, banning hunting. Working with international bodies, Greenland has moved to protect many mammals by limiting hunting, including whales, narwhals, seals, reindeer and polar bears. This has been difficult and controversial in a land where people still rely on hunting to survive.

There has also been a huge effort to protect trails from litter; Greenlanders and visitors alike are required to 'leave no trace' and to carry out everything they carry in, from gas canisters to toilet paper. In Nuuk, volunteers can join boat excursions along the fjord to collect litter (page 87).

As our desire for hard data on global warming has increased, so the environment of Greenland has become one of the most monitored places on earth. Greenland Ecosystem Monitoring (w g-e-m.dk) runs and co-ordinates a long-term monitoring programme and Greenland's Institute of Natural Resources (w natur.gl) monitors all animals, plants and the environment. These bodies advise government on how well laws and regulations are working, as well as offering guidance on how to improve the island's environment.

ARCHAEOLOGY

Remnants of ancient Inuit and Norse civilisations have been discovered around the coastal regions of Greenland, and the cold, dry climate has preserved many of the remains found. However, with climate change and rising temperatures, scientists are concerned that any undiscovered finds are at risk of deteriorating. The main sites to visit are described below.

AASIVISSUIT–NIPISAT UNESCO WORLD HERITAGE SITE (Between Nipisat, near Sisimiut, on the west coast & Aasivissuit, near the ice sheet, south of Kangerlussuaq) This ancient Inuit hunting ground contains the remains of 4,200 years of human history. There are seven sites which include prehistoric camps, ruined buildings, cairns and trails, as well as colonial ruins on the coast which reflect the arrival of Europeans in the 18th century. Many of these sites can be reached by boat from Sisimiut (page 143).

QILAKITSOQ (On the peninsula above Disko Bay) In 1972, two brothers discovered beneath an outcrop of rocks eight mummies: a baby boy, a boy of four and six women. It is believed they died around 1475. Owing to very cold temperatures, the bodies have been well preserved, including their tattoos and clothing: their boots were made from sealskins and they wore two coats, the outer one made from sealskin and the inner one from birds' feathers. Four of the mummies can be seen in the Greenland National Museum in Nuuk (page 82).

KUJATAA UNESCO WORLD HERITAGE SITE (Between Qaqortoq & Narsarsuaq in south Greenland) There are five sites where Norse settlements dating from the

10th to the 15th century have been discovered, of which there are two main sites to visit. **Qassiarsuk** (Brattahlið), 5km southwest of Narsarsuaq, is where Erik the Red and his descendants lived in the 15th century. Here an impressive replica of a Norse longhouse and reconstruction of one of the first churches of the New World can be seen. You can visit this site by taking a boat or ATV from Narsarsuaq (page 91). At **Qaqortukulooq** (Hvalsey) you can see the remains of a 14th-century early Christian church, probably the best-preserved Norse ruin in Greenland. It is best visited by boat from Qaqortoq or Igaliku (page 104).

HISTORY

THE FIRST INUIT SETTLERS The earliest-known settlers in Greenland were Inuit, a semi-nomadic people, travelling in extended family groups to hunt. They lived in transportable camps which might be on sea ice or on land depending on the season and where they wanted to hunt. Igloos (igloo just means house) could be temporary or semi-permanent, a small single room or a few rooms, with a dome as much as 4m across. They came to the island in small boats and sleds from northern Canada and settled on Greenland's northwest coast. At least five waves of Inuit came across Baffin Bay before Europeans even knew that Greenland existed, but the dates are sketchy. The first two groups are known as the Independence I and the Saqqaq – named after the locations in which their remains were first found. They both arrived around 2500BC, following the migration of their main food source – reindeer and musk ox. The Independence I group lived on the Greenland coast for at least 1,000 years, the Saqqaq group for perhaps 1,800 years. The third and fourth Inuit groups, Independence II and 'Dorset', arrived around 1000BC and, again, stayed for at least 1,000 years, living on the coasts and, maybe, interacting with the last Saqqaq survivors. No remains of Independence, Dorset or Saqqaq people have been found after AD1.

Over 600 years later, a fifth wave of Inuit arrived from Canada, the late-Dorset people. Again living on the coast, the late-Dorset people are known to have stayed for at least 700 years, from approximately AD700 to 1380. Not all the incomers were successful, but many developed the tools and skills that enabled them to establish temporary settlements. The Inuit learned these skills over hundreds of years: sleds were constructed, initially pulled by men; ways of extracting oil from blubber and seal meat were developed and this oil was burned to create heat and light, making the long winters easier to survive.

NORSE SETTLERS Meanwhile, on the east coast, Norse settlers were arriving, the first Europeans to be aware of Greenland. There had long been Norse settlements in Iceland and now they crossed the sea to reach the Greenlandic coast. These first Norse settlers found it too inhospitable to stay – those who tried perished. Around AD982 the Norse explorer Erik the Red was forced to flee Iceland due to a blood feud; he and his father had already been forced to flee Norway. He headed for Greenland and landed near Tasiilaq on the southeast coast before making his way around Cape Farewell and up the west coast until he found a place where he could establish a farm at Qassiarsuk.

On his return to Iceland, Erik described the new lands that he had found as the 'Green Land', an extraordinarily audacious piece of marketing, and thus he persuaded more settlers to join him. Over the next 400 years, the Norse settlers established farms, villages and even churches and their population peaked at around 6,000. The King of Norway claimed Greenland as Norwegian in 1261 and demanded the settlers paid him their taxes. In 1397 Norway was merged into the Kingdom of Denmark, meaning that Greenland was then under the rule of the Danish crown.

The settlers grew crops, kept cattle, sheep and goats and hunted polar bears, narwhals and walruses. They struggled with the lack of wood, something plentiful in Norway, so they travelled to Newfoundland and brought timber from there to use. They also exported skins and tusks to Europe and this was critical to the settlers' success, but a period of global cooling – the Little Ice Age – may have been their downfall.

Starting in the early 1400s, the North Atlantic cooled rapidly and this would have impacted on the success of both farming and hunting. If the Norse settlers were already only just surviving, then failing crops and an inability to hunt may have proved fatal. Records show that Norse traders found it harder to sail to Greenland due to the larger ice floes and many moved on to other markets.

And nobody knows what happened next. The last reports of Norse settlers in Greenland date from the early 1400s and then nothing. Even today, researchers and scholars debate on the demise of the Norse in Greenland.

LATER INUIT SETTLERS The late-Dorset Inuit were still living in northwest Greenland into the late 14th century, and during that period the final group of Inuit began to settle on Greenland. The Thule arrived from Canada between 1200 and 1400 and settled in northeast and northwest Greenland. Over time, the Thule culture overtook the late-Dorset culture and became dominant, although it is likely that the two cultures interacted for many years. The Thule tribal group probably became dominant due to their superior technologies – harpoons, kayaks and skin-covered boats and trained dogs to pull their sleds. The Thule excelled in hunting both on land and sea and archaeological evidence shows that they understood how to survive this harsh climate with not only hunting tools but even basic snow goggles, snow shovels and different types of knife for different tasks. Today's Greenlanders are largely descendants of Thule Inuit.

EXPLORERS AND COLONISERS When the English explorer John Davis visited Greenland in 1585 and wrote a report about Greenland and the Inuit, the Norse had disappeared. It is probable that the Inuit were able to survive the climate change that the Little Ice Age brought where Scandinavian incomers were not. There is no evidence of conflict or disease – the Norse settlers had just vanished.

Davis was one of many explorers in the late 16th century seeking the Northwest Passage, a navigable route west from Europe to Asia. These explorers were joined by Dutch whalers, primarily hunting bowhead whales. Between them, these two groups mapped the west coast of Greenland for the first time. The Inuit were largely left to hunt and farm the land without interference from outsiders, although there appears to have been some trade of food and water.

There is no record of Norwegians nor Danes having any significant governmental contact with Greenland for many years, and yet Denmark continued to claim sovereignty over the island. In the 18th century a new wave of Europeans became interested in Greenland, many seeking to trade with the Inuit and some seeking to establish Christianity on the island. The Lutheran priest Hans Egede arrived in Greenland from Norway in 1721 with three ships, 45 other colonists and a few portable houses, and in 1728 they established the settlement of Godthaab. It is worth noting that the entire population of Greenland at this time – Inuit and European – numbered fewer than 10,000.

Nomadic Inuit hunters were already using the Godthaab/Nuuk area as a seasonal settlement because it was relatively sheltered in winter. Hans Egede had come to Greenland to convert the Norse settlers to the Lutheran religion but he was 300 years too late. He did take a great interest in the Inuit, not only attempting to convert them but also trying to understand their language and how they lived, but he found it very difficult. The Inuit resisted Egede's attempts to convert them to Christianity, the Dutch whalers were antagonistic towards the new Scandinavian settlers and Egede's trading company went bankrupt. On top of all this, smallpox repeatedly hit the colony and in 1735 Hans Egede's wife, Gertrude, succumbed to the disease. The following year Hans Egede left Greenland to take his wife's body to Denmark for burial and he never returned. By 1733, Moravian missionaries had arrived from Europe and established a string of missions along the west coast; merchant Jacob Severin persuaded the Danish king to give him the monopoly of trade between Greenland and Europe. For the first time, the Inuit saw the attraction of trading skins and tusks for tea and coffee, candles and lanterns, and interesting foods. The Danes redoubled their claims to the island, claims disputed into the 20th century by their now independent Norwegian neighbours.

In the 19th century, with the end of the Napoleonic Wars, there was a boom in European exploration of the area (page 194). The search for the Northwest Passage was restarted and there was a desire by explorers to map the 'far north'. One of these explorers was American Robert Peary, the first person to prove that Greenland was an island and who gave his name to Peary Land, the northernmost tip of Greenland. Peary also went on to claim that he was the first person to reach the North Pole, a claim that is unlikely to be true.

The Danish government now started to have a more formal presence in Greenland and in the mid-1800s held elections for local Greenlandic councils, but all decisions were still made in Copenhagen. One has to remember that there were very few Greenlanders at that time – perhaps 15,000 or so. It wasn't until 1951 that Greenland had its own elected parliament, by which time its population had doubled.

WORLD WAR II World War II brought the American forces to Greenland. Germany had occupied Denmark in 1941 but the Americans established air and naval bases in Greenland, partly to protect their supply of minerals and partly as a staging post for them to get supplies and flights into Europe. This was, perhaps, the first time that the Inuit's traditional lives were impacted by external values – the Americans brought such a different, materialistic way of life to this hunter-gatherer nation. The American bases of World War II never completely went away. The strategic importance of Greenland during the Cold War meant that the Thule air base in the northwest became permanent, and in 1946 US Secretary of War Robert Patterson offered US$100 million (more than $1.5 billion today) to buy Greenland. The offer was rebuffed by Denmark.

DENMARK AND EUROPE In 1953 the Danish constitution was changed to give all Greenlanders Danish citizenship for the first time. The Danes were interested in exploiting both fishing and minerals and were also concerned about the living conditions of Inuit hunters in small settlements as seals were becoming harder to hunt. Jobs were available in the new industries, so Inuit were moved out of the small remote communities and into larger towns, rehoused in apartment blocks with health care and education for their children. But the new housing did not suit the Inuit. They could not get through the doorways when wearing sealskin suits; seal blood congealed in the drains and blocked them; there was nowhere to store kayaks, equipment or clothing. The well-meant change had destroyed both their turf huts and their lifestyle.

In a 1972 referendum, Denmark decided to join the European Economic Community (EEC), even though Greenlanders voted heavily against joining, fearing that foreign fishing boats would come and 'steal' their fish. After joining the EEC, and as the Greenlanders predicted, British and German fishing boats arrived and the cod stocks decreased rapidly. The Greenlanders pressed for change and, in 1979, Greenland was granted a degree of self-government. Four years later another referendum was held, resulting in Greenland leaving the EEC and the island gaining control, once more, of its territorial waters.

THE WHISKY WAR Denmark and Canada share a border that runs down the Kennedy Channel between the northwest coast of Greenland and Ellesmere Island, and in 1973 Denmark and Canada formally agreed precisely where that border should be drawn. Unfortunately, tiny Hans Island straddled the newly agreed border and the two countries were unable to agree to whom this unpopulated 1.3km² lump of limestone belonged. Inuit from both Canada and Greenland had hunted in the area for hundreds of years so both countries felt they had a legitimate claim.

The dispute became known as the Whisky War after a group of Canadian soldiers planted their flag on the island in 1984, and left, beside the flag, a bottle of Canadian whisky. Later the same year, Denmark retaliated by removing the Canadian flag, planting a Danish one and leaving a bottle of Danish schnapps. Over the following years this ritual was repeated by both sides. Finally, after nearly 50 years, in June 2022 Canada and Denmark agreed that the border would go down the middle of the island and that Canada and Denmark would now have a land border.

GOVERNMENT AND POLITICS

Greenland is part of the Kingdom of Denmark. Since 1979, Greenland has had a degree of self-government and this increased greatly when the Self-Government Act was agreed in 2008 and extended in 2009. All Greenlanders retain Danish citizenship and Greenland's affairs are represented around the world by Danish embassies and consulates, although Greenland does have independent representatives in Washington DC and at the EU in Brussels.

In 2016, Greenland's parliament set up a commission to come up with a draft constitution for an independent Greenland. The resulting document was published in the spring of 2023 and is not revolutionary, more evolutionary. Many have welcomed the draft constitution, though there are detractors on both sides – those who say it does not drive the move to independence fast enough and those who say that it will create too much distance between Denmark and Greenland.

DENMARK Denmark has three parts to its country: the continental Europe section, colloquially called 'Denmark proper', and the two self-governing countries of Greenland and the Faroe Islands. In terms of size, Greenland makes up 98% of the Danish landmass but in terms of population continental Denmark has over 98% of the population with the remaining 2% split fairly evenly between Greenland and the Faroe Islands.

Denmark's parliament is the Folketing where 179 members sit, including two each from Greenland and the Faroe Islands. Members from continental Denmark are democratically elected using a hybrid method of constituencies and proportional representation. This usually results in the government being a coalition of parties who are willing to support the largest party. Typically there are more than 15 parties represented in parliament, as well as some independent members.

Denmark does still have a royal family, and the current monarch, Frederik X, came to the throne in 2024. The monarch takes no part in the political life of Denmark apart from attending the first session of the Folketing.

The Danish government appoints a high commissioner to represent Denmark in Greenland and this commissioner has a seat in Greenland's parliament, where they can speak but not vote.

GREENLAND Greenland's parliament is the Inatsisartut and has 31 members, who are democratically elected to serve for four years by proportional representation. There are just over 41,000 registered voters in Greenland. Though there are seven political parties, normally some of these do not receive enough votes to get representation in parliament. Independent candidates do also stand for parliament but seldom get elected. There is a separate election for the two representatives who sit in the Danish parliament.

Greenland's political parties can roughly be ranged from left to right starting with the Community of the People (Inuit Ataqatigiit), then Forward (Siumut) and the Descendants of Our Country (Nunatta Qitornai) parties. More in the centre ground are Point of Orientation (Naleraq) and the Democrats (Demokraatit), and slightly further right are Cooperation (Suleqatigiissitsisut) and Solidarity (Atassut). As well as spanning the left–right spectrum, the parties also differ on their views on the union with Denmark, from supporting the status quo to wanting full independence. The parties are all relatively young when compared with most European political parties and, therefore, some fail and new ones are born with more frequency than might be expected elsewhere.

The government is led by a prime minister (*naalakkersuisut siulittaasuat*) who heads up their chosen cabinet. The government is, invariably, a coalition and the ministerial posts are divided between the parties in the coalition. The government has responsibility for all Greenland's domestic affairs but does not have responsibility for monetary policy, defence or international affairs.

Greenland is now split into five municipal governments (at one time there were more than 60) which cover the entire island except the immense Northeast Greenland National Park which, although encompassing over 40% of Greenland's landmass, does not have a permanent human population. The US base at Thule is also excluded, although it is surrounded by the municipality of Avannaata.

ECONOMY

The Royal Greenland Trading Company (RGTC) was created by the Danish government in 1774 to run both Greenland's trade and Greenland's administration. In 1908, the Danish government took over running government affairs from the RGTC but it retained its monopoly on trade right up to 1950. In 1979 the RGTC, which was still a virtual monopoly, was split up into smaller organisations. The largest part of the business became KNI (Greenland Trade) which is wholly owned by the Greenland government. Because of this heritage and the necessity to subsidise many services, Greenland's government is involved in much of the country's commercial life; the state is Greenland's largest employer. All of the following companies are Greenlandic state owned: **Royal Greenland**, Greenland's largest fishing and fish-processing company; **Royal Arctic**, the monopoly sea transport company for cargo which also operates most of the harbours, the lighthouses and the Arctic Umiaq ferry; **Air Greenland**, the international and domestic airline with subsidiaries including Greenland Travel, Arctic Excursions, Hotel Arctic, Norlandair and World of Greenland; **Polaroil**, the largest oil supply company in Greenland and part of KNI; and **Pilersuisoq** (also part of KNI), which has the largest chain of retail shops in Greenland. Pilersuisoq stores are found in practically every town and village – their shops, more than 60 across the country, not only sell everything from rice to rifles but also incorporate offices for Post Greenland and for the Bank of Greenland. If the state did not run these stores, which are generally not profitable, many towns and villages would have neither a shop nor access to a post office or bank.

There are two major retail chains that are not state-owned: Pisiffik is a chain of retail stores which became fully independent from the state in 2015 and is owned by a Scandinavian retail group (Pisiffik stores are found only in the larger towns and have a variety of trading names, including SPAR); Brugseni is a co-operative, owned by more than 30,000 of its customers.

The largest independent company in Greenland is Polar Seafood, which markets and sells prawns caught by independent trawlermen. Its fishing fleet also catch cod, halibut, redfish, mackerel and snow crab.

Greenland's economy is heavily based on fishing, which accounts for over 90% of the country's exports, making it extremely vulnerable to lowering fish and prawn stocks and to price fluctuations. The value of fish exports is estimated to be around DKK4.4 billion annually. The economy is also dependent on the subsidy from the Danish government which is also around DKK4.4 billion. The dependence on a single industry and a subsidy from Denmark makes Greenland's desire for independence difficult. The population want better schools, better health care and better retirement options, but these all cost money, money that comes largely from Denmark. Every infrastructure project, including the new and improved airports, is underwritten by Denmark.

Tourism is expanding but it is never going to be Greenland's economic answer, though minerals might be. Greenland is thought to have significant reserves of rare earths, vital for many high-tech devices, and may have other metals and even hydrocarbons. The challenge is whether these can be economically exploited without harming the environment and without most of the benefits, and most of the control, going overseas.

Infrastructure, drilling and mining projects have attracted interest from across the world, including the USA and China, raising concerns over how Greenland can improve its economy while also increasing its independence.

PEOPLE AND CULTURE

Greenland's culture is an Inuit culture with links to the Inuit of northwest Canada, Alaska and Siberia. In all these lands, the Inuit have developed a way of life that thrives in the challenging conditions of the Arctic. Over 80% of Greenland's population identify as Inuit and nearly 90% were born on the island.

Greenlanders are warm and welcoming; they know it is cold outside and the idea of not welcoming a stranger into their home is unthinkable. Indeed, when the weather forces a change in their plans, or yours, then everybody just gets on with it, accepting that this is how life is in the Arctic. This adaptability may also mean that, because the weather and the tide are just right, they just leave their office and head for the harbour, jump into their boat and go fishing.

Traditionally Greenlanders saw themselves as living in a tribe rather than a family and relationships could be fluid. Polygamy, partner swapping, divorce and adoption of children were all accepted practices and, indeed, may have helped lower the risk of inbreeding and expanded the gene pool. Missionaries spoke against all these practices, which may be why the missionaries were more warmly received by women than men. Even today, family bonds are cast much wider than in many cultures and it is not unusual for children to be raised outside of their biological family, perhaps by the mother's sister or aunt or, even, a family friend.

In Inuit culture, women play a crucial role in ensuring the survival of the group. Men and women have traditionally had different roles: men hunt; women cook and make the home. While in small rural settlements these roles are still there for some, women are now often at the head of programmes and organisations; efforts to keep Greenland 'green', including blocking new mining projects, have been led primarily by women.

STORYTELLING Inuit culture is an oral one and traditions were never written – there was no written Inuit language until the concept was introduced by foreigners. Storytelling is used in Inuit culture not only to entertain but also to educate about traditional values and skills. Most traditional stories have, of course, now been written down and new technology has stepped in to reinvigorate the oral tradition; traditional Inuit tales can now be heard as podcasts worldwide.

INUIT TECHNOLOGY Inuit are masters of adaptation and invention. The earliest sunglasses, or snow goggles, ever found belonged to the Inuit, used to protect their eyes from snow blindness. The 'glasses' were fashioned from wood or bone, with a narrow horizontal slit cut in a solid band that covered both eyes to restrict bright light. The band was then attached to sealskin leather which was tied around the back of the head.

Inuit developed a range of knives, the most well known today being the *ulu* or women's knife. The earliest ulu were made of stone and bone but now most are made of metal with a wooden handle. They were used for the skinning of animals, particularly polar bear, seal and reindeer, and then used to clean the skins to make them thin enough to be dried and used as material. Ulu come with a T-shaped or D-shaped handle, depending on the region of origin. There is an interesting collection of ulu in the Kittat Economusée (page 83) where these knives are still used.

There are few trees on Greenland so animal bones and driftwood were used to make tools and to strengthen structures. The Inuit learned how to get oil from whales and seals and, thus, had oil lamps which provided light and heat in the long dark winters. The Inuit also made complex harpoons, or *unaaq,* and fishing spears, designed to fly true through the air and then not fall out of the fish, seal, walrus or whale when it tried to escape. The best harpoons had points that were sharp but not brittle and shafts with multiple barbs which were then attached to a line made from seal or walrus gut.

Kayaks, or *qajaq* in Greenlandic, were perhaps the Inuit's greatest invention and are used all over the Arctic. Each kayak was made for its owner, of stitched sealskin stretched over a frame of wood and bone. As an Inuit your father would make your first kayak frame with you; your mother would cover it with three or four harp sealskins. The kayak's length should be three times the span of your arms, the hole in the cockpit just large enough for your hips and the height such that the top of the kayak was level with your waist when you sat in the boat. Many hunters would have two kayaks, the winter kayak being lighter to allow it to be carried further, and attached would be an array of hunting equipment. At the bow, a harpoon on its own

1

support was secured with a line; also up front, a detachable white blind to hide the hunter from his prey. If the hunter had to continue his hunt over the ice, he would take the blind with him. Also on the front of the kayak would be a rifle and, in a dry bag, ammunition. Behind the hunter would be a float made from inflated seal bladders, the *avataussaq*, and a towline, the *kautit*. The caught seal or walrus would be attached between the kayak and the float in such a way that it stayed horizontal in the water, enabling the hunter to tow it home. Finally, there was the paddle, or *pautik*, which was very narrow. This may have been because of the lack of wood or it may have been because narrow paddles work better in open water.

The Inuit also had a large open boat shaped rather like a giant canoe, the *umiak*, often called the women's boat. Like the kayaks, these boats had a wood and bone frame covered with sealskins. Umiaq were up to 10m long and 1.5m wide with four to six women rowing and were often used to move home. The Inuit were semi-nomadic and the boat would carry all their belongings, including children and dogs, travelling up to 40km each day.

To travel across snow and ice, the Inuit used dog sleds and different designs were developed to suit local conditions. Longer sleds were used in northern Greenland and the dogs were arranged in a fan with one lead dog in front. Further south, the *kitaa* sled was shorter and had a high handle at the back to assist with manoeuvrability; dogs were usually in a wide fan, sometimes two deep. In east Greenland, the *tunu* sled was even shorter and the handle higher with the dogs tied in pairs.

HUNTING

> The Inuit culture is the most pure hunting culture in existence. Inuit are not even hunter-gatherers. Inuit are hunters, pure and simple.
>
> Henriette Rasmussen, Greenland government minister

Greenland is a country where the only real agriculture is sheep farming and this on less than 1% of the land. The only way to survive in Greenland is to hunt.

Wherever Greenlanders live, most hunt. The further north the community, the more traditionally Inuit the lifestyle is likely to be, but many town dwellers still hunt for reindeer and other meat. Around 85% of Greenlanders now live in the 16 larger towns, the remaining 9,000 being spread over more than 60 smaller settlements which may have as few as 40 residents. In these small communities, the members of each family, men and women, split their time between paid employment and hunting and fishing. Paid employment is necessary to pay for electricity, internet access and even ammunition but it is fishing and hunting for seal, walrus, narwhal, musk ox, polar bear and reindeer that provide most of the family's food. Animal skins are still cleaned and dried to be made into clothing and boots.

The reindeer hunt is considered by many Greenlanders as the best activity of the year. Hunts take place in autumn when the weather can be particularly beautiful and the hunt becomes the great social event of the year, raising people's spirits before the darkness of winter. And, of course, reindeer meat is many Inuit's favourite meal.

In the last 50 years, the dependence on hunting has declined but there can be no doubt, hunting is still at the heart of Greenland's culture. No matter what their job is, most Inuit see themselves as hunters. Hunting is not, of course, without its detractors and many of us would not choose to see a wild animal hunted and killed; but if the Inuit had not been successful hunters, they would not have survived. Pressure from environmental and conservation groups has led Greenland's Home

Rule Government to set hunting limits for most species; many are still unhappy about these restrictions to their traditional lifestyle.

LANGUAGE

West Greenlandic or Kalaallisut has been the official language of Greenland since 2009. Kalaallisut was the dominant language until the 1950s, when Danish became the language used and taught in schools. In 1979, when Greenland achieved home rule, Kalaallisut was reintroduced as the primary language for schools but there is still, today, a tension between the use of Kalaallisut and Danish. Many feel that Danish is used by the more educated classes as a way of enhancing their status. There are now moves to make Kalaallisut mandatory for all government communication.Greenlandic is an Inuit language and is closely related to the native languages of the northern regions of North America and Siberia. There are three distinct dialects of Greenlandic: Kalaallisut is the West Greenland dialect used by 85% of the population; Inuktun is the dialect of the Thule region; and the Tunumiit oraasia dialect is used in east Greenland. The three dialects are significantly different and people using one are generally not understood by speakers of another.

Only Kalaallisut has an agreed written, as opposed to oral, form. This means that in east Greenland and around Thule you may see the same word spelt in more than one way, which is at times confusing. Public notices are written in Kalaallisut throughout the country.

Greenlandic is a polysynthetic language in which words are made by stringing together roots and suffixes. This allows the creation of long words which might be a whole sentence in most other languages. The longest word in Greenlandic we came across contained 92 letters: *nalunaarasuartaatilioqateeraliorfinnialikkersaatiginialikkersaatilillaranatagoorunarsuarrooq*, which can be roughly translated as 'again they tried to build a radio station but it appears that it is actually still only on the drawing board'.

RELIGION

TRADITIONAL BELIEFS In the smaller communities of Greenland, as in villages throughout the world, everybody knows everybody else and, indeed, there are complex family relationships within every community. These bonds are part of the way that Greenlanders survive; community is everything and mutual respect is the norm.

The traditional religion of the Inuit is animist, believing that everything, living and non-living, has a spirit. Every animal and bird, every stone and every piece of earth, the rain and the snow all have a spirit and a right to be respected. To disrespect the spirit of anything is to invite bad luck.

Many Inuit myths and legends have been passed down through the generations by word of mouth. Even today, these stories are retold to the younger generation. Often the tale will involve a mythical creature such as a **Qivittoq**, a wandering ghost who lives in the mountains. The story goes that if a Greenlandic person committed a crime, their community might banish them to the hills. Their chances of survival in such a harsh climate are remote and it is believed that the ghosts of these people continually roam the mountains. If you are out on your own in the wilderness, you may of course meet a roaming Qivittoq and although some are said to be friendly, others are evil and may attack.

A FOLK TALE: 'THE COMING OF MEN, A LONG, LONG WHILE AGO'

The Danish explorer Knud Rasmussen (page 164) travelled all across Greenland, northern Canada and Alaska, writing down stories and poems told to him by the 'Eskimo people' he met. He collected 52 stories in his book Eskimo Folk-Tales. *The stories were translated from Greenlandic and Danish by W Worster, whose English-language book was published in 1921. The book is illustrated with drawings by the Inuit who told the stories.*

Our forefathers have told us much of the coming of earth, and of men, and it was a long, long while ago. Those who lived long before our day, they did not know how to store their words in little black marks, as you do; they could only tell stories. And they told of many things, and therefore we are not without knowledge of these things, which we have heard told many and many a time, since we were little children. Old women do not waste their words idly, and we believe what they say. Old age does not lie.

A long, long time ago, when the earth was to be made, it fell down from the sky. Earth, hills and stones, all fell down from the sky, and thus the earth was made.

And then, when the earth was made, came men.

It is said that they came forth out of the earth. Little children came out of the earth. They came forth from among the willow bushes, all covered with willow leaves. And there they lay among the little bushes: lay and kicked, for they could not even crawl. And they got their food from the earth.

Then there is something about a man and a woman, but what of them? It is not clearly known. When did they find each other, and when had they grown up? I do not know. But the woman sewed, and made children's clothes, and wandered forth. And she found little children, and dressed them in the clothes, and brought them home.

And in this way men grew to be many.

And being now so many, they desired to have dogs. So a man went out with a dog leash in his hand, and began to stamp on the ground, crying 'Hok–hok–hok!'

Some of the stories told are quite bloodthirsty. The mythical creature **Erlaveersiniooq** is a woman who entices travellers into her hut. Some say she is beautiful; others claim she is ugly. She will beat her drum and try to make you laugh, at which point she will jump on you and cut out your intestines. Your only chance of survival is to eat your own intestines before she prepares them for her meal. These scary tales are definitely a warning to take care when walking into the wilderness.

Shamans, *angakkuq*, are the link between humans and this spirit world and have the power to influence the spirits. They act as a medicine man, judge and priest and, while most are men, some angakkuq are women. Angakkuq wear masks, usually of animals, when performing rituals to enable them to cross into the spirit world. Angakkuq still perform rituals and visitors to Greenland are most likely to witness them at a festival, perhaps the return of the sun or at midsummer. When things were going badly – illness or poor hunting perhaps – the angakkuq had to travel to the spirit world to understand why the spirits were unhappy. A drum dance would be held with the whole village drumming or singing and assisting the angakkuq in entering a trance state in order to travel to the spirit world. Angakkuq could also imbue an item with magical powers: a falcon's talons

Then the dogs came hurrying out from the hummocks, and shook themselves violently, for their coats were full of sand. Thus men found dogs.

But then children began to be born, and men grew to be very many on the earth. They knew nothing of death in those days, a long, long time ago, and grew to be very old. At last they could not walk, but went blind, and could not lie down.

Neither did they know the sun, but lived in the dark. No day ever dawned. Only inside their houses was there ever light, and they burned water in their lamps, for in those days water would burn.

But these men who did not know how to die, they grew to be too many, and crowded the earth. And then there came a mighty flood from the sea. Many were drowned, and men grew fewer. We can still see marks of that great flood, on the high hilltops, where mussel shells may often be found.

And now that men had begun to be fewer, two old women began to speak thus: 'Better to be without day, if thus we may be without death,' said the one.

'No; let us have both light and death,' said the other.

And when the old woman had spoken these words, it was as she had wished. Light came, and death.

It is said, that when the first man died, others covered up the body with stones. But the body came back again, not knowing rightly how to die. It stuck out its head from the bench, and tried to get up. But an old woman thrust it back, and said:

'We have much to carry, and our sledges are small.'

For they were about to set out on a hunting journey. And so the dead one was forced to go back to the mound of stones.

And now, after men had got light on their earth, they were able to go on journeys, and to hunt, and no longer needed to eat of the earth. And with death came also the sun, moon and stars.

For when men die, they go up into the sky and become brightly shining things there.

might thus be blessed and sewn into a hunter's clothing; or a whale bone might be built into the frame of a kayak.

When an Inuit dies, their personal soul goes either down to the 'land of the dead' at the bottom of the sea, where hunting is plentiful and the soul can be reunited with its ancestors, or up to a cold hell where food is scarce. Everybody has many souls and one of these, the name soul, would be passed to a child in the next generation. Nowadays, children are still often given the name of a dead ancestor. This ensures that the spirit of the ancestor's name lives on and it is for this reason that, in the past, Inuit graves were unnamed. Traditionally most bodies were buried under stones – the ground was too hard to dig – resulting in a flat-topped stone cairn. The grave site would be chosen in an area of good hunting, with an unobstructed view of the land or sea.

Although only 1% of the population are practising animists, the presence of angakkuq customs and culture is everywhere and lies at the core of much of Greenland's culture.

CHRISTIANITY Today, most Greenlanders identify as belonging to the Church of Greenland, a Protestant Christian Evangelical Lutheran church. This is Greenland's official religious institution and is led by the Bishop of Greenland and, like so many Greenlandic institutions, is governed by, but largely autonomous from, the Church of Denmark. There are 17 parishes in Greenland and each should have a resident priest but it has proved difficult to find enough Kalaallisut-speaking priests for many years. Some parishes are very large with poor transport links, meaning that it is only possible for the priest to visit some settlements' churches two or three times a year. For this reason, many services are now led by lay volunteers. Lutheranism split from the Roman Catholic church in the 16th century. There are many similarities between the practices of the two faiths but there are also substantial differences. Lutherans do not accept the Pope and they have different beliefs on how salvation is achieved and on the sacraments.

EDUCATION

All children receive free and compulsory education between the ages of 6 and 16. Children learn the West Greenlandic Kalaallisut language, as well as Danish and often also English. Most lessons are taught in Kalaallisut, but a shortage of teachers and teaching materials means that some classes are taught in Danish. The language taught in schools has changed over the last few generations; at one time, parents saw Danish as being better than Kalaallisut, but now children learn both languages and even speak both languages in a single sentence. Textbooks are increasingly available in either language and some use both languages in the same book. East Greenlandic is not taught in schools, even in east Greenland.

In small communities, the school usually teaches only the first seven grades. Children from these communities then have to move away to complete the final three years of education, staying in the homes of local families or school dormitories. Home-schooling is permitted in Greenland and is regulated and assessed by the government. Some families, or groups of families, employ tutors to enable the provision of this type of education.

Education from the age of 16 may take place in Greenland, where four towns – Aasiaat, Sisimiut, Nuuk and Qaqortoq – have upper secondary schools (high schools), or in Denmark and lasts between one and four years. Vocational education is also possible for the over-16s and can last between one and five years and always includes work as an intern with a company. Only one in seven students stays in any form of education after the age of 16.

There is a small university, Ilisimatusarfik, in Nuuk which offers 11 first-degree programmes and four Masters programmes. About a third of degree-level students study in Greenland, the remainder choosing to attend university in Denmark.

ART AND CRAFTS

The Inuit had no paper, no ink and few dyes. They were semi-nomadic hunters – everything had to be carried with them and everything that was carried had a purpose. Traditional Inuit art, therefore, focused on decorating tools and skins used as clothing or tents. Stone, driftwood and bone were carved, often with the images of the animals or fish that they hunted and these carvings form most of the early Inuit art that survives.

The marking of people's skin was also common and most 'tattoos' had meaning. For example, a line drawn from a girl's lower lip to her chin marked her transition from a child to an adult woman. Further tattoos would indicate other life events, such as childbirth or the mastering of a new skill. For men, tattoos might be used to bring luck when hunting or to indicate that a man was a successful hunter. Both men and women might have tattoos that relate to Inuit folk tales and these have, in recent years, become increasingly popular. The tattoo you are most likely to notice is a set of lines across the fingers which relates to the legend of Sedna, whose fingers were cut off by her father (page 83).

Most early art was more handicraft than pure art: craft with a purpose. The traditional *qajaq*, forerunner of the modern kayak, is surely a work of art? The frame was made from driftwood and bone, tied with animal sinews and covered with sealskins to make it watertight. The hunters in the qajaqs would be wearing suits of waterproof animal skins, again sewn with sinews, and in their hands would be handmade paddles and spears. Many of these tools and skins would be decorated with carvings or dyes.

Inuit decorated their clothes with beadwork, and beads were also used to make amulets for good luck and to ward off evil spirits. Traditionally, beads were made from animal and fish bones and teeth, crustacean shells, wood and soft stone and might be dyed using herbs, berries or blood. Glass beads were introduced by whalers in the 17th century. Beadwork is still a popular art form today and is often used to decorate household items, as well as clothing and for earrings.

Some early art was religious or had mystical links. The *tupilak* is a case in point. Tupilaks, or ancestors' spirits, were invoked for protection or to cause injury, or even death, to one's enemy. A small package was made with parts of creatures, perhaps birds of prey or a whale, and something from their enemy, all carefully bound together. After being given magical powers in a religious ceremony held by the angakkuq (shaman), the package was thrown into the sea, freeing the tupilak, the ancestor's spirit, to go on its way. Tupilaks are invisible to ordinary people – only angakkuqs can see them – so angakkuqs traditionally carved what they saw out of bone, enabling others to picture the spirit. These tupilak figures are still carved today from a variety of materials and can be bought as souvenirs. If you are thinking of buying one, check what it is made from. CITES regulations restrict the export and import of some animal parts (page 58).

Masks also have a mystical or religious origin. Traditionally there were many types of mask. Dancing masks were used in drumming ceremonies, theatrical masks were worn while performing entertainments and house masks represented the spirit of the house, protecting it and the household. Most masks were made from driftwood and painted in just three colours: black, the colour of magic; red, the colour of love and life; and white, the colour of ancestors' bones. While the masks were modelled on the human face, the features were distorted to amuse or shock. A few very early Inuit miniature masks survive and can be seen in Greenland's museums. At festivals today, Inuit may use black, red and white face paint to imitate traditional masks.

It is only in the last 200 years that there have been significant outside influences on Inuit arts and crafts; indeed arts like painting barely existed before Europeans arrived. The impressionist Hans Lynge, in the early 20th century, was perhaps the first internationally recognised Greenlandic painter and, a little later, Jens Rosing is noted for his portrayal of animals, birds and nature.

Since home rule in 1979, many of Greenland's artists have followed more political or cultural themes, seeking to represent their views in their work. Today's work by many young artists takes the Inuit cultural background, particularly the relationship between mankind and nature, and seeks to interpret it in a much more international way. A traditional knife (*ulu*; page 21) might still be the article being decorated but the decoration may owe as much to African or Chicago art as to Inuit tradition.

In Nuuk, the Greenland National Museum and Archive (page 82), Katuaq (page 80) and the Nuuk Art Museum (page 84) are great places to look at and learn about Greenlandic art. There is also an excellent Art Museum in Ilulissat (page 162) and many smaller towns have their own museums.

MUSIC

Drumming and singing form the core of traditional Inuit music and Greenlanders will still break into song with just a little encouragement. Drum and dance ceremonies have always been an important part of the culture, bringing together a village for celebrations. The dancers not only wore masks but also painted their faces and held or wore objects that caused the audience to be scared or amused. The dances also had a sensual, even sexual, element – which is probably why the Christian missionaries tried to ban them in the 1700s, but the tradition survived in north and east Greenland where the church was less active.

Mask dances are still popular and performed at many celebrations and at cultural centres. The drums (*qilaat*) are frame drums and look like very large tambourines. The frame, of wood or bone, is attached to a small handle, and the membrane is made from the skin or intestines of an animal, usually seal or polar bear. The drum is hit with a small drumstick, again of either wood or bone.

Drumming may be accompanied by singing and song duels were used as a way of managing conflict. The objective of the song duel was to resolve a dispute without serious harm and could include participants slapping each other's faces or even joining each other in a wrestling dance. It was socially unacceptable to refuse the invitation to resolve a dispute this way. Some more traditional Inuit still feel that drumming has a mystical element and may be unwilling to allow non-Inuit visitors to play their drums.

ARCHITECTURE

Despite being semi-nomadic, the Inuit did build some permanent structures from peat and rock. These small huts with skin-covered windows appear to offer very basic shelter and were probably occupied when hunting was impossible. When travelling, Inuit often carried skin tents for temporary shelter or built igloos.

Igloos appear to be very simple domes of snow but, in fact, successful igloo building requires great skill. The shape of the igloo is not a simple hemisphere but is a complex curve called catenary – the same curve that is made by the wire hanging between telegraph poles. This curve, and the way the ice blocks are cut, makes the structure much stronger. The type of ice the blocks are cut from is also critical, as is the depth that the igloo sits into the snow and the way the blocks are laid, a three-dimensional spiral. The direction and curve of the entrance tunnel ensures that the interior of the igloo stays warm – there can be as much as a 50°C temperature difference between outside and inside a good igloo.

Norse settlers brought building techniques from their homes with them. Norse farmsteads were single storey and usually built from local rock that was then covered in peat to improve insulation. A farmstead building might be quite large and accommodate not only two or three generations but also their livestock – a good way for everyone to stay warm in winter. Norse also built log houses in southern Greenland, either from local or imported wood. These were very similar to the trappers' cabins built by hunters in North America.

In the 1950s, the Danish government started a programme to improve the housing in Greenland and introduce the now ubiquitous multicoloured 'tract house'.

There were a few designs, all gable-roofed and very similar, and the houses came to Greenland as plywood kits. Tract houses dotted across the landscape have come to typify Greenland's settlements; no two houses are allowed to be less than 10m apart to lower the risk of fire spreading. The settlements are also unusual as there are few fences; in Greenland the householder owns only the house, not the land that it sits on.

The 1950s also brought the first apartment blocks to Greenland and these became a source of great friction between the Greenlanders who were moved to them and the Danish government. The apartments were designed in Denmark without any consideration for the lifestyle of Greenlanders. One infamous Nuuk apartment block, 'Block P', was said to house 1% of Greenland's entire population.

Most settlements had no road system so houses were numbered chronologically as they were built. Today most settlements do have streets with street names and houses have numbers that relate to their location in the street, but you will see the old chronological numbers too; these are identified by the letter B before or after the number. These B-numbers can be useful to reassure you that you have come to the right place as not all hotels, cafés or shops have signs.

In these fast-growing settlements of near-identical buildings, a colour-coding system was introduced to assist in distinguishing one from the next. All buildings that were connected with religion, education or retail were painted red; all health buildings were yellow; green buildings were for power, communications and transport; blue for factories – mostly fish processing; finally, the black building was the police station. This colour-coding scheme no longer exists, and houses are painted in whatever colour the owner chooses, but the code's influence lingers on – the local hospital will still be yellow.

2

Practical Information

WHEN TO VISIT

A trip to Greenland will take your breath away whatever time of year you choose to visit. Whether you dream of dog sledding across endless snow-covered tundra or kayaking among gigantic icebergs, you won't be disappointed. At times you will find yourself overwhelmed, awestruck and having just to stand and stare to take it all in. Travel in Greenland is challenging and amazing in equal measure.

Greenland is accessible all year and the best time for your trip will be determined by which activities and sights interest you most. Dog sleds and snowmobiles have greater range in the winter, but in summer the sea ice opens up to allow kayaking and the west coast ferry is able to travel further north. In summer, the days seem endless and in midsummer it is never really dark; in winter, the days are short but the dark night sky is pierced by a million stars and may be lit up by the northern lights.

In coastal areas, where most people, sights and activities are based, the snow starts to melt in March or April; wildflowers spring up to carpet the tundra and migrating birds return to build nests. The temperature starts to rise and the ice in the fjords begins to melt, but there is probably still enough snow for that dog-sled adventure.

High season for tourism is June to August when Greenland is warmest, busiest and most expensive. In June you are likely to witness the midnight sun and, if you like to party, you can join in the midsummer celebrations; on Midsummer's Day there is music, singing and dancing in every settlement across Greenland, no matter how small. High season means everything is open, transportation is easier and more trips are running; but it is also the season for mosquitoes, so bring your repellent and buy a head net. While some birds and whales live in Greenland all year, others arrive from the south in spring as the land and waters warm up.

The shoulder seasons of May and September offer better value and these are good times for hiking, taking wildlife trips and sailing or kayaking in the bays to see icebergs and glaciers. By October the tundra flora is turning to burnished gold and slowly the snow returns to cover the land in a white blanket. Greenlanders, however, love to be outside whatever the season and many activities are available all year round. February and March are perhaps the best months for ice fishing, skiing, dog sledding, snowmobiling and snowshoeing. At the end of the day, you can enjoy long cosy evenings dining on your freshly caught fish and drinking local beer.

A list of public holidays, festivals and major sporting events can be found on page 56. Climate charts for areas of Greenland are on page 6.

HIGHLIGHTS

THE NORTHERN LIGHTS Greenland is one of the best locations in the world for viewing the northern lights as they usually occur between 60° and 70°N, directly

The northern lights, or aurora borealis, have inspired, fascinated and frightened people for many centuries. Legends have grown up around this magical natural phenomenon. Ancient Greenlandic tales relate that when the lights are dancing in the sky, the dead are playing 'football' with a walrus skull. It was believed that if you conceived a child under the green glow of the northern lights then the child would be exceptionally intelligent. Others believed that the lights were a sign from the heaven that ancestors were trying to contact the living or that the dancing lights were the spirits of children who died at birth, dancing in the heavens.

The scientific explanation of the northern lights gives a more prosaic account. These haunting lights are caused by energised particles from the sun crashing into the atmosphere about 100km above the earth. The protective magnetic field around the earth shields us from most of these particles but some are deflected down the magnetic field lines to the north and south poles. These particles then interact with the gases in our atmosphere and different gases emit different lights when heated by the particles – oxygen gives us a range from green to yellow and nitrogen gives us colours ranging from blue to purple to crimson.

Greenland is one of the best locations in the world for viewing the northern lights. Its northern location and its sparse population means that there is very little light pollution, increasing the chances of witnessing this magical sight. Auroras occur throughout the year but the light of summer evenings makes them invisible to the eye. A dark clear night between September and April is the best time to enjoy the shimmering curtains of dancing light.

Aurora Reach (w aurorareach.com) provides a forecast for the likelihood of seeing the northern lights over the next three days for most locations in Greenland.

over Greenland. The lack of light pollution here also increases the chances of witnessing this magical sight. Auroras are most visible on dark, clear nights between September and April. Dog-sled and snowmobile trips into the wilderness offer a wonderful way to see the aurora.

WHALE WATCHING White beluga whales, huge bowhead whales and narwhals all overwinter off the coasts of Greenland. In summer you have the chance of seeing ten more species, all here to feed in these rich waters. Take a whale safari boat trip from anywhere on the west coast between May and September or keep your eyes on the sea as you travel on the ferry…or even just look across the water from your hotel room window. The sight of these giants of the deep is always a moving experience.

ICEBERGS, GLACIERS AND THE ICE SHEET Where else in the world can you walk on, and camp on, an ice sheet with nothing ahead of you but ice for thousands of kilometres? Where else can you watch icebergs the size of tower blocks float past your hotel room? Where else can you lay in bed and hear the crack and bang of glaciers calving? Greenland offers easy access to ice in its many forms.

DOG SLEDDING There are more than 17,000 sled dogs in Greenland – there are even laws to protect their purity. Dog sledding is part of the Inuit way of life and has been a means of transport for more than 4,000 years. North of Nuuk and on the east coast, there are many locations that offer dog-sledding trips which can last a couple of hours or many days, staying in huts or igloos on the way. It is quite magical to race silently across the frozen snow with just a team of dogs, skilfully commanded by their musher.

INUIT PEOPLE AND CULTURE This is not an empty land, it is a country where the Inuit people have lived for thousands of years. You will continually wonder how they do it, how they flourish in such a challenging environment. Learn more in the country's excellent museums, especially in Nuuk, Sisimiut and Ilulissat; and chatting with any Greenlander over coffee will give you an insight into their daily life.

WILDERNESS No settlement is very large and wherever you are, even in Nuuk, the wilderness is only minutes away. Hills and mountains, fjords and glaciers are all part of a vast untouched landscape – and there are no roads. Here are many cabins where you can stay and immerse yourself in this wildness. Whether you choose to walk, snowshoe or ski, kayak, climb or just sit and fish, you cannot help but be overwhelmed by the raw grandeur of Greenland.

SUGGESTED ITINERARIES

Greenland is a huge island and it can take time and money to get between different areas. Beware of trying to cram too much into your visit; instead, think about concentrating on one or two regions. Tour operators, both those that operate across all of Greenland (see opposite) and regional operators, listed in each regional chapter, can organise tailor-made multi-day packages.

The itineraries described on the following pages are only suggestions. Typically they are about ten days long, but there are numerous alternatives. Travel between regions is most easily done using internal flights or the excellent weekly coastal ferry which links many towns. When planning your trip, don't forget to include a 'buffer day' before your flight home.

SOUTH GREENLAND More than likely you will land at the international airport at Narsarsuaq, so take a day here to visit the museum and hike to Hospital Valley or even the ice sheet. The next day, take a 10-minute boat ride to Qassiarsuk for a guided tour of Erik the Red's farmstead and church. Spend the night in the settlement or at one of the sheep farms before heading down the fjord to Qaqortoq, either by boat or by scheduled helicopter from Narsarsuaq. Spend the next day exploring Qaqortoq walking the Stone and Man sculpture trail and visiting a café or two. A boat from here will take you to Nanortalik, calling at the Uunartoq hot springs; or you can take the scheduled helicopter, which gives you a unique view of the mountains, fjords and glaciers. Allow a day in Nanortalik to explore the colonial harbour and the open-air museum before taking a boat up the Tasermiut Fjord, where, if you have time, you can spend a night or two in a cabin in remote and beautiful Tasiusaq. Back in Nanortalik, a helicopter flight will return you to Narsarsuaq.

NUUK AND THE ARCTIC CIRCLE Fly into Kangerlussuaq International Airport. The next day take a drive across the tundra to the ice sheet, spotting reindeer and musk oxen en route. Walk on the ice sheet using crampons and walking poles and, for the full experience, camp on the ice overnight. Return to Kangerlussuaq, flying the next day to Sisimiut; or if you are an experienced walker, you could spend a week or more walking the Arctic Circle Trail. Spend two days in Sisimiut: in the summer go whale watching and hiking, or in the winter enjoy the backcountry on a snowmobile, skis or dog sled. Then take a flight to Nuuk, where you can easily spend two or three days, sailing down the fjord and maybe doing some fishing, visiting the excellent museums or taking a tour around Nuuk's own brewery and of course enjoying the restaurants and cafés. Fly home via Kangerlussuaq.

ILULISSAT AND DISKO BAY Arrive in Ilulissat and the next day take a boat around the stupendous icebergs and along the fjord to the face of the Jakobshavn Glacier. On your second day, walk to the splendid Icefjord Visitor Centre and then take one of the marked trails along the side of the UNESCO-listed Icefjord. After two days, take a boat across Disko Bay to Qeqertarsuaq on Disko Island, watching for whales all the way. Disko Island is great for a day's hiking or wandering the black-sand beach. In winter, you can try dog sledding or snowmobiling. Then take a second boat trip across the bay to lovely Aasiaat, or maybe take the scheduled helicopter. Aasiaat has lots of easy backcountry walking or perhaps try kayaking or sea fishing. In winter, you can cross-country ski or learn to ice fish. After two days in Aasiaat, take a plane back to Ilulissat.

EAST GREENLAND AND NUUK You'll probably arrive into Kulusuk's tiny international airport from Iceland and then transfer to a helicopter for the short but spectacular flight to Tasiilaq. You can easily spend four days in this beautiful remote location. In winter you can dog sled, visit ice caves, sleep in an igloo or snowshoe; while in summer you can kayak, hike, visit a glacier and look for whales. After all this fun and activity, return to Kulusuk by helicopter and then fly across the ice sheet to Nuuk for some culture and interesting restaurants and cafés. Three days in Nuuk will give you time to sail down the fjord, visit the excellent museums and maybe spend a night camping in a tentsile tent in the mountains. Fly home via Kulusuk or Kangerlussuaq.

TOUR OPERATORS

UK

All Iceland ✆01904 406534; w all-iceland.co.uk. All Iceland, despite its name, offers packaged & tailor-made holidays to Greenland, all using Iceland as a stopover on the way in.

Arctic Direct ✆01793 279921; w arcticdirect.co.uk. Three package trips are offered – musk ox viewing from kayaks, a short but upmarket visit to Disko Bay and a longer diving-oriented trip to east Greenland.

Baltic Travel ✆020 8233 2875; w baltictravelcompany.com. Independent & group package tours from 5 to 16 days covering many different regions.

Best Served ✆020 4586 1015; w best-served. co.uk. Summer, winter and autumn tailor-made trips based in Ilulissat or south Greenland.

Discover the World ✆01737 214250; w discover-the-world.com. A variety of trips ranging from a short low-cost trip to east Greenland to a gourmet visit to the Icefjord.

Nordic Experience ✆01206 708888; w nordicexperience.co.uk. A selection of summer & winter package tours plus trips that offer a taste of both Iceland & Greenland.

Regent Holidays ✆020 7666 1290; w regent-holidays.co.uk. Good selection of year-round short & longer trips either packaged or tailor-made. Trips include dog sledding & northern lights in winter & the midnight sun in summer.

Travel Local w travellocal.com. A UK-based website where you can book direct with selected local travel companies, allowing you to communicate with an expert ground operator without having to go through a 3rd party travel operator or agent. Your booking with the local company has full financial protection, but note that travel to the destination is not included. Member of ABTA, ASTA.

GREENLAND

Albatros Arctic Circle Kangerlussuaq 3910; +299 841648; w albatros-arctic-circle.com. Day-trip operator based in Kangerlussuaq & Ilulissat who are also able to arrange accommodation.

Arctic Excursions +299 244789; w arcticexcursions.com. Part of the Greenland Travel group, Arctic Excursions enable you to book with small specialist operators that are otherwise hard to find or hard to deal with. Direct links with the specialist operators enable Arctic Excursions usually to confirm your booking immediately. They also offer a selection of multi-day packages.

Greenland Travel Aqqusinerssuaq 3A, Nuuk 3900; +299 701107; w greenland-travel.com. Probably the largest tour company in Greenland with package tours & tailor-made trips, as well as business & group travel. They have a reputation for delivering excellent service.

Guide to Greenland Inspektorbakken 8, 3900 Nuuk; +299 582014; w guidetogreenland.com. A large selection of tours & packaged multi-day trips throughout Greenland. There is a guide to what is available each month.

Taavani +299 385490; w taavani.gl. Experienced Greenlandic travel company that is primarily focused on business travel & trips for large groups. Taavani also develops tours in Greenland for international travel agents.

Travel by Heart +299 550905; w travelbyheart.gl. Founded by Greenland travel expert Elise Bruun, her first question will be 'What do you want to see & do?' She offers a few regular trips but really specialises in travel tailored to your needs & has the in-depth knowledge to keep costs down without sacrificing content or comfort.

OTHER EUROPE

50 Degrees North +47 21 040100 (Norway); w fiftydegreesnorth.com. Tailor-made trips including remote camping & glamping.

Greenland Tours Reykjavik Iceland; +49 30 364 283620 (Germany); w greenlandtours.com. Wide selection of tours running from Feb to Sep, individual & guided.

Topas Travel +45 7370 9339 (Denmark); w greenlandbytopas.com. Independent & guided tours throughout Greenland. Part of the same group as Blue Ice Explorer & Disko Line.

NORTH AMERICA

Collette +1 800 340 5158 (Canada); w gocollette.com. Travel company with over 100 years' experience. Offices in both Canada & USA.

Great Canadian Travel +1 204 949 0199 (Canada); w greatcanadiantravel.com. Travel agency that specialises in personalised travel tours.

Natural Habitat Adventures +1 800 543 8917 (USA); w nathab.com. Nature tourism specialist with small group tours.

CRUISING AROUND GREENLAND

Expedition or adventure cruising is one of the fastest growing sectors of travel and Greenland now has a number of cruise lines visiting its waters (see opposite). Cruising offers a different experience to land-based travel and may be more suitable for some visitors.

Cruise ships, especially the smaller ones, can get you to hard-to-reach parts of Greenland and can get you close to wildlife, including polar bears. Being ship-based, however, means that you will have less interaction with Greenlanders and get less sense of living in this extraordinary environment. Choosing a cruise that starts or finishes in Greenland offers the option of doing both, as land-based travel can be added on to the beginning or end of the cruise.

Most cruise ships in these waters are reasonably small but they can still seem quite large when moored off a Greenland settlement. A 'small' ship may have as few as 30 passengers or as many as 500 and this hugely affects the ability of the ship to tailor the trip to the specific interests of passengers. It also impacts the ability of the ship to get into smaller bays and fjords and affects how onshore excursions operate.

On a small ship, it will always be possible for everyone who wants to take part in an excursion to do so; on large ships numbers or time may be more limited. Onshore excursions are essential when cruising in Greenland if you are to get a real feel for the coastal communities and the lives of those who live in them.

One downside of a small ship, however, is that you are more likely to be aware of the movement of the vessel; larger ships tend to be more stable. Large ships are also likely to have more facilities – if something like a gym or a pool is important to you then check that the ship has what you need. Restaurant facilities and entertainment also vary hugely, as do the size and type of cabins available.

Most ships cruising around Greenland will have experts on board who will give talks on Greenland, wildlife and similar interesting subjects. If there is something you are particularly interested in, then check out who is on your ship.

Finally, especially if you are a first-time cruiser, carefully check what is and is not included in the price as this differs greatly between cruise operators.

Albatros Expeditions ℡+45 36 989796 (Denmark); w albatros-expeditions.com; ☉ Jul–Sep. Around 9 cruises that cover every part of Greenland including the remote coast of the national park & the far northwest coast. Cruises last 1–2 weeks on board their own 189-passenger ship with gym, pool, spa & jacuzzi & start in Iceland or Kangerlussuaq.

Aurora Expeditions ℡+61 2 9252 1033 (Australia); w auroraexpeditions.com.au; ☉ Jun–Sep. A variety of cruises that visit both of Greenland's coasts & travel the entire Northwest Passage in 2 ships, each carrying 132 passengers, with gym, spa & jacuzzi. Cruises start in Canada or Iceland & last 2–4 weeks.

Hurtigruten Expeditions ℡+44 208 846 2666 (Norway); w hurtigruten.com; ☉ Jun–Sep. Cruises along Greenland's east & west coast using 3 ships with 250–400 passengers on board. Cruises last 2–3 weeks & start in Iceland.

Oceanwide Expeditions ℡+31 118 410410 (Netherlands); w oceanwide-expeditions.com; ☉ Aug–Sep. A variety of cruises to south & east Greenland for 1–3 weeks accommodating 108–170 passengers. Oceanwide also offers cruises from Constable Point near Ittoqqortoormiit on

their 3-masted sailing schooner in Scoresby Sound. This ship sleeps up to 33 passengers & cruises last about 10 days.

Polar Quest ℡+46 31 333 1730 (Sweden); w polar-quest.com; ☉ Jun–Sep. Luxury 10–14-day cruises on their small 12-passenger expedition ship visit many parts of the Greenland coast.

Poseidon Expeditions Limassol Cyprus; ℡+44 20 3369 0020 (UK); w poseidonexpeditions.com. Cruises based out of Reykjavik & Svalbard. A small selection of trips lasting 10–14 days to east, south & west coasts with about 100 passengers on board.

Silversea ℡+44 844 251 0837 (UK); w silvesea.com; ☉ Jun–Oct. Luxury cruises visiting Greenland in 2 ships each accommodating 220–280 passengers. Cruises last 10–42 days & also visit Alaska, Canada, Iceland & continental USA.

Quark ℡+1 802 357 5112 (USA); w quarkexpeditions.com. Cruises based out of Iceland, Canada & Kangerlussuaq including a northern lights cruise & the Northwest Passage. They use 2 ships accommodating 130 & 200 passengers for cruises lasting 2–3 weeks. Spa, sauna & gym on board.

RED TAPE

VISAS Citizens of Denmark, Finland, Iceland, Norway and Sweden are free to enter, reside and work in Greenland and only require an ID card; everybody else must have a passport. Visitors from many countries do not need a visa to visit Greenland for up to 90 days. The Danish Immigration Service's website (w nyidanmark.dk) has the definitive list of visa-free countries, which currently includes all EU countries plus the UK, Canada, USA, Australia and New Zealand.

Greenland is in neither the EU nor the Schengen Area. As you are likely to be travelling through either Iceland or Denmark, you may need a separate visa for one of these countries. In general, if you qualify for a Greenland visa, you will also qualify for an Iceland or Denmark visa and, in the case of Denmark, you can apply on a single form for both the Danish and Greenlandic visas. Check before you travel.

Visas are issued by Danish embassies abroad or by the Danish Immigration Service. The authorities will generally issue visas provided they can assess that you intend to return home before your visa expires. The process is extremely transparent and details are given on their website.

CUSTOMS Customs, on entering Greenland as a tourist, are relaxed; illegal drugs, weapons and ammunition, knives, animals and pornography are all banned, although you can obtain a permit to import a hunting rifle. When leaving Greenland, there are restrictions regarding animal products (page 57) and cultural artefacts that are more than 75 years old.

The following, interesting, list shows what you can currently bring in duty-free if you are over 18:

200 cigarettes
2.25 litres of wine
1 litre spirits or 2 more litres of wine
2 litres of beer
2 litres of carbonated drink containing caffeine
1 litre of water
40g perfume
1,000kr worth of cosmetics
4kg chocolates and sweets
4kg tea and coffee
5kg meat and meat products

EMBASSIES Denmark has around 100 embassies around the world. The Foreign Ministry website (w um.dk/en/about-us/organisation/find-us-abroad) lists all of them.

GETTING THERE AND AWAY

BY AIR Greenland has six international airports and most flights to Greenland arrive from Copenhagen, in continental Denmark, or from one of Reykjavik's airports in Iceland. There is one summer-only, weekly route from Iqaluit in Canada to Nuuk, flown by Canada North. Air Greenland and Icelandair fly most of the routes and flight prices are relatively high.

Today, Kangerlussuaq is the major hub for international flights and the only airport with a runway that is long enough to accommodate large aircraft. This will change in 2024/2025 as both Nuuk and Ilulissat airports' runways are being increased in length to 2,200m. New control towers and new navigation equipment are also being installed to provide safer landings, particularly in bad weather conditions, which can currently disrupt flights. Lots of other facilities are also being upgraded with new terminal buildings, access roads and, in Nuuk, an airport hotel.The official opening of Nuuk's new airport is planned for late November 2024 but timelines on such large projects – this is the largest project ever in Greenland – are always challenged. It is anticipated that Nuuk and Ilulissat will become the main hubs for international travellers during the lifetime of this guidebook.

Via Denmark (Flight time 4–5hrs) From Copenhagen, Air Greenland flies daily to Kangerlussuaq and once or twice a week to Narsarsuaq. Copenhagen Airport has direct flights from Europe, Asia, north Africa and North America, including European low-cost carriers. For those flying from Asia or Africa, flying via Copenhagen is likely to provide the more convenient and cost-effective routing. For those coming from Europe, there is also the option of using rail or coach connections to reach Copenhagen.

If you have spare time in Copenhagen Airport, there are excellent and frequent train and metro links into the city, taking just 15 minutes. There is a left luggage locker facility in the parking P4 building; the lockers will accommodate small- and medium-size bags for up to 24 hours. If you need, or wish, to spend the night, there are hotels just 5 minutes' walk from the terminals, as well as a huge selection of accommodation in the city.

From March to September, Air Greenland also flies weekly between Kangerlussuaq and Billund in Denmark. Billund Airport has direct flights to most of Europe, making this a useful alternative route for European travellers. Billund is connected to Copenhagen by plane and by train, the train journey taking under 3 hours and costing around 200kr.

Via Iceland (Flight time 3–4hrs) Reykjavik has two airports: Keflavik (IATA code KEF) is Reykjavik's main international airport and is about 1 hour's drive southwest of the city; Reykjavik (RKV) is the second and mainly domestic airport and is just 5 minutes' drive south of the city.

From Keflavik Airport, both Icelandair and Air Greenland fly to Nuuk with at least one flight a day. Icelandair also has flights every week to Ilulissat, Kulusuk and Narsarsuaq. Keflavik Airport has direct flights from Europe and North America, including European low-cost carriers. Reykjavik Airport does not have any international flights other than those to Greenland. For those flying from North America, flying via Keflavik is likely to provide the more convenient and cost-effective routing.

Norlandair flies weekly from Akureyri in northern Iceland to Ittoqqortoormiit's airport (CNP) in the northeast of Greenland. The Ittoqqortoormiit airport is also called Nerlerit Inaat Airport and is actually 40km from Ittoqqortoormiit across a fjord. An Air Greenland helicopter is permanently stationed at the airport to ferry passengers to Ittoqqortoormiit heliport (OBY), which is located just 500m north of the town. This means that it can take quite a long time after landing at Nerlerit Inaat Airport for you to actually get to Ittoqqortoormiit if the flight from Akureyri is busy.

Icelandair fly between Akureyri and Reykjavik (RKV) airports several times a day, a flight of less than 1 hour. There is also a good Strætó coach service (w straeto. is/en) that does the same journey; it takes 6–7 hours and travels through some spectacular scenery in northwest Iceland.

Via Canada (Flight time 2hrs) Canada North flies weekly in summer from Iqaluit, the only city in Canada's Nunavut territory. Iqaluit has a connecting daily flight to Ottawa.

BY SEA The only way to travel to Greenland by sea is on a cruise (page 34) or by private charter. There are no scheduled international ferry services.

PREPARATIONS You do not need any immunisations to travel to Greenland although it is advisable to be up to date with all the usual recommended vaccines, including Covid-19, influenza, MMR, tetanus, diphtheria and polio.

Comprehensive health insurance is an absolute necessity for all visitors except Nordic citizens, who do have the right to necessary health care while in Greenland. Residents of the EU and the UK who carry the correct health card (EHIC/GHIC) have the right to health care but not to transportation to hospital from places where there is no permanent population; this transportation, if needed, can be very expensive.

It is advisable to carry a basic first aid kit, which should include any medication that you take regularly or periodically. Also consider packing:

- plasters/band-aids
- blister plasters for hiking
- antiseptic wipes and cream
- paracetamol and ibuprofen
- wound dressing (gauze and tape)
- anti-diarrhoea pills
- insect repellent, especially from June to September
- a 'space blanket' for rewarming

If you need to bring prescription medicines to Greenland, it is wise to bring them in their original packaging with the instruction leaflet and, if possible, carry a copy of the prescription or a letter from your doctor. This will prevent any misunderstandings on arrival when passing through customs.

TRAVEL CLINICS AND HEALTH INFORMATION A full list of current travel clinic websites worldwide is available on w istm.org. For other journey preparation information, consult w travelhealthpro.org.uk (UK) or w wwwnc.cdc.gov/travel (USA). All advice found online should be used in conjunction with expert advice received prior to or during travel.

MEDICAL PROBLEMS
Altitude sickness Most of Greenland is reasonably low lying but the mountains of the ice sheet exceed 2,500m, the height above which altitude sickness can occur. The highest point in Greenland is Gunnbjørn Fjeldat, 3,694m in the Watkins Mountains on the east coast. To minimise the risk of developing altitude illness, sensible precautions should be adopted and you should always trek with experienced guides when at altitude. Ascents should be gradual, with scheduled rest days for the body to acclimatise to the lack of oxygen in the air. Ascending too quickly carries with it a number of risks: **acute mountain sickness** (AMS), with symptoms including headache, loss of appetite, nausea, vomiting, poor sleep, fatigue and weakness; **high-altitude cerebral oedema** (HACE), whose symptoms include confusion, altered consciousness and poor co-ordination; and **high-altitude pulmonary oedema** (HAPE), whose symptoms include breathlessness even when resting, a dry cough which may become wet, and frothy, blood-stained saliva and mucus. All of these are medical emergencies which require urgent treatment. The affected person must be accompanied to descend to a lower altitude and seek help. Altitude sickness can be fatal if untreated.

Climate-related issues The climate can be a health hazard in Greenland, especially in winter when temperatures may not get above freezing. Snowfall can be heavy, even around the coast. Good-quality windproof and waterproof clothing, warm layers and thick-soled shoes with a good grip will ensure that you stay safe, warm and dry. A warm hat and gloves are also necessary to prevent heat loss. Even more warm clothes are required if you are contemplating dog-sled expeditions or excursions in small boats. Add and remove layers as appropriate for the temperature and your level of exertion. Remember, cold or wet weather is only a problem if you are not wearing the right clothing, so be prepared.

Hypothermia Hypothermia (low core body temperature) is unusual in travellers who are physically fit and properly clothed, but can occur rapidly in people who are injured or immobilised. Someone whose torso feels cold to the touch with symptoms including uncontrollable shivering and confusion or loss of co-ordination should be taken to shelter and evacuated. Remove any wet clothing and wrap the casualty in dry insulation eg: a sleeping bag. Rewarming should be gradual, using another person's body heat if necessary.

Frostbite Frostbite (the freezing of a specific body part such as fingers, toes, nose or earlobes) is another reason to head for warmth and shelter. Frostbitten skin can appear waxy, cold to the touch, or discoloured. Anything beyond mild frostnip requires medical assessment. Treatment includes:

• handling the affected areas gently; do not rub
• bandaging the affected parts loosely with a sterile dressing
• not walking on frostbitten feet or toes if possible
• rewarming gently in water at around 40°C, once you have reached shelter

If there's any chance the frostbitten areas will freeze again, **don't thaw them**. Pain relief will become necessary as the tissue rewarms.

Sunburn It is very easy to get sunburned or chapped lips in Greenland even when there is cloud cover, particularly between March and September. Most of your body may be covered, but remember to protect your face and any other exposed skin with high-factor sunscreen, factor 30 or above.

Dehydration Greenland's air is often dry and windy, so drinking enough water and avoiding dehydration are important in all seasons. Water in Greenland is some of the cleanest in the world. In small settlements, it may come from a central supply and have to be carried in cans to the house or accommodation.

Mosquitoes and ticks Mosquitoes are a nuisance in July and August and their bites are irritating, but Greenland's mosquitoes are not known to carry any diseases. You may want to avoid bites by covering up, wearing light-coloured long-sleeved shirts and long trousers, using a face net and covering exposed skin with insect repellent, preferably DEET-based. The local remedy is Labrador tea (*Qajaasat*); the leaves are rubbed between your hands and then the extracted juice spread on to any exposed skin.

The seabird tick (*Ixodes uriae*) is the only tick found in Greenland. It is not known to transmit disease to humans. As the climate changes, it is likely that other ticks and biting insects will expand their range.

Rabies Rabies is extremely rare in Greenland. As far back as 1859, rabies was found in sled dogs. In 1960, a vaccination programme was instituted which eradicated the disease from the dogs, though it is believed that rabies may still be present in some Arctic foxes. Your chances of encountering an Arctic fox that is within biting distance is minuscule.

Rabies is spread through the saliva of an infected animal and is usually transmitted through a bite or a scratch. If this unlikely event should occur, wash the wound with soap and water for at least 10 minutes and then immediately seek medical advice.

Seasickness Much of the travel between settlements is by boat, and the waters can be choppy. Some practical tips to reduce motion sickness include:

- reducing motion – sit in the middle of the boat
- looking straight ahead at a fixed point, such as the horizon
- closing your eyes and breathing slowly while focusing on your breathing
- avoiding reading or exposure to unpleasant smells

If you are susceptible to motion sickness, various medications are available including tablets and patches. Common remedies include cinnarizine, scopolamine, domperidone and prochlorperazine. Speak to your pharmacist or primary care doctor. If you need to vomit, using a bucket is safer than leaning over the side of a rocking boat.

Sexually transmitted diseases Sexually transmitted diseases are on the increase in Greenland and, indeed, most Nordic countries. Condoms are available in pharmacies and many general stores.

MEDICAL TREATMENT All settlements have some level of health-care provision. There are five hospitals – in Aasiaat, Ilulissat, Sisimiut, Qaqortoq and Nuuk – and there are clinics in most towns, but the treatment available in these clinics can be fairly limited. Hospitals and clinics are, by tradition, in yellow buildings and their logo is a stylised family next to a yellow igloo. Similarly, there are dentists in all the main towns, but not in smaller settlements. Larger settlements have pharmacies but these have limited supplies, so make sure you pack sufficient quantities of your medication. In small settlements, the general store will sell some drugs.

The phone number for all health **emergencies** is ☏ 112, but there may also be a local number that will get you through to the local nurse or doctor in a small settlement. Bearing in mind the size of the country and the distances between towns, assistance may not arrive very quickly. Serious health issues will generally mean evacuation to a hospital by plane, helicopter or boat.

SAFETY

Crime rates in Greenland are low relative to the rest of the world and crime against visitors to Greenland is even lower. The most dangerous things in Greenland generally are cold weather, the terrain and polar bears. In settlements the most dangerous thing is ice; locals are used to this and visitors are not. In addition, steep roads, gusty winds and ice can be the recipe for a fall if you don't take extra care.

Beware too of snow on top of invisible meltwater rivers and lakes in spring; test the snow in front of you with a pole if you have any doubts.

If you are heading out of town, make sure that you ask someone local whether your route is safe and tell someone you are going and when you expect to get back. This is a landscape with few landmarks – it is easy to get lost. Ensure you have a GPS device, or a mobile phone with GPS and maps, with you and that you know where you started. If possible, borrow or rent a radio (emergency calls are made on VHF channel 16). You may have a satellite SOS feature on your phone, but on the iPhone 14 and above, for example, it does not at the time of writing work in Greenland. The advertised service limit is 62°N, and Greenland and Denmark are not on Apple's list of countries that support the service.

You are very very unlikely to meet a polar bear, but make sure you know what to do if a bear does appear (page 118).

WOMEN TRAVELLERS

Women travelling alone will find Greenland safer than most countries and are unlikely to encounter any issues; crime against all travellers is extremely low.

TRAVELLING WITH A DISABILITY

Greenland is a challenging place to travel in if you have a physical disability. The terrain is almost universally difficult for people who use wheelchairs or other walking aids, even in summer, and there are few disability-friendly facilities. With prior agreement, Air Greenland allows blind and visually impaired passengers to bring their guide dog on to the aircraft with them.

Greenlanders are very happy to help those with a disability but may have very little experience in this area. Many activities do require quite a lot of physical interaction; even riding on a snowmobile or a dog sled requires the passenger to hold on, sit upright and brace their body. Tour operators will often go out of their way to make a tour successful for any guest with a disability where that is possible, but they may need guidance as to your individual needs and how to meet them. It is wise to discuss fully any physical disabilities with tour providers before booking.

A dialect of Danish Sign Language is used in Greenland; this is very similar to sign language in Iceland, Norway and the Faroe Islands.

The UK's **gov.uk** website (w gov.uk/government/publications/disabled-travellers/disability-and-travel-abroad) has a downloadable guide giving general advice and practical information for travellers with a disability (and their companions) preparing for overseas travel. The **Society for Accessible Travel and Hospitality** (w sath.org) also provides some general information.

LGBTQIA+ TRAVELLERS

Greenland enjoys some of the best rights for LGBTQIA+ people in the world. Same-sex activity, relationships and marriage enjoy the same rights as heterosexual relationships. Discrimination is illegal under Article 100 of Greenland's Criminal Code, and reports of discrimination are rare. There is, however, virtually no gay scene anywhere in Greenland as the population is just too sparse. There is a well-attended Nuuk Pride (⬛) festival every June which ends with a parade of people, floats and flags.

TRAVELLING WITH KIDS

Greenlanders treat children as adults in many ways; children are given a lot of freedom and responsibility from quite a young age. A child of 12 using a rifle or being on a boat alone is not unusual. Visitors may feel that the safeguards that they are used to having around children are missing.

Many activities that are attractive to adults are equally attractive to children and, provided children are wearing the right clothes and taking the right precautions, there is no reason why visiting Greenland with children should present any significant problems.

Do be sure to discuss the age, size and abilities of your children with any tour operators to ensure that they are able to provide suitable clothing and equipment. Be sure to ask whether each child will be able to take part fully in the activity and, if not, what restrictions there will be.

WHAT TO TAKE

LUGGAGE When travelling in Greenland you may be using small planes, helicopters, ferries and boats; so it is important you check the weight and size limits for luggage as these vary. Also bear in mind that you may be carrying your own luggage and often over rough ground, so think carefully about what you really need. Few hotels and hostels have lifts.

Air Greenland prides itself on being a full-service airline, which means that every ticket includes 20kg of checked baggage and 8kg of hand luggage, even on helicopter flights. Checked baggage can be divided into one or more suitcases, and excess baggage can be purchased if necessary but is expensive and, of course, space is limited. Even on helicopter flights, there may be space for odd-size baggage, so make a special service request when booking, giving the airline time to find a solution. Skis, for example, can usually be accommodated provided you advise Air Greenland in advance.

CLOTHING

There's no such thing as bad weather, only bad clothing.

Scandinavian saying

The secret to keeping warm and dry is layers as this enables you to increase or decrease your warmth according to the weather. It is also important to make sure you do not get too hot and sweaty, particularly when working hard at an activity. A sweaty body cools down really fast when you stop the activity, so expect to be continually taking layers off and on to keep yourself comfortable. Carrying a small backpack, with a rain cover, to put those spare layers in may be a good plan.

For clothing there are three layers to think about. The first is the thermal base layer with long sleeves and long pants. This layer absorbs your sweat and takes it away from your skin. Over this is the mid-layer, a shirt or a thin jumper, perhaps. This is the insulation layer and you may choose to actually have two mid-layers – a fleece over a shirt maybe – to achieve the right level of warmth. Over this is the protection layer, which needs to be waterproof and windproof and include a hood. To achieve this, you may choose to wear a windproof fleece under a waterproof jacket or just one jacket that does both.

Don't forget to protect your legs: long thermal pants under heavyweight walking trousers or padded trousers under waterproof over-trousers. Your head will need a warm hat, one that won't blow off, and your hands need gloves or mittens – liner gloves under warm gloves add that extra layer, and water-resistant gloves will keep your hands dry.

Finally, feet. Waterproof hiking boots with sturdy, thick soles and thick, warm socks to go in them are a must. Thermal-lined wellingtons or snow boots are good too but, whatever you choose, your footwear must be waterproof and have non-slip soles. Consider, also, wearing thin liner socks to add an extra layer of insulation. Make sure you walk your boots in before you travel.

EQUIPMENT Everyone has their own favourite 'necessities', but here are a few things that we think are necessary in Greenland.

- Sunglasses
- Sunscreen and lip balm
- Moisturising face and hand cream
- Eye drops
- Water bottle
- Towel to take trekking to dry your feet after river crossings
- Sleeping eye mask if you are travelling in summer
- Mosquito repellent and head net if you are visiting in summer (both available in Greenland)
- Camera and/or binoculars
- Mobile phone
- Power-bank battery
- Walking poles

ELECTRICITY Greenland's power is 230V 50Hz which is the predominate standard in Europe but not in North America. Some devices work on more than one voltage, but many do not, and it may be dangerous to plug a North American device into a Greenland socket, even with an adaptor.

Electricity plugs have two round pins, the same as most of continental Europe, sometimes with a third earth pin or earth strips, technically classed as types C, E, F and K. If you need an adaptor, you will be able to purchase one in Greenland but you will save money if you buy one before you travel.

MONEY AND BUDGETING

Greenland, being part of Denmark, uses the Danish krone, written DKK or kr, which is split into 100 ore. Bank notes run from 1,000kr down to 50kr and coins from 50kr to 1kr, as well as 50 and 25 ore.

There are no money exchange counters at Greenland's airports, but there are banks in large towns where you can change foreign currency. If you are flying in from Denmark then you can, of course, get Danish krone in cash there, either from an ATM or a bureau de change.

There are ATMs in many settlements including Nanortalik, Narsaq, Qaqortoq, Paamiut, Nuuk, Maniitsoq, Sisimiut, Kangerlussuaq, Aasiaat, Qasigiannguit, Ilulissat, Qeqertarsuaq, Uummannaq, Upernavik and Tasiilaq. You will also find them in the larger airports and supermarkets. ATMs support cards from the international card networks including Visa, MasterCard, Eurocard and American Express. Be aware, though, that ATMs may run out of money at the weekends when they are not restocked.

Credit cards are widely accepted in larger towns, usually contactless if your card supports this. In smaller stores and in more remote towns, you may be charged a small percentage if you pay with a credit card, and there is also the risk of connection failures in bad weather. Always have krone cash available as a backup.

Some tourist shops and most Pilersuisoq stores will accept foreign currency notes, but the exchange rate offered is usually very poor.

Some typical prices for everyday items are:

Loaf of bread	35kr	250g cheese	25kr
1 litre of milk	22kr	1kg apples	25kr
6 eggs	20kr	Mars bar	15kr
500g pasta	16kr	Cappuccino	30kr
1kg rice	28kr	Bottle of beer	24kr

BUDGETING Greenland is an expensive country to visit, but with a little planning there are ways to reduce the cost of your trip without sacrificing your experience.

The most expensive time to visit is June–August when hotels raise their prices and cheap rooms and good deals on activities are difficult to find. If you can travel during the winter months or the shoulder seasons of April/May or September/October, you'll find it is quieter and, often, cheaper.

It is important to consider where you stay, and eat. Hostels – often called guesthouses – are a good budget option. The majority of hostels are comfortable, with bunk beds or private rooms and well-equipped kitchens. Many towns have houses and apartments to rent, which present good value for families and small groups. Most accommodation offers free transfers from the airport or harbour if you ask. To keep costs down you may not want to dine out every night. There are pizza and Thai take-away restaurants in most towns and, sometimes, very reasonably priced cafés in supermarkets; but if you really want to keep prices down self-catering is the best option. Every settlement has a surprisingly well-stocked supermarket and many even have a bakery. Larger communities also have a fresh fish and meat market, usually down by the harbour. It is always cheaper to eat what the locals eat, but bear in mind that the local meat is likely to be seal, whale or reindeer. There is no need to buy bottled water – the water from the tap is crystal clear and tastes wonderful.

Travelling is definitely part of the experience. Restricting the places you visit to one or two regions will reduce the number of expensive flights you need to take; and after you arrive in a region, you can often use scheduled boats to get about which are less expensive than flights. If you travel a little slower, you can cut your costs. The coastal ferry, the Arctic Umiaq, runs from Qaqortoq to Ilulissat calling at ten ports along the way. On board there is a wide range of accommodation from bunk beds to private en-suite cabins. Disko Line runs many local ferry services: up Nuuk Fjord; around south Greenland; from Sisimiut and Maniitsoq to small local settlements; and around and across Disko Bay. These are subsidised by the government so a little cheaper. Nuuk, Sisimiut, Ilulissat and Kangerlussuaq all have a local bus service. The cheapest way to travel, though, is on foot, bringing your own tent and wild camping. Organised camping sites are rare, but you are allowed to camp anywhere that is not in a settlement or is cultivated land.

There are several activities that are free – hiking, photography, some museums and events (check the events calendar at **w** visitgreenland.gl). From the shore, you can

TYPICAL DOMESTIC TRAVEL PRICES

AASIAAT TO ILULISSAT
Flight (25mins) 950kr
Disko Line ferry (2hrs 50mins) 780kr
Arctic Umiaq ferry (4hrs 30mins) 600kr

QEQERTARSUAQ TO ILULISSAT
Helicopter flight (25mins) 1,400kr
Disko Line ferry (2hrs 15mins) 780kr
Arctic Umiaq ferry (5hrs 15mins) 700kr

NUUK TO SISIMIUT
Flight (55mins) 1,700kr
Arctic Umiaq ferry (21hrs, overnight in couchette) 1,200kr

iceberg watch all year, and at certain times of year you can even whale watch this way. A few places hire out equipment – kayaks, paddleboards, skis and bikes – at reasonable prices, and some hotels and hostels provide this type of equipment free to guests.

Once you have a plan for your trip, it is worth contacting local tour operators. If you want to do several activities, they may offer a package trip that is cheaper for you than if you buy everything individually; and if the weather disrupts an activity or journey, a local operator is well placed to change the itinerary or arrange an alternative. There are lists of local tour operators in the regional chapters. Air Greenland (w airgreenland.com) and its sister travel agency Greenland Travel (w greenland-travel.com) sometimes offer special deals like their Fly 'n' Sleep scheme, which includes a flight from Copenhagen to Nanortalik, Narsaq or Qaqortoq with an overnight stopover in Kangerlussuaq. This means you visit two regions while only paying for one flight.

GETTING AROUND

The climate can be harsh in the Arctic and this can delay all forms of transport with little notice. While an individual carrier, like Disko Line or Air Greenland, will always reorganise your journeys, this is not so if your late flight means you miss the boat or vice versa. It is wise only to make hotel bookings that can be changed and to have insurance that covers you if you do miss a connection and have to buy a new ticket. For similar reasons, it is wise to have a buffer day in your itinerary before your international flight home.

BY AIR All domestic flights are provided by Air Greenland (w airgreenland.com) with many of these routes operated by helicopter. Air Greenland has the largest helicopter flight network in the world, currently boasting 19 Airbus helicopters, a mix of H125s, H155s and H255s. They also have nine Dash 8 fixed-wing aircraft. The helicopters are more frequently delayed by weather than the Dash 8s, something to bear in mind when planning your itinerary.

There are around 14 airports and 42 heliports in Greenland, with Nuuk, Ilulissat and Kangerlussuaq the major hubs for domestic flights. Work is ongoing at Nuuk and Ilulissat airports to increase runway lengths and improve terminal facilities, all of which are planned to open in late 2024/early 2025.

2

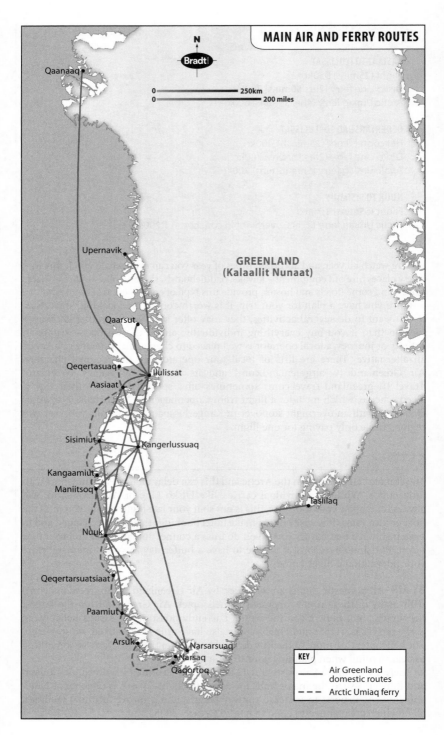

Since Air Greenland is a full-service airline, your ticket always includes 20kg of luggage and 8kg of hand luggage even on helicopter flights. On longer flights, over 2 hours, you'll even get a drink and a snack. Few routes are flown every day, so it requires some patience and flexibility to put an itinerary together. On the upside, every flight is a sightseeing trip – you may be flying over icebergs in Disko Bay or passing calving glaciers while flying along the coast where whales, especially beluga, can also be spotted.

Unusually, flights do sometimes leave ahead of schedule, so don't leave it to the last minute to check in. On helicopter flights, there may be limited space for odd-size baggage so, if you need to check in something unusual or large, make a special service request to Air Greenland at the time of booking. They are amazingly accommodating; for example, carrying skis is nearly always possible.

Passenger check-in for Air Greenland helicopter flights from very small settlement 'helistops' is performed at a check-in counter inside the local Pilersuisoq supermarket. You will not receive a boarding pass but your checked baggage will be taken from you and tagged and you will be able to wait in the warm. Checked baggage is transported between the Pilersuisoq store and the helistop by whatever form of transport is suitable given the terrain and the weather.

When there are flight delays, Air Greenland's staff are excellent at providing information and, if you have a Greenlandic network phone number, you will receive SMS notifications to inform you of changes. We recommend you invest in a local SIM card (page 66), and make sure that your new local mobile number is registered against your Air Greenland bookings. Air Greenland will always rebook you and provide you with food vouchers, taxi vouchers and accommodation; these are absolutely guaranteed for all delayed passengers. Greenlanders are very chilled when delays happen, fully aware that the airline and its pilots are specialists in Arctic flying and that they only delay flights when it is necessary. Delays are always a chance to talk with local travellers – we've chatted while sharing strawberry cake with reindeer hunters, talked football with the players from Greenland's top team on their way home complete with medals and a huge cup, and, most bizarrely, sung 'Here comes the sun' with a gentleman who told us he loved everything about Liverpool and its famous sons, the Beatles.

BY FERRY The M/S *Sarfaq Ittuk* coastal ferry, operated by Arctic Umiaq (w aul.gl), is an economical and interesting way to travel all along the west coast of Greenland. It is a passenger ferry only; it does not carry vehicles.

From late April until early January, the ferry travels once a week from Ilulissat in the north to Qaqortoq in the south. The whole route, top to bottom, is 1,330km (718 nautical miles). There is a shorter service during the second half of March and early April when the ferry does not travel as far north, stopping at Sisimiut, due to sea ice. The timetable does change with the seasons, and the extension of the service further north in the spring depends on sea-ice conditions being favourable. Check the Arctic Umiaq website for the latest times for the period when you plan to travel. You can generally board an hour before departure; make sure you are there at least 30 minutes early.

There are many highlights to the ferry trip. Just north of Nuuk, between Maniitsoq and Kangaamiut, there is a region of ragged peaks and glaciers. Further north, in Disko Bay, you will pass gigantic icebergs and, if you are lucky, spot whales as the ferry crosses the bay. In the south, halfway between Arsuk and Paamiut, the ferry passes the Paamiut Glacier, its huge sheet of ice reaching down to the sea. Further south still, the fjords along the south Greenland coast

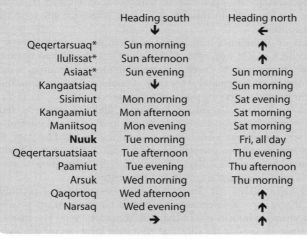

FERRY DEPARTURES

The ferry does not always call at the towns marked * and in summer, for a few weeks, also calls at Qasigiannguit, Uummannaq, Upernavik and Itilleq.

	Heading south ↓	Heading north ←
Qeqertarsuaq*	Sun morning	↑
Ilulissat*	Sun afternoon	↑
Asiaat*	Sun evening	Sun morning
Kangaatsiaq	↓	Sun morning
Sisimiut	Mon morning	Sat evening
Kangaamiut	Mon afternoon	Sat morning
Maniitsoq	Mon evening	Sat morning
Nuuk	Tue morning	Fri, all day
Qeqertarsuatsiaat	Tue afternoon	Thu evening
Paamiut	Tue evening	Thu afternoon
Arsuk	Wed morning	Thu morning
Qaqortoq	Wed afternoon	↑
Narsaq	Wed evening	↑
	→	↑

(Narsaq to Arsuk) are spectacular and so remote that you may spot grazing reindeer and musk oxen. Binoculars are a boon on board to get a closer view of the coast, for birdwatching and to spot whales and seals in the water. From June to August, the ship's guide gives lectures about Greenland and about what to see in the smaller cities and settlements.

The ferry itself was purpose-built for this route and is, therefore, designed to sail in icy waters. There are two open decks, both with seating, from which the view is truly breathtaking and there is also a lounge at the rear of the ship which offers a panoramic view without the need to go outside. There are 26 four-berth cabins which you can book exclusively for fewer people. Each cabin has a window, an en-suite shower and toilet, and a kettle. Bed linen and towels are provided. The 134 bunk beds are in cabins of up to eight beds and called, confusingly, couchettes; for this accommodation there are shared showers and toilets. Couchette bedding is not provided, but you can rent blankets and towels on board; having your own sleeping bag is a better option. Not all couchette rooms have a window or porthole. There are also three suites: two Junior Suites and one Igloo Suite. All three have double beds and TV and include free Wi-Fi. The Igloo Suite also comes with three meals a day, while a Junior Suite includes breakfast.

There is one restaurant on board, café Sarfaq (⏰ 07.00–22.00), which serves a reasonable range of food all day including open sandwiches, rolls and cakes. Breakfast plus a hot lunch and dinner are also served. There are machines selling hot and cold drinks, snacks and sandwiches. You can bring your own food and drink on board the ship but you may not consume it in public areas. If you are travelling on the ship through Qaqortoq, Nuuk, Ilulissat or Sisimiut, and the ferry is running to schedule, then you may have time to leave the ship and eat in the town. The café and lounges are great places to meet and talk to local Greenlanders and other travellers. There is always a sense of camaraderie on board and the locals are likely to be as interested in your life as you are in theirs. While for you this is an unforgettable cruise, for them it is an essential transport connection.

Online booking of tickets, cabins, couchettes and meals can be done on the website, and it is advisable to book as early as you can. The refund policy allows for cancellation up to 2 hours prior to departure with a full refund, but this is not a process we have actually tested. For a small charge, you can also bring bikes, kayaks and similar items on board. There are also safe deposit boxes if you wish to lock away your valuables. Wi-Fi is available on board but it is expensive (unless you have booked a suite) and slow, and comes and goes depending on the ferry's location.

Although the ferry travels up the coast, the seas can be rough and being prepared for seasickness is wise. Pressure point wristbands, pills and patches can all help; they may be available on board, but you are better advised to come prepared. If you do feel seasick then get outside and look at the horizon; this helps the body adapt to the motion.

BY LOCAL BOAT Small boats operate between many coastal and fjord settlements. The most comprehensive booking website is that of Disko Line (w diskoline.gl/ en) where you can buy tickets for travel in the Disko Bay area, for the west coast from Qeqertarsuatsiaat to Sisimiut and around south Greenland. In many coastal communities there are tour companies that run boat trips as well as companies who just charter boats. Asking around will often find you someone who is happy to take you in their boat to wherever you need to get to. The operating range of boats can be limited due to ice, particularly during the winter or just when the icebergs get stuck in awkward locations. In this case, you may be able to use a dog sled or snowmobile.

BY BUS AND TAXI There are no long-distance bus services. There are city buses in Nuuk, Sisimiut, Ilulissat and Kangerlussuaq and some of the smaller towns, typically operating on a circular route around the town on a regular basis and inexpensive. These services can be useful if you are staying on the edge of town.

Large towns have plenty of taxis and, to make life easier, some have phone apps which enable you to request a taxi at a particular location. The apps do not require you to specify your destination, nor do they enable you to pay. Some of the apps are in Danish only, but they are simple enough to understand. Even small settlements usually have one or two taxis but, while most taxis accept card payments, this cannot be guaranteed in small settlements.

BY CAR Driving in Greenland is unlike anywhere else in Europe or North America. The longest road runs for about 50km, and there are no roads between towns. There is no ferry to bring your vehicle to Greenland nor between towns in Greenland. If you rent a car, you are therefore confined to a small area around that town. Given the small size even of Nuuk, think twice before planning to rent. That being said, with Greenland's Arctic weather conditions, hiring a car may be practical for some visits where there is a particular need. On the upside, you'll never experience traffic congestion and other drivers are very courteous.

The minimum age to drive in Greenland is 18 and you must hold a full driver's licence; most rental companies will stipulate a minimum time that you must have held the licence, maybe one or two years. Any licence from your home country must be in the Latin alphabet, otherwise you must also hold an international driver's licence.

At any time of year, weather conditions must dictate how you drive. Cars are always on winter tyres and roads are either ploughed or laid with salt, gravel or sand. Despite this, slow and steady is the only way to drive here; braking distances

2

are huge compared with normal conditions. Cars drive on the right and are required to give way to any non-motorised vehicle, including dog sleds. Don't underestimate the speed of a dog sled, nor its ability to turn suddenly and unexpectedly.

Pedestrian crossings are marked with lines on the road and with a blue-and-white sign on both sides of the road. Drivers are required to give way to pedestrians waiting to cross. The speed limit is 40km/h on most roads and all cars must have their headlights on all the time. Everyone in the car must be wearing a seatbelt and it is illegal for the driver to use, or even touch, a mobile phone. Finally, you may not drive while under the influence of alcohol – the limit is 50mg per 100ml of blood – or drugs.

BY DOG SLED AND SNOWMOBILE If you travel north of the Arctic Circle then you will see plenty of **dog sleds** – they are the traditional way to travel in this region and the primary form of transport for many Greenlanders in winter. The Inuit have survived in Greenland partly because their skill with dog sleds allows them to move home and to hunt over a wide range. Today, most dog-sled teams are not there for tourists: they are working dogs. All through the winter, they pull their owner's sled for hunting or fishing, and are also used to transport locals and visitors between settlements.

There are strict rules governing the dogs that pull the sleds. They are pure-bred Greenlandic sled dogs, not huskies. To preserve the purity of the line, importing dogs to Greenland north of the Arctic Circle or to east Greenland is forbidden, even for short periods, except in exceptional circumstances.

Snowmobiles are, perhaps, the dog sled's modern equivalent. They are basically motorcycles on skis, just as useful and just as noisy. They are relied on as a basic form of transport by many Greenlanders and can, unlike a motorcycle, pull a trailer or even two. No driving licence is required to drive a snowmobile but you must be at least 18 years of age. Driver and passenger must both wear helmets.

ON FOOT Walking is the way most people get around inside towns and settlements, and there are a few things to be aware of. First, because nobody owns land, you can walk almost anywhere. This means that taking a shortcut between roads is normal practice – just watch out for hidden holes. Watch out, too, for pipes. Nearly all pipes are overground and carry everything – water, grey water, sewage, gas, fuel, electrical cables, phone cables and internet fibre optics. Many pipes are fragile and you should never step on them.

You can use any walkways and staircases that you see. Staircases are used by everyone and are really useful to get up hills or across boggy ground. Sometimes you will end up passing close to a house, and this is alright provided you don't look in the windows.

There are a few places you can't walk and these are generally fenced-off pasture grown for hay and rare private gardens.

FINDING YOUR WAY ROUND Identifying a building, even when it contains a business, is sometimes tricky. There may be no sign with the business name, nor even a street name. However, the building will have one or two numbers on it, near the door. One of these is the building number (it is preceded or followed by the letter B) and the other is the building's number in the street. At least one of these numbers should be in any address; often both are given. Building numbers are unique in a town and are issued sequentially when the permission is given to build. For some towns the Open Street Map (w openstreetmap.org) does number most buildings. Google Maps does not; indeed, Google Maps seems to have some confusion over which parts of Greenland are land and which are sea but it gets it right if you switch from the basic 'Map' view to the 'Earth' satellite view.

MAPS AND NAVIGATION There are two good maps that show all of Greenland: International Travel Maps' 1:3,000,000 map *Greenland & North Pole*; and Sagamaps' *Greenland*, which is available in a choice of scales from 1:11,800,000 to 1:2,500,000. These maps, and those listed below, are usually available from good map stores including Stanfords (7 Mercer Walk, Covent Garden WC2H 9FA; w stanfords.co.uk).

Sagamaps (w sagamaps.dk) also produces more detailed maps. Its Blue Series of 13 1:500,000 maps covers all of the west coast and the easily accessible parts of the east coast. The Yellow Series of three maps covers the far north of Greenland at the same scale. The more detailed Red Series comprises 23 maps at 1:250,000 and, again, covers all the west coast and accessible parts of the east coast. All Sagamaps are available in a choice of finishes: flat or folded, plain paper or laminated.

Greenland Tourism Trekking (w compukort.dk/Compukort/Grnlandskort. html) produces 22 even more detailed maps, most at 1:100,000 and a few at 1:75,000. These cover selected coastal areas and give a lot of detail including 25m contours, recommended hiking and snowmobile trails, camping places and hostels. The map's grid gives UTM co-ordinates plus latitude in steps of 5' and longitude in 10'. The maps are available on waterproof and tear-resistant paper or downloadable to smartphones and tablets using the Advenza app. Advenza is a mapping app whose store contains many publishers' maps from all over the world. As well as the Greenland Tourism Trekking maps, it does also offer some free maps published by the Greenland Institute of Natural Resources (search for 'Greenland Institute' in the Advenza store). These are good for terrain but not for tracks and paths.

Using a **compass** in Greenland requires care because Greenland is a long way north and compass needles point to magnetic north rather than true north. At more southerly latitudes, the difference between the two, the magnetic declination, is small enough that it can be ignored – in London it is less than one degree. In Greenland, the difference between magnetic north and true north is quite large and needs to be taken into account when navigating. Today the magnetic declination in Nuuk is −20°, but it will be different in a month's time as the magnetic north pole drifts. There are a number of websites (eg: w magnetic-declination.com) that offer accurate and up-to-date information.

ACCOMMODATION

Accommodation in Greenland ranges from dormitory beds in hostels to private cabins with helicopter transfers, and the costs reflect this. In the larger towns, prices fluctuate according to demand but in small towns and settlements there is likely to be fixed, seasonal pricing. At peak times and for small places, it is always best to book ahead but with the ability to change your booking. In Greenland, you never know whether your plane or boat will be delayed.

HOTELS The words hostel and hotel are often used quite loosely and it is difficult sometimes to distinguish between the two. All large towns have at least one hotel that we would rate as 3- or 4-star, where you will find a comfortable en-suite room. Many hotels have a Scandinavian feel to them, clean and simple, while others reflect the Greenlandic culture with animal skins, lots of wood and bright colours. Most rooms have Wi-Fi, normally free, and a TV, usually with only Greenlandic and Danish channels.

All hotels have a restaurant or café, and breakfast is usually included in the rate. In smaller settlements, it may be the only restaurant in town. Hotels offer transfers to and from the airport or harbour, usually at no additional cost.

HOSTELS The quality of hostel accommodation in Greenland is surprisingly good. They are a great option for budget travellers and many offer excellent, clean accommodation. Most hostels in Greenland have more single and double rooms than dormitories, generally sharing shower and toilet facilities. There will also be a communal kitchen and, usually, laundry facilities. Some hostels offer optional cooked meals, though usually these must be booked ahead of time. Many hostels are run by tour operators and others by private individuals; none is affiliated to the International Hostel Association.

GUESTHOUSES A guesthouse in Greenland means a house that you can rent, either the entire house or a room in the house. It can be hard to distinguish between the smaller hostels and the larger guesthouses which rent their rooms out individually. There will usually be between two and four bedrooms in a house, sharing one or two bathrooms, a kitchen and a dining/lounge area. Some guesthouses are in exceptional locations and have wooden terraces from which to enjoy the views.

Guesthouses are all self-catering and every settlement has at least one good supermarket for you to shop at but check that it will be open when you arrive. In the larger towns, some of this type of accommodation is on Airbnb and similar booking sites, but the majority is offered through individual's or tour operators' websites. Tour operators will usually also arrange transport to and from the accommodation.

RURAL HOUSES, FARMS AND CABINS Across the whole country, the range of isolated cabins is huge. There are basic, self-catering cabins; more comfortable cabins with heating and lots of facilities; upmarket cabins with hot tubs, views of glaciers and gourmet dining. What they all have in common is that they enable you to get right out into Greenland's wild and rugged backcountry. Most cabins can organise transport on request.

In south Greenland, many farms have rooms, cabins and hostels where you have the option of taking your meals with the family. This is a great way to understand the life of the sheep farmers and their families, and eat very well.

Hunters and fishermen have private cabins in the wilderness. These are generally only bookable as part of a trip with them.

CAMPING There is no private land ownership in Greenland so there are few restrictions on camping. You may camp anywhere except inside a settlement, a designated UNESCO World Heritage Site or a bird breeding area; and you can only stay one night before moving on, though it seems this is rarely checked. There are very few organised campsites, but some hostels allow camping in their grounds and use of their facilities for a small fee. Camping is not an option in east Greenland nor in the far north due to the risk of polar bears.

Small settlements have service houses whose primary purpose is to provide laundry and shower facilities to local people whose homes have no running water. If you are camping, you can use the service house for a small fee. Some service houses will allow you to sleep in them if there is no other accommodation available in the settlement – but it should be a last resort.

UNIQUE LOCATIONS With an organised trip, you can camp on the ice sheet; you need a permit, so this is difficult to arrange yourself. You can also sleep in an igloo. In both cases, you are provided with lots of warm bedding and reindeer skins. If you walk the Arctic Circle Trail, there are free huts in amazing locations all the way along the route. You will need to bring your own bedding, and a tent in case you find the hut is full.

EATING AND DRINKING

Food has often been scarce in Greenland's past. Winters were especially difficult and settlements suffering famine was not unusual. When food was available, even abundant, communal feasts and sharing were common. The Greenlandic explorer Knud Rasmussen (page 164) explained to a European colleague, 'To eat eight huge meals of meat with coffee to follow, one meal after another, is a thing which you only grow accustomed to after living among us for sometime.'

Traditionally raw, smoked and fermented meat and fish have always been part of the diet; raw foods contain more nutrients and fermented foods last longer. The most common meats were musk ox, reindeer, polar bear, whale and seal and are still popular today – don't miss the opportunity to try them. Vegetables and fruit were, traditionally, unavailable. They can only be grown in the very south of Greenland and even there it is a short growing season.

Today, there is no shortage of food. You will find supermarkets in every town and settlement filled with every type of food that you would expect and the Danish influence means that you will probably find a bakery in there too. Even in the smallest of settlements there is always a good supply of breads, cakes and pastries to go with all that coffee. The Greenlandic diet did not, traditionally, contain dairy products and even today you may notice less use of cheese and yoghurt than you are accustomed to. Many Inuit are lactose intolerant and lactose-free dairy products are commonly found.

EATING OUT The 3- and 4-star hotels usually have good restaurants, but you may find equally high-quality food in a slightly scruffy café in the middle of town,

RESTAURANT PRICE CODES

Meal price codes are based on the average cost of a main course.

$$$$	Expensive	over 300kr
$$$	Upmarket	225–300kr
$$	Reasonable	151–224kr
$	Budget	up to 150kr

Greenlandic coffee is a speciality coffee usually served after a meal. Freshly brewed coffee is mixed with whisky and Kahlúa, a coffee liqueur, in a wine glass. Then a spoonful of Grand Marnier, an orange and brandy liqueur, is set alight and poured over the top. Finally, it is topped with a pyramid of whipped cream. It is said that the ingredients represent Greenland – it requires a little imagination:

Kahlúa Warm and soft, representing the animals, the scenery and the women.
Whisky Rough, representing the rugged landscape, the hunters and the men.
Grand Marnier When set alight, its flames represent the northern lights.
Coffee A drink that brings everyone together to talk and tell their stories.
Whipped cream Shaped like the icebergs in the seas and fjords.

so don't be put off by the exterior. Cafeteria-style restaurants often offer a very good-value basic meal at lunch and dinner – always meat, gravy, potatoes and vegetables.

Most restaurants serve a fusion of international and Greenlandic food. Alongside beef steaks, a menu may offer reindeer or musk ox. Similarly, a pasta dish may include smoked Arctic cod, a pizza may be topped with minced musk ox, as well as chorizo, and the risotto may be made with whale meat. In better restaurants local herbs – Labrador tea, mountain sorrel and Arctic thyme – will also be evident. There are a few excellent Thai restaurants, too, which serve a Thai-Chinese-Greenlandic fusion menu, using pork, chicken or Greenlandic meats and mild curry sauces. And chips!

A typical local restaurant meal might start with a platter of dried fish. The most traditional is dried capelin, a small fish that can be either chopped into small sections or split and peeled back, rather like a pea pod. Dried cod, white and full of flavour, is also popular, as is narwhal skin which is white or pink with a mild fish flavour. Dried fish is often served with a bowl of black berries, similar to blueberries. The main course might be local lamb, which is excellent, musk ox or reindeer steak, often served with a rich sauce. Alternatively, fish may be served, typically Arctic char, Greenland halibut or trout, or snow crab. Potatoes are a common accompaniment, along with other vegetables which may include red cabbage, celeriac and cauliflower. These are all vegetables least affected by their journey from Iceland or Denmark. Pickled vegetables are also popular, particularly red onion. Some vegetables are now grown in south Greenland in the summer and new enterprises are growing salad vegetables all year round in managed environments – heated and artificially lit greenhouses.

The most common dessert is traditional Greenlandic cake, a cross between cake and bread mixed with dried fruit. It is sometimes sliced and spread with jam. After your meal, Labrador tea may be served, perhaps flavoured with locally picked thyme, or Greenlandic coffee (page 54).

VEGETARIAN AND VEGAN DIETS Vegetarians and vegans are not going to starve in Greenland but it is going to be tricky. Most restaurants in Nuuk will have a vegetarian dish on the menu, but outside of the capital, most restaurants will have neither vegetarian nor vegan dishes, though asking for a dish to be made without the meat or fish will usually be possible. Organising your travel to stay in accommodation with a kitchen will make life much easier. The supermarkets do sell a selection of fruit, vegetables, nuts, eggs and cheese and, in Nuuk, you will find vegan alternatives for milk, cheese and so forth in the larger supermarkets. Outside of Nuuk, soya milk is probably the only product of this type that will be available. There will be lots of food that is inherently vegan, of course.

DRINKS Greenlanders drink a lot of coffee and it is usually excellent. Many cafés have espresso machines while supermarkets sell cups of filter coffee. You will also be offered teas, including those made with freshly picked herbs, and water is free, clean and served everywhere. Soft fizzy drinks like Coke are widely available, but the drink that Greenlanders grow up with is Faxe Kondi; it tastes much like Sprite or a sweet lemonade.

Greenlanders, like many indigenous peoples, have had a difficult time with alcohol and in some parts of the country you cannot buy spirits. Wine and beer are available in most supermarkets and restaurants and many cafés. Supermarkets can sell alcohol only at restricted times (typically, noon–18.00 Mon–Fri, 11.00–13.00 Sat), but hours can vary.

There are two good Greenlandic breweries, Qajaq in Narsaq and Immiaq in Ilulissat, which both offer a wide range of bottled and draft beers. There is also a micro-brewery in Nuuk, Godthaab Bryghus (page 80), which only sells its draft beers in house, on tap.

FESTIVALS AND ANNUAL EVENTS

6 January	**Mitaartut** An Inuit winter festival where children dress up as ghosts or any scary character and sing and dance outside homes in the hope of receiving sweets. A Greenlandic Halloween.
February/March	**Nuuk Snow Festival** (w snow.gl; free entry) Teams of four from all over the world take part in this snow sculpture competition, with four days to complete their sculpture from a cube of snow. The festival also has children's workshops, daily 'snow concerts' and street food. You can volunteer to help.
March/April	**Arctic Circle Race** (w acr.gl) This ultimate 160km cross-country skiing race is held each year in Sisimiut. The route passes through magnificent, varied and sometimes harsh terrain, and involves three days of skiing and two nights in tents. Dog sleds and snowmobiles are used to transport competitors to the camp. There is also a shorter 100km route and a one-day race for children.
April	**Avannaata Qimussersua** (f; free) More than 200 people, many families, climb aboard their dog sleds and spend three days following one of the training routes of Knud Rasmussen, a famous Greenlandic explorer (page 164). The venue varies from year to year but is always in west Greenland above the Arctic Circle.
	Arctic Sounds (w arcticsounds.gl) This five-day music festival with artists from many Nordic countries is based in

1 January	New Year's Day
6 January	Epiphany
March/April	Easter: Maundy Thursday, Good Friday, Easter Monday
April/May	Common Prayer Day (4th Friday after Good Friday)
April/May	Ascension Day (6 weeks after Maundy Thursday)
May	Whit Monday (7 weeks after Easter Monday)
21 June	National Day, or Ullortuneq
24 December	Christmas Eve
25 December	First Day of Christmas
26 December	Second Day of Christmas
31 December	New Year's Eve

Sisimiut, but it is also celebrated on the coastal ferry, where musicians board at Nuuk and entertain the passengers until they reach Sisimiut.

May — **Nuuk Nordic Culture Festival** (Biennial, next in May 2025; tickets 350kr for all events, free for under 12s; w nuuknordisk.gl) A week-long festival in the capital, with exhibitions of contemporary art and culture, theatre, dance and visual arts, music and literature held in several venues around the city. Volunteers welcome (if you volunteer, you get free entry to all events).

21 June — **Greenland's National Day** Held on the longest day of the year, National Day is a celebration of Greenlandic culture. Festivals take place in all the towns and settlements with singing, hoisting the flag, church services, folk dancing and more. Many people wear national costume.

June — **Marathons** To make the most of those long summer days, there are several marathons in various towns including Aasiaat (Midnight Sun Marathon and Half-Marathon; ■), Qaqortoq (■; rather hilly!) and a half-marathon in Nuuk (w sportstiming.dk/event/12954).

July — **Sheep Farmers' Festival** Held over the first weekend of July in either Qaqortoq or Narsaq in the sports field to celebrate the end of the lambing season. Competitions include horseback riding and lasso throwing, and there are lots of free family activities. There are also handicraft stalls, delicious local lamb to feast on and a dinner dance in the sports hall in the evening.

Nuuk Pride (■) A colourful LGBTQIA+ festival of concerts and films culminating in a parade.

Arctic Hiking Festival (w arcticcirclehike.com) A six-day festival near Sisimiut where you can not only hike but also improve the trails and make the area more accessible in the future.

August — **Qooqqut Festival** (■; free) A weekend music festival for all the family at this small settlement on the side of Nuuk Fjord.

	KangNu race (**f**) This extreme running race across rough terrain on the edge of Nuuk has a choice of distances – 56km, 35km or 20km.
September	**Akisuanerit Festival** (**w** atlanticmusicshop.gl) Concerts and other music events held on the edge of Nuuk and featuring many local bands.
September/October	**Polar Circle Marathon** (**w** polar-circle-marathon. com) Known as the coolest marathon on earth, the race begins with a section of the route on the ice sheet above Kangerlussuaq. The track is sometimes covered in snow. A half-marathon is also run on the next day.
24 December	**Santa Claus lands in Nuuk** (**w** visitnuuk.com/santa-lands-in-nuuk) Santa arrives in Nuuk in a bright red helicopter and distributes sweets among the children. If the weather is bad, Santa cleverly comes on his red fire engine instead.

SHOPPING

Every settlement has a supermarket and a post office. In larger towns, there will be a selection of supermarkets, but in small settlements there will be just the government-run Pilersuisoq supermarket which will also house the post office. Supermarkets are open at least five days a week, usually with shorter hours on Saturdays. Only in larger towns are supermarkets open on Sundays.

Fresh food at the best prices can be found at the local markets, which are nearly always beside the harbour. Shoppers can purchase fresh fish, sea mammal meat and berries directly from the people who hunted, caught or picked them that day. Market traders generally only accept cash.

Nuuk has a good bookshop and a good stationery shop; both sell maps and guides (page 81). Outside of the capital, maps and English-language books are hard to find.

GIFTS AND SOUVENIRS Most tourist information centres and some hotels sell a selection of local handicrafts, souvenirs and gifts. In the larger towns, you will also find high-quality craft shops and boutiques, some selling traditional clothing. Sealskin handbags, shoes, boots and clothes are particularly interesting.

A popular gift is a tupilak (page 27), a small statue with a scary face, once believed to protect you from enemy attack. Today, they are carved mostly from horn, bone or stone by craftspeople who wish to preserve the Inuit myths and keep their ancestral stories alive. You will also find beautifully decorated ulu, knives traditionally used by women to clean animal skins or trim blocks of snow and ice. These are also good for chopping herbs when you get home. Both tupilak and ulu can be bought from craft workshops in many towns including Nuuk, Tasiilaq, Sisimiut and Ilulissat. The craftspeople are very happy to show you how they work and explain the meaning of each particular piece. Many will also make a special piece just for you.

Beaded jewellery and decorated clothing can have traditional or very modern designs. Beaded earrings are very popular. Also worth seeking out are hats, gloves, scarves and socks made from musk ox wool or *qiviut*, claimed to be the warmest wool in the world but it is also extremely expensive. You can also buy skincare products made using local ingredients and Greenlandic herbs – thyme, Labrador tea, juniper and chamomile.

The export of some animal products is restricted by CITES regulations (see above). Check before you buy.

ACTIVITIES

Local tour operators can be found throughout Greenland and offer a huge selection of activities. Many have an informative website, while others just rely on a Facebook page. Information on these local tour operators can be found in all the regional chapters.

If you plan to do an activity that requires specialist equipment or clothing, then most operators will be able to provide you with what you need – but check before you travel. Although Nuuk and larger towns do have an outdoors store, the range of items will be limited, so don't assume that you will be able to buy what you need in Greenland. If you do need to bring equipment with you, check that it will fit into the plane, helicopter or boat that you are travelling on.

On the following pages, we have given a rough guide to the best months for each pursuit. Greenlanders are very flexible, though, so you will find that activities are offered whenever conditions permit.

ARCTIC CIRCLE TRAIL (May–Oct, Feb–Apr for skiers & snowshoers; see also page 140) The Arctic Circle Trail is Greenland's most popular long-distance walking trail, running 165km between Kangerlussuaq and Sisimiut, from the ice sheet to the ocean, and part of the trail is within the Aasivissuit-Nipisat UNESCO World Heritage Site. Where you actually start is open to debate. It adds 37km to the start of the trail if you start on the ice sheet or reduces the walk by 13km if you get a ride to the end of the road. The trail takes 7–12 days to walk, is remote and only suitable for experienced walkers. There are nine basic huts en route, all free to use, and you will need to carry all your bedding and food. It is also possible to ski or snowshoe the trail in winter.

BIRDWATCHING (Apr–Oct) There are believed to be more than 200 different bird species in Greenland; however, only about 30 live here year-round. Many of the more common birds are described on page 12, but you may wish to seek out some of the unusual species including Brünnich's guillemot, a black-and-white seabird that stands upright like a penguin. Three of the rare 'high Arctic gulls' may also be found, the ivory gull, Sabine's gull and the Ross's gull. Another favourite is the snowy owl, a distinctive bird that feeds on lemmings, but it is hard to spot. Well adapted to Arctic conditions, its feet are protected by feathery pads to keep them warm. There are a few particularly good locations for sighting birds and these are mentioned in the regional chapters. Many tour operators offer special birdwatching trips.

BOAT TRIPS (Year-round) Whether it is on the coastal ferry, a fishing boat or a water taxi, boat trips are a 'must do' in Greenland. The range of trips is vast, lasting from a half-hour shuttle to a few days on the ferry. Boat trips are an excellent way to see the country's coastal scenery, glaciers and giant floating icebergs; they will also get you up close to the wildlife – from polar bears and whales to seals and seabirds.

Before booking, give some thought to what kind of boat you want to be on. Small open boats get you up close to nature but can be cold – wear several layers of warm clothing and take any more offered to you by the trip operator. Fully closed-in boats are warm but you are restricted in your movement and can feel a bit remote from the scenery. Trips in boats that have space inside and out are often best.

CLIMBING (May–Aug) Climbing in Greenland is challenging and only for the experienced. Permits are required to climb in most areas and there are no reliable guidebooks or mountain rescue service. There are, however, a few specialist tour companies which employ excellent, experienced mountain guides to take individuals or small groups climbing; these are listed in the regional chapters, especially in south and east Greenland.

COASTAL FERRY (Mar–Jan; see also page 47) From late April to early January, the Arctic Umiaq passenger ferry travels once a week up and down the west coast from Ilulissat in the north to Qaqortoq in the south. Owing to the presence of sea ice, there is a slightly shorter route during the second half of March and early April when the ferry does not travel as far north, stopping at Sisimiut. The trip takes just over three days in one direction or a week to make the round trip, calling at ten settlements on the way. The ferry provides not only comfortable transport but also offers great opportunities for visitors to watch wildlife, see glaciers and icebergs and meet local people over lunch in the restaurant.

CYCLING (Year-round) Greenland has no road network, but cycling is possible in towns and settlements and on some trails. It takes no time to get out of any town into the wilderness – just ask a Greenlander where you can find the nearest trail that you can cycle. In a few locations you can also rent 'fat bikes', mountain bikes with extra-large tyres; these are designed to make it easier to cycle on the Arctic terrain and are popular for winter cycling. Being designed for this environment, their tyres cut a groove in snow and give better grip on ice.

DOG SLEDDING (Nov–Apr) Dog sledding is part of the Inuit way of life and has been a means of transport for thousands of years. Many locations offer dog-sledding trips which can last a couple of hours or many days, staying in huts or igloos on the way. In winter, you may even find that the transport from your flight to your accommodation is by dog sled.

You will hear the howling dogs before you see them. Always eager to run, these strong animals will be jumping around waiting for the musher (sled driver) to harness them up. There can be up to 12 dogs pulling a sled and it takes time for the musher to assemble them in the correct formation. Depending on the location, the dogs might be harnessed in pairs or a single- or double-fan formation, always with the lead dog at the front. As you watch the musher prepare the sled, you will appreciate the special bond they have with their dogs.

Even if you are wearing warm clothes, you may be offered skin trousers and a skin anorak, plus insulated boots. It will be cold on the sled, so take up the offer. The wooden sled will be covered in reindeer skins for extra warmth.

Once all the dogs are harnessed, they jump around straining to be away. The musher will stand at the back of the sled and, with a brief command, you are off. Racing across the snow or maybe along a frozen fjord, the endless icy landscape stretches out ahead. Silent, apart from the rhythmic beat of the dogs' paws and the occasional command from the musher. There may be a chance to stop for a hot drink or some ice fishing, an opportunity for the musher to explain how they control the dogs and how they are cared for. However long your journey, the experience of joining a musher and their team of dogs will be one of the most treasured memories that you take home.

FISHING (Year-round: fly fishing and sea fishing in summer; ice fishing in winter) Fly fishing for Arctic char starts in salt water in May and then in rivers from July to September. All fishing requires a fishing licence from a post office (from 75kr/day to 500kr/month). Most rivers are open to be fished by anyone, but there are nine private rivers, so make sure you check before fishing. Some tour operators offer single and multi-day fishing trips throughout the season.

Ice fishing is a totally different experience. After drilling a hole in the ice or chipping a hole with a *tupa*, you can fish for redfish, Greenland halibut and cod. You may use a single short line or a long, multi-hooked line depending on the fish that are to be caught. When long lines are used, a reel in a stand is positioned over the hole to wind in the up to 2km of line that has been played out. Tour operators typically use snowmobiles or dog sleds to get you to the best fishing spots.

FLIGHT-SEEING (Year-round) You may feel that with so many albeit short flights in aircraft and helicopters to get from place to place, you don't need to go up in a plane to see more. However, a tour in the air can allow you to see specific sights or spend time over a chosen location and enable you to see herds of musk ox, roaming polar bears or a mass of icebergs in the bay. From the air, you can get a greater understanding of just how huge the ice sheet really is. Many helicopter flights offer the option of landing on the ice sheet or on a glacier.

HELI-SKIING (Mar–May) Heli-skiing is most popular in east and west Greenland with helicopters being used both to get into the area and to the top of each run. The vast mountain slopes offer endless opportunities for long downhill runs. Experienced ski guides make it possible to ski new routes in areas where only Inuit have travelled before. As well as extraordinary skiing on virgin snow, heli-skiing offers the opportunity to enjoy incredible views across this vast untouched landscape.

HIKING (Year-round) Even in Nuuk, the countryside is always on your doorstep. Whether you want a stroll with friends after lunch or to spend more than a week alone on the Arctic Circle Trail, Greenland has hiking everywhere and for every ability. There are a number of mountains that can be hiked up in a day and hiking trail information can be found in tourist information centres and bookstores. All land is owned by the state and you are free to hike anywhere you wish as long as you respect the people around you and their possessions.

Greenland's landscape is unlike anywhere else and it is easy to get disoriented. Before you leave, make sure somebody knows where you are going, that you have a good map (page 51) and a GPS device with a full battery. Weather is also a critical factor; make sure you always have warm, waterproof clothing with you, even on a sunny cloud-free day, as the weather can change in an instant. Regional tour companies are able to provide experienced guides who can take you off the beaten track and help you spot wildlife.

HORSERIDING (Apr–Oct) In south Greenland, you can ride Icelandic horses, typically between the sheep farms and small settlements. Horses were first brought in by Norse settlers and riding is still an easy way to visit the Norse ruins. Rides can last just a few hours or for up to eight days.

HOT SPRINGS (Year-round) There are a few hot springs dotted around Greenland especially in volcanic and geothermal areas including on the island of Qeqertarsuaq in Disko Bay and at Uunartoq in south Greenland. None of the hot springs is developed; you can just turn up and join in – bring your swimwear, a towel and a drink. There is something quite special about sitting in a hot spring while watching icebergs float by.

ICE SHEET (Year-round) Greenland's ice sheet can be visited most easily from Kangerlussuaq, from where a 37km road runs to the edge of the ice sheet. It is also accessible from other towns and settlements by walking in, by boat up a fjord or by helicopter. Tour operators are able to offer trips to the ice sheet with the option of staying the night on the ice in a tent. You will need to put on crampons once you reach the ice sheet, so wear hiking boots or tough outdoor shoes. It is possible, with the correct permits and support, to hike across the ice sheet. The 600km crossing takes about 30 days and is tough (page 194).

KAYAKING (May–Oct) Kayaks, *qajaq* in Greenlandic, have been used for hunting and for travel for 4,000 years. Today, the kayak is still an everyday means of transport, as well as a symbol of the traditional Inuit way of life, and kayaking is enjoyed as recreation by locals and visitors alike, affording great views of icebergs, birds, seals and whales. While traditional skin-and-frame kayaks are still used for hunting in northern regions, modern lightweight kayaks are now used for fun and for travel. In many towns and settlements, you will find kayaks available to rent. Whether you are a beginner or experienced, always ask the locals about sea and fjord conditions before you go out.

Practical Information ACTIVITIES

2

Until recently, taking good photographs of the northern lights required sophisticated equipment but today this can be done with most modern mobile phone cameras. It is amazing what they can produce.

We do recommend you undertake some trial runs at home before you leave. You will need a tripod with a phone clamp that will enable you to hold the phone in a horizontal position. A little 'Gorillapod' tripod is fine, though you may have to crouch down or find a rock to put the tripod on. Before you start taking the photos, get away from all sources of light and any source of vibration or movement.

1. Turn the flash off.
2. Turn the shutter timer on, 5 seconds is fine. This gives time for the phone to be still after you have pressed the shutter button on its screen.
3. Select night or fireworks mode.

This may be all you need to do – it depends on your phone and how bright the northern lights are. Try this out at home by taking photographs of the moon in a big night sky, not zoomed in. This is a good way to learn how to operate the settings on your phone. If you are not getting good pictures, then there are a few more things that you can try.

4. Turn the camera to manual mode.
5. Turn off auto focus and, if you have the option, set the focus to infinity.
6. Set the ISO setting to 800 or 1600. This makes the camera more sensitive to light.
7. Set the white balance to 3200K. This makes the colours of the northern lights truer.
8. Set the shutter speed to 10 seconds. Increase it in 5-second steps if the photos are too dark; decrease it in 1-second steps if they are too bright.
9. If you are using an iPhone 11 or newer, set the exposure to –0.7.

The golden rule is to try things out on your phone, experiment to see what works. The moon and sky are good test subjects. When you are happy with your photos, try taking some video, again on night or fireworks mode and using your tripod. Good luck.

MIDNIGHT SUN (May–Aug) Wherever you are in Greenland in summer, you will experience very long summer days, but for true midnight sun you must be north of the Arctic Circle. Like everywhere in the northern hemisphere, the longest day is 21 June but, if you are north of the Arctic Circle, the sun will not set. The further north you travel, the more days of midnight sun you will experience. In Ilulissat, the sun does not set from 21 May until 24 July and in Siorapaluk, in the far north, the sun does not set for four months.

THE NORTHERN LIGHTS (AURORA BOREALIS) (Sep–Apr) Greenland is one of the best locations in the world for viewing the northern lights. Its northern location and lack of light pollution increases the chances of witnessing this magical sight. Auroras are most visible on dark, clear nights between September and April. Dog-sled and snowmobile trips into the wilderness offer a wonderful way to see the aurora.

PADDLEBOARDING (Apr–Sep) Stand-up paddleboarding is another way to see Greenland from the water. Like kayaks, SUPs offer an alternative way to see Greenland's animals and birds while paddling up a fjord. The near silence of an SUP is a great advantage – you'll clearly hear the creek of the ice, the cries of the seals and unmistakable sound of a whale blowing before taking a breath.

PHOTOGRAPHY (Year-round) Whether you are taking photos with your mobile phone or have a bag of sophisticated camera bodies, lenses and filters, Greenland is a photographer's dream destination. With icebergs and snow-capped mountains, multicoloured villages and blue-eyed dogs, there is no shortage of subjects and the pure air means the light is crystal-clear. A few tour operators offer photography tours, often focused on a particular area or subject and accompanied by a professional photographer.

Always ask before taking photographs of people and respect them if they say no. As it can be cold all year, keep your spare batteries charged up and inside your jacket to keep them warm. If you are taking photographs with a mobile phone, then it may be worth investing in a portable power bank so that you can recharge while on the move.

There are laws regulating the use of drones (w droneregler.dk/english) which ban them in many places including all urban areas, in the national park and near airports.

SKI TOURING (CROSS-COUNTRY SKIING) (Feb–May) The ski touring season usually starts in late February and runs into May. Most ski touring is done without any use of lifts or helicopters; it is just you and your skis. On a crisp spring day, there is no better way to see the landscape. Ski tours can last just for one day or for multiple days, going from hut to hut and supported by teams on snowmobiles or dog sleds. Adhesive 'skins' are used on your skis to enable better grip when going uphill. At night on multi-day trips, the sky is inky black and full of stars and, if you are lucky, full of the dancing northern lights. In Eternity Fjord (page 153), you can ski tour from a moored boat into areas that are, even by Greenland's standards, remote and untouched.

SNOWMOBILING (Oct–Apr) For many Greenlanders, the snowmobile is part of everyday life. While we use a car or motorcycle, many Greenlanders use a snowmobile. Typically, snowmobiles are used from October to March but this season extends as you travel north. You must be over 18 years of age to drive a snowmobile, though no licence is needed. A guided snowmobile tour is recommended for first-timers, available in many places. If you rent a snowmobile without a guide, make sure you understand the traffic laws, especially regarding where you can and cannot drive and who has priority. See also page 50.

SNOWSHOEING (Oct–Apr) Snowshoeing enables hiking to continue when deep snow covers the ground. It is a bit more aerobic than hiking but well worth it for the silent beauty of stepping out into an endless expanse of snow. The snowshoes – oval plates or nets that strap to the bottom of your boots – spread your weight, so that you end up walking on top of the snow rather than sinking into it. Most snowshoeing is done on short trails, but the Arctic Circle Trail is a long-distance option. While staying in a hut during an overnight snowmobile or dog-sled trip, you may have the opportunity to snowshoe in the surrounding area.

NAJA P – GREENLAND POP'S AWARD-WINNING MUSICIAN

Oscar Scott Carl

Naja P's inspiration may come from within, but her latest album points outward and emphasises how cool Greenland's history and culture are. When asked where her interest in music comes from, her answer is almost cinematic: the childhood memory of her mother singing the famous Greenlandic lullaby 'Innarta Anaanaga' to her when she was going to sleep as a little girl.

According to her mother, Naja P was making melodies before she could talk, and her grandmother says she was making songs as soon as she could speak. Her very first release, the five-track album *Naasunnguusunga*, which means 'When I was a little flower', won Greenland's biggest music award at the Koda Awards in the spring of 2023, and her hit with the same name has become almost ubiquitous with over 300,000 plays on Spotify. Naja P has quickly established her name in Greenland's music landscape.

Behind the artist's name 'Naja P' is 23-year-old Nuumthmioq Naja Parnuuna Sofia Vahl Olsen. She previously studied anthropology at Aarhus University and briefly considered becoming an academic like many others in her family. But there was something that didn't quite feel right. One day, she had a conversation with her mother and received a piece of advice to follow her own dreams. This advice led her to follow her musical dream and also led her to attend drama school in Nuuk. Her résumé now includes being a comedian, singer and actress.

The starting point in Naja P's music is her own emotions. She is determined that her music should mean something to someone, to convey her feelings to others. Following your own dream is advice that she wants to pass on to everyone.

While her first album was more melancholic and primarily focused on emotions related to her love life, Naja P is now heading in a new direction. She has created

WHALE WATCHING (Year-round, but best May–Oct) This is a must-do when visiting Greenland. If you have never been whale watching before, then you are in for a treat as this is one of the best places in the world to see whales. Three whales overwinter off Greenland's coast and, in summer, you have the chance of seeing up to 13 different whale species, all here to feed in these rich waters. Nuuk, Ilulissat, Tasiilaq, Aasiaat and Uummannaq all have whale-spotting boat trips.

The easiest whales to spot are humpbacks and bowheads as they both breach and their tails are flipped up into the air before they dive. Narwhal are easy to see when they put their heads above water because of their long tusk. Belugas are tricky to spot as they are only 3m long and show only their grey-and-white backs above water; but being white, they can be seen from the air. Fin whales act in a similar manner but are dark grey and up to 27m long; the little dorsal fin that gives them their name is about two-thirds of the way along their back which does have a distinctive ridge along its entire length. Minke whales can be confused with fin whales: they both have fins but minkes are only about 10m long and much darker in colour.

ARTS AND ENTERTAINMENT

In Nuuk **evening entertainment** is centred at the Katuaq Cultural Centre (page 80). Other towns have occasional concerts and there is often **live music** in cafés and bars, especially on Friday and Saturday night. It is likely to start late and go songs with English lyrics which will be released at a later date, but first an album for the Greenlanders. Once she was not proud of being Greenlandic, but then she spent some time in Portugal and saw everything from the outside, in a different light. She saw how cool it actually was to be Greenlandic and how Greenlanders have been able to survive in an extraordinary way.

The album, released in 2024, was made in collaboration with photographer and artist Inuuteq Storch and was produced by fellow musician and producer Tûtu. The goal is clear. They want to convey a message to all Greenlanders. The new album says, 'Look at how cool our history and culture are.'

Naja P is part of a new wave of young musicians who create music themselves, from a fledgling idea to the release of a fully produced song. And, although she would like to have a manager for the 'boring paperwork', she and Tûtu, who produces all of Naja P's music and is an important part of Naja P's success, are personally responsible for all the music released under her name. That they are not dependent on anyone does, they believe, give a great feeling of ownership to their music.

Naja P is part of the new wave who have found that, with a studio and a laptop, it is easy to release high-quality music. Quality is something that Naja P believes is central to the story of musicians and creative people in Greenland. When she spoke to other creatives in her acceptance speech at the Koda Awards, she stressed the incredible talent in Greenland that needs to be shown to the world.

Oscar Scott Carl is a documentary writer and photographer who is working with Visit Nuuk to draw portraits, in words and photographs, of interesting Nuuk residents.

on into the morning. **Traditional drum and dance music**, which does also have a choral element, may be heard at festivals and at occasional events put on for tourists. There is also a more modern tradition of **church choir music**, introduced by the Danish missionaries. You may be able to listen to choir practice in a local church; ask at your accommodation. **Modern music** is influenced both by tradition and by European and American music with interesting results. If you fly in with Air Greenland on their new Airbus, you can listen to a good selection of modern Greenlandic music on the flight in.

There are a number of **music festivals** across the country including Arctic Sounds in Sisimiut (page 55), Nuuk Nordic Culture Festival (page 56), the Akisuanerit Festival in Nuuk (page 57) and the Qooqqut Festival (page 56). On Greenland's National Day, there is music, singing and dancing in even the smallest settlements.

The two best **art galleries** in Greenland are the Nuuk Art Museum (page 84) and the Art Museum in Ilulissat (page 162). Art is also often exhibited in Nuuk's Katuaq centre and Sisimiut's Taseralik Cultural Centre. And many hotels have impressive local art hanging on their walls. There are **art trails** in Nuuk, Qaqortoq and Aasiaat, and it is quite common to see artwork on the outside of buildings.

Only Nuuk has a **cinema**, again in the Katuaq centre, and films are occasionally shown in Sisimiut's Taseralik Cultural Centre. Both these venues are frequently used by Greenland's National Theatre (w nuis.gl), who also have their own theatre in Nuuk.

MEDIA AND COMMUNICATIONS

TELEPHONE *Country code +299*
Telephone landlines started being phased out in Greenland in 2021 and very few remain in service. Everywhere has moved to mobile-phone technology. There is only one mobile phone operator in Greenland, Tusass (formerly TELE Greenland). Every settlement with more than 70 inhabitants is guaranteed at least 2G coverage and, in practice, nearly every settlement has at least a 4G service, and 5G is being rolled out to larger towns.

There are two options if you want to use your mobile phone away from Wi-Fi in Greenland. The first is roaming on your home provider's tariff, if they support roaming in Greenland. Check before you leave home and check the costs too – these vary dramatically. The second option is to get a pre-pay SIM card from any Tusass shop and then put money on to the card, either online (**w** tusass.gl) or purchased from a Tusass shop. If you plan to be in Greenland for any length of time, this can be an attractive and lower-cost alternative. Tusass do offer specific plans aimed at visitors. For 499kr you can get 20GB of data plus unlimited calls and texts, valid for two weeks or, for 249kr, 3GB of data plus unlimited calls and texts, valid for one week. Unless you expect to use a lot of data when not connected via Wi-Fi, both deals are likely to be more expensive than just pay as you go. A spend of 199kr will get you unlimited calls and texts for a month, with no data.

INTERNET Internet is available on the mobile-phone data network, but for visitors Wi-Fi provided by hotels, cafés and many public buildings is faster and generally free. Internet browsers are unable to translate pages in Greenlandic but there is often the option to have the page in Danish and most browsers will translate these Danish pages into your native language reasonably well.

NEWSPAPERS AND MAGAZINES There is only one newspaper published in Greenland. The *Atuagagdliutit/Grønlandsposten* – universally known as the AG –

KAFFEMIK

Whenever there is a reason to celebrate, or even when there isn't, Greenlanders will hold a *kaffemik*, a social event to which everyone is invited and where the idea is to meet people, chat, eat and drink and generally have a good time. If you get the chance to attend a kaffemik, don't miss it.

You'll know you are in the right house when you arrive to see 30 pairs of shoes in the hallway and you're met with the aroma of coffee, cake and lots of other, maybe unfamiliar, foods. There will be a lot of food – always cake, probably a few different kinds, but there may also be soup, dried fish and seal, crab legs...the list really is endless. As a visitor, it is a chance to try a lot of different titbits that have been carefully home cooked.

You don't need to dress up for a kaffemik, though, if you are lucky, the host may be wearing the Greenlandic national costume. You can bring a small gift, but this is not essential. There is no set time to arrive or leave. Eventually, when you have met a lot of people and eaten a lot of cake, the room will be full to bursting and that is the time for you to go to make room for other visitors who are just arriving.

is published on Tuesdays and Thursdays. Its online version (**w** sermitsiaq.ag) is updated at least daily.

TELEVISION AND RADIO The Greenlandic Broadcasting Corporation (KNR) broadcasts two television channels and one radio station (90.5FM, 570AM). There are a number of other radio stations including ICE (93.5FM – modern music) and Nanoq (100.0FM – modern and Greenlandic music) and many towns have local radio stations. Nearly all broadcasting is in Greenlandic or Danish, but you can also find films in English, shown with subtitles.

POST Tusass is the Greenlandic postal company; its headquarters are located in Nuuk. There are Tusass post offices in every community in Greenland but in small settlements it will be hidden in the back of the Pilersuisoq supermarket. It costs 23kr to send a letter or postcard (under 20g) to Europe or 32kr for the rest of the world.

CULTURAL ETIQUETTE

Greenlanders are friendly and welcoming, but they are more restrained in their social interaction than most Westerners. If you are entering a local's home, always take your shoes off even if they say it doesn't matter – they are just being polite. If you are invited for a meal, bringing a bottle of wine, a box of chocolates or a small gift from your home country is a nice gesture but not a requirement.

Greenland is often a land of silence and Greenlanders are happy not making conversation for quite long periods, worryingly long for most visitors. If they are not speaking, it is just because they have nothing particular to say at that moment and they are quite comfortable with the silence. When they do speak, Greenlanders are quite direct in their comments and opinions rather than hedging around a subject. This can be quite disconcerting at first but does, in some ways, make life easier as you know immediately where you stand.

It is not usual to ask a person's age; it is more polite to ask which year they were born in. If you are taking photographs of people, always ask the person concerned and if they say 'no', then respect their choice.

As a foreigner it is better to use the word Inuit (singular Inuk) rather than Eskimo. Some people are sensitive about being called an Eskimo and find it insulting.

Greenlandic sled dogs – seen by Greenlanders as working dogs and not as pets – should not be approached unless you are invited. The dogs may give you a nasty bite to scare you away.

TRAVELLING POSITIVELY

VOLUNTEERING All volunteers, whether paid or not, need a work visa. This requires a written application to be sent to the Danish Agency for International Recruitment and Integration. Only the residents of Nordic countries (Norway, Denmark, Iceland, Sweden and Finland) have the automatic right to work in Greenland.

The main year-round work is teaching English. In school the children learn Greenlandic and Danish, but there are a few opportunities for them to learn English. During the winter there is little work for outsiders but in the summer (June to September) help is needed in museums and shops, DIY skills for repairs, guides are needed to lead walks and there is always work on the reindeer farms. Useful websites for finding job opportunities are: **w** workaway.info and **w** workingtraveller.com.

A Dutch company has set up greenhouses in Narsaq where they propagate Greenlandic plant cuttings and seeds. Local schools are then involved in planting these trees. You can donate money to buy trees or contact them to volunteer your help (w greenlandtrees.org).

Nuuk Water Taxi (page 75) organises periodic rubbish clear-ups in the fjord and are usually able to accommodate a few volunteers to help them. It can be a fun day out and a chance to meet and chat to the locals.

Annual festivals throughout the country are often very happy to take on volunteers. You can join in the fun and might get free entry. Contact the festival organisers through their websites.

SPEND LOCAL This guidebook lists many small local businesses where the money you spend will go directly into the local economy.

One hotel chain, with hotels in Nuuk, Sisimiut, Aasiaat and Ilulissat, is 'not-for-profit'. Hotel SØMA has, for more than 50 years, supported local seafarers, fishermen and local communities, and if you stay or eat there then you too will be supporting those in need. The hotels and restaurants are just as good as any other in Greenland.

Tap water in Greenland is crystal clear, so don't buy water and do bring a refillable water bottle or two with you.

There are few large souvenir shops, but there are lots of very small cabinets in hotels, in cafés and restaurants and in tour operators' offices where handicrafts made by local people are displayed and sold. They can probably tell you the maker's name and even point out their house.

Part Two

THE GUIDE

3

Nuuk and the
Nuuk Fjord

On the western coast of Greenland, 250km below the Arctic Circle, Nuuk is the most northerly capital city in the world. Nuuk means 'tip' in Greenlandic and is so named because it sits on a rocky promontory at the entrance to the world's second largest fjord system. Nuuk Fjord stretches 170km inland from the Labrador Sea, an arm of the North Atlantic, to the ice sheet, cutting a large gash into a brutal landscape of ancient mountains. There is only one other settlement in the whole fjord system, tiny Kapisillit, which is accessible only by boat or helicopter.

NUUK

Nuuk is a young, vibrant city full of local culture and art with more than 80% of the 20,000 population being of Inuit lineage. It is the fastest-growing region of Greenland and now houses more than one-third of the country's population, and there are plans for it to expand further.

Even though it is 'the big city', this is still a very Greenlandic place. The airport is tucked in against a mountain on one of the few pieces of flat land and on the drive into town you pass traditional multicoloured wooden houses. Parked on every piece of spare land is a boat or a snowmobile. There are some higher-rise buildings and there are areas that are busy with cars and vans, almost unheard of outside of Nuuk. Surprisingly, a lot of vehicles are electric but it is a smart choice as the hydro-electricity is cheap.

Even if you are passing through the city on your way to another destination, it is worth spending a few days in Nuuk before moving on. You will find excellent museums and an art gallery, where you can delve into the fascinating history and culture of this isolated country. There is accommodation for every budget and restaurants range from pizzerias to fine dining, with some interesting interpretations of traditional Greenlandic food. If you are self-catering, then the supermarkets will surprise you with the range of goods on offer – from fresh bread and Danish pastries to mangoes and pineapples. They may, unfortunately, also surprise you with their prices.

There are no roads into or out of Nuuk, not even a gravel track: a 12-minute drive from the city centre literally brings you to the end of the road. Everything in this city has come in by boat or plane, including everything in the shops and restaurants unless it was caught or hunted in the fjord. Standing in the centre of cosmopolitan Nuuk with a cappuccino, a mobile phone signal and Wi-Fi, it is easy to forget how remote this is.

The people may live in the city but much of their lives are spent in the 'backcountry' where the season and the weather dictate what you can do. This means that there

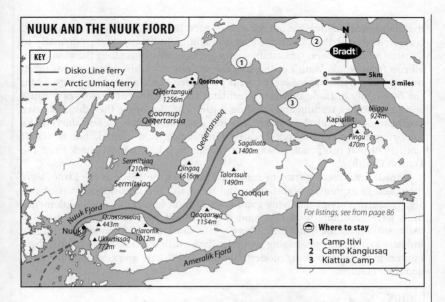

NUUK AND THE NUUK FJORD

KEY
— Disko Line ferry
- - - Arctic Umiaq ferry

Qeqertanguit *1256m*
Qoornoq
Qoornup Qeqertarsua
Qeqertarsuaq
Kapisillit
Nijggu *924m*
Pingu *470m*
Sagdliata ▲*1400m*
Sermitsiaq *1210m*
Qingaq *1616m*
Talorssuit *1490m*
Sermitsiaq
Qooqqut
Nuuk Fjord
Quassussuaq ▲*443m*
Qaqqarsuq *1154m*
Oriarorfik
Nuuk
Ukkusissaq *1012m*
772m
Ameralik Fjord

For listings, see from page 86
◐ **Where to stay**
1   Camp Itivi
2   Camp Kangiusaq
3   Kiattua Camp

is a real buzz in the city at certain times of year. In April, everyone is talking about their boats, cleaning and repairing them and getting them back into the water. Boats are the only way that most people are able to get out of the city. In July, the talk is of reindeer hunting; guns are cleaned, ammunition bought and plans made for August trips with friends and family – every Greenlander has a quota that they are allowed to hunt each year. Finally, in October, winter preparations start, when boats come out of the water to be stored and the covers come off snowmobiles ready for overland journeys.

HISTORY Hans Egede (page 16) arrived in Greenland from Norway in 1721 with three ships, 45 other colonists and a few portable houses; Norway was part of the Kingdom of Denmark at this time. They set up home across the fjord from Nuuk at Hope Colony, but during the first winter many were ill with scurvy and, in spring, returned home. Egede's mission was to find the descendants of Erik the Red but he found that they were long gone, having either perished or returned home.

Hope Colony was a poor choice for a settlement, a windy headland beset with storms. In 1728, the colonists moved across the water to present-day Nuuk and called it Godthaab. Nomadic Inuit hunters were already using this area as a seasonal settlement because it was relatively sheltered in winter.

Egede tried hard to make a life in Godthaab, but it was tough. The Inuit came and went and resisted all attempts to convert them to Christianity, the Dutch whalers were antagonistic to the new Scandinavian settlers and the trading company that King Frederick IV had established for the settlers went bankrupt. On top of all this, their biggest issue was disease, particularly scurvy and smallpox, which repeatedly hit the colony in deadly waves; even Egede's wife, Gertrude, died of the disease in 1735. The next year, Hans Egede left Greenland to take his wife's body to Denmark for burial. He never returned, but his sons, Niels and Paul, who had learned Greenlandic as children while growing up, stayed and continued his work. Paul became a missionary while Niels became a merchant, working in Sisimiut for many years. By 1733, Moravian missionaries had arrived and they converted an influential Inuit angakkuq (shaman) to Christianity; the Moravians established a string of missions along the west coast, all run from Nuuk. With Egede gone, the settlement's administration was taken over by merchant Jacob Severin, who persuaded the Danish king to give him the monopoly of trade between Greenland and Europe. For many years Nuuk was just another trading and whaling settlement, but being the administrative centre for trade and the church laid the foundations for present-day Nuuk's importance. In 1950, Nuuk became Greenland's first capital, but it wasn't until 1979 that it officially changed its name back to the Inuit Nuuk from the Danish Godthaab.

Danish investment started to come into Nuuk in the 1950s as the Danes were interested in exploiting both fishing and minerals. The Danish government was also concerned about the living conditions of Inuit hunters in small settlements. Seals were becoming harder to hunt and the Inuit were in danger of dying of malnutrition. At the same time, there was a shortage of labour for the mining industry and the fish-processing factories. The Danish solution was to resettle these hunters in towns, providing modern housing, health care and education for them and their families.

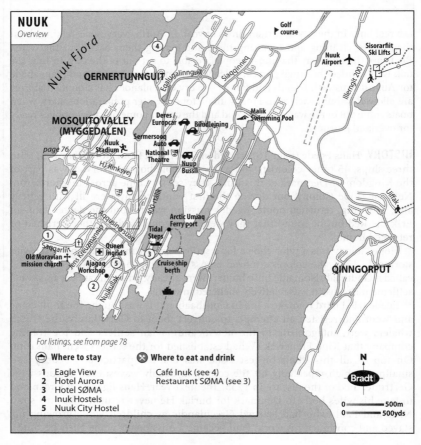

NUUK
Overview

Golf course

Nuuk Airport

Sisorarfiit Ski Lifts

Illerngit 2001

QERNERTUNNGUIT

Eqaluqalinnguit

Siaqqinneq

Malik Swimming Pool

MOSQUITO VALLEY (MYGGEDALEN)

Derés/Europcar

Biludlejning

Sermersooq Auto

Nuuk Stadium

page 76

National Theatre

Nuup Bussii

HJ Rinksvej

400-rallik

Uilfak

Aqqusine staq

Arctic Umiaq Ferry port

Tidal Steps

QINNGORPUT

Saqqarliit

Old Moravian mission church

Jens Kreutzmannip

Queen Ingrid's

Ajagaq Workshop

Nuukullak

Cruise ship berth

For listings, see from page 78

🛏 **Where to stay**
1 Eagle View
2 Hotel Aurora
3 Hotel SØMA
4 Inuk Hostels
5 Nuuk City Hostel

✗ **Where to eat and drink**
Café Inuk (see 4)
Restaurant SØMA (see 3)

N

Bradt

0 ——— 500m
0 ——— 500yds

This did not go well. The housing that was built was designed for Danes not Inuit, with nowhere to store fishing equipment, outdoor clothing nor, indeed, the day's catch. Men whose lives had previously been determined by their needs, the seasons and the weather were required to turn up on time for shifts in a factory; many had never had to use money before.

The 1960s and 70s apartment blocks that you see today are the result of these well-meaning reforms. Repeatedly modernised, they still provide low-cost housing and many are now decorated with huge murals, all by local artists, which soften their stark outlines.

By 1977, Nuuk's population had grown to more than 8,000 and it has continued to rise steadily every year since; in the last 20 years, Nuuk's population has doubled.

GETTING THERE AND GETTING AWAY

By air There are daily flights to Nuuk from Keflavik (3hrs 30mins), Iceland's main international airport, flown by either Icelandair or Air Greenland. **Keflavik Airport** has direct flights from Europe and North America, including European low-cost carriers. There is a weekly flight (summer only) flown by Canada North to Iqaluit (2hrs) which then connects onwards to Ottawa.

All **domestic flights** are flown by Air Greenland. Nuuk is well served with flights to Kangerlussuaq every day, and flights on most days to Narsarsuaq, Maniitsoq, Ilulissat and Sisimiut. There are services to Kulusuk and Paamiut at least twice a week.

Nuuk Airport is about 6km northeast of the city. It is served hourly by the Nuup Bussii's route 3 bus service (06.00–17.30 Mon–Fri, noon–15.30 Sat; 20kr) which takes about 20 minutes to get you into the city, though most accommodation will be happy to organise an airport transfer. Nuna Taxa taxis also meet flights (✆363636; about 200kr). It is planned that much will change at Nuuk Airport as the runway is being extended to 2,200m, a new control tower is being built and new navigation equipment will provide safer landings in bad weather, which can currently disrupt flights. The large new terminal building has cafés, shops and ATMs; an airport hotel is also planned. The 'new' airport is all due to be officially opened in late November 2024.

By sea From the second half of March until early January, the Arctic Umiaq passenger ferry (w aul.gl; page 47) travels once a week up and down the west coast of Greenland. The timetable does change with the seasons but typically, on Friday evenings at 20.00 the ferry heads north to Sisimiut and, from late April when the ice permits, on to Ilulissat. The ferry then heads south once more, reaching Nuuk on Tuesday at 07.00. After 2 hours in port, the ferry continues its journey south, eventually reaching Qaqortoq. The ferry usually calls at 11 ports in its complete journey along the coast and returns to Nuuk at 07.30 on the following Friday morning, ready to leave again that evening. On Fridays there is, therefore, time for passengers on the ferry to make a quick visit to the city.

Disko Line organises a scheduled, subsidised small boat ferry (it is actually a Nuuk Water Taxi boat) service to and from Kapisillit about three times a week (500kr). It is a cheap way to see the fjord, but there are no stop-offs or commentary along the route. It is possible to get to Kapisillit and back in a day, and booking is essential.

ORIENTATION
The Colonial Harbour in Old Nuuk was once the centre of the settlement and it is only a couple of minutes' walk inland from here to the centre of

the modern city, with the Katuaq Cultural Centre at its heart. Immediately north of these areas is Mosquito Valley (Myggedalen). This was the second area that was colonised and the term 'mosquito' referred to the poor, emaciated workers who lived in this slum area of the settlement. Today, ironically, it is one of the most expensive parts of the city as it is sheltered and has views across the fjord. Further up the coast is Qernertunnguit, a recently developed suburb where, initially, nobody wanted to live – it had been an area of Inuit graves and Greenlanders are very superstitious about these things.

The area south of Old Nuuk and the centre used to be home to low-cost housing and light industry. Today, this area is being redeveloped for residential use, industry being squeezed out to the northern outskirts. At the very southeastern point is the port, Greenland's biggest and recently extended to handle the increasing volume of container traffic. The older area of the port is now used for fishing boats, and some trip boats leave from the Tidal Steps (Tidevandstrappen) here, particularly in winter. Fishing boats sometimes sell fish and sea mammal meat on the quay; news of its arrival spreads quickly across social media, attracting a queue within minutes.

Across the bay from the port is an area of new housing called Qinngorput. This was once an Inuit hunting ground and many Nuuk residents will tell you they used to pick berries there every autumn. In the last 20 years it has been developed with modern, almost Scandinavian-style houses and apartments complete with supermarkets, the new Malik swimming pool and the city's new waste incinerator (which produces heat for the pool and some houses).

GETTING AROUND Nuuk has a **bus service** with yellow buses operated by Nuup Bussii (office: Industrivej 10; w bus.gl). Routes 1 and 2 run daily from 06.00 to midnight. Route 3 runs every day except Sundays, and routes X1 and X2 run on weekdays only. All bus services are less frequent at the weekends. The Nuup Bussii website has timetables, route maps and even a real-time tracker that shows you where the buses currently are.

You can buy the ticket for a single journey (20kr adult, free for under 15s) on the bus and this is then valid for 1 hour – the expiry time is stamped on the ticket. Locals use yellow plastic cards (30kr) which can be pre-loaded with single tickets (20kr each) or a voucher for ten tickets (150kr). If you intend to use buses a lot, it is cheaper to get a card. Cards can be bought and loaded with tickets in Pisiffik and Brugseni stores in Nuuk and at the Nuup Bussii office. Cards are not available on buses but, once you have a card, you can purchase vouchers for it on any bus. Bus stop signs are yellow and many bus stops have small shelters, usually green, with a timetable on the wall.

There are many **taxis** in Nuuk (✆ 321321, 363636) which you can hail on the street, or at the (only) taxi rank outside the Hans Egede Hotel. There are also apps – Taxagut (in Danish) and Nuuk Taxi (in both Danish and English) – both of which can identify where you are, usually accurately, and you tell the driver where you want to get to.

There are a number of **car rental** companies in Nuuk, but do you really need a car in such a small place? The good thing is that, if you do hire a car, you will never hit a traffic jam nor have any trouble parking. The biggest three companies are: Deres/Europcar (Industrivej 43; ✆ 314800; w deresauto.gl), Biludlejning (Industrivej 18; ✆ 314314; w biludlejning.gl) and Sermersooq Auto & Marine (Industrivej 29; ✆ 323705; w sams.gl). Typical car hire costs are 400–750kr per day, or 2,500–14,000kr per week.

TOURIST INFORMATION AND TOUR OPERATORS Nuuk has an all-encompassing tourist information website (w visitnuuk.com), which includes a frequently updated events calendar. Nuuk's tour operators are well organised, with informative websites, so it is easy to book an activity or tour. A must is a boat trip down the fjord – only then can you appreciate how vast and remote this really is.

The tour operators listed below specialise in the Nuuk area. For Greenland-wide tour operators, see page 33.

Arctic Boat Charter \533880; w abc.gl. A boat charter company with a fully licensed Targa 37+ 12-passenger boat with a fully enclosed & heated cabin. Ideal for large group travel up the fjord.

Arctic Excursions \244789; w arcticexcursions. com. Part of the Greenland Travel group, Arctic Excursions enables you to book with specialist operators including Air Greenland Charter, who offer helicopter flights around Nuuk with the option of landing on Sermitsiaq, with great views of Nuuk & the fjord.

Greenland Escape \384040; w greenland-escape.com. This small family-run company offers city tours either on foot or in a minibus. The knowledgeable guides will enable you to understand Nuuk's history & how it is changing today. They also own 2 hostels, a hotel & some apartments.

Greenland Travel \701107, +45 33 131011 (Denmark); w greenland-travel.com. This large tour company offers a packaged multi-day trip to Nuuk from Europe year-round. Your trip can be customised or you can add on extra tours from local operators.

Inuk Travel \534245; w inuktravel.gl. Gerth Poulsen has been organising travel in Greenland for more than 20 years & his travel agency offers a range of services. Inuk Travel also owns and runs Inuk Hostels and their Aurora glass igloo (page 78).

Nuuk Water Taxi [76 B3] Imaneq 27; \388777; w watertaxi.gl; ⏰ 10.00–14.00 Mon, Tue, Thu & Fri. There are 6 boats operating a wide selection of excursions & activities. A boat trip to the north of the fjord can include a hike to see the glacier – using snowshoes in winter. In summer, a guided kayak tour along the fjord is spectacular & you are likely to get up close to icebergs. For the less energetic, try the Icefjord cruise among those

icebergs, a whale safari to spot humpback whales or 'catch & eat' where you fish for your dinner (Jun–Sep). 'Puffin Express' trips run for a limited period (May–Aug) to the only island where puffins nest, about an hour south.

Qajaq Seaway \241010; w qajaqseaway.com. A boat charter company with a fully licensed Targa 25.1 partially enclosed 6-person boat. Ideal for small group travel around the fjord.

Tupilak Travel [76 D3] Imaneq 18; \313218; w tupilaktravel.com; ⏰ 08.30–17.00 Mon–Fri, 10.00–13.00 Sat. A good selection of day trips with half-price tickets for children up to 11 years. City tours, deep-sea fishing & local family visits are available all year round. They also offer guided hikes, or you can pick up a free hiking map from their travel office & explore by yourself. Between May & Sep, they'll take you paddleboarding or kayaking around the icebergs, on a 3hr whale safari or a 'Puffin Express' boat trip. In winter, Tupilak can take you by car to the edge of the city to view the northern lights…but no guarantees!

Two Ravens \584110; w tworavens.gl. 2 passionate & experienced outdoor guides offer some unusual tours all year round, including an overnight trip sleeping in tentsiles (tents that 'hover' above the ground) or a 2-night sleepover on a deserted island. They also offer the options of reaching the summit of Quassussuaq (430m) for amazing views, either hiking in summer or using snowshoes in winter, when it can be combined with some northern lights viewing. The more adventurous could take a helicopter to the top of a mountain for a high-altitude snowshoe heli-hike, a 2-day adventure hike in the fjord or some cross-country skiing. Adam & Thorlax are extremely knowledgeable & they are able to put together an adventure just for you.

FESTIVALS There are many festivals in Nuuk including the **Nuuk Snow Festival** (February to March), **Nuuk Nordic Culture Festival** (biannually, in May), **Nuuk Pride** (July), the **KangNu** race (August), the **Akisuanerit Festival** (late September) and **Santa Claus**, who arrives on Christmas Eve. For further details, see page 55.

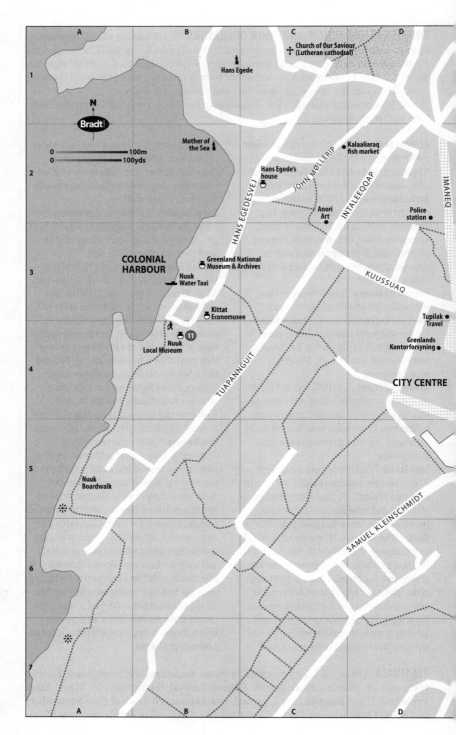

N

Bradt

0 ——————— 100m
0 ——————— 100yds

COLONIAL HARBOUR

Church of Our Saviour
(Lutheran cathedral)

Hans Egede

Mother of
the Sea

Kalaaliaraq
fish market

Hans Egede's
house

Anori
Art

Police
station

Greenland National
Museum & Archives

Nuuk
Water Taxi

KUUSSUAQ

Kittat
Economusee

Tupilak
Travel

Nuuk
Local Museum

Grønlands
Kontorforsyning

CITY CENTRE

HANS EGEDESVEJ

JOHN MØLLERIP

INTALEEQQAP

IMANEQ

TUAPANNGUIT

Nuuk
Boardwalk

SAMUEL KLEINSCHMIDT

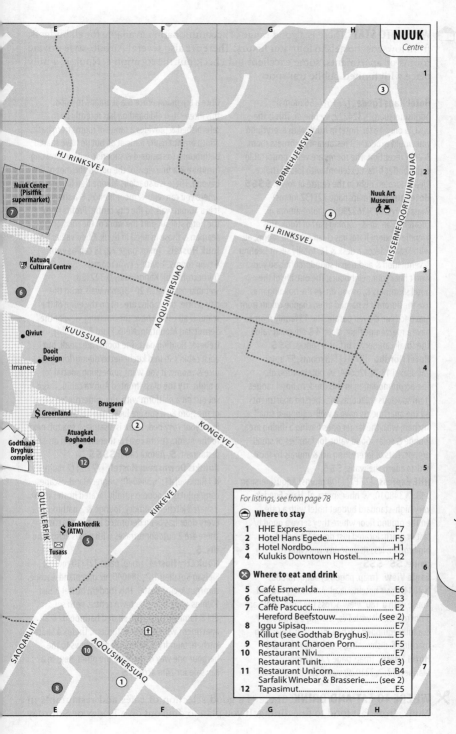

HJ RINKSVEJ

BØRNEHJEMSVEJ

Nuuk Center
(Pisiffik
supermarket)

Nuuk Art
Museum

HJ RINKSVEJ

KISSERNEQQORTUUNNGUAQ

Katuaq
Cultural Centre

AQQUSINERSUAQ

Qiviut

KUUSSUAQ

Dooit
Design

Imaneq

Brugseni

KONGEVEJ

Greenland

Atuagkat
Boghandel

Godthaab
Bryghus
complex

KIRKEVEJ

BankNordik
(ATM)

QULLILERFIK

Tusass

SAQQAARLIIT

AQQUSINERSUAQ

Nuuk and the Nuuk Fjord   NUUK

3

77

WHERE TO STAY There is a good range of accommodation available for all budgets, from low-cost hostels to four-star luxury. There are also several Airbnb-style private rooms or apartments, some excellent but check out the location – Nuuk is a hilly place with limited public transport.

Hotel Hans Egede [77 F5] (156 rooms) Aqqusinersuaq; ☎324222; w hhe.gl. This is the best, & only 4-star, hotel in Nuuk with everything you would expect – 3 restaurants, a fitness room & 24hr reception. The rooms are very comfortable & the buffet b/fast excellent with lots of choice. Ideally located right in the centre of town. **$$$$**

Hotel Aurora [map, page 72] (32 rooms) Paassaasivik 8; ☎362290; w hotel-aurora.gl. Located in an up-&-coming part of Nuuk, this friendly modern hotel has clean & bright rooms, all with Scandi décor, a desk & TV, totally silent heating & ventilation & additional soundproofing so you won't hear your neighbours. The outside of the hotel shimmers &, as you arrive the building may, like the aurora it is named after, change colour from green to blue & even purple. The 13 family rooms have a mezzanine floor, sleep 4 & are great value. The small café serves b/fast & snacks. **$$$**

Hotel Nordbo [77 H1] (18 rooms, 57 apts) Vandsøvej 13; ☎326644; w hotelnordbo.gl. The accommodation in this modern hotel ranges from spacious sgl rooms to 5-person apartments. All the apartments have a well-equipped small kitchen, with the larger ones having a dining area, lounge & sofas. Good value for families or small groups. Lots of interesting art & murals by local artists adorn the walls. **$$$**

HHE Express [77 F7] (108 rooms) Aqqusinersuaq 14B; ☎348010; w hheexpress.gl. Hans Egede's very high-standard budget hotel with a café on the ground floor where they serve a good b/fast or lunch; located just down from its 4-star big brother, less than 5mins' walk into the centre. **$$–$$$**

Eagle View [map, page 72] Saqqarliit 80; ☎484400; w hotelnuuk.gl. Amazingly located house with a 180° view across the fjord. There are 5 dbl rooms, all with TVs, sharing 2 bathrooms & a fully equipped kitchen including a washing machine & dishwasher, and living room. **$$**

Hotel SØMA [map, page 72] (44 rooms) Marinevej 3; ☎321029; w hotelsoma.gl/nuuk.

Once a telegraph office & a seaman's mission, this interesting old building has recently been refurbished & provides a range of rooms from basic, which are not really basic at all but do have shared bathrooms, to standard & superior, with interesting furniture & a fine view of the port & the mountains beyond. There is a spacious Marine Den lounge, where you can relax & meet friends, & a small spa. It is a 10min walk to the city centre. Profits from the hotel still support the work of the mission for seamen & those in need in Nuuk. Good value. **$$**

Inuk Hostels [map, page 72] (3 cabins with 4 twin rooms, 1 with 2 twin rooms) Qernertunnguit Kangerluat; ☎322128; w inukhostels.gl. A 20–30min walk from the city centre, the cabins are set on the edge of the water & all cabins have the amazing view of the Sermitsiaq Mountain, Nuuk Fjord &, possibly, icebergs floating past. The rooms are small, but each cabin's shared kitchenette/dining/lounge is nice & roomy. If you want something special for a night, try the glass-fronted Aurora cabin. This is set out on a platform with an uninterrupted view of the fjord &, if you are lucky, the northern lights from your cosy bed. There is a sauna & spa tub next to the Aurora (extra cost) & there is a good on-site restaurant. **$**, Aurora cabin **$$$$**

Kulukis Downtown Hostel [77 H2] (7 rooms) H J Rinksvej 41; ☎384040; w greenland-escape. com/kulukis. A good centrally located hostel with a shared kitchen, laundry, lounge & 2 bathrooms. Every door has been decorated by a local artist. There are 2 outdoor terraces with views across the city. **$**

Nuuk City Hostel [map, page 72] (10 rooms) Sipisaq Kujalleq 1; ☎384040; w greenland-escape. com/nuuk-city-hostel. This modern hostel is just 15mins' walk from the town centre, with sgl, dbl & family rooms with shared bathrooms & an apartment with private bathroom. There's a shared kitchen, laundry & lounge; & nice views to the harbour one way & the fjord the other. Keys in a key safe for 24hr access. **$**

WHERE TO EAT AND DRINK There is a good selection of cafés and restaurants in Nuuk, from fast food to fine dining. If you plan to dine out on a Friday or Saturday night, you may be wise to book. Many good restaurants struggle to meet demand on these weekend evenings.

Hereford Beefstouw [77 F5] Hotel Hans Egede; +299 324222; w hhe.gl/a-hereford-beefstouw; ⏰ noon–15.00 & 18.00–22.30 daily. A steak restaurant with an astonishing selection of cuts, located on the top floor of the hotel. Similar to the restaurants of the same name in Denmark but here you can also get reindeer or musk ox steaks & finish with a Greenlandic coffee. **$$$**

Killut [77 E5] Imaneq 30, at Godthaab Bryghus complex (page 80); ⏰ 17.00–22.00 Tue–Sat plus noon–15.00 Sat. A popular restaurant, centrally located on pedestrianised Imaneq. Their short menu includes snow crab, recommended, as well as hunter's pie, the Greenlandic version of shepherd's pie made from reindeer & musk ox. On Sat, the restaurant is open for a smorgasbord lunch. Being part of the brewery complex, there is a range of good beer on tap, as well as wines & spirits. **$$$**

Restaurant Tunit [77 H1] Hotel Nordbo; 546644; w hotelnordbo.gl/en/restaurant-bar; ⏰ 06.00–10.00 daily, 11.30–15.00 & 17.30–23.00 Wed–Sat. The restaurant is in a bright room with a striking mural of the northern lights. The menu changes every month to reflect the seasons, combining Greenlandic & Danish cuisine. Small bar, friendly service & reasonably priced. Open to non-residents. **$$$**

Restaurant Unicorn [76 B4] Colonial Harbour; 329190; e unicorn@outlook.com; 🅵; ⏰ 17.00–21.00 Mon–Sat. The Unicorn has a view over the Colonial Harbour & the colonial buildings of the museums. The lamb & reindeer steaks are particularly good, as is the Thai-influenced seafood soup. If you 'catch and eat' in the winter, this is probably where your catch will be cooked for you on your return. In summer, the owners also run the restaurant at Qooqqut in Nuuk Fjord. **$$$**

Sarfalik Winebar & Brasserie [77 F5] Hotel Hans Egede; 324222; w hhe.gl/restaurant-og-bar; ⏰ 18.00–22.00 Mon–Sat. Located on the 5th floor of the hotel with fine views across the city, this is one of Nuuk's best fine dining restaurants. The menu is international with a Greenlandic twist, & includes redfish & musk ox. Extensive wine list. **$$$**

Café Inuk [map, page 72] Qernertunnguit Kangerluat; 322128; w inukhostels.gl/en/cafe-inuk; ⏰ 09.00–16.00 Mon & Tue, 09.00–21.00 Wed–Fri, noon–21.00 Sat, 10.00–21.00 Sun. Set above the rooms of the Inuk Hostel, this café shares the same amazing views of the fjord, icebergs & mountains. Seasonal Greenlandic specialities including fish soup, a selection of local dried fish – capelin, cod – & narwhal &, our favourite, reindeer steaks. Malu, the knowledgeable owner, will happily explain to you the role these dishes traditionally played in the local diet & offers a Greenlandic 'Tasting & Storytelling' experience. **$$–$$$**

Restaurant Nivi [77 E7] Aqqusinersuaq 12; 329222; w nivi.gl; ⏰ 17.00–late daily. Set over 3 floors, the theme is 'sharing' in this new restaurant so there are lots of small, as well as large, dishes. The menu is mostly European; there are cocktails (& mocktails) too. **$$–$$$**

Restaurant Charoen Porn [77 F5] Aqqusinersuaq 5; 325759; w charoenporn.gl; ⏰ 17.00–22.00 daily. The dark interior of this great Thai restaurant seems somehow out of place in Nuuk. It serves excellent Thai food with some interesting Greenlandic fish specialities. Take-away available. **$$**

Tapasimut [77 E5] Aqqusinersuaq 6; 329222; 🅵; ⏰ 11.30–21.00 daily. Above Bar Maximut & entered by the door on the right, this restaurant serves Greenlandic & international food in small tapas-style portions, which is good if you want to sample a few new dishes. There is a well-stocked bar & a large window looks down on the street. **$$**

Cafetuaq [77 E3] Imaneq 21, inside the Katuaq Cultural Centre; 363779; e cafe@katuaq.gl; 🅵; ⏰ closed Sun. Local & international dishes, including the Hot Sled Dog, a Greenlandic spin on the hot dog, &, our favourite, Greenlandic tapas, which gives you the chance to sample narwhal, smoked lamb, musk ox plus local smoked salmon, prawns & scallops on a single platter. It is a popular place for locals to meet for coffee or lunch. **$–$$**

Restaurant Soma [map, page 72] Marinevej 3; 321029; w hotelsoma.gl/nuuk; ⏰ cafeteria 08.00–20.00 daily, restaurant 17.00–21.00 Wed–Sat. 1 restaurant, 2 personalities. The cafeteria part has been serving cake, coffee & the very reasonably priced 'dish of the day' to locals for over 50 years. In 2023, Chef Jacob arrived to add the fine dining restaurant . The local lamb with celeriac & new potatoes is outstanding. $–$$

Café Esmeralda [77 E6] Aqqusinersuaq 7; ☎329095; ▓; ⊕ 09.00–22.00 daily. It may not look much from the outside, but this small, friendly restaurant is much smarter once you are inside & serves good food including omelettes, paninis, pizza, pasta & tortillas. The Brunch Buffet (⊕ 09.00–14.00; $$) at w/ends & holidays is particularly popular. Good value. $

Caffè Pascucci [77 E2] Imaneq; ☎326065; ▓; ⊕ 08.00–23.30 Mon–Sat, 08.00–21.30 Sun. Busy coffee shop on the edge of the Nuuk Center serving good coffee, cakes & snacks. Friendly service & a few outside tables in the sun. $

Iggu Sipisaq [77 E7] Avannarieq 10; ☎329555; e info@cafeiggu.gl; ▓; ⊕ 11.00–23.00 Sun–Thu, 11.00–02.00 Fri–Sat. Tucked away just off the main street, Iggu serves a huge range of proper Italian-style pizzas & calzone. Good value. Eat-in, take-away or delivered to your accommodation. $

ENTERTAINMENT AND NIGHTLIFE
Right in the centre of town is the **Katuaq Cultural Centre** [77 E3] (Imaneq 21; ☎363779; w katuaq.gl; ⊕ closed Sun), perhaps the most striking building in the city centre. It was designed by the Schmidt Hammer Lassen partnership, their first major project. The façade was inspired by the rippling colours of the northern lights and the interior feels rather like an indoor public piazza. The café, **Cafétuaq** (page 79), is to the right and to the left are two auditoria, which can be transformed to host rock and classical concerts, weddings, conferences and art exhibitions. One auditorium is also home to Nuuk's only **cinema** (Katuaq Bio). Films are usually shown in their original language, sometimes with subtitles. Check the centre's website to see what's on.

The **Godthaab Bryghus** [77 E5] (Imaneq 30; w bryghuset.gl) complex in the centre of Nuuk has something for everyone including bars, restaurants, a discotheque and a brewery, which runs a fascinating tour in English on Fridays (⊕ 17.00; 250kr). Master brewer Luca takes a small group round Greenland's largest brewery – it's still very small – explaining the ingredients and processes that result in a range of beers, which can be tasted during your visit. The tour ends with a dinner of 'hunter's pie' in the Killut restaurant (page 79).

Bars, pubs and clubs

Daddy's [77 E5] Godthaab Bryghus complex, Imaneq 30; ☎348080; ▓; ⊕ 15.00–midnight Mon–Thu, noon–04.00 Sat, noon–midnight Sun. Further back from Takuss & past the Killut restaurant, Daddy's is a classic, old-fashioned pub with good beer, a billiards table (with local rules!), dartboards & snacks, which include reindeer burgers. The dark, cosy atmosphere attracts locals after work & into the night.

Garagen Discotheque [77 E5] Godthaab Bryghus complex, Imaneq 30; ☎348060; ▓; ⊕ 17.00–midnight Thu, 17.00–04.00 Fri–Sat. Hidden in the corner & looking like a garage is the Garagen Discotheque, the place for the young at heart to dance till dawn.

Skyline Bar [77 F5] Hotel Hans Egede; ☎324222; w hhe.gl/skyline-bar; ⊕ 17.00–midnight Sun–Thu, 17.00–03.00 Fri–Sat. Located on the top floor of Hotel Hans Egede, a smart bar with a huge view & live music at w/ends.

Takuss [77 E5] Godthaab Bryghus complex, Imaneq 30; ☎348080; ▓; ⊕ 20.00–04.00 Fri–Sat. Clearly aimed at the more mature drinker, this bar has 4 or 5 beers on tap & live music most nights.

SHOPPING
Many shops are open every day but with shorter hours at the weekend; some are closed on Sundays. There are **supermarkets**, small and large, throughout the city; the dominant brands are Pisiffik, Brugseni, AKIKI and SPAR.

Kalaaliaraq [76 C2] (John Møllerip; ⊕ 09.00–17.00 Mon–Fri, 09.00–15.30 Sat–Sun) is Nuuk's **fish market**, where you will find not only freshly caught fish but also sea mammals – seal and walrus. When we were at the market in April, the first lumpfish roe was arriving to much excitement. The arrival of the roe is a sign of spring and Greenlanders will freeze it, to be used throughout the year.

In the city centre, shops are concentrated around the **Nuuk Center** [76 E2], Greenland's only shopping mall, and pedestrianised Imaneq. There are a few souvenir shops dotted around the city and many hotels sell souvenirs too.

Books and stationery

Atuagkat Boghandel [77 E5] Aqqusinersuaq; w atuagkat.com; ⏰ 10.00–17.30 Mon–Fri, 10.00–14.00 Sat. Situated opposite Hotel Hans Egede, this is the largest & oldest bookstore in the country, founded in 1976. It is a good place to buy local maps, as well as English-language books & Greenlandic books on history, culture & politics. There is also a range of fiction.

Grønlands Kontorforsyning [76 D4] Greenland Office Supplies; Imaneq 24; ⏰ 09.00–17.30 Mon–Fri. Opposite Qiviut, with a good selection of maps & stationery.

Souvenirs and crafts

Ajagaq Workshop [map, page 72] Nuukullak 18; w sermersooq.gl/da/ajagaq; ⏰ 08.00–17.00 Mon–Sat, 10.00–15.00 Sun. Ajagaq is a 20min walk from the city centre but it is worth the effort as it really is a workshop, not just a shop. There are 20 workstations on 2 floors that are rented by local craftspeople working with soapstone, bone &

wood. Every piece in their tiny shop is handmade & unique. Work for sale includes carvings, tupilaks, keyrings & jewellery. They will also make a piece especially for you.

Anori Art [76 C2] Indaleeqqap 14; f; ⏰ 10.00–17.30 Mon–Fri, 11.00–14.00 Sat. Just above the Colonial Harbour, Anori Art has a wide selection of local craftwork.

Dooit Design [77 E4] Imaneq 27; f; ⏰ 11.00–17.00 Mon–Fri, 11.00–14.00 Sat. One of 2 rather good shops in pedestrianised Imaneq (the other is Qiviut), this art & crafts gallery specialises in glass.

Qiviut [77 E4] Imaneq 27; w qiviut.gl; ⏰ 10.00–17.30 Mon–Fri, 10.00–14.00 Sat. Offering a wide range of traditional & modern clothing made locally from skins & fur.

Tupilak Travel [76 D3] See page 75. The tour operator has its own souvenir shop on the same street which also sells postcards & some maps.

SPORTS AND ACTIVITIES With a roof shaped like a wave, Nuuk's award-winning **swimming pool**, Malik (Sarfaarsuit 4; ☏ 696969; w malik-nuuk.gl; ⏰ 08.00–20.40 Mon–Fri, 08.00–15.40 Sat–Sun; 50kr, children free), has several pools and two hot tubs with a view over the bay.

Nuuk's nine-hole **golf course** (w en.nuukgolf.com; 600kr inc clubs & balls) is set among the rocky cliffs on the outskirts of the city. The golf club has an agreement with Tupilak Travel (page 75), who will transport you to the course where you can rent equipment and balls; your clubs will include a special 'rock club' in case you get caught in the rough. There is also a golf simulator in the clubhouse. Who knew you could play a game of golf so close to the Arctic Circle?

But what could be more iconic than skiing in Greenland? The three **Sisorarfiit Ski Lifts** (off lllerngit 2001; ☏ 327805; w skilift.gl; f), located to the east of the airport, run only when the snow and wind are right; check their Facebook page for the latest news. A day's ski pass is 200kr (half price for under 17s) and you can hire all the equipment you need.

There is no longer a Nuuk marathon but there is an annual **Half-Marathon** (w visitgreenland.com/event/nuuk-halvmarathon; f; 150kr) every summer on the Saturday before or after midsummer. There is also the **KangNu race** (f) which is an extreme running race across rough terrain that starts on the edge of Nuuk. The event is held in late August and you can choose to run 56km, 35km or 20km; alternatively, you can choose to walk the 20km route.

OTHER PRACTICALITIES There is a branch of **Greenland Bank** [77 E4] (✆ 09.30–15.30 Mon–Thu, 09.30–15.00 Fri) at Imaneq 33 and a Tusass **post office** and phone shop [77 E6] (Qullilerfik 2; ✆ 10.00–17.00 Mon–Fri, 10.00–13.00 Sat) at the top of Imaneq. There is also a **BankNordik** ATM [77 E6] here; ATMs can also be found in most supermarkets and in the Katuaq Cultural Centre (page 80).

Nuuk has its main **police station** [76 D2] (✆701448) on P H Lundsteensvej, near the Nuuk Center, and the country's largest **hospital**, Queen Ingrid's, is south of the city centre on Jens Kreuzmannip. For ambulances call ✆344112; for the fire service, the national number is ✆113.

WHAT TO SEE AND DO

Old Nuuk The oldest part of Nuuk is the picturesque **Colonial Harbour** [76 B3] which looks out over the mouth of the Nuuk Fjord. This is where Hans Egede established the Godthaab colonial settlement in 1728, and his modest yellow house [76 C2] – the oldest house in the country – still stands. It is now the ceremonial home of the prime minister and is used for wining, dining and entertaining visiting dignitaries. Hans Egede, dressed as a Lutheran preacher, still stands above it all, his **statue** [76 B1] high on the hill beside the harbour. It is worth the walk up to the top to share his view of ever-expanding Nuuk and across the fjord to the islands and peninsulas beyond. Also on the hill, but not as high as Hans Egede, is Nuuk's prominent cathedral.

The cathedral, the **Church of Our Saviour** [76 C1], was built in 1849 and had its clock tower and steeple added in 1884. It is a fine example of a wooden Lutheran church, becoming a cathedral only in 1994. Its interior is white-painted wooden panelling and on the end of each pew is a candle, giving the old cathedral rather an elegant feel. The church is lit by chandeliers that hang over the aisle, interspersed with two votive ships. These were given to the church by shipowners and must have been the focus of many prayers from seamen's families over the years.

As you walk down the cobbled lane back to the sea, the buildings of the Colonial Harbour ahead still look like a small fishing village. It is easy to imagine looking out to sea, trying to spot the first supply ship of the summer or, perhaps, one's husband returning in his kayak. In the waves here is the impressive *Mother of the Sea* [76 B2] sculpture. It is hard not to compare this with the smaller and less impressive *Little Mermaid* in Copenhagen. The Mother of the Sea (Sassuma Arnaa in Greenlandic) is a central character in Inuit mythology and in this statue she is surrounded by all the creatures that the Inuit hunted to survive – walrus, seal, fish, eel and polar bear – and the shaman who is combing these creatures out of her hair. Every Inuit knows the folk tale associated with the Mother of the Sea (see opposite).

On the shore here you will see a kayak drying rack. The traditional kayaks drying here are very different to the modern lightweight kayaks that we are used to today. The Kayak Clubhouse is just to the left, where, lying outside, you may spot whale bones and driftwood – these will be used to build and repair the boats.

Walking back past Hans Egede's house you soon reach, on your right, an extended 1936 warehouse that now houses the **Greenland National Museum and Archives** [76 B3] (Hans Egedesvej 8; ✆322611; w en.nka.gl; ✆ Sep–May 13.00 –16.00 Tue–Sun, Jun–Sep 10.00–16.00 daily; 50kr/free adult/under 16). This was Greenland's first museum and remains the largest and most impressive museum in the country; it is worth at least a couple of hours of your time. It has a huge number of well-presented exhibits and clearly maps the history of Greenland from the first Inuit settlers to the present day. We recommend that you start by walking all the way through to the far end of the museum in the second building – this enables you to

SEDNA, MOTHER OF THE SEA

As with all good myths and fables, there are many versions of the Mother of the Sea story. Here is one.

Sedna, the Mother of the Sea, was a giant, the daughter of Anguta, the god who created the world. Sedna and Anguta frequently argued. One day, Anguta took his daughter out to sea and threw her into the water. Sedna clung to the side of the boat, but Anguta cut off her fingers and she, and her fingers, sank to the bottom of the sea. There, she became its ruler, the Mother of the Sea, and her fingers became the creatures of the world – polar bear, Arctic fox, reindeer, musk ox, whale, seal, walrus and narwhal; all creatures that are hunted by Inuit.

After some time, Sedna found that her long hair was getting matted because, without fingers, she was unable to comb it and all the creatures were getting caught in it. On land, the Inuit were starving to death because there were few animals to hunt and few fish to catch. The Inuit asked their best angakkuq (shaman) to visit Sedna, whom they believed controlled everything that lived in the sea, and to seek her help.

The angakkuq entered a state of trance which enabled him to talk to the spirits, who warned him that Sedna was furious because her hair was matted, and that he would have to hold on to her hair very tightly or she would kill him. He travelled to her house and, upon entering, immediately grabbed her hair and wrapped himself in it. Sedna wrestled with the angakkuq, but when she realised he wanted to help her, she let him start to comb out her hair. As he combed, so she calmed down and the creatures reappeared from the tangled mess.

When her hair was cleaned, the Mother of the Sea told the angakkuq that the reason her hair had become matted, the reason the creatures had become caught up in it, was that the Inuit were not respecting nature enough. If they didn't hunt and fish responsibly, then all the creatures would disappear and the Inuit would starve once more.

begin at the oldest exhibits and walk towards the present day. There is one complete hall dedicated to transport, including kayaks, umiaks and sleds. While we view the kayak as a boat for sport or, perhaps, transport, the Inuit built kayaks for the sole purpose of hunting (page 21).

The 'must-see' in the museum are the Qilakitsoq mummies (page 184). The sight of them, lying on reindeer skins and dressed in their furs, will take your breath away and, alone, would warrant your visit. The mummies were preserved for more than 500 years, walled up in a dry cave. That one can still see the tattoos on one of their faces is extraordinary.

Opposite the entrance to the National Museum is **Kittat Economusée** [76 B3] (Hans Egedesvej 29; 📞366398; 🇫; ⊕ 10.00–17.00 Mon, Wed & Fri; free), the home of Greenland's National Costume (page 84). This is a workshop and hire shop, where a dedicated group of women work on the manufacture and restoration of Greenland's national costumes. The women are very happy to talk you through how the garments are made, which starts with preparing the skins – you may see these drying on racks outside the workshop – and ends with an ornate costume, covered in intricate decoration.

GREENLANDIC NATIONAL COSTUME

The national costume is today worn only for festivals and on special occasions such as a child's first day at school, their confirmation and, later, their wedding. While some costumes are handed down through families – often repaired at communal workshops – others are rented.

In the traditional Greenlandic costume, both men and women wear long *kamik* boots made from seal or polar bear skin and reaching high up the thigh. The boots are highly decorated with pieces of coloured animal skin or embroidery. The man's costume is quite simple with black trousers, which are now worn instead of animal skin trousers, and a white shirt with a hood, called an *anorak*. The women's costume varies. In west Greenland, it is called the *kalaallisut* and the women wear a red anorak, which is decorated with a deep collar of coloured beadwork (called pearls), and sealskin shorts, decorated with embroidery and pieces of coloured animal skin. The east Greenlandic costume, called the *tunumiutuut*, has a white anorak with a small amount of embroidered decoration and sometimes trimmed with a fringe of beadwork. They also wear shorts, made from polar bear, seal or walrus fur.

In both east and west Greenland, the women's anorak may have an optional hood and the shorts are very short, only just reaching the top of their long kamik boots.

At the far end of the quay is the **Nuuk Local Museum** [76 B4] (Nuutoqaq; Hans Egedesvej 29; \ 366031; w nuuk-lokalmuseum.com; ⊕ 13.00–16.00 Wed–Sun). This small museum, housed in the old colonial boatyard building, opened in 2017 and records the modern history of Nuuk, from the arrival of Hans Egede to the present day. The early photographs show just a few buildings, the same buildings that today form the historic Colonial Harbour area. The museum also covers the influx of Inuit hunters in the 1960s and 70s when they were resettled from their villages to Nuuk to work in fish factories. There is a focus on the history of local families, many of whom have donated artefacts. One room shows local art and crafts, particularly pottery, in an exhibition that changes frequently; most items in these exhibitions can be purchased.

For a breath of fresh air, there is a fine walk with lots of good viewpoints from the Colonial Harbour along the wide wooden **Nuuk Boardwalk** [76 A5], which heads southwest along the coastline. The boardwalk starts outside the front of the Nuuk Local Museum and continues for 1km to Nuuk's most westerly headland. From here the small road Saqqarliit brings you back into the top of the town centre, passing on the way the **Old Moravian mission church** and its photogenic graveyard. There is also a good view from the beach behind the church.

City centre Nuuk city centre is small and has one pedestrianised street, Imaneq. At the bottom of Imaneq is the **Katuaq Cultural Centre** [77 E3] (page 80), opened in 1997 with its own café making a great place for lunch or a coffee. Around this area are many shops, a bank and some good dining options. Partway up the street is the **Godthaab Bryghus** [77 E5] brewery complex where you can get a drink, a meal and evening entertainment. The brewery runs a fascinating tour (page 80).

The **Nuuk Art Museum** [77 H2] (Kissarneqqortuunnguaq 5; \ 327733; w nuukkunstmuseum.com; ⊕ 13.00–17.00 Tue–Sun, until 21.00 Thu; 30kr, free on Thu) is a 10-minute walk east. This is probably the best art gallery in Greenland with, on the left as you enter, its permanent collection and, on the right, a guest exhibition that changes four times a year. Passing through the rooms, it is striking how differently local and foreign artists have portrayed Greenland and its people over the years. The museum also offers a thought-provoking insight into the local culture and how the art has been influenced by politics and activism. There is a large mix of media here – sketches, watercolours and oils, ceramics, sculptures and video. The craftsmanship exhibited is exquisite, particularly the carved tupilaks. If you pick up their free leaflet 'the Nuuk Art walk', also available as an audio download, you can use it as a guide to walk yourself around the city, while also seeing all 19 pieces of art, including the iconic *Mother of the Sea* (page 82).

Nuuk's backcountry Nuuk may be the largest city in Greenland but the backcountry is always close. The easiest access points are along Siaqqinneq, which turns into a gravel track after it passes the prison, on Illerngit 2001, where the ski lifts start opposite the airport; and at the end of Uiffak, where a barrier blocks the road when it turns to gravel – this is the access to Nuuk's drinking water supply.

Some tour operators guide groups on **hiking trails** from Nuuk, including to the top of the closest two mountains – Quassussuaq (433m) and Ukkusissaq (772m). Perhaps more fun is to stay the night and camp but, for most tents, the ground is too rough, too rocky and the odd flat patch is a wet bog. **Two Ravens** (page 75) have solved this problem with their hovering tents. These 'tentsiles' are hard to describe – you sling your tent between the boulders like a giant hammock, except it becomes an almost-rigid structure rather than a sagging sling. Once inside, they are remarkably comfortable and the views across the fjord mouth and islands are extraordinary. Add to this an expedition dinner around the camp fire and breakfast watching the sun rise from behind the mountains…it's hard to believe the city is only just over an hour away.

While hiking is possible all summer, snowshoeing and skiing make different routes possible in winter. Many tour operators have experienced guides and can provide equipment and transfers for these day adventures. Another popular outing in winter is by vehicle to high and dark locations around the city to see the northern lights. This can also be done in a boat; there is something very special about a night cruise lit only by the stars and the fantastical colours of the aurora borealis. Seeing the lights cannot be guaranteed but some websites (w aurorareach.com) provide predictions of likely success.

If you wish to walk on your own, despite the fact that many trails are well marked, we recommend that you buy a map and carry a GPS device. A compass may also be useful, but remember that compasses do not point to true north in Greenland (page 51). With a map, it is an easy walk up Quassussuaq (433m) from either Uiffak (about 4km each way) or Illerngit (about 2km each way). You can find more information on marked trails on the Visit Nuuk website (w visitnuuk.com). The best map of the area is probably Greenland Tourism Trekking map 11 – Nuuk (1:75,000).

It is also possible to walk between Uiffak and the end of Siaqqinneq, near the prison, round the back of the Quassussuaq mountain and through Paradise Valley (about 10km). The navigation for this walk is easier if you start at Uiffak, and the views are better too. Using buses to get near the start (bus stop 41) and back from the airport adds a couple more kilometres.

NUUK FJORD

Nuuk Fjord system (Kangerlua) – a network of deep fjords running between the near vertical walls of snow-capped mountains – is the second largest fjord system in the world, the largest being Scoresby Sound (page 130) in east Greenland. This fjord system is fed by three glaciers, all fingers of Greenland's ice sheet, whose meltwaters merge partway to the sea. Here, three long mountainous islands – Qoornup Qeqertarsua (Bear Island), Qeqertarsuaq (Big Island, which rises to 1,616m) and Sermitsiaq (home to the 1,210m-tall mountain of the same name) – split the waters again into three parallel fjords that run for more than 40km. The three fjords meet again just before Nuuk to flow into the Labrador Sea and, thus, the North Atlantic.

Taking a boat trip is the only way to really appreciate the grandeur of this fjord system. As your small boat moves up the fjord, the scale of the soaring rock cliffs that sweep down to the water is impressive. The fjord is home to millions of birds – cormorants, terns, ducks and sea eagles – but to very few people. Kapisillit is now the only active settlement, with a population of just 40. There are a number of abandoned villages, once home to seal hunters; most were cleared in the 1960s and 70s, their population relocated to work in the fish factories of Nuuk. Many of these settlements have, rather ironically, become reinvented by Nuuk city dwellers as ideal locations for their summer houses and this, in turn, has caused some rather good restaurants to pop up for just a few months each year in the most unlikely locations.

There are many myths and legends that relate to the history of the fjords, stories passed down from generation to generation. When near Kiattua, our captain related a legend, told to him by his grandfather.

Many, many years ago two friends, an Inuit and a Viking, both fell in love with the same girl. She refused to choose between them so the two men decided to settle the matter by a trial of their archery skill. They pinned a reindeer skin on the island's beach and then climbed to top of the mountain. Whoever managed to hit the skin with his arrow first would win the girl. To prevent any chance of revenge, the winner would then push the loser off the mountain to their certain death.

The story's ending depended on whether an Inuit or a Viking was telling the story.

Most of the year, it may be possible to travel up the fjord to the very edge of the ice. Embedded in the sheet ice are blue icebergs that have calved off the glaciers; ice that is, therefore, millions of years old. If you can manage to chip off a piece of this ice, you will see that it is clearer than glass, due to being compressed for so long. It works very well in a glass of gin or whisky.

 WHERE TO STAY AND EAT *Map, page 71*
It is possible to stay in Nuuk Fjord, by camping or by renting a cabin. A few Greenlanders rent out their cabins on Airbnb and similar platforms, but most accommodation is available through tour companies or other small businesses who will also organise your boat transfer and food – the only shop in the whole fjord is in Kapisillit.

Camp Itivi \277769; w campitivi.gl; ☼ May–Aug. Located on the north side of the fjord opposite Qoornup Qeqertarsua, or Bear Island. There are just 3 cottages, each sleeping up to 4 with solar power & gas heating. Nikolaj provides the boat transfer in a small open boat or you can get there using a water taxi. You can bring your own food & cook, or Nikolaj's chef can cook for you in the restaurant cabin. The fjord here is huge & beautiful, & lazing in the hot tub with a glass of wine is an experience you'll never forget. **$$$$**

Camp Kangiusaq \545690; w watertaxi.gl/en/side/camp-kangiusaq; ☼ Jun–Sep. This camp is even further north up the fjord & is run by Nuuk Water Taxi. Every stay includes a transfer in one of their heated Targa boats & all meals at the camp. The 15 fixed tents are on individual platforms, all with dbl beds. There are kayaks, paddleboards

Discover Greenland

With the leading travel specialists

- Small-ship Expedition Cruising
- Hiking Adventures
- Off-the-beaten-track Breaks

Always exploring
Personalised adventures. Trusted expertise.

01737 428 663
discover-the-world.com

above
(VP/S)

Icebergs, like this one in Disko Bay, are coloured pink, red and orange by Greenland's midnight sun PAGE 154

left
(MB/S)

Wherever you walk in Ilulissat, the view is dominated by majestic icebergs floating down the icefjord PAGE 154

below
(S/D)

In spring, as the temperature rises, the tundra bursts into life and meltwater from the glaciers and snow-covered mountains cascades into the fjords. Pictured: Disko Island PAGE 177

Greenland's national flower, purple dwarf fireweed (*Chamerion latifolium*), grows in the flooded gravel beds where winter snow has melted PAGE 13 above (CZ/S)

The Elephant Foot Glacier in the Northeast Greenland National Park is over 5km wide and visible from space PAGE 133 below (NL/S)

above
(W/D)

Strap on a pair of crampons and experience the unique Greenland ice sheet; you can even camp for a night on the ice beneath a sky full of stars PAGE 140

below left
(TZ/S)

The Arctic Circle Trail is Greenland's most popular long-distance walking route, running 165km from the ice sheet to the ocean PAGE 140

below right
(MP/VG)

Mountain biking past the Russell Glacier, a finger of the ice sheet PAGE 140

On a crisp spring day, there is no better way to explore the landscape than on skis; trips can last for one or multiple days, overnighting in huts or igloos. Pictured: skiers ascending the mountain behind Kuummiut in east Greenland PAGE 63

Kayaking among the icebergs allows you to get up close to seals, and even whales, and to watch white-tailed eagles hunting for fish PAGE 61

above left (ARC/VG) In Nuuk's Kittat Economusée, women still make Greenland's national costumes, finished with intricate embroidery and beadwork PAGE 83

above right (MP/VG) Believed to protect from enemy attack, tupilaks – today a popular souvenir – are carved from horn, bone or stone by craftspeople, keeping their ancestral stories alive PAGE 27

below (OF/D) Qeqertarsuaq Museum's collection includes the dog sled once used by north Greenland's most important government officer to carry out his duties PAGE 180

After drilling a hole in the ice, a long, multi-hooked line is lowered into the deep fjord water to catch redfish, cod or Greenland halibut PAGE 60   above left (ARC/VG)

Dried fish have always been part of the Inuit diet, often served with berries; even today, a local meal may start with a platter of dried fish PAGE 54   above right (C/D)

Drum and dance ceremonies have always been important in Greenlandic culture, bringing together the whole village PAGE 65   below (MP/VG)

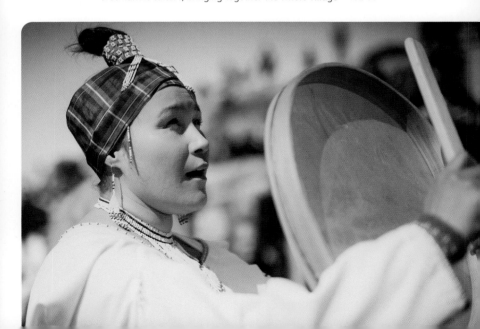

above left (BMJ/S) Polar bears (*Ursus maritimus*) inhabit the remote north and northeast of Greenland PAGE 7

above right (DD/S) Reindeer (*Rangifer tarandus groenlandicus*), also known as caribou, are common all over Greenland PAGE 8

left (SS) Musk oxen (*Ovibos moschatus*) are well adapted to extreme Arctic conditions PAGE 7

below left (DD/S) Arctic hares (*Lepus arcticus*) are easiest to spot in the spring, when the snow has melted but their coats are still white PAGE 8

below right (APP/S) Arctic foxes (*Vulpes lagopus groenlandicus*) have brown-grey coats in summer, which in winter thicken and turn white, providing excellent camouflage against the snow PAGE 8

& endless trekking opportunities, including to visit an icefjord. **$$$$**
Kiattua Camp [not mapped] 🔌529530; **w** nomadgreenland.com; ⏱ Jun–Sep. Transfer is by boat or helicopter to this camp located 90km up Nuuk Fjord in a secret location.

This is off-grid luxury glamping – with no more than 10 guests at any time. It is fully catered & there is an outdoor hot tub & a sauna tent. Activities offered include kayaking, paddleboarding, fishing & foraging for wild plants. **$$$$**

WHAT TO SEE AND DO Most of Nuuk Fjord stays ice free all year so you can always explore it by boat. The water is 800m deep in places and teeming with fish. Several tour operators in Nuuk will take you **fishing** year-round and you may have the option of a 'catch-and-eat' trip. These combine a boat trip up the fjord with a stop to fish. Every line is equipped with multiple hooks and everyone is likely to catch many fish – Arctic char, Atlantic cod, Greenland halibut or redfish. With the catch in, the trip then heads off to the restaurant in Qooqqut, or Nuuk, where the chef prepares and cooks your catch. It is a splendid way to spend the day.

In the summer you can **kayak and paddleboard** among the icebergs. If you are lucky enough to be in Nuuk between May and September, there are boat trips to see the **puffins** nesting on a small island near the mouth of the fjord. There are also **whale-watching** trips from Nuuk, a chance to spot humpbacks and sometimes fin and minke whales.

There are a few **hiking trails** that can be reached by boat. One option is to take a boat to Qooqqut and then hike to Kapisillit where you can then catch the scheduled boat back to Nuuk. The hike takes about three days and you'll need to bring everything with you, including a tent. There are three shorter options, all recently waymarked: the first is to hike from Kapisillit to the ice sheet which takes about 3 hours; the second takes you to the top of Pingu, the mountain behind Kapisillit; and the third takes you around the base of Pingu. You can also hike between Qooqqut and Nuuk; it's the route used by the Nuukkap Race (**w** greenlandarcticxplorers. com/adventure-races). It is about 70km – two days for extreme runners but three to four days' trekking – and you'll need a good map. The best map for this whole area is Sagamaps Red Series map 6 – Nuuk (1:250,000).

In winter, it's best to take a boat with a heated cabin but you will still need lots of warm clothing. It is possible to be dropped off near a settlement or trail for some **snowshoeing and skiing**. If a boat is not for you, how about a scenic **helicopter** flight to give you an overview of the whole area? And if the weather is good you can land on a mountain summit. The large windows give you a tremendous view right down the fjord.

Nuuk Water Taxi periodically organises a rubbish clear of the fjord. You can join a group of **volunteers** who will target a beach or bay and spend a few hours cleaning it up. The rubbish collected is being monitored by researchers to understand where this litter is coming from. Extra volunteers are always welcome – contact Nuuk Water Taxi (page 75).

KAPISILLIT Kapisillit is a traditional hunting and fishing village 75km northeast of Nuuk, the only settlement in the Nuuk Fjord with a permanent population, which numbers just 40. The word 'Kapisillit' means salmon in Greenlandic language, as the nearby river is the only known location in Greenland with a spawning salmon population (visitors are not allowed to fish for salmon here).

Since it is a recognised settlement, Kapisillit is supported by the government, which provides power, fuel, health care, education and a shop. The village tumbles down the hillside to the fjord's edge with the 470m Pingu Mountain towering over it.

Walking in from the jetty, the main track leads uphill towards the church, which could accommodate the entire population four times over. The simple church is probably the village's oldest building, but it has been rebuilt and refurbished many times. Kapisillit also has a school, with just eight students. The teacher lives on the other side of the fjord, commuting to school by boat in summer and by snowmobile in winter.

Next to the jetty is the state-supported Pilersuisoq supermarket (⊕ 10.00–15.00 Mon–Fri, 10.00–noon Sat); its location makes restocking from the supply boat easier. There is a list of around 400 items that every settlement store must try to stock and this one, like many, also has a small bakery and post office at the rear of the shop.

The families that live here rely on hunting and fishing, as well as a little tourism. The Greenlandic government is also supporting an experimental sheep farm on the other side of the fjord; the sheep are kept in the red barn during the worst of the winter. Across the country there are many pilot schemes to produce more food in Greenland and, thus, reduce reliance on imports.

Getting there and around Kapisillit is accessible only by boat or chartered helicopter. Disko Line, in co-operation with Nuuk Water Taxi, runs a small, scheduled and subsidised boat service to and from Nuuk sometimes as often as three times a week, a trip of about 90 minutes. You can also get here with any of the boat charter companies and many tours of the fjord visit Kapisillit.

 Where to stay

Asimut Tours & Camp ☏553404; w asimut. gl; ⊕ May–Sep. 3 modern cabins in the village sleeping 2–5 people all with kitchens, lounges, terraces & TVs. Some even have saunas. The owners also offer transfers and several optional trips while you are there. (Asimut plan to build more cabins in Kapisillit and, maybe, even a small hotel.) **$$$$**

Inuk Travel Page 75. Inuk Travel has recently opened a 5-person cabin & another small cabin across the water at the sheep farm. **$$**

QOOQQUT Beware, there is more than one Qooqqut in Greenland! This one is situated about an hour's boat ride northeast from Nuuk up the fjord, and as there is no permanent population here, the government does not provide a shop or any services. The settlement is accessible only by boat using the usual Nuuk boat companies.

The small, rather ramshackle, landing stage leads you to a main track up through the cluster of holiday houses; there are more than 50 spread around Qooqqut and many more dotted along the fjord shore wherever a small boat can get in. From October to April you are more likely to see reindeer than people as most homes will be unoccupied. But for one weekend in August this tiny settlement is transformed for the **Qooqqut Festival** (w katuaq.gl/en) with tents and marquees and lots of live music and dancing. This is a family-friendly event, with no alcohol and free entry.

 Where to stay and eat There are sometimes homes available to rent on Airbnb and similar platforms. Remember you will also have to organise your own travel to and from Qooqqut and bring in all your food and water.

Qooqqut Nuan Cabins (5 cabins) ☏313218; w tupilaktravel.com/visit-beautiful-qooqqut-nuan; ⊕ Jun–Sep. Located in the centre of the village, each heated cabin has room for 5 guests in 3 beds. There are shared toilets & showers at the restaurant where all meals are served. The 1hr boat transfer is best organised with Nuuk Water Taxi who also offer the cabins as a full-board package. Rental options include tents, sleeping bags & rifles! **$$$**

Qooqqut Nuan Restaurant \313218; w tupilaktravel.com; ⊕ Jun–Sep. This is the sister restaurant to the Restaurant Unicorn in Nuuk & is only open in the summer. The setting is excellent, the food is wonderful, & the service is friendly. It is particularly good for preparing & serving the fish you caught on the way here – but not cheap. B/fast for guests only; lunch & dinner for non-residents too. **$$$**

4

South Greenland

In south Greenland, real high and mighty granite mountains pierce the sky. Between them, massive glaciers hang from the ice sheet's edge and feed deep fjords, which run over 100km to the sea. Take a boat up a fjord, or better still a helicopter, and you'll get a real feel for the extraordinary grandeur of this region's scenery, and admiration for those who come here every year to attempt Greenland's toughest climbs.

On the edge of these narrow fjords are tiny settlements serving just 37 sheep farms, where a single family may be raising more than 1,000 lambs every year. The sheep roam freely across the lowland fells which are snow-covered in winter but turn every shade of green in summer, with lush pasture and hillsides covered in native shrubs and flowers. Ancient farm tracks link the farmsteads and these tracks open up the area to hikers and horseriders. South Greenland has a milder climate than the rest of the country; they even grow vegetables here, but there are still icebergs and sea ice. These have been carried by the currents all the way down the east coast. Occasionally, that sea ice carries polar bears.

This is where Erik the Red first landed in AD982 and, if you fly in from Iceland, Narsarsuaq in south Greenland may be your first stop too. Many travellers will come to see the Kujataa UNESCO World Heritage Site, an area that celebrates and preserves the first places in the Arctic to be farmed and the oldest evidence of Norse culture outside Europe.

Qaqortoq, with its photogenic old town, is the largest settlement in south Greenland and a good base from which to explore the area. Few people venture as far as pretty Nanortalik and the extreme southern tip, but this area has one of the most unbelievably stunning landscapes in all of Greenland.

TUNULLIARFIK FJORD

Narsarsuaq is set at the top of the 60km-long Tunulliarfik Fjord and has the only international airport in the south. It is a good base for hiking, visiting the sheep farms and Qassiarsuk, home of Erik the Red. Across the fjord from Qassiarsuk is tiny Itilleq, from where a short walk takes you to Igaliku and its interesting Norse remains, part of the World Heritage Site. To the south, at the entrance to the fjord is Narsaq, a town that is served by the northbound coastal ferry.

NARSARSUAQ Before 1941, this was just an area of flat land between a small glacier, a finger of the ice sheet, and the fjord. On 6 July 1941, an American convoy of eight ships led by an icebreaker, brought in supplies, 447 military personnel and 23 officers. Their mission was to build an air base to be called Bluie West One. This base served as an intermediate landing place for war planes crossing over the Atlantic to join the battle against Germany. Reminders of this war activity still exist – the airport runway and many of the buildings in use today were built in the 1940s. There is still a strategically important weather station south of the airport which releases a balloon twice a day to enable data to be collected and sent to weather forecasters across the world. The small population of 139 mainly work at the airport or the hotel.

Narsarsuaq's only paved road leads from the fjord harbour in the south, past the hotel and airport, through Hospital Valley to the edge of the ice sheet. A gravelled road turns off this, crossing the river to Qassiarsuk and the sheep farms.

Getting there From Copenhagen, Air Greenland flies once or twice a week to Narsarsuaq, and Icelandair flies at least once a week from Reykjavik's main international airport, Keflavik. Domestic flights fan out from here to other parts of Greenland.

Air Greenland flies six domestic routes from Narsarsuaq: to Nuuk, by plane, and Qaqortoq, by helicopter, on most days except Sunday; to Nanortalik and Narsaq, both by helicopter, on most weekdays; and to Kangerlussuaq and Paamiut two or three times a week, by plane. The airport is in the centre of town. There is a small refreshment kiosk and, for international departures, a duty-free shop.

Getting around You can walk everywhere in Narsarsuaq; the centre of town is very small and flat. All accommodation providers will take you to and from the airport or harbour or, indeed, anywhere you need to get to.

Narsarsuaq is on Greenland's second longest road, or rather gravel track, useable only by All Terrain Vehicles (ATVs) and only for part of the year. The track hugs the west shore of the fjord all the way to Qassiarsuk and then over the ridge to Tasiusaq, a distance of over 50km. All along the shore are sheep farms, now linked by their new road. Being driven along the road in an ATV is a hair-raising experience through extraordinary glacial terrain.

Disko Line runs scheduled ferries to and from Narsarsuaq, linking most towns and settlements; their ticket office is in the Blue Ice café. Local boat owners, including Blue Ice Explorer and Polar-tut, also provide boat taxi services. The journey time from Narsarsuaq to Qassiarsuk is just 6 minutes by boat and Itilleq is only 15 minutes away. The boat to Qaqortoq takes around 2 hours.

The water this high up the fjord comes from two glaciers which makes the fjord water almost fresh, rather than saline, so it freezes more easily. In some winters, it is possible to walk or drive across the frozen fjord between Narsarsuaq and Qassiarsuk.

Tourist information and tour operators Visit South Greenland is a good source of up-to-date visitor information and ideas. Check their website: w visitsouthgreenland.com.

ATV udlejning Narsarsuaq ☎294507; f.
This is a small company that rents out all-terrain vehicles (ATVs) from as little as 2hrs to a full day (350–1,300kr). You must be over 18 to hire a vehicle, but no driving licence is needed & you get to drive wherever you want. Maps are provided, along with some ideas of interesting routes to take. Each ATV can take up to 2 people. It is a great way to get out into the backcountry.

Blue Ice Explorer Near the airport terminal; ☎497371; w blueiceexplorer.gl. Blue Ice offers a wide range of guided & self-guided trips, as well as boat transfers between towns & settlements. They have their own boats, accommodation & vehicles, & sea kayaks to rent. Tours may include visiting UNESCO sites, fishing for Arctic char or hiking between farms & settlements.

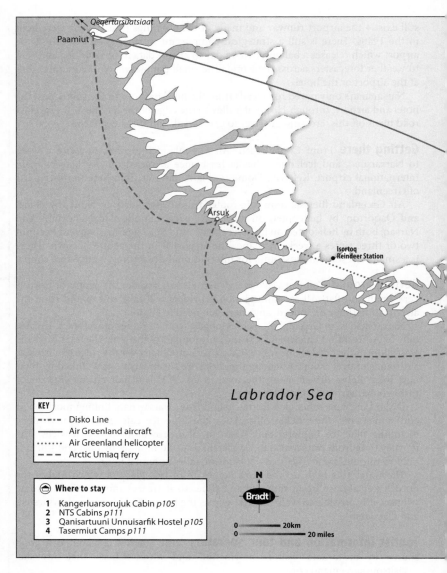

KEY

----- Disko Line
——— Air Greenland aircraft
······ Air Greenland helicopter
– – – Arctic Umiaq ferry

Where to stay
1 Kangerluarsorujuk Cabin *p105*
2 NTS Cabins *p111*
3 Qanisartuuni Unnuisarfik Hostel *p105*
4 Tasermiut Camps *p111*

N

Bradt!

0 ——————— 20km
0 ——————— 20 miles

Labrador Sea

Isortoq Reindeer Station w wildgreenland. com. This is a commercial reindeer farm where 2,000 reindeer roam over a huge area. The owners now offer wilderness & fishing trips in this remote location, staying either in the farmhouse or camping. Your trip begins & ends in Narsarsuaq & if you want to be left totally alone in the wild for a few days, then they can arrange that too.

Tasermiut South Greenland 665010; w tasermiutgreenland.com. Local experts with more than 25 years' experience & a range of tours including kayaking, hiking & biking. Their excellent 8–15-day packaged tours around south Greenland offer good value.

Travel by Heart 550905; w travelbyheart.gl. Greenland travel expert Elise Bruun offers riding & hiking holidays around the fjord using sheep farms & hostels for accommodation. Trips are tailored to your needs; she has in-depth knowledge of this area.

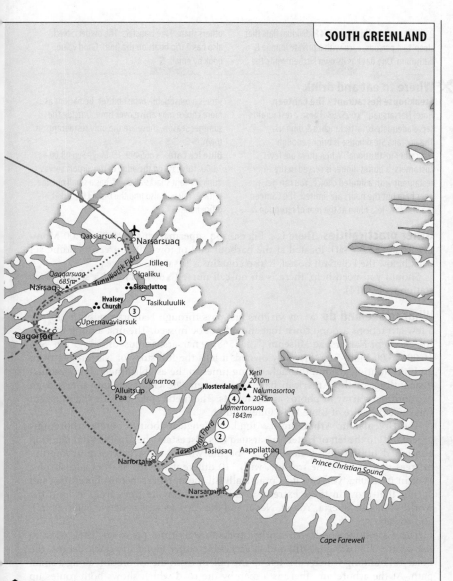

Where to stay

Hotel Narsarsuaq (95 rooms) ☏665253;
w hotelnarsarsuaq.gl. This is the big hotel in town
& is perfectly adequate but rather tired & lacking
in character. It is conveniently located within
walking distance of the airport. Most rooms have
bathrooms. Wi-Fi is neither fast nor free. **$$**
Narsarsuaq Hostel (Sleeps 36) ☏497371;
w blueiceexplorer.gl/accommodation/narsarsuaq-
hostel; ⊕ May–Sep. The hostel overlooks the

fjord with eight 4-bed & 6-bed dorms; bring your
own sleeping bag or rent one of theirs. Shared
bathrooms, kitchen, lounge & a small shop. **$**
Polar-tut hostel & flats ☏565415; e polartut@
gmail.com; w visitsouthgreenland.com/polar-
tut-narsarsuaq-new. Polar-tut can be found to
the right of the hotel in a long 2-storey building.
Inside, downstairs, is the bright hostel with a
kitchen & TV lounge. There are 10 rooms, 7 sgls,

2 dbls & a triple. Upstairs are 4 individual flats that sleep 1–4 persons, each with a private lounge & bathroom. One flat has its own kitchen while the others share. Free transfers. The owner, Storch, also has 2 trip boats on the fjord. Good value; book by email. **$**

Where to eat and drink

Steakhouse Restaurant / The Canteen
Hotel Narsarsuaq; ☎665253. These 2 restaurants serve adequate b/fasts, lunches & dinners. The upstairs Steakhouse is bright enough but rather institutional. When there are few customers, a buffet dinner is served in the restaurant with a limited choice. You can get a beer here but the hours are limited. The Canteen is a window-less room at the rear of reception & serves a reasonable b/fast buffet; be patient as more choice may arrive over time. Outside the summer season, these are the only restaurants in town. **$$–$$$**

Blue Ice Café ☎665499; ⏲ May–Sep 08.00–18.00. This café on the edge of the airport serves drinks & light snacks all day & has a small outside terrace. You will also find the Disko Line ticket office here. **$**

Other practicalities There is a Pilersuisoq supermarket (⏲ 10.00–17.00 Mon–Fri, 10.00–13.00 Sat), located at the harbour end of town, in a green building set back below the Polar-tut hostel. It also contains a Tusass post office.

Should you need help, there is an on-call nurse (☎664541) and a small police station (☎497414).

What to see and do Many visitors just pass through Narsarsuaq, but there are a few attractions around town that should not be missed. The first among these is the excellent **Narsarsuaq Museum** (☎234568; w narsarsuaqmuseum.gl; ⏲ Jun–Sep 10.00–16.00 Mon–Sat). Privately owned, it tells the full story of Narsarsuaq from an Inuit hunting ground through Viking times to the establishment, and eventual dismantling, of the American base. The owner, Ole Guldager, has amassed an extraordinary array of photos and artefacts. The metal spike outside the museum was once the spire of Bluie West One's church.

The **Greenlandic Arboretum** (w ign.ku.dk/english/about/arboreta/arboretum-greenland) to the left of Hotel Narsarsuaq was first established in 1954 but planting continued until 1999. Today, it may be the world's most extensive arboretum of trees that grow at the treeline, with 110 different species of trees and shrubs. Within its 200ha, you can find practically all the northern hemisphere trees and shrubs that grow in these extreme conditions. There are trees from around the world – Alaska, Siberia, Yukon, Nepal and the Alps, as well as native willow, birch and rowan.

There are some good, well-marked **trails** to walk from the town. The closest to the centre climbs **Signal Hill** and is accessible either along the track behind the Polar-tut building which curls left up the hill, or from the arboretum along a small path. At the arboretum, there is a map by the road which shows both routes up the hill; each is about 4km long and, on a clear day, you do get a view north of the ice sheet.

Back on the road, you'll no doubt spot the **monument** to Japanese explorer Naomi Uemura (1941–84). The monument marks where, in the summer of 1978, he started his lone journey by dog sled across the ice sheet from south to north, a journey of over 2,600km. Earlier the same year he had driven a dog sled to the North Pole, becoming the first person to reach the pole solo.

Heading out north along the paved road, there are three interesting trails, all signed. The first forks off left just outside town, signed to **The Ridge**. This trail ends at a great viewpoint with the ice sheet straight ahead. If instead you continue on the main track, you reach **Hospital Valley** and its sole remaining chimney. Once there was a huge American hospital here and rumours abound as to why. The most plausible explanation is that it was used to treat severely injured GIs returning from the Korean War. It is a 4km walk to this valley from town.

Continuing further, the track leads to **Flower Valley**, a beautiful area of coarse grass, Arctic plants and stunted bushes. In summer, it is a sea of bright green grasses and colourful flowers. Walking on, you will reach a waterfall, and this is where the walking becomes climbing. The path up the side of the waterfall is only suitable for the fit, wearing the right footwear and then only if conditions are good. The reason to undertake this climb is that you can get up close to the **ice sheet**. We would

KUJATAA UNESCO WORLD HERITAGE SITE: NORSE AND INUIT FARMING AT THE EDGE OF THE ICE CAP

In 2017, five areas of south Greenland were designated a UNESCO World Heritage Site. These were the first areas of the Arctic to be farmed and they contain the oldest evidence of Norse culture outside Europe. It is interesting that, when the Norse settlers arrived in the 10th century, they had to adapt their farming to the local conditions. When their sheep farms failed, they changed to raising goats. When cereal crops failed, they took up hunting. Soon a trade developed, exchanging grain and flour for walrus tusks and sealskins.

The last evidence of Norse settlers is a marriage contract from Hvalsey Church dated 1408. After this period, nobody really knows whether they died out or moved on.

Two of the most visited parts of Kujataa are **Qassiarsuk** (page 96), which contains Erik the Red's Brattahlið farmstead and church; and **Igaliku** (page 98), seat of the 12th-century bishopric in Greenland. Further south, down the Igaliku Fjord, is **Sissarluttoq**, the smallest section of Kujataa, which contains the remains of more than 40 ruined structures including a large Norse manor house built with thick stone walls. All the ruins are set within a beautiful valley – it is easy to understand why it was chosen as the place to settle. There is no tourist infrastructure here. Most people visit Sissarluttoq by boat from Igaliku or Qaqortoq. It is also possible to walk to Sissarluttoq from Igaliku and on to Qaqortoq – it is a beautiful walk of about 80km and takes around three days. Greenland Trekking Map No 2 – Narsaq (1:100 000) covers the entire route.

Across the fjord from Sissarluttoq is **Tasikuluulik**. This was the Norse Vatnahverfi or Eastern Settlement and is generally regarded as having the very best pastoral land in the area. Today, there are still farms dotted across the landscape but there are few visible signs of Norse habitation.

The fifth area, **Qaqortukulooq** is best known for the **Hvalsey** medieval church, although there are actually 11 Norse and two Thule Inuit sites in this area. Hvalsey is the largest, and the best-preserved Norse ruin in Greenland with thick walls up to 6m high. This was the area settled by Erik the Red's cousin Thorkel Farserk. He became rich, and the ruins here include a banqueting hall, stables, barns and storehouses. In 1410, it was reported in Iceland that, on 6 September 1408, a well-attended wedding took place in Hvalsey. The site can be visited from Qaqortoq by boat; it takes about 30 minutes to get there.

recommend using a guide; it is 14km to the ice sheet from town. Blue Ice Explorer's website (see below) does give good navigation information for all these walks and they offer guides.

There is also an interesting short walk in the opposite direction to the **harbour** on the fjord, originally built by the Americans to land their building materials. It is about 2km each way and you might spot the weather station on your right.

QASSIARSUK Across the Tunulliarfik Fjord from Narsarsuaq is the tiny settlement of Qassiarsuk with a population of just 62. Snowy mountains and icy fjords form the backdrop for a land of rolling green hills, ideal for walkers and horseriders. The present settlement was founded only 100 years ago by the Frederiksen family and most of today's farmers can trace their roots back to Otto and Tiioaaraq Frederiksen who were the first people to live off sheep farming in Greenland.

Otto and Tiioaaraq weren't, of course, the first settlers to be attracted to this area and its temperate climate. Erik the Red settled here in AD982 and there are Norse ruins all around the settlement. A bronze statue of Erik's son, Leif Eriksson, stands above the village, looking out to the fjord. In some ways not a lot has changed in the intervening thousand years. This is still farming country and a boat is the essential form of transport. Farmers now have ATVs, but they still walk or ride Icelandic horses and have dogs to round up their sheep.

Qassiarsuk is a place to relax and to enjoy the slow pace of life. Many farms and settlements are linked by gravel tracks and narrow paths. This network gives visitors the opportunity to walk or ride the trails while staying in farms or hostels.

There is a small **Pilersuisoq** (⊕ 10.00–15.00 Mon–Fri, 10.00–noon Sat) supermarket in the centre of the settlement.

Getting there Disko Line runs scheduled boats between Qassiarsuk and Narsarsuaq, Qaqortoq, Narsaq and Itilleq. Polar-tut and Blue Ice Explorer both offer boat taxi services.

At some times of the year, it is also possible to access Qassiarsuk by ATV along the gravel road from Narsarsuaq. It takes about 2 hours, though the rivers have to be low and the snow has to have melted to make this possible. Ask your accommodation or contact Riding Greenland (see below) if you want to do this – it is quite a ride and gives you a wonderful view of the countryside.

Tourist information and tour operators Visit South Greenland's website (w visitsouthgreenland.com) provides a lot of excellent information on this area including suggested itineraries for hiking and horseriding; look for 'sheep farms' on their Destinations page.

Blue Ice Explorer Office in Narsarsuaq; see page 91 for contact details. Blue Ice offers easy self-guided hiking trips around the sheep farms & settlements based on hostel accommodation. Trips include luggage transfer & variable meal options.
Riding Greenland \253444; w riding-greenland.com. The original horseriding tour company in Greenland offering trips, typically of about 8 days, through the sheep-farming areas, visiting Norse ruins on the way. Naasunnguaq & Piitaq Lund, who are the 3rd generation to be running their farm, also provide ATV buggy tours & accommodation in their hostel (see opposite).
Travel by Heart See page 92 for details.

Where to stay

In Qassiarsuks

Illunnguujuk Hostel (4 rooms) ☎497185; e farmhouse309@outlook.com; ■. A farm on the outskirts of the settlement with 4 dbl rooms sharing 2 bathrooms & a kitchen. B/fast & other meals can be provided. **$$**

Leif Eriksson Hostel (10 rooms) ☎522822; w qassiarsuk.com; ⏲ May–Sep. Just 100m from the jetty, in front of the Leif Eriksson statue, this hostel has 7 dbl rooms & 3 dorms. There is a shared kitchen, bathroom & lounge. Run by Tasermiut South Greenland (page 92) who offer kayaking, hiking & biking tours. **$**

Riding Greenland Hostel (13 rooms) ☎253444; w riding-greenland.com/kontakt. A selection of sgls & dbls, 4 bathrooms plus a shared kitchen & laundry. All meals available if booked in advance. Lovely sunny terrace overlooking the fjord. **$**

Sheep farms in the area

Qorlortup Itinnera Guest House (2 rooms, 8 beds) ☎261548; e aaqqioqkleist@gmail.com. Located in a settlement of the same name, 8km north of Qassiarsuk within the boundaries of the World Heritage Site. Shared bathroom, kitchen & living room. Optional b/fast, packed lunch & evening meal. This guesthouse also offers UTV (utility terrain vehicle) buggy tours & transfers. **$$**

Sillisit Hostel (14 beds plus 2 cabins) ☎497377; e sillisithostel@hotmail.com; w sillisit.dk; ⏲ Jun–Sep. Located in a settlement of the same name, 14km south of Qassiarsuk. Hostel on a large sheep farm, with shared bathroom, kitchen & terrace. Also 2 private 2-person cabins that share a WC/shower cabin. Meals available if pre-booked. **$$**

Inneruulalik Farm (Sleeps 8) ☎253444; w riding-greenland.com. Part of Riding Greenland – this is Naasunnguaq & Piitaq Lund's farm. Shared bathroom & kitchen; meals available if pre-ordered. Walkers are also welcome, not just horseriders. **$**

Sermilik Hostel (24 guests) Tasiusaq; ☎199202; w sermilikhostel.com. 2 houses in Tasiusaq, 7km along the trail from Qassiarsuk, run by Aviaja Lennert & Klaus Frederiksen. Transport available if pre-booked. Each house has a shared kitchen & bathroom. There are also two 2-person cabins which use the main farmhouse bathroom facilities. Meals are available if pre-booked – the cabins do not have kitchens. Small shop. **$**

Tasiusaq Kayak Hostel (5 rooms with 2–6 beds) Tasiusaq; ☎243540; w tasermiutgreenland. com/greenland-hostels. A small hostel right on the Bay of Icebergs with a shared lounge, kitchen & shower/WC. Meals & transfers available if booked in advance. Bring your own sleeping bag or rent one. Kayaks to rent. **$**

Where to eat and drink

Nearly all the accommodation providers in this area have kitchens and, if you make a request in good time, most will buy in food for you. While they can buy lamb and some fish and vegetables from farmers and hunters, all other food will have to be brought in. Most of the accommodation providers will also offer meals, including a packed lunch if you request the meals in good time.

Riding Greenland Hostel See above. Provides meals for non-residents; booking essential. **$$**

Café Thorhildur ☎497377; e cafe.thorhildur@ gmail.com; ■. A seasonal café set on the fjord shore serving coffee, cakes & light meals using locally produced lamb & beef. There is a good range of locally made souvenirs here, including natural skin creams, jewellery & musk ox wool garments. **$**

What to see and do

Brattahlið Erik the Red's farmstead, Brattahlið, and his wife, Tjodhilde's, church are the focal points of this part of the Kujataa World Heritage Site (page 95) although there are many other Norse ruins around the settlement. The church is believed to be the first Christian church anywhere on the North American continent and measured only 2m by 3.5m. It was built of stone and turf, with wooden panelled walls and a sandstone floor.

The remains of a circular cemetery were discovered here by archaeologists, with men and women buried in separate areas; the remains of 155 people have been found, some dating back to the 10th century. This date ties in with tales of Tjodhilde's church written in the Icelandic sagas.

In 2000, to help visitors visualise how the settlement once looked, reconstructions of both the farmstead and the church were built. When you enter these replicas, you realise how small houses were around AD1000. You can explore the ruins without a guide but the reconstructions are open only as part of a tour (☎274607; ⊕ Jun–Aug 09.00–16.30 Mon–Fri; 50kr) led by the resident UNESCO guide, whose knowledge brings the ruins to life.

Hiking and riding Around Qassiarsuk, there are a number of farms and hostels offering accommodation and this allows visitors to walk or ride between them. Distances are not large and the land is hilly rather than mountainous so the walking or riding can be enjoyed at a leisurely pace. You are likely to see Arctic hare and lots of birds, including white-tailed sea eagles. Walkers can extend the area by taking a boat across the fjord to Itilleq, from where a walk across a narrow neck of land brings you to Igaliku. Most people spend one or two nights on each farm before moving on; luggage can be either backpacked or transported for you by ATV or, in winter, by snowmobile.

The farms and hostels are all heated and insulated and many are open most of the year. Walking and snowshoeing the trails in winter, when there is snow on the ground and ice in the fjord, is an unforgettable experience – you may even get to be transferred across the frozen fjord by snowmobile.

We recommend using either Sagamaps Red Series No 2 – Narsarsuaq (1:250,000) or, better, Greenland Hiking Maps 2 – Narsaq (1:100,000). Both cover the area, the latter in greater detail. It is, of course, possible to book all of the accommodation and transfers individually but it is easier booked through one of the local tour operators.

ITILLEQ AND IGALIKU Itilleq is a tiny settlement with a jetty on the Tunulliarfik Fjord. Around the village are hay fields; hay is crucial to farmers as a foodstuff for their sheep in winter. From spring to autumn the hay fields are fenced off to keep the sheep out and you must stay out too or risk the wrath of the farmers. Itilleq is a useful place for visitors as a gravel track, 'the King's Road', runs over the narrow isthmus, linking the jetty with Igaliku, 4km away to the east. The road is named after a Danish king, either King Christian X, who visited Igaliku in 1921, or his son, King Frederik IX, who visited in 1952 – nobody seems quite sure which.

Igaliku has a population of 35. In summer this is a green and beautiful farming settlement, and you begin to understand why Erik the Red named this country Greenland. The village curves around a bay of blue water; colourfully painted houses are dotted apparently randomly across the slopes and a skyline of snowy peaks completes the scene. There are, in fact, more houses than people most of the year; many of the houses are holiday homes for well-off Greenlanders.

Back in 1125, this settlement was named Garðar and became the Episcopal residence for the Norsemen of Greenland. There was already a large farm here, probably the largest Norse farm in Greenland. The whole area is still dotted with the ruins of more than 50 different types of building from the Norse era but they are all hard to discern as much of the stone of the buildings was reused by later residents.

The ruins do include a cathedral, St Nicolai's, where a bishop's grave was found. In the grave was the bishop's staff made from the tusk of a walrus, and this enabled archaeologists to establish that Igaliku was, indeed, the Norse Garðar.

In 1782, Anders Olsen and his wife, Tuperna, came to Igaliku from Norway; Anders was Norwegian but Tuperna was Inuit. The farm they established was the first in all of Greenland since the Norse had left over 300 years before. To build their houses and stables, they used the stone from the old Norse Episcopal buildings.

> 60 people live in Igaliku. All except 2 men and 7–8 women are descendants of Anders Olsen. Here, a clan of people live isolated from mid-September to mid-May, with no connection to the outside world. Three or four times a year, one of them travels to the Colony to sell their produce. In harsh winters, the cattle are fed with dried fish but turnips grown in fenced fields are used as well. The cows give milk in abundance and the Bottom-dwellers make good cheese and butter. They also go hunting in the fjords.
> Louis Bob, Danish historian (1914)

Anders and Tuperna Olsen's descendants still live and farm in Igaliku today.

There is a Pilersuisoq shop (⊕ 10.00–14.00 Mon–Fri, 10.00–noon Sat) with a surprisingly good selection of food for such a small settlement. As ever, there is a Tusass desk in the shop.

Getting there and around Disko Line runs a scheduled service from Narsarsuaq and Qassiarsuk to Itilleq. Local boat companies including Polar-tut and Blue Ice Explorer run boat transfers to Itilleq from Qaqortoq, Narsarsuaq, Sillisit, Qassiarsuk, Tasiusaq or any sheep farm. From Itilleq, your Igaliku accommodation will transfer your luggage, and you if you wish, by ATV to Igaliku; it is a 4km walk across the isthmus.

Where to stay and eat You can **camp** anywhere in Igaliku that is not fenced off and is not a cultivated field, as in all of Greenland. The settlement does have a good service house where you can wash your clothes or get a shower. **Igaliku Café ($$)** in the Igaliku Hotel is the only option for meals if you are not cooking for yourself. The café serves three meals each day but you must order the day before to be sure of being served. They also make good coffee.

Igaliku Hotels & Lodges (21 rooms & cabins) \665499; w blueiceexplorer.gl/accommodation/igaliku-hotel-lodges; ⊕ May–Sep. Blue Ice offers a variety of accommodation options: there is a guesthouse, a villa, some cabins & a hotel. The large wooden cabin, the 'guesthouse', has 4 dbl rooms sharing a bathroom & lounge but no kitchen. The villa, which is rented out as a single unit, is another wooden cabin with 3 dbl rooms, kitchen, lounge & a lovely sun terrace. There are 6 small cabins, on the hill above the hotel, all dbl rooms with heating, their own bathrooms but no kitchens. The hotel has 8 small rooms with shared bathrooms & there is a restaurant here available for residents of all the properties. **$$$**

Igaliku Farm Holiday (3 houses, 3 camping pods) \531961; e tatsipkitaa@gmail.com; �[f]; w igaliku.gl. Malene & Kaava offer a selection of properties around Igaliku. Their summer lake cottage is a little outside the settlement. Beautifully set with a great view of the fjord, it sleeps up to 4 in 2 bedrooms with a lounge/kitchen, running water & WC but no shower. Their other 2 houses are located in Igaliku itself, 1 sleeps 3 & the other 4. Both have kitchens, living rooms & WCs but only the larger house has a shower. The 3 camping pods each sleep 2 & share the use of a house with a communal kitchen & bathroom facilities including a shower. Book by email. **$**

What to see and do Taking the **Garðar tour** (☏220504; ☉ Jun–Aug 09.00–16.30 Mon–Fri; 50kr) led by the resident UNESCO guide really brings the ruins of the Igaliku's old Norse settlement to life. The guide explains the ruins, earth mounds, worked stone and ditches which still remain and puts them into the context of Norse settlements in the 12th century when this was their religious heart.

Igaliku is an excellent location for **hiking** with a few marked trails. The Lake and Plateau Hike (also known as the red route) is the one that everyone wants to do, and with good reason as it ends at an amazing viewpoint that overlooks the Qooroq Glacier and the Tunulliarfik Fjord. Mainly on sheep trails, passing lakes on the way up to the view, the hike is 17km long with a rise of 266m and is waymarked all the way with red dots. It takes about 6 hours. There is a downloadable route for this hike on the Blue Ice Explorer website (**w** blueiceexplorer.gl/hiking).

While this 'red route' heads north, it is also possible to walk south to the top of Nuuluk, about 5km each way but with a 823m climb. It will take about 6 hours there and back, and the route is not waymarked – you will need a map. Again, we recommend the same maps for walking around Igaliku as for the Qassiarsuk area (page 98).

NARSAQ Narsaq is on a headland between the Tunulliarfik and the Sermilik fjords, at the foot of the Qaqqarsuaq mountain. It was an early Norse settlement and then, in the 18th century, became a centre for seal traders, attracted by its sheltered, deep-water harbour. Around 1900, this trade started to die out due to a lack of seals and the hunters turned their attention to fishing. This did not really take off until a fish factory was built in 1953 and fish and shrimp became the main industry. Unfortunately, as waters warmed so the shrimp moved north and in 2010 the factory closed. By this time, sheep farming had become a major industry in south Greenland and the old fish factory became a sheep slaughterhouse, processing more than 20,000 animals every year.

The population of Narsaq grew from 25 in 1870 to nearly 2,000 in 1990, but since the closure of the fish factory it has declined by a third to 1,312. In a town where jobs are scarce, a potential new industry is, of course, welcomed but, in Narsaq, the potential new industry is uranium mining, the 'Kvanefjeld Project'. This has been under development for many years and, in 2020, the mine was granted preliminary approval to extract rare earths and uranium, but two years later the Greenland government changed and the mining permit was not renewed. The exploitation of minerals is a controversial subject in the whole of Greenland, offering the potential of greater independence but at the cost of greater industrialisation and potential pollution.

Getting there and away Air Greenland has **helicopter** flights on most weekdays from Narsaq to Narsarsuaq and Qaqortoq. The heliport is about 1km northwest of town.

The Arctic Umiaq **ferry** (page 47) usually calls every Wednesday evening on its way north, visiting towns and settlements all the way up to Nuuk and onward to Disko Bay. Disko Line runs boats from the town to nine settlements including Narsarsuaq and Qaqortoq, both journeys taking about an hour.

 **Where to stay and eat** *Map, opposite*

There are also some rentals on Airbnb.

Hotel Narsaq (16 rooms) Alangunguup Saqqaa; ☏661290; **e** info@hotelnarsaq.gl; **f**. Located on the southeastern side of town, this is the only hotel in Narsaq. Basic en-suite rooms but friendly staff.

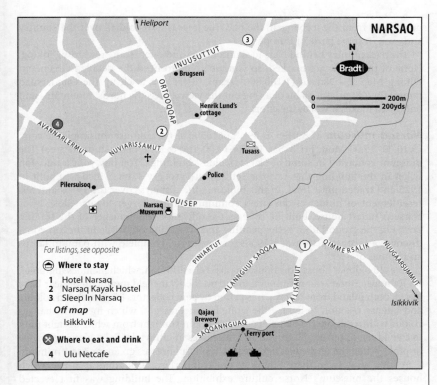

N

| 0 | | | 200m |
| 0 | | | 200yds |

For listings, see opposite

⊖ **Where to stay**
1 Hotel Narsaq
2 Narsaq Kayak Hostel
3 Sleep In Narsaq
   Off map
   Isikkivik

⊗ **Where to eat and drink**
4 Ulu Netcafe

Labels on map: Heliport, INUUSUTTUT, Brugseni, ORTOOQQAP, Henrik Lund's cottage, AVANNARLERMUT, NUVIARISSAMUT, Tusass, Pilersuisoq, Police, LOUISEP, Narsaq Museum, PINIARTUT, ALANNGUUP SAQQAA, QIMMERSALIK, NUUGAARSUMMUT, AALISARTUT, Isikkivik, Qajaq Brewery, SAQQANNGUAQ, Ferry port

---

There is a restaurant, Klara, in the hotel (**$$**) with a limited menu. **$$**

Sleep In Narsaq (2 dbls, 3 sgls) Inuusuttut B 866; ☎496497; w sleepinnarsaq.dk. Helle has 5 bedrooms in an attractive guesthouse in a residential area on the edge of town. The rooms share a large living room, kitchen & 2 bathrooms & a terrace on the 1st floor runs the whole length of the house. **$$**

Isikkivik (Cabin for 2) Inuusuttut; ☎252426; w silamut.com/english/index-eng.htm. A cabin on the edge of town with a small bedroom, a bright & comfortable living/dining room with a view of the fjord & a small terrace. It has hot & cold running water but no shower, & a compost toilet. Rented by the week. **$**

Narsaq Kayak Hostel (10 4-bed rooms) Ortooqqap; ☎265440; w tasermiutgreenland. com/greenland-hostels. This blue hostel, centrally located just 5mins' walk from the harbour, is owned by Tasermiut South Greeenland. Basic with shared facilities, & 1 bathroom. Bring your own sleeping bag or rent one. **$**

Ulu Netcafe Avannarliit B-1032; ☎580394; w ulu.care; ⬛. A small café that sells drinks & burgers. It is also a shop that sells health products like soap, herbal balms & oils made from Greenlandic ingredients. **$**

Other practicalities The two supermarkets in the town are Pilersuisoq (Louisep; ⊕ 07.00–18.00 Mon–Fri, 07.00–14.00 Sat–Sun) and Brugseni (Inuusuttut; ⊕ 07.00–20.00 Mon–Sat, 07.00–16.00 Sun). The **Tusass** post office and phone shop is at Erik Egedes Plads (⊕ noon–15.00 Mon–Fri).

What to see and do Narsaq's small red-and-white timber **church** has a very impressive blue-and-white interior but your only chance of seeing inside is at a Sunday morning service. Narsaq also has a **brewery**, Qajaq, but unfortunately it is not open to the public – you can, of course, try their excellent beers, brewed using pure water from the icebergs in the bay. The beer is now sold all over the country and even in some parts of Europe.

The backcountry behind Narsaq is untouched and offers some rewarding **hiking**. None of the tracks are marked, so you are going to need the detailed Greenland Hiking Map 2 – Narsaq (1:100,000) again. There is a track up the Qaqqarsuaq mountain (685m) – it's a bit of a slog but the view across the fjords, mountains and out to sea makes it worth the effort.

Narsaq museum (Louisep B-49; ☏ 661659; w narsaqmuseum.simplesite.com; ⏱ 10.00–15.00 Mon, Fri & Sat, 09.00–14.00 Tue & Thu; 60kr, students free) The museum is housed in some of Narsaq's oldest buildings. You buy your admission ticket in the building that was the settlement's grocery store, which was built in 1925 and traded until 1960. In this building, the displays cover the 1950s and 60s resettlement of hunters from small communities into larger towns. Close by is Narsaq's oldest house, built in 1850 as the office for the manager of the trading post. On the ground floor is the printing and art exhibition; while in the loft you'll discover a reconstruction of a 1950s grocery store, complete with paraffin lamps and bottles of beer.

The old blubber house now houses a mineral exhibition, which includes tugtupite, or 'Reindeer Stone' – a rare mineral found on the Kvanefjeld mountain or near Lake Taseq, both inland from Narsaq. It is prized by gem collectors for its rich red colours and intense reaction to light – the stone is 'tenebrescent', which means it changes colour within minutes of being exposed to bright sunlight from white or light pink to a vivid red or purple. Tugtupite also fluoresces in ultraviolet light, glowing orange or pink. When the ultraviolet light ceases, it phosphoresces green for a few minutes.

A little away from these buildings on Avannarlermut is building B-84, which houses the museum's Norse culture exhibition. The building was first erected in 1774 in Alluitsoq and didn't arrive in Narsaq until 1907, having been moved several times. This was not unusual; buildings were often demolished, moved and reconstructed particularly in the 1950s to 70s when settlements were being abandoned. The building has been a church, home to a language researcher and missionary, and a school.

Across town, the museum also runs the little red cottage of the Greenlandic pastor **Henrik Lund** who died here in 1948. Lund was also a poet, songwriter and a politician; he wrote one of Greenland's national anthems 'Nunarput, utoqqarsuanngoravit'. A man of many talents, he built this house with his son Dolfi. It is still furnished with the Lunds' possessions and is a window into life in Greenland in the 1940s. Outside is a splendid bronze bust of the man himself.

QAQORTOQ

Qaqortoq's colourful houses climb the hillside behind the harbour, their bright blues, pinks and yellows contrasting with the rugged grey mountains; it really does look like the quintessential Greenlandic town. Down in the port, red and white fishing boats unload, between the stranded icebergs. The fish market is on the edge of Qaqortoq's colonial centre, set around the charming town square and Greenland's oldest fountain. Here locals meet and you'll find some good cafés, including the Inugssuk where once a cooper made barrels for seal and whale oil. Among the preserved old buildings, you'll also discover the 1832 St Saviour church and two museums. From this colonial centre, the more modern town rises steeply, clinging to the hillside. Qaqortoq is home to 50% of south Greenland's population – but still that is only 3,000 people. Everywhere is within walking distance; even the heliport is just a short walk away along the quayside.

When exploring the town you are bound to notice some of the 31 sculptures on the Stone and Man sculpture trail (page 107). Qaqortoq is home to many artists and is a centre for Greenland's traditional and modern arts. There is local art and craft on display everywhere from large wall murals to tiny bone carvings. The walls of private houses, even their window frames, may be decorated with traditional designs.

HISTORY Saqqaq Inuit first settled in the Qaqortoq area more than 4,000 years ago. Dorset Inuit arrived some 1,500 years later, and Norse settlers arrived in the 10th century. The Norse era lasted almost 500 years, during which time (12th century) the Thule Inuit arrived in the area. There is evidence that, for a while, the Norse and Inuit lived and worked together.

The present-day city was founded in 1775 when the Norwegian Anders Olsen established a trading centre for saddle-back sealskins. By the early 20th century, the town had a thriving cod fishing industry, and most of the old buildings date back to this era. Cod fishing has declined and today Qaqortoq is an administrative centre and the location of Greenland's only tannery.

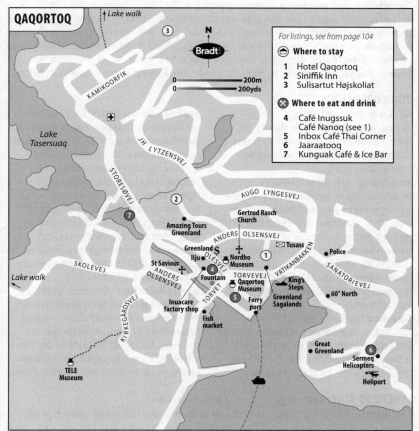

GETTING THERE Despite being the biggest town in the area, getting to Qaqortoq is not simple as there is only a heliport at the moment, although an airport is planned in the future. The upside of this is that arriving by air involves a scenic Air Greenland helicopter ride from Narsarsuaq's international airport across south Greenland's dramatic fjords and snow-capped mountains – it is 'free seating', so get on board first to get one of the window seats. Air Greenland flies four domestic routes from Qaqortoq: Narsarsuaq most days except Sunday, Nanortalik and Narsaq most weekdays and Alluitsup Paa at least weekly. The heliport is about 1km southeast of the town.

The Arctic Umiaq ferry (page 47) usually calls every Wednesday afternoon on its way north, visiting towns and settlements all the way up to Nuuk and onwards to Disko Bay.

GETTING AROUND Qaqortoq is a walkable town and your accommodation will almost certainly transport you to and from the port or the heliport. There are a few taxis (388888, 641111, 644444) and even a little local bus (operating 07.00–19.00), which wanders in a loop around the town every 20 minutes or so – it does pass the harbour but not the heliport. The bus stops are yellow with a bus logo.

Disko Line operates a scheduled boat service, subsidised by the government, to and from 13 settlements and towns including Qassimiut, Nanortalik and Narsaq. Their boats, and most tour boats, depart from the King's Steps. It is an interesting and economic way to see the sublime scenery while getting from A to B and it's a chance to chat with local people. The Disko Line website makes it easy to book but it takes a little effort to work out where the boats go to and when. Many tour operators, including Blue Ice Explorer (page 91), have boats and can arrange transfers to almost anywhere, including individual sheep farms or cabin locations.

TOUR OPERATORS

60° North Havnevej 1132; 643187; w 60north.gl; ⊕ 08.00–16.00 Mon–Fri. 60° North is a boat charter service with a wide range of boats & ships, offering boat transfers, boat tours & fishing trips.

Arctic Hiking e einar@arctichiking.gl; w arctichiking.gl; ⊕ Jun–Aug. This is a complete guiding service for everyone, from travellers who would like a guided stroll around town to explorers who wish to cross the country's ice sheet.

Gardar Charter e aho@qaq.gl. A small family concern with a closed boat offering trips to hot springs at Uunartoq, small farms & settlements & all parts of the UNESCO site including Hvalsey Church.

Greenland Sagalands Vatikanbakken; 642444; w sagalands.com. Sagalands are located in the centre of town next to the small boat jetty in the red building. Run by knowledgeable locals, they are able to offer lots of advice & ideas for

your time in the area. Sagalands organise multi-day trips including walking or riding trips around sheep farms, as well as day trips to Hvalsey, the hot springs at Uunartoq & the ice sheet at Qalerallit. A popular experience is to enjoy dinner, or a kaffemik, with a local family in their own home.

Hunter's Eye 646880. Jens Peter is a hunter who runs guided fishing trips where you might catch halibut, salmon, Arctic cod or Arctic trout. All trips start in Qaqortoq & often use Jens's Qassimiut House for overnight accommodation. He also offers day boat trips to watch whales or visit the Uunartoq hot springs.

Sermeq Helicopters Jaaraatooq; 494230; w helicopter.gl. These small helicopters take up to 6 passengers on pre-planned tours including landing on the ice sheet, visiting the Uunartoq hot springs & to the UNESCO World Heritage Site at Hvalsey. Or, it may be just the most scenic and exciting way to reach your remote hut in the fjord.

 WHERE TO STAY *Map, page 103, unless otherwise stated*
Outside the town, there are many cabins dotted about the fjords and a few can be rented by visitors. Most people get to their cabin by boat taxi but you can use a

helicopter transfer which is, of course, more affordable for groups. Make sure you know what you need to take in with you – your cabin may be so remote that you must take in all your food. Some locations offer the option of meals cooked in the local farmhouse or in a restaurant cabin.

In Qaqortoq
There are also some rentals on Airbnb.

Hotel Qaqortoq (40 rooms) Anders Olsensvej; ✆642282; w hotel-qaqortoq.gl. A splendid modern 4-star hotel set slightly up the hill in the centre of town. There are a variety of rooms & it is worth asking for a room with that great view of the bustling harbour & the icebergs in the fjord. This is the premier hotel in town, with good facilities including comfortable common areas decorated with local arts & crafts. There are large windows to make the most of the view & even a small sunny terrace. As well as rooms, there are also a few serviced apartments with kitchens. Laundry service. **$$$$**

Siniffik Inn (11 rooms) Aaninngivit; ✆642728; w siniffik-inn.dk. This is the large white house at the very end of the road. Owner Heidi has a wealth of knowledge about local culture & entertains b/fast guests with conversation, information & even poems. All the rooms are dbl, some with their own bathrooms, & every room has views of the fjord or the lake. There is a small bar & dining area where evening meals are served in the summer. **$–$$**

Sulisartut Højskoliat (50 rooms) Kamikoorsik; ✆642466; w sulisartut.gl; ⊕ Jun–Aug. 20mins walk northwest of town, this college offers rooms when the students are away in the summer. There is a strong student vibe about the place. Sgl & dbl rooms with bathroom come with full board & access to a shared kitchen & laundry. In a separate wing there are sgl rooms with shared bathrooms & kitchen; no meals are included in this wing but you can eat at the college canteen. **$–$$**

60° North Apartments [not mapped] (17 houses & flats) ✆643187; e booking@60north. gl; w 60north.gl/hotellejligheder. 60° North has a range of self-catering accommodation all over town. All the houses & flats have kitchens & sleep 2–6 people. Min 2 nights' stay. **$**

Out of town
Kangerluarsorujuk Cabin [map, page 92] (Sleeps 4) ✆199207; e larsmakkak@gmail. com; ⓕ. Just a 30min boat ride or 10min by helicopter from Qaqortoq, this cosy cabin is beautifully furnished & has a full kitchen, flushing toilet, running water & solar electricity. Meals are available. No Wi-Fi; no mobile phone signal. **$$**

Qanisartuuni Unnuisarfik Hostel [map, page 92] (Sleeps 10) ✆199243; e aqqalund@gmail. com; w visitsouthgreenland.com/qanisartuuni-unnuisarfik; ⓕ. On the side of the Igaliku Fjord, this was once the home of the sheep farm owners and is now a hostel with sgl, dbl & trpl rooms. There are shared facilities & it is also possible to order meals. Kayak rentals & lots of hiking options; no Wi-Fi; no mobile phone signal. **$**

✕ WHERE TO EAT AND DRINK *Map, page 103*
For a small town, there is a good range of places to eat, although some are hard to spot as their outdoor signs are small. In the summer, many have outdoor tables. Booking is a good idea for weekend evenings.

Café Inugssuk Torvevej; ✆580163; e inugssuk. qaqortoq@qajaqbeer.com; ⓕ; ⊕ noon–23.00 Tue–Thu & Sun, noon–03.00 Fri–Sat. A cosy bar & restaurant on the edge of the town square. Local specialities include reindeer or musk ox steak with Waldorf salad & a whisky sauce. They also serve large fruit smoothies. Later in the evening, the café becomes more of a bar, sometimes with live music. Outdoor seating in summer & more room upstairs. **$$**

Café Nanoq Hotel Qaqortoq, Anders Olsens Vej; ✆642282; w hotel-qaqortoq.gl/eng/brasserie/ brasserie.htm. A smart, reasonably priced café with coffee, cakes, pasta & steaks. There is also a small bar. The café has its own terrace with a great view over the harbour. **$$**

Inbox Café Thai Corner Torvet; ✆484788; e inbox3920official@gmail.com; ⓕ. This small Thai place is rather hidden on the edge of the port. Take the road behind the museum & the restaurant is on your left; there are signs in the 1st-floor windows. The small white door leads you upstairs to quite a large restaurant which has an extensive Thai menu where you will find interesting Thai-Greenlandic fusion dishes with seal, musk ox & red fish. Ask about the day's special. $$

Jaaraatooq Next to the heliport; ✆493782; w jaaraatooqshop.com; ⏰ 11.00–17.00 Mon–Fri, 11.00–15.00 Sat. Small coffee & souvenir shop conveniently located next to the heliport – you can watch your helicopter coming in across the fjord. $

Kunguak Café & Ice Bar ✆275077; w kunguak.com; ⏰ 11.00–21.00 daily. Set above the river on the edge of the town centre, this is a popular & friendly café. It serves an interesting selection of sandwiches, burgers & pizza plus hot & cold drinks, all at reasonable prices. At the side is the café's own ice-cream parlour with a wide selection of flavours including the local favourite, liquorice. There is indoor seating plus outdoor seating next to the river. $

SHOPPING There are a number of general stores including two large supermarkets. On the quayside by the square you will find an indoor **fish market** (⏰ 08.00–15.00 Mon–Fri, 08.00–14.00 Sat), which may be full or empty of fish and seal meat depending on whether a boat has arrived in the last few hours. Everything is labelled, telling you not only what the fish is but also when it was caught and by which fisherman or hunter. Next door, in the summer, is a small outdoor market for fruit and vegetables where local farmers sell whatever they picked that day.

Also next to the fish market is **Sissami** (⏰ 08.00–17.00 Mon–Fri, 08.00–13.00 Sat), good for camping and fishing equipment. Below the Qaqortoq Hotel, **Tamat Sports** (Torevej; ✆642576; ⏰ 11.00–17.00 Mon–Sat) also stocks a range of outdoor clothing, thermals and boots.

On the side of the square is the factory shop of **Inuacare**. They produce natural skincare products in Qaqortoq, all the herbal ingredients hand-picked in Greenland. Above the square, just across from the Greenland Bank, is **Iiju** (Olesvej B409; ⏰ 10.00–17.00 Mon–Sat), which sells wool, candles and gifts – they are not all Greenlandic but they are all beautiful. Further up the hill is **Amazing Tours Greenland** (Aaninngivit; 🅕), in a long, yellow house, where you will find a wide range of local souvenirs, particularly wood carvings, traditional beaded jewellery and a huge range of Inuit earrings. Or you could climb the hill just for the view.

At the far end of the quayside, **Great Greenland** (Havnevej; ✆642433; e info@great-greenland.gl; w great-greenland.com; ⏰ 10.00–16.00 Mon–Fri & when cruise ships are in port) is Greenland's only sealskin-processing factory, with an on-site shop which sells a wide selection of sealskin jackets, bags, shoes, boots and throws. There are guided tours of the factory (booking essential), which explain characteristics of the five main types of seal that are hunted. Skins are brought in by hunters to the rear of the factory and the tour takes you through the complex multi-stage process of cleaning and treating the skins and then how they are transformed into very high-quality clothes and footwear. The factory also processes musk ox, polar bear and sheep skins. It is not to be missed.

OTHER PRACTICALITIES There is a branch of the Greenland Bank (⏰ 09.30–15.30 Mon–Thu, 09.30–15.00 Fri) on Anders Olsensvej with two ATMs, one indoor, and the Tusass post office (⏰ 10.00–17.00 Mon–Fri) is on the same street.

WHAT TO SEE AND DO Next to the town square is the **Qaqortoq Museum** (✆641080; e qamu@kujalleq.gl; ⏰ 14.00–17.00 Tue–Fri & Sun; 60kr); the building was built in 1797, having been designed and assembled in Denmark before being dismantled, shipped and reassembled in Qaqortoq. You can still see that all the wooden sections making up the walls were numbered to enable its reconstruction. Your museum entry ticket gets you into all three of the town's museums.

In the first room of this interesting museum there are three sealskin kayaks – it is hard to believe that anyone could hunt seal and walrus from these tiny boats. There are also some old harpoons, as well as a collection of carved bone. In the next room, fine carved tupilaks created by master carvers Aron and Cecilie Kleist are displayed. Further into the museum, mannequins show off traditional Inuit clothing made from seal and polar bear skin and finely decorated with colourful beadwork. Upstairs is a collection of newspaper cuttings from 1959 which tell the tragic story of the M/S *Hans Hedtoft*, which, on her maiden voyage, sank with all hands off the south Greenland coast. In the attic are two rooms: one where Knud Rasmussen (page 164) spent time in 1932 when he was preparing for his later expeditions; Charles Lindbergh occupied the other room in 1933 while he was scouting around Greenland for the PanAm airline which planned to build a refuelling airport somewhere nearby.

Across the road behind the Qaqortoq Museum, in the low yellow house, is the **Nordbo Museum** (⊕ 13.30–17.00 Mon–Fri); this house was once home to the town's blacksmith and dates back to 1804. The small museum focuses on the lives of Norsemen in this area, including a Norse stone grave. There is also a lot of information about the Kujataa UNESCO World Heritage Site (page 95). A climb up the hill takes you to the **TELE museum** (⊕ May–Oct noon–17.00 Tue–Fri, but check it is open before you start the climb). The museum tells the story of Greenland's role in the development of transatlantic communications. On a clear day, an added benefit of that climb is a huge view across the whole area.

The small red church in the colonial centre is **St Saviour Church**, usually closed to the public unfortunately. It was built in 1832 and inside is a lifebelt from the ill-fated M/S *Hans Hedtoft*, the only piece of wreckage ever found. Overlooking the whole area is the modern white **Gertrud Rasch Church**, which is usually open; the views through its windows might distract one's attention from the sermon.

A pleasant way to walk around Qaqortoq is to follow the Stone and Man **sculpture trail** (leaflets available in the museum). The trail was established by local artist Aka Hoegh, who had the idea of turning existing rock faces into a sculpture gallery. There are 31 works including some by artists of international renown. For a bit more of a hike, there is a 10km well-trodden trail around **Lake Tasersuaq**, very popular with local walkers.

Small boats and helicopters can also take you to any of the sites in the Kujataa UNESCO World Heritage Site, including Hvalsey Church (page 95), as well as to and from remote cabins. Helicopters may also offer the option of landing on the ice sheet – not cheap but an amazing experience. **Fishing** for Arctic char and cod is also possible on most boat trips; catch your own dinner. If you would rather enjoy a **home-cooked meal**, there are a few local families who will happily cook for you in their own home. It is probably the best way to really understand the south Greenlandic way of life and to hear their family stories. Ask at your accommodation or a tour operator.

Fruit and vegetables in Greenland are expensive as they have to be imported from Denmark or Iceland. In 1959, a research farm was set up by the Danish and Greenlandic governments, 7km east of Qaqortoq. **Upernavaviarsuk experimental farm** (❧ 649306; w nunalerineq.gl) experiments with the conditions needed to grow crops in Greenland. The question is, with the long summer daylight hours and with climate change increasing the spring and summer temperatures and extending the growing season, what can be grown? As well as trying out various perennial grasses and grains for sheep, they have set up a nursery and gardens where new horticultural techniques are trialled. Raised hot beds and greenhouses are now being used to increase the variety of crops that can be grown. By discovering varieties that suit the conditions and the climate, the farm is successfully growing tomatoes, lettuce, cucumber, carrots, rhubarb and strawberries. Assisted by this research, some farmers in south Greenland are now growing fields of potatoes and cabbages. Greenland is virtually disease free, so they can produce high-quality organic fruit and vegetables – the challenge is to roll this out on a larger scale. If you would like to visit these nurseries, it is often possible to combine a visit with a boat trip to nearby Hvalsey Church. Kim Neider will be very happy to show you around.

For the more energetic, Qaqortoq usually has an annual, and rather hilly, **marathon** (e qaqortoqmarathon@hotmail.com; f) on the first weekend in July, which is part of the **Sheep Farmer Festival**. Lambing season is over and the farmers are ready to have a bit of fun with lasso and horseriding competitions. It is also an opportunity to buy local crafts and, of course, enjoy some locally raised lamb. During the day lots of family activities are on offer around the sports field, and in the evening you can go to the official dinner dance in the sports hall (tickets required). Occasionally the festival moves location to Narsaq.

ALLUITSUP PAA AND UUNARTOQ Alluitsup Paa is a traditional fishing and hunting village of 164 people situated halfway between Qaqortoq and Nanortalik. The church was burned down in 2007 and the nearest church is now in Qaqortoq, but the settlement does have a school, shop, post office and first aid clinic. There is one hotel, **Seaside Whale** (619209; e whaleseaside@outlook.com; f; **$$**) with en-suite rooms and balconies offering great views over the water and a chance to spot whales. Alluitsup Paa has a heliport with flights to Narsarsuaq and boat connections to Qaqortoq, Nanortalik and the hot springs at Uunartoq.

On the uninhabited island of **Uunartoq**, about 15km northeast of Alluitsup Paa, there are some bathing pools fed by hot springs. There is no infrastructure, just the bathing pools made by damming the streams, so it really is just you and nature. Lay back and watch the icebergs float by and marvel at the snow-capped mountains – these just might be the most beautiful hot springs in the world, and they are free. This is a truly rejuvenating experience for body and soul.

Uunartoq hot springs can also be reached by boat or helicopter from Qaqortoq or Nanortalik and may be combined with visits to other areas. It is wise to bring a full water bottle, some waterproof shoes and a towel.

TASERMIUT FJORD, NANORTALIK AND THE FAR SOUTH

With vertical granite cliffs rising sheer out of the waters, Tasermiut Fjord takes your breath away, whether you arrive here by boat or by helicopter. These mountains present climbers with some of the world's toughest climbs and, at over 2,000m, some of the highest climbing walls. The landscape is dominated by sheer and jagged granite spires; between them huge glaciers flow down from the ice sheet. In high valleys, you may spot pale blue lakes of cloudy meltwater caught among the peaks. This is utterly forbidding and unforgiving terrain, and the only way in is by boat along a fjord or by helicopter.

Further southeast, in a vast area of sea channels, islands and fjords, are the tiny settlements of Narsarmijit (population 57) and Aappilattoq (population 93). Remote and difficult to reach, very few tourists get this far south. At the very southern tip of Greenland is the uninhabited Cape Farewell archipelago, isolated from Greenland's mainland by the spectacular Prince Christian Sound.

TASERMIUT FJORD Tasermiut Fjord runs 70km north from Nanortalik to the Sermeq Glacier, which once reached the fjord but has now receded and its meltwater flows across a strip of gravel moraine. Locally, the glacier is known as the Devil's Horns Glacier because of the two rock horns that protrude partway up its slope. The narrow fjord is hemmed in by the mountains – Ketil (2,010m) and Nalumasortoq (2,045m) are the highest, but Ulamertorsuaq (1,858m) is agreed to be the most difficult to climb. At their foot are the sparse ruins of Klosterdalen, a Norse monastery which is practically impossible to find without a guide.

A little further south is the fjord's only settlement: **Tasiusaq** at the end of the Nuugaarsuk peninsula. This headland is a rare piece of flat land and has a sheep farm, a few cabins (page 111) and an unbelievably beautiful location. Tasiusaq has a Pilersuisoq shop (🕐 10.00–15.00 Mon–Fri, 10.00–noon Sat) and is served by a weekly Air Greenland helicopter in winter or a weekly Disko Line service in summer, both weather dependent. Otherwise, if you are staying in the cabins, transfer can be organised by chartered boat or helicopter.

Near the mouth of the fjord, on a small island, is Greenland's southernmost town, Nanortalik, with a population of 1,120. It is the largest town in the region and acts as a service centre for the whole area.

NANORTALIK In a stunning setting on a rocky peninsula near the entrance to the Tasermiut Fjord, Nanortalik's cluster of brightly coloured houses are framed by a backdrop of mountains. This quaint, isolated town is surrounded by pristine wilderness and has always been a strong and independent community.

Set on an island of the same name, Nanortalik is a fishing and hunting community; hunting for hooded seals on the ice every spring is still a major source of food and income. Nanortalik means 'place with polar bears' and the Norse called the island Bear Hunt Island (Hrakbjarnarey). If you are very lucky, you might see a polar bear on sea ice in spring, but you are highly unlikely to see a polar bear on land today at any time of year.

The town has a splendid natural harbour, and at the end of the 18th century the port became a trading centre for whale blubber and seal products; in recent years, there has been some mineral extraction – graphite on the island and gold on the mainland. Neither mine is currently operating although further prospecting for gold in the area continues.

Getting there and around Air Greenland flies helicopters from Nanortalik to Narsarsuaq and Qaqortoq on most weekdays, and weekly to Alluitsup Paa and Tasiusaq in winter. The heliport is about 250m east of the town.

When possible, Disko Line runs boats from the town to 11 settlements on the south Greenland coast and its fjords, including Narsaq, Narsarsuaq and Qaqortoq. The boat and helicopter services work together so the small settlements get served by one or the other each week if at all possible. It is also possible to use local boats for transport to and from almost anywhere, including remote cabins. Check tour operators' Facebook pages for offers of empty seats when they are running transfers between settlements.

Most people get around the town on foot but there are some local taxis.

Tour operators

Guide in Greenland ✆ 269386; e guideingreenland@gmail.com. Erneeraq

Benjaminsen is a licensed guide who offers guided tours around Nanortalik and its

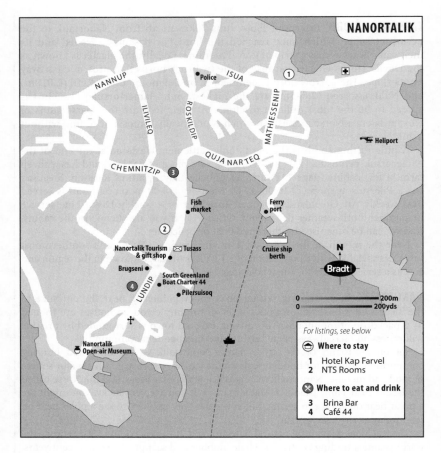

NANORTALIK

Police · ISUA · MATHIESSENIP · NANNUP · ILIVILEQ · ROSKILDIP

Heliport

QUJA NARTEQ

CHEMNITZIP ③

Fish market

Ferry port

②

Nanortalik Tourism & gift shop · ⊠ Tusass

Cruise ship berth

N

Brugseni ●

Bradt

South Greenland Boat Charter 44

④ · Pilersuisoq

LUNDIP

✝

Nanortalik Open-air Museum

| 0 | | 200m |
| 0 | | 200yds |

For listings, see below

🏠 **Where to stay**

1   Hotel Kap Farvel
2   NTS Rooms

❌ **Where to eat and drink**

3   Brina Bar
4   Café 44

---

backcountry. He also can act as your guide on any boat tour.

Nanortalik Tourism Lundip Aqqutaa B 128; ☎613633; w nanortaliktourism.com. This is the largest souvenir shop in town & they can also organise boat tours for groups.

NTS boat charter ☎490691; w nts.gl. A local family company with 3 boats who can organise local boat tours or transport to cabins. NTS also has rooms in Nanortalik & cabins in the fjord.

Serano Boat Tours ☎246549; e seranonoah@ icloud.com; ⨍. Serano has open boats for a variety of tours.

South Greenland Boat Charter 44 Ulissannguit B-4b; ☎613444; e info@ tasermiutcamp.gl; ⨍. Charter 44 has several closed boats for tours to nearby settlements, the fjords & to the southeast coast. In Oct 2023, SGBC44 were granted a 5-year concession starting in Jan 2024 for polar bear sightseeing on the southeast coast. More details will be announced on their Facebook page, or contact them via email.

 Where to stay and eat *Map, above, unless otherwise stated*
In Nanortalik

Hotel Kap Farvel (10 en-suite rooms, 10 with shared bathroom) Isua B304; ☎613294; w kapfarvel.gl. This is a standard hotel where all the en-suite rooms share the view out to sea.

The more basic rooms are in a separate wing referred to as 'the hostel'. It is all clean, comfortable & well run, which is impressive given the isolated location. The restaurant (⊕ 07.15–09.30, noon–13.00 & 18.00–19.00 daily; **$$**) serves 3 meals

a day & is normally only open for guests of the hotel but they may be able to accommodate you if you are staying elsewhere. The food is fine; dinner must be ordered before noon. **$$$**
NTS Rooms (8 apts) ☎490691; w nts.gl. Centrally located next to the Nanortalik Church, all these smart modern apartments have private bathrooms, TVs & their own entrance. The larger 2 apartments that sleep 2–4 people have kitchens, the remainder have kitchenettes. **$–$$**
Brina Bar Qujanarteq B340; ☰; ☺ 20.00–midnight Mon–Thu, 21.00–04.00 Fri–Sat. A bar with live music at w/ends. **$**
Café 44 Lundip Aqqutaa B44; ☰; ☺ 19.00–midnight Sun–Thu, 20.00–03.00 Fri–Sat. More of a bar than a restaurant, often with live music. Popular with the town's youth. **$**

Outside town
Tasermiut Camps [map, page 92] (2 sites) ☎286650; w tasermiutcamp.gl. Tasermiut Camps has 2 sites in the fjord, one near the ruins of the Klosterdalen monastery & one north of Tasiusaq. Both are offered as packages which include transfers in a closed & heated boat, tented accommodation, activities, all meals & evenings around the fire with some storytelling & singing. **$$$$**
NTS Cabins [map, page 92] (3 cabins) Tasiusaq; ☎490691; w nts.gl. Each of these 3 insulated wooden cabins, with gas heating & kitchen, sleeps 2. The location is hard to beat & the cabins face the fjord with views of snowy mountain peaks. Bring some fishing gear & you are sure to catch your dinner. The cabins are 7km north of Tasiusaq (page 109) along a reasonable track. **$$$–$$$$**

Other practicalities Nanortalik has two supermarkets and a **fish market** (near Brina Bar) where today's catch of fish and sea mammals is on display – here you will almost certainly find fish and seal meat and, perhaps, whale. The road ahead of the fish market has most of Nanortalik's shops on it including the supermarkets, Nanortalik Tourism's souvenir and gift shop – the best place in town for locally made souvenirs – and a couple of clothing shops. There is a Tusass post office and phone shop (☺ 09.00–15.00 Mon–Fri) at Lundip Aqqutaa B-128.

What to see and do If you arrive by boat, it will probably be the new harbour you step on to. There is an interesting walk along the water's edge, connecting the old and new harbours, which takes you past the sights of the town. The **new harbour** is very much a working harbour, with huge containers stacked everywhere. Following the water's edge, turn left at the first junction and immediately you'll get the view of the harbour mouth. If you were to keep straight on at that junction, the road would take you across the island to Hotel Kap Farvel, 200m away.

Turning left again brings you past a long blue building which is Brina Bar, and then to the **fish market**, and then, up ahead, is the striking white **church**, built in 1916. The wooden building looks rather like a stave church but with a single, very steep, tiled roof to the nave and, at the front, an integrated squat clock tower with porches on two sides. The interior is rather plain in a Lutheran way but the alter is splendid with a lot of gold ornamentation. Make sure you don't miss the little organ, built in 1861 and the oldest in the country, nor the local artwork on the walls. If you are lucky, you may get to see and hear the choir. Choral singing is something of a tradition in Nanortalik and all the singers will be dressed in their finest Greenlandic costumes. Just in front of the church is a boulder carved into the likeness of Knud Rasmussen, Greenland's greatest explorer; the small building to the side is a chapel of rest.

Keeping ahead, the road ends at the old colonial harbour, now used by small boats, and to the right the buildings of the **Nanortalik Open-air Museum** (☎613406; w museum.gl/Nanortalik-1). The museum overlooks the old colonial harbour in an area that is unchanged since the 19th century. It occupies ten buildings, making it Greenland's largest museum. The scope is vast – industry, health care, clothing, technology and sea-going boats, including an umiak that is over 500 years old. There are also reproductions of turf huts and summer camps.

The rest of **Nanortalik Island** is easily walked. There are lots of **trails** and, at 7km by 5km, it would be hard to get lost but a map is still a good idea. Beware that the Greenland Hiking Maps do not cover Nanortalik Island, even though map 5 is called Nanortalik. Sagamaps Red Series No 1 – Qaqortoq (1:250 000) is the best map of the island.

The island's **west coast** is particularly spectacular with 500m-high cliffs, which makes it a great place to look for whales. Walking along the east coast is more beach and boulder hopping but extremely pleasant on a sunny day. You can also walk straight up the middle to the Quaaik mountain (308m). It is a steady climb and the top has a 360° view. Keep your eyes open for stone circles and rectangles under the vegetation – remains of Inuit camp circles and Norse homesteads. If you are walking in spring, do check with someone local about any polar bear activity. This is extremely rare and the local people will know if there are any current issues.

PRINCE CHRISTIAN SOUND Prince Christian Sound is a waterway loved by cruise ships in summer, when the water is ice free. Stark, majestic yet beautiful, the sound is flanked by high granite peaks rising precipitously 2,220m from the icy water; waterfalls cascade hundreds of metres into the fjord below, glaciers flow down from the vast ice sheet above. If you are lucky, you might even spot minke, fin or blue whales.

The rock walls of the sound display bizarre geological patterns created over millions of years. The strata are folded back and forth, split by huge dark cracks. Black lichen appears to pour down the rock as if someone had spilt ink and then, around every corner, there is another white glacier, slashed with neon blue crevasses. There are seven glaciers, all part of the ice sheet and all moving slowly down into the sound. These glaciers calve icebergs, which makes navigation difficult as the icebergs float out to sea along the channel, or sometimes don't. Icebergs often get trapped at either end of the channel, earning them the name 'gatekeepers', until they finally break loose. Recent warmer winters have made the sea ice disappear more quickly in the spring, so the icebergs are trapped for less time. The waterway is up to 300m deep but only 500m wide in places, resulting in strong, unpredictable tidal currents. A ship may take 6 hours to make its way along the Prince Christian Sound, passing just one village on the way, Aappilattoq.

AAPPILATTOQ Set at the junction of fjords and the Prince Christian Sound, Aappilattoq sits perched on a narrow shelf of land beneath the 1,457m Issuttussoq mountain. It does feel that you have reached the furthest tip of Greenland's massive island.

This tiny Inuit village – whose name means 'sea anemone' and refers to the rough mountain it sits below, whose rock has an unusual red hue – is the only human habitation in the whole of Prince Christian Sound, a dot in this stark landscape. It is a real village, with a population of around 93 but this is less than half the number of people who lived here 25 years ago. Aappilattoq has its own little red church, a small cemetery, school, health centre, general store, repair shop, service house for washing, fire station and heliport. In winter the only way in is by Air Greenland's weekly helicopter flight from Narsarsuaq, which can only fly when the weather permits. In summer, the fjords and sound are free of sea ice, so Disko Line boats make the weekly trip. All the families here fish and hunt, living isolated most of the time from the outside world.

The settlement is visited by cruise ships in the summer, an event that can easily swamp the community, but you can visit with a local boat operator from Nanortalik on a day trip or take the cheaper weekly Disko Line boat (880kr, half price over 65 or under 16) out and back, but this does not offer you any time to get off and see the village.

The Disko Line boat also calls at **Narsarmijit** (population 57), the southernmost settlement in Greenland and just 50km north of Cape Farewell. There was once a failed Norse settlement here, but a Moravian missionary founded the present settlement in 1824. Remarkably, the government supports the village with the necessities of life, including a church and a small shop (⊕ 10.00–15.00 Mon–Fri, 10.00–noon Sat). In winter, weather permitting, the heliport is visited weekly by Air Greenland.

WESTERN COASTAL PORTS

There are three ports – Arsuk, Paamiut and Qeqertarsuatsiaat – between Narsaq and Nuuk, all called at by the Arctic Umiaq ferry and by some cruise ships. All three are very small and isolated.

ARSUK The first people to settle here were the nomadic Saqqaq Inuit. By the time Norse settlers arrived, the Saqqaq had left and soon the Norse moved on too. It was only in the 15th century that the Thule Inuit came to Arsuk and established a permanent settlement. In the late 18th century, a British engineer started mining silver at Ivittuut in the Arsuk Fjord, but soon the silver ran out. Some 60 years later, a group of Danes found cryolite (used in the aluminium extraction process) in the same mine, which then remained in operation for over 100 years, eventually closing in 1987. The population of Arsuk has been declining ever since, from over 300 in 1991 to just 72 today.

Arsuk's few tiny houses are dotted around the port and, set on the hill, is a fine little red-and-white church, built in 1830, with a steep green roof. Directly behind the church is the Kuunnaat mountain (1,418m), blocking any way out over land. The settlement is still supported by the government and has a shop, open every day except Sunday, a school and a health centre.

The Arctic Umiaq ferry (page 47) usually calls early every Wednesday and Thursday morning. On Wednesdays it is on its way south to Qaqortoq and Narsaq; on Thursday it is heading north again on its way back to Nuuk and onward to Disko Bay. There is also a heliport in Arsuk with weekly flights to Qaqortoq.

PAAMIUT Paamiut sits at the end of a long rocky peninsula which juts out into the Labrador Sea. Its nearest neighbours are Arsuk, 112km south, and Qeqertarsuatsiaat, 132km to the north. Off the coast is an archipelago of over 100 uninhabited islands; travel 50km inland and you reach the vast deserted ice sheet.

The town was established in 1742 as a small trading centre for seals and whales. In the 20th century, cod fishing became the main industry and, in 1967, a cod factory was built and Paamiut became somewhat of a boom town. Unfortunately, the cod did not last, but the factory didn't close down: it now processes crab and shrimp. Paamiut's boom times did not last either; the population, now 1,173, has been in decline for more than 20 years.

Paamiut has two supermarkets, Pilersuisoq and Brugseni, and a Tusass post office but limited tourist infrastructure, though it is visited by the occasional cruise ship. Air Greenland flies two domestic routes to Narsarsuaq and Nuuk twice a week; the airport is about 2.5km north of the town. The Arctic Umiaq ferry (page 47) usually calls just before midnight on Tuesdays on its way south to Arsuk

4

and beyond. It returns early on Thursday afternoons on its way back north to Nuuk
and onward to Disko Bay.

 Where to stay and eat *Map, below*
Two hotels, with attached cafés, serve those who venture this far. And for evening
entertainment there is one bar in the town, the Nano Baari (Illoqarfiup Qeqaa;
╲596433).

Hotel Ivaana (13 rooms) Illoqarfiup Qeqaa B
580; ╲498560; e amtoaps@gmail.com; ￼. Hotel
Ivaana's rooms are split over 2 floors with every
room having a TV & the 8 largest rooms private
bathrooms. There is a shared kitchen & the Café
Paamiut is in the basement. **$$**

Hotel Paamiut (11 rooms) Kirkegårdsvej 13;
╲586633; w hotelpaamiut.com; ￼. Located just
south of the church, Hotel Paamiut's 4 sgl & 7 dbl
rooms all have a private bathroom; rates include
b/fast. The Café Tamu, same owners, is next door.
The hotel also has 5 houses to rent, 4 with 3
bedrooms each & 1 with 5; & all have a kitchen,

bathroom & washing machine. The website has a
map showing the houses' locations. Rooms **$$**,
houses **$$$**

Café Paamiut In Hotel Ivaana; ￼. Serves Thai &
fast food such as burgers & sausages. Eat in or take
away; large portions. **$**

Café Tamu Kirkegårdsvej 11; ⏲ 11.00–14.00 &
16.00–19.00 Mon–Sat. Next door to Hotel Paamiut,
this is where you'll find Jessie or Ane-Marie if they
are not in the hotel. The café serves b/fast (hotel
guests only) plus lunch & dinner. It's an interesting
menu including excellent reindeer curry & hot
chocolate with cream & marshmallows. **$**

What to see and do Paamiut is the place to see white-tailed eagles, with the
largest number of this species in Greenland. Minke, fin, killer and humpback
whales all swim along the coast here, as do seals. There are no organised boat trips
but local fishermen may be happy to take you out to see whales or, in summer, to
fish for trout and salmon.

Many ancient trails head out of town into the backcountry, great for walking in
summer or cross-country skiing in winter. No trails are marked, so go equipped

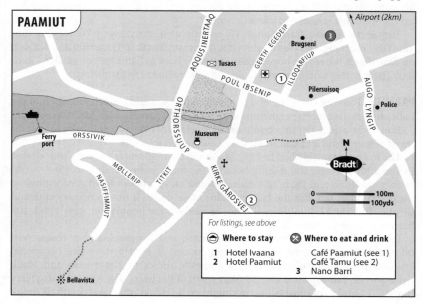

with a map. We'd recommend Greenland Hiking Maps 21 – Paamiut (1:75,000). There are two easy trails to viewpoints. One, the 'bellavista', is on top of the hill to the south of town along a path at the end of Nasiffimmut. You can reach the second viewpoint if you walk along Kirkegårdsvej, the road on the right side of the church, and, directly after passing the main cemetery, turn left up Qipoqqaq. At the very end of this road take the path up to the viewpoint on top of the hill that is slightly to your left for a view across the sea and mountains.

A Norwegian-style stave **church**, in the centre of town, the Palaseqarfik was built in 1909 and is claimed to be one of the most beautiful in Greenland. Its red walls, green roof and ochre woodwork is certainly striking. The inside is typically Lutheran, with a votive boat hanging over the aisle.

Practically next door to the church is the Paamiut **museum** (✆366615; ⊕ 13.00– 16.00 Tue–Fri & Sun) which consists of a number of buildings – we never did quite work out how many of the buildings were actually part of the museum. The former colonial manager's house, built in 1839, contains the main museum displays, as well as the ticket office and a small shop. Also worth visiting are a peat house, a cooper's workshop, a sheep shed which was once used as the hospital, two salt-storage buildings, an old shop and post office and the carpenter's house.

QEQERTARSUATSIAAT It takes the ferry more than 7 hours to get here from Nuuk on Tuesdays, heading to south Greenland, and it returns late on Thursdays on its way back to Nuuk. Boat is the only way in as there are no roads; nor is there an airport or heliport. The town is situated at the very northern point of the island of the same name, which means 'rather large island' – it has an area of 8km by 6km.

As with so many coastal towns, Qeqertarsuatsiaat started life as a trading port and became an early centre for cod and salmon fishing. For many years it had a population of over 300, but today it is reduced to only 177. There is some hope of a revival of Qeqertarsuatsiaat's fortunes as, in 2016, a Norwegian company took over a troubled ruby and pink sapphire mine 18km east of the town. Mining into rock that is around 3 billion years old, they are extracting the oldest rubies and pink sapphires on earth; each stone can be identified as Greenlandic by the trace elements that it contains. Although the mine is owned by a large Norwegian family, the mine is very Greenlandic: it has a 100% local workforce and three-quarters of its operating costs are spent in Greenland.

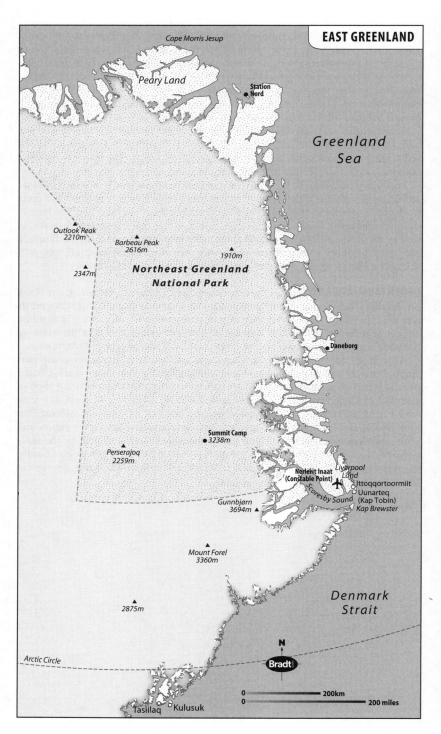

EAST GREENLAND

Cape Morris Jesup

Peary Land

Station
Nord

Greenland
Sea

Outlook Peak
2210m

Barbeau Peak
2616m

1910m

2347m

Northeast Greenland
National Park

Daneborg

Summit Camp
3238m

Perserajoq
2259m

Liverpool
Land

Nerlerit Inaat
(Constable Point)

Ittoqqortoormiit

Scoresby Sound

Uunarteq
(Kap Tobin)

Kap Brewster

Gunnbjørn
3694m

Mount Forel
3360m

Denmark
Strait

2875m

N

Arctic Circle

Bradt

0   200km
0   200 miles

Tasiilaq   Kulusuk

5

East Greenland and the Northeast Greenland National Park

East Greenland is one of the most remote and wild places left on earth. Only 3,000 people live on this 10,000km coast, and two-thirds of them live in one town, Tasiilaq. It is a land of extremes with the world's largest national park, the world's longest fjord system, the northern hemisphere's coldest temperatures and the world's lowest population density.

The interior is covered by Greenland's ice sheet, which in places extends all the way to the coast. Other parts of the coast are extremely mountainous, including Gunnbjørn Mountain, Greenland's highest at 3,694m. The mountains frame a labyrinth of fjords, some extending more than 300km to the very edge of the ice sheet. It is an Arctic paradise of silence, untouched and rarely visited.

Even today the area is very isolated. Ice makes navigation extremely hazardous and, at times, impossible. Supply ships are few and far between, perhaps twice a year, and even they can get stuck in the sea ice for days. There is no coastal ferry and only two civilian airports. Kulusuk has flights from Nuuk and Iceland, but Ittoqqortoormiit, further north, only has flights from Iceland.

Western culture has had less impact on east Greenland than elsewhere in the country and life here is more traditional. The people speak East Greenlandic as their first language, which to the outsider is totally different to West Greenlandic. The language has no agreed written form, although people do send each other phonetic text messages on their mobile phones. In addition to East Greenlandic, most people speak West Greenlandic, Danish and some English; all signs and posters are in West Greenlandic. They even have their own national costume (page 83), which they proudly wear on special occasions.

Tasiilaq and Kulusuk have the area's best tourist infrastructure, including a choice of accommodation and experienced tour operators who can open up this challenging wonderland with a wide variety of exciting adventures.

HISTORY

East Greenland has always been isolated, and the continual year-round stream of polar sea ice flowing down the coast kept European hunters and settlers away until the late 17th century. It is probable that early Inuit did populate the area for short periods thousands of years ago, but none stayed long. They either moved on, as nomadic people do, or they perished. In the 15th century, Thule Inuit coming from the north were the first to settle permanently. They used the land and sea both to hunt and for travelling and settled around the Ammassalik and Scoresby Sound regions, both good areas for hunting and fishing. Along the whole 10,000km coast, these are still the only regions with settlements.

By the late 17th century, European whalers were hunting off the east coast and, despite the pack ice, they made landings to trade with the Inuit and to take on drinking water.

In 1885, Gustav Holm led the first successful Danish expedition to the area, using traditional umiaks which could be paddled in water and dragged across ice. They reached the community of 413 Inuit living on the side of the Ammassalik Fjord in the Tasiilaq area. These Inuit believed that they were the only people left on earth as their Inuit contacts to the north and south had all died out. They were barely surviving and a second expedition just seven years later found that the population had dropped by more than 100. The Danes founded a trading and missionary

POLAR BEARS

Above everything else, the polar bear (*Ursus maritimus*) is the animal most associated with Greenland and the animal that every visitor would like to see. Of all the areas in Greenland, the east coast is where you are most likely to see one.

Most polar bears live in the remote north and northeast of Greenland. In the late spring, as the sea ice breaks up, they travel south on the ice down the east coast. When the sea ice starts to break into ever smaller pieces and seal hunting becomes impossible, the polar bears retreat to the mainland to find birds and berries to eat while they slowly walk back north.

Even in east Greenland, you are unlikely to see a polar bear unless you are on a guided trip with the specific purpose of seeing them. Specialist tour operators are licensed to offer trips to see bears, but there are never any guarantees. Being on a boat or cruise ship probably offers the best chance to spot a polar bear, perhaps when it is hunting from the sea ice. Snowmobile and dog-sled trips can also be successful.

A polar bear can be up to 3m long and weigh as much as 500kg. They are equipped with sharp claws, large teeth and strong jaws. Being carnivorous, they will attack anything that they think can be eaten, and that includes people. Nobody has been killed by a polar bear in Greenland for many decades because Greenlanders are very aware of the danger they pose. Towns have polar bear watches and protocols that dictate what happens when a polar bear is sighted near a settlement.

You are extremely unlikely to meet a polar bear inside a settlement, but there is a risk once you leave town. While researching this guidebook, we asked repeatedly what should be done if you see a polar bear and you have neither a gun nor flares. The advice was always the same: *You must never, ever be in that situation.*

A local guide in Kulusuk told us, 'If you see a polar bear on land, unless you have a rifle, flares or dogs, then it is too late. The bear will have already smelt you; he can outrun you and once he picks up your smell, he can hunt you down.'

Polar bears are hunted in east Greenland, controlled by strict quotas. Outside the supermarket you may spot the 'Piniagassat anginerit killilersukkat' notice informing everyone how many animals are left on this year's hunting quota. *Nanoq* are polar bears.

settlement at Tasiilaq two years after that and used it as their base to explore and map the coast further north. When their maps linked with those made by Peary, who started from Thule and mapped the far north coast, the whole of Greenland's coast had been mapped for the first time.

Danish influence after 1900 changed the culture of the east Greenlanders; Christianity was introduced and slowly they moved from a life of nomadic subsistence hunting and fishing to an economy based on settlements, where sealskins and cod were sold for cash. In 1925, the Danish settlement at Scoresby Sound, present-day Ittoqqortoormiit, was established.

The change in the economy saw the gradual introduction of motorboats and snowmobiles. Although many hunters across east Greenland today still use traditional equipment like umiaks, kayaks and dog sleds, this is in decline.

KULUSUK

Once an Inuit hunters' summer settlement, Kulusuk is today a small community of around 220 people who live by fishing and hunting seals and polar bears.

The first European contact with the Thule Inuit hunters of Kulusuk wasn't until the early 1900s and Kulusuk wasn't officially founded as a Danish settlement until 1909. However, there were Europeans living here before this, as the church was built in 1908. In 1956, the US army built an air base here as part of their

KEY
······· Air Greenland helicopter

⊜ Where to stay
1 Ice Camp Greenland *p128*
2 Tasiilaq Mountain Hut *p126*

KULUSUK AND TASIILAQ

5

It's early morning as I sit writing this, our sled's dogs still asleep as the sun slowly begins to rise. After months of uninterrupted daylight, the first frosts, night skies and aurora borealis of autumn are on us. Sitting in our wooden cabin in the small Tunuumi community of Kulusuk, I'm looking out over the wind-riffled fjord that surrounds this village, small icebergs adrift on the tide, steep gneiss mountains and the Apusiaajik Glacier rising from the far shore. Our boat lies on its mooring, the same spot from which we travelled out over the sea ice only a handful of months ago.

I turned up here in my late teens, searching for adventurous climbing and skiing, stumbling on a place and community that has since totally captivated me. It's here that my wife Helen and I have made our home and where we mountain guide through the year.

Thousands of kilometres of wild coastline extend either side of our village, a band of alpine mountains running much of that length. Inland lies an ice cap that can take many weeks to cross, extending 2,500km from south to north. But it's the sea that is surely the beating pulse of Kulusuk. The subsistence-hunting community that belong here have lived in deep connection with the migrations of sea mammals, fish and ice that come and go as each year rolls on. Modern changes, not least to the climate, threaten this way of life, but the roots go deep, something that's apparent when I see the children dog sledding, fishing and hunting.

Taken under the wing of Geo and his family a couple of decades ago, I've had the privilege of learning in the only way knowledge is handed on here: countless days spent with elders quietly pointing out the intricacies of ice patterns, underwater rocks and storm cycles. From the cold months when we ski, dog sled and snowmobile over a skein of ice, through late spring when vast fields of drift ice open and close around our boats, to the ground swell and storms of autumn, change is perhaps the only constant.

With nothing a given and only friends and family (maybe) in a position to help, every journey out from the village is a committed undertaking. Intergenerational intimacy with the waters, ice, animals, land and weather, combined with an alertness to thousands of factors that could add up to bringing food back to family – or returning safe – lies at the heart of life here, a vibrancy of connection that is spell-binding to me.

Matt Spenceley is co-founder of Pirhuk and has lived in Kulusuk for more than 20 years. He is passionate about living, climbing and skiing in Greenland and about the bonds he and his wife Helen have made with the people of Kulusuk.

Cold War early-warning defence system; they left in 1991 and their air base is now the area's airport.

From the airport, the track to the village meanders around hills and lakes and passes a small rocky cemetery of white crosses. Cresting the final hill, Kulusuk sits below you – clusters of brightly coloured houses beautifully set around the fjord shore and framed by huge snow-capped mountains. The fjord bay is dotted with dog sleds in winter and boats in summer but there are always icebergs not far away.

Few houses here have running water or flushing toilets. Water is collected from the blue communal 'tap house'. The drinking water is drawn from the centrally located lake on the hill and is available all year round through the central pump and above-ground pipes, which avoid the permafrost. The village has a kindergarten, a small school with 40 pupils, a shop with a post office, a church and one hotel. The community has to be self-sufficient as, even as late as May, supply boats may still be unable to sail into the dock.

GETTING THERE No ferries serve the port but, bizarrely, Kulusuk does have an international airport. It is served at least twice weekly by an Air Greenland flight from Nuuk and also, at least once a week, by an Icelandair flight from Keflavik. It is less than 2 hours from Iceland by air. There is a helicopter shuttle to and from Tasiilaq, timed to work with the incoming and outgoing longer-haul flights.

The airport has a small café and is about 2km southeast of the settlement. It is something of a culture shock when you step out of the two-room terminal into the wild, bare landscape, the only other building in sight the garage for the airport vehicles. There are no roads, just a narrow gravel track, and no taxis or buses wait to take you into the village. It is not recommended that you walk, at least not without a guide, as you are in polar bear country – your accommodation will provide an airport transfer on request; or you might get a ride on a quad bike (see below).

A boat transfer from Kulusuk to Tasiilaq, on the other side of the fjord, is available, weather and ice permitting. It takes about 1 hour and can be booked through Guide to Greenland (w guidetogreenland.com) or your accommodation.

GETTING AROUND Walking is the most common way to get around in the village itself, with dog sleds, snowmobiles, skis and snowshoes coming out in the winter. Outside the village, local people always travel with a gun or in a vehicle because of the small but real risk of meeting a bear. There is a quad bike taxi run by Georg Utuaq (✆230958), which takes one or two passengers, depending on luggage and how good you are at hanging on.

TOUR OPERATORS

Arctic Wonderland Tours Suulup Aqqulaa B724 Tasiilaq; ✆981293; w arcticwonder.com. Established in 1973, this may be the longest-running family business in Greenland. They own the hotels in Kulusuk & Tasiilaq. Boat trips include crossing the fjord to the Apusiaajik Glacier in an open boat (wear warm clothes). They also offer a walk around the village & a trip up to the old American radar station for panoramic views of the area.

Nunatak Adventures ✆281591; w nunatakadventures.com. Their most popular trip is to walk on the glacier and explore an ice cave with 2 excellent guides. They also offer a full-day trip with 2hrs walking on Greenland's ice sheet. A selection of mountain trips reach untouched, unclimbed & even unnamed peaks.

Pirhuk Greenland Mountain Guides B1014 Kulusuk; ✆234275; w expeditiongreenland.com. A team of professional mountain guides with over 20 years' experience; there are impressive biographies of all the guides on their website. They offer ski touring, mountaineering, trekking, dog sledding & custom expeditions & organise all their own logistics. As well as guiding groups, they also support independent projects. All trips are based in their Nanoq Lodge, which sleeps 15 in dbl & trpl rooms & is exclusively for trip participants. This is a comfortable, cosy & practical hand-built wooden lodge with lots of space for storing clothing & equipment. There are hot showers & flushing toilets in the shared bathroom…& Helen makes great scones.

WHERE TO STAY AND EAT Both Nanoq Lodge and Hotel Kulusuk serve meals to guests but generally not to non-residents.

Hotel Kulusuk (34 dbl rooms) B 1500; 986993; w arcticwonder.com/hotel-kulusuk. Located between the settlement & the airport, this hotel is owned by Arctic Wonderland tours, as is the hotel in Tasiilaq. The hotel feels rather like a mountain lodge, decorated with polar bear skins & local pictures & photographs. Its facilities include a sauna & hot tub, both with views across to the snow-capped mountains. There is even a resident masseuse during the winter & summer seasons. All rooms are en suite with a TV & kettle. You can choose to stay with just b/fast, FB or HB (there is nowhere else to eat unless you buy food at the settlement store). There is a range of equipment to rent; ask before you come if you need something specific. $$$

OTHER PRACTICALITIES If you have found a house or room to rent, then you'll need to find the Pilersuisoq store (⊕ 09.00–16.00 Mon–Fri, 09.00–noon Sat) in the middle of the settlement, which does include a good bakery.

There is medical help available in the village from the resident nurse and her helper.

WHAT TO SEE AND DO The village is extremely photogenic, so take some time to wander around with your camera. The small red Lutheran **church** was built in 1908 by the surviving crew of a Danish ship that was wrecked on the shore, using timbers salvaged from the ship. Its construction is, therefore, a little odd. A model of the original sailing ship still hangs above the church organ. The elegant stained-glass windows were donated by a German glassworks owner who visited Kulusuk in 1970.

The small **Kulusuk Museum** (531245, 276849; w kulusukmuseum.gl; ⊕ by prior appointment only) is owned and run by Justine and Frederik Boassen, and most of the items inside come from local families. The museum gives a real insight into Inuit life on the east Greenlandic coast, very different from that of the west coast. The collection includes local traditional costumes, beadwork and even polar bear skulls. Jewellery, gifts and postcards are also sold here.

Villagers sometimes put on traditional **drum dance** performances, mostly when the settlement has a number of tourists visiting.

There is an old American **radar station** above the village which you can drive up to for panoramic views of the area. Travelling further afield, the most popular trip is to cross the fjord to the **Apusiaajik Glacier**, which you can walk on and explore an ice cave. In the winter a dog sled is the way to travel; with frozen lakes and extensive backcountry there are numerous routes to enjoy. For the more adventurous, there are mountains, glaciers and fjords that would take a lifetime to explore, many seldom visited. Expert local guides can tailor an itinerary to suit your abilities and ambitions. If you are the first to climb a mountain, you do get the right to name it!

A private helicopter operates from Tasiilaq (see opposite) and this can drop you, and collect you, from almost anywhere making the extreme skiing and mountaineering options infinite.

TASIILAQ

Tasiilaq is set in a sheltered bay off the Ammassalik Fjord and, as you sweep in by helicopter from Kulusuk – the only way in or out of east Greenland's largest town for much of the year – the view is breathtaking. The blue bay, frozen solid for six months every winter, is studded with icebergs in summer. Snow glints on the magnificent, jagged mountains that drop steeply to the water. It could be the opening sequence of a film about extreme Arctic exploration.

Tasiilaq's colourful houses climb the steep hillside from the harbour and the main hotel is right at the top. All the houses look across the bay to the snow-covered mountain ridge. With a population of 1,900, the town has all the amenities of modern life – shops, internet, mobile phone service and an astroturf football field – but you can never forget how remote this close-knit community is. Everything that isn't hunted or caught comes in by ship, the first in June, the last in October. Offshore pack ice blocks the bay for seven months of the year and the arrival of the first supply ship in spring is received with a three-cannon salute and much celebration. At last there will be chocolate and fresh fruit in the shops.

Tasiilaq is an outdoor adventurer's paradise with a well-developed tourist infrastructure and a very helpful tourist information office. There is a good choice of accommodation here, most with their own tour operations, but you can pick and mix: staying in one company's accommodation does not mean you have to do all, or any, of your trips with them.

The wilderness is never far away. A few days before our last visit, a polar bear had strolled to the edge of town. Despite attempts to make him leave, he repeatedly returned, coming too close and had to be shot. The polar bear skin was hanging up to dry at the back of the hunter's house.

During the same visit there was a katabatic wind warning. These winds, locally called *piteraqs*, sweep down from the ice sheet under the force of gravity. Wind speeds can exceed 300km/h and temperatures can drop below –20°C. Locals prepare for the winds by moving everything to the leeward side of a building and tying it down. Shutters are closed and even helicopters are parked undercover. For 12 hours the streets are empty, but the next morning, when the wind has dropped, life resumes as if nothing remarkable has happened.

GETTING THERE AND AROUND There are helicopter flights with Air Greenland every day except Sunday to Kulusuk, mainly to feed passengers to, and retrieve them from, the Nuuk and Keflavik flights. There are also helicopter flights each week to Isortoq, Tiniteqilaaq, Kuummiut and Sermiligaaq. The heliport is to the east of town about 2km from the centre. A boat transfer to Kulusuk is also available when ice conditions permit.

There are two **taxi** companies in town: Avi's (✆598313) and Sylvia's (✆581070).

TOURIST INFORMATION AND TOUR OPERATORS There is an excellent tourist information office (✆587646; w eastgreenland.com) in the centre of the town. This is the place to go for information on tours, trips and events in the area.

Arctic Dream B578; ✆584171; e info@ arctic-dream.com; w arctic-dream.com. Lars Anker-Møller founded Arctic Dream because he wanted to enable visitors to have an authentic east Greenlandic experience – local cuisine, local culture delivered by local people. Arctic Dream offers boat trips to small settlements including Tiniteqilaaq, as well as a trip to visit the Knud Rasmussen Glacier, calling at the ruined US base Bluie East Two at Ikateq. Longer multi-day trips include an 8-day winter adventure, 5 days of which are spent travelling by dog sled between local houses & mountain huts. A 6-day summer adventure explores an ice cave, visits Ikateq, sails down the Sermilik Fjord & much more.

Arctic Wonderland Tours In Hotel Angmagssalik; ✆981293; w arcticwonder.com. Arctic Wonderland offers a range of local walking tours including to the Valley of the Flowers. They also offer boat or dog-sled trips visiting the Sermilik Fjord & the village of Ikateq or to the 6km-wide Helheim Glacier.

Dines Tours Gentoftevej B924; ✆982143; w dinestours.com. A small company offering dog sledding in winter to Qorlortoq Lake or Ukiverajik & boat trips in summer in the Tasiilaq Fjord or to Kulusuk.

Greenland Copter ✆547574; w greenlandcopter.com. Tim Nicolaisen's helicopter company (his brother Mikki owns Hotel

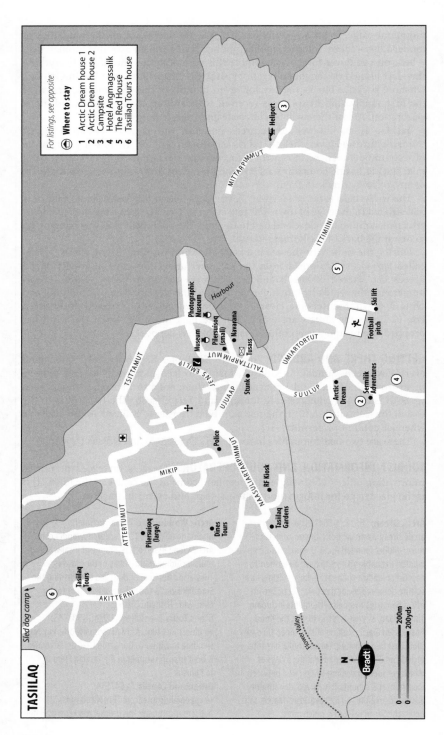

TASIILAQ

For listings, see opposite

Where to stay

1 Arctic Dream house 1
2 Arctic Dream house 2
3 Campsite
4 Hotel Angmagssalik
5 The Red House
6 Tasiilaq Tours house

Sled dog camp

Heliport

MITTARPIMMUT

ITTIMIINI

Harbour

Photographic Museum

Pilersuisoq (small)

Museum

Navarana

Tusass

TSIITIAMUT

JENS EMILIP

UJUAAP

TALITTARPIMMUT

Stunk

UMIARTORTUT

SUULUP

Arctic Dream

Sermilik Adventures

Football pitch

Ski lift

Police

MIKIP

NAASULARTARPIMMUT

RF Kiosk

ATTERTUMUT

Pilersuisoq (large)

Dines Tours

Tasiilaq Gardens

Tasiilaq Tours

AKITTERNI

Flower Valley

N

Bradt

0   200m
0   200yds

Angmagssalik) supports heli-skiing & specialist charter flights, as well as offering sightseeing tours to the Helheim & Mittivakkatand glaciers & the Johan Petersen Fjord. All flights can land on the glaciers as well as overfly the majestic mountains & ice-studded waterways; visibility in the clear Greenlandic air can exceed 200km. Your time walking on a silent glacier will never be forgotten.

The Red House Napparngummut B1025; 🌐981650; **w** the-red-house.com. Very experienced guides. Winter activities include dog-sled trips of 3–7 days, spending the nights in a settlement with a local family; a 1-week photography trip (Feb–Mar) to see the northern lights, staying in their own cabin; ice fishing for cod, redfish & sea scorpion; & snowshoeing or ski-trekking over mountains & glaciers to old Inuit settlements. In summer they offer boat & kayak tours, hiking with overnight camping, rock climbing & glacier tours. The Red House also supports projects, including film-making & extreme expeditions.

Sermilik Adventures 🌐230558; **w** sermilikadventures.com. A small local company run by hunter Tobias and Line, who ensures all trips run smoothly. Line is also a good cook and a trained nurse. Their speciality is exciting & unusual multi-day trips. In Mar–Apr a 4-day trip combines dog-sled journeys, sleeping in an igloo & a boat trip around the icebergs on the Sermilik Fjord. You may see polar bears, or at least their tracks. In summer, a boat trip up the fjord takes you whale & iceberg watching, & allows you to catch fish for dinner, & the next day brings you to Nattivi on the edge of Greenland's ice sheet. From here, a traditional dog sled transports you on to the ice sheet. On the final day there is the opportunity to kayak in the fjord. Sermilik is also one of the very few tour operators licensed to run polar bear safaris. From Jun to Sep, they offer all-inclusive multi-day trips from Tasiilaq. Travelling by boat along the coast, & camping overnight, the trips travel to wherever Tobias believes the bears are to be found. Tobias recently took explorer Levison Wood on a similar journey for British television broadcaster Channel 4.

Tasiilaq Tours 🌐252302; **w** tasiilaqtours.com. Rasmus & his wife run this small local company that offers dog-sled tours & boat trips. They can also rent out a wide range of equipment – from fishing rods & tents to satellite phones & kayaks.

 WHERE TO STAY AND EAT *Map, opposite, unless otherwise stated*
Next to the heliport is the **campsite ($)**, run by the Red House. It has on-site toilets and you can walk up the hill to the Red House to use the shower if you wish.

Hotel Angmagssalik (40 rooms) Suulup Aqqulaa; 🌐981293; **e** yewlin@arcticwonder. com; **w** arcticwonder.com/hotel-angmagssalik. Owned by Arctic Wonderland Tours, this hotel is right on the very top of the hill, so the views are terrific – and the walk up from the harbour or town is breathtaking too. There are some lovely public rooms with interesting local arts & artefacts, including a huge narwhal tooth & a polar bear skin, & lots of books & photos. Dbl & sgl rooms, with shared or private bathroom. Most people opt for HB or FB as the options for eating out are minimal. All food is served buffet-style & is pretty good considering how far it has all come. The hotel restaurant ($$), open also to non-residents, spans the front of the hotel building & has a great view of the town below & the fjord beyond. There is a set menu for b/fast, lunch & dinner with a couple of choices. The bar serves a limited selection of beers & wines. **$$–$$$**

The Red House (26 rooms) **w** the-red-house. com/en/accommodation.html. The Red House (it says 'Aapalartoq' on the outside) has both a guesthouse/hostel & 4 other houses offering accommodation in a mixture of dbl & trpl rooms. The guesthouse/hostel has 16 dbl rooms & a shared kitchen, a dining room, a library & 2 bathrooms. B/fast is served every morning in the summer season & other meals are available if requested in advance. The other houses sleep 4–6 in dbl rooms & all have a kitchen, dining room & bathroom. You can rent an entire house, if you wish, & all guests can take their meals in the Red House, again if requested in advance. **$$**

Arctic Dream (2 houses) 🌐584171; **w** arctic-dream.com. Arctic Dream has 2 houses with 5 & 6 bedrooms. Both houses can be rented in their entirety if desired. Houses have fully equipped kitchens, bathrooms & dining rooms. **$**

Tasiilaq Mountain Hut [map, page 119] (Sleeps 14) w arctic-dream.com/hc-mountain-hut. 700m up & set on a cliff overlooking the fjord, this is a unique location to spend a night or 2 while exploring the mountains. The views are, as you might expect, simply breathtaking. There is a kitchen, a seating area & a toilet. Access is by boat up the fjord & then a 5hr hike to reach the hut. The hut is booked through Hotel Angmagssalik (page 125) & the boat transfers with Arctic Dream (page 123). **$**

Tasiilaq Tours (Sleeps 4) Akitterni B1554; ☎252302; w tasiilaqtours.com/guesthouse. Tasiilaq Tours has a house to rent with kitchen, bathroom with flushing toilet, a washing machine & a lounge with a TV. There is a small terrace & a great view of the fjord. **$**

SHOPPING Above the harbour, just to the right of the two museums is the smaller of the two Pilersuisoq **supermarkets** (⊕ 07.00–22.00 daily); it has a smaller range than the big one but it does have a bakery and an ATM. The larger Pilersuisoq (⊕ 10.00–18.00 Mon–Fri; 09.00–14.00 Sat) is just 10 minutes' walk away and also sells clothes and footwear (upstairs) and camping gear (downstairs), including tents, sleeping bags, stoves, lamps and disposable camping gas cylinders. There is also a selection of rifles and ammunition on sale – you must be over 12 years old to make a purchase. The **RF Kiosk** in town is also good for camping gear, including gas.

Next door to the small Pilersuisoq, you will come to **Navarana** (⊕ 10.00–17.00 Mon–Fri, 11.00–17.00 Sat–Sun), an interesting shop for craftwork, including pottery, tupilaks, jewellery and souvenirs. It also sells clothes and some food. Continuing along this haphazard row of shops, the next building is the **Tusass** post office and phone shop (⊕ 09.00–15.00 Mon–Fri). Across the road is the **Stunk workshop** (⊕ 08.00–16.00 daily), where local craftspeople work on bone and horn. It is a proper workshop and you get to see how your carving was made and have the opportunity to buy from the maker. If you don't see quite what you want, many artists are willing to make a piece especially for you.

OTHER PRACTICALITIES Emergency numbers in Tasiilaq are ☎981211 for the hospital, ☎701224 for the police, and ☎113 for the fire service.

WHAT TO SEE AND DO The town is split in two by the ravine that leads to the harbour. It should take only about 30 minutes to walk across town, but the hills slow you down. All around town you may spot benches to rest on, some looking like sleds and all carefully positioned for good views.

The most prominent building in Tasiilaq is the 1985 pentagonal **church** (⊕ variable but always for Sun mass & you may be able to sneak in to choir practice: 19.00–21.00 Tue & Thu), set on a promontory overlooking the sea. Inside there is a selection of traditional and modern Greenlandic art, notably a striking picture behind the altar. A votive umiak hangs over the central aisle.

A little below the church, to the east in a small red building, is the tourist information centre; then the next building down the hill is the old 1908 church, which is now home to an interesting **museum** (⊕ May–Sep 10.00–16.00 Sun–Thu, 13.00–16.00 Fri–Sat, Oct–Apr 13.00–16.00 Sun–Thu). It displays artefacts from the area and interesting old photos of the first expeditions by Europeans to the east coast in the 1800s. There is also a very fine collection of tupilaks by Gedion Qeqe. In the grounds, there is a peat house, once home to 25 people, which the museum staff are happy to open on request. Further down the hill is the **Photographic Museum** with seasonal exhibitions all summer – check on east Greenland's website (w eastgreenland.com) for what's on and opening hours.

Behind the football pitch in the centre of town is a **ski lift** (⊕ Fri–Sun). It runs only at weekends when there is enough snow and not too much wind. You can rent all the skiing equipment from the house at the bottom; there are two runs, one on each side of the lift.

At the northern edge of town, after passing the last houses, you reach the **sled dog camp.** This is where all the town's dogs are chained up and where you may start your dog-sled trip. They are all working dogs so don't be tempted to pet them unless invited to by their owner.

To the west of town is **Flower Valley**, considered to be 'in the town' by locals, so you don't need to carry a gun. It is, of course, possible that a polar bear might be in the area but locals will know if this is the case. To be sure, ask at your accommodation or at the tourist information office before you go. Before you start the walk, we recommend visiting **Tasiilaq Gardens**, just to the left at the start of the valley. This community project is running a crop-growing trial using south-facing cold frames. So far they have successfully grown salad, edible flowers and root vegetables. You can learn more about the project at the tourist information office.

Back at Flower Valley, the noticeboard provides a good outline map of the area. On the back of the same sign is a more detailed map of the actual valley. The track leads to the cemetery and then becomes a path that wanders up the valley marked with red dots and arrows from time to time. After cresting a small ridge, the first lake is reached. At the top of this lake is a small waterfall; it is possible to cross the river above the waterfall and return on the opposite side of the water. If you keep ahead around the second lake, then you reach a rather more impressive waterfall, above which you again have the option of crossing the stream to return on the far side. If you are here in spring or summer, then Flower Valley will live up to its name with cotton grass, pink saxifrage, snow buttercups and purple willowherb. In the autumn look for the small black Arctic blueberries.

On your return, after passing the cemetery, you can take a boardwalk right, which leads towards the hotel. The route takes you to a small hillock and a wooden bridge across the river. Now keep forward to meet the path that is heading diagonally up and left to the crest of the hill. At the top, you'll cross some reasonably flat ground to reach the road just below the hotel. Don't tread on the pipes please, as they contain everyone's internet and satellite TV cables.

Out of town there is a wealth of adventures to experience any time of the year. During the winter, Tasiilaq is a centre for ice climbing, ski touring and heli-skiing, with unclimbed mountains, snow-filled valleys and vast swathes of unfenced wilderness. There are many exciting options for day trips or longer expeditions. Snowmobiles and dog-sled adventures are also magical at this time of year, a chance to experience the pure air and raw grandeur of the backcountry and try your hand at ice fishing. As the weather warms up and the snow melts, the boats are launched in the harbour and you can venture out along the ice-studded fjords to visit glaciers and possibly spot a whale. On a multi-day trip you have the option of staying in an igloo or small mountain hut and experiencing the silence and amazing skies in this pristine wilderness.

Some trips call at **Ikateq** on their way to the Knud Rasmussen Glacier. This was the site of the US World War II air base Bluie East Two. From 1942 to 1947 this airfield was used as a refuelling stop and had a medical station for the wounded. Sadly, when the base was closed, nothing was cleared away, leaving buildings and vehicles to slowly disintegrate. Rusting fuel drums – there may be as many as 25,000 – soon started to leak, but it was not until 2019 that the Danish and Greenlandic governments started to clean up the mess. It is interesting to wander around the abandoned site; it is bleak and windswept and some of the old buildings are now used as occasional shelters by passing hunters and fishermen.

TINITEQILAAQ (TIILERILAAQ)

Tiniteqilaaq is the official name for this settlement but many people still use the old traditional name Tiilerilaaq, and you will find this used on many maps. Diilerilaar is the phonetic East Greenlandic name; there is no agreed written name, and some people call it Tinit for short.

The settlement sits on a shelf on the edge of the Sermilik Fjord; behind it rise huge mountains and in front is the narrow waterway. Even by Greenlandic standards, this is remote. The fjord is always full of icebergs from the Helheim Glacier, less than 50km further up the fjord. This is wild country and the scenery ensures that you will never forget how remote you are. It is this unique location that has attracted local tour operators to establish basic accommodation here and to provide local guides so that visitors can explore this unspoilt wilderness.

Tiniteqilaaq is very small with just 93 people living there, mostly hunters and fishermen. There is a school, one room of which is used as the church, but there is no running water – everyone collects what they need from the tank. There is a Pilersuisoq supermarket (⊕ 09.00–15.00 Mon–Fri, 09.00–noon Sat).

GETTING THERE In summer, most visitors arrive by boat from Tasiilaq, 40km or 3–4 hours away. In winter, travel is by dog sled or snowmobile across a glacier and a frozen sea (2–3hrs). There is a heliport (IATA code TQI) on the edge of the village with up to three Air Greenland flights a week to Tasiilaq.

 WHERE TO STAY

Egon House (Sleeps 6) ✆584171; w arctic-dream. com/egon-house-tinit. Egon House has 3 bedrooms, a good kitchen, dining area & seating area. There is an indoor bathroom but no running water. **$**
Gert's Hut (Sleeps 8) ✆584171; w arctic-dream.com/gerts-hut. Constructed by local craftsman Gert, this hut sits 1km above the village & has amazing views in every direction. There is a kitchen & seating area & an outside toilet. **$**

Ice Camp Greenland [map, page 119] (5 2-person cabins) ✆584171; w arctic-dream. com/ice-camp-greenland. Just when you were thinking that Tiniteqilaaq was as remote as it gets, these 5 simple cabins, creating a tiny village of their own, are even further into the wilderness. They are painted in traditional colours & each has a toilet & 2 beds, & there is a communal main house with a shower. The camp is mostly used by tour operators bringing in small groups for whom they provide transfers & meals. **$**

WHAT TO SEE AND DO Tiniteqilaaq is in an excellent location for exploring the Sermilik and Johan Petersen fjords and it is possible to reach the glaciers at the head of both of these from the village. Travel is by boat or kayak in summer or by dog sled or snowmobile in winter. Many multi-day trips from Tasiilaq visit Tiniteqilaaq on their way north.

The **Sermilik Fjord** is 81km long from the sea to the **Helheim Glacier** at the head of the fjord, one of the three main glaciers that feed the fjord with icebergs. The glacier has a face more than 6km wide and is the fastest-moving glacier on Greenland's east coast. The calving face has retreated more than 3km in recent years, although at one time it had retreated twice this far and then recovered. NASA has been monitoring the glacier since the 1990s.

Branching west off the Sermilik Fjord, just south of Tiniteqilaaq, is the Johan Petersen Fjord, which runs for about 20km up to the Bruckner and Heim glaciers. It is navigable only in summer and is strewn with icebergs all year. It is sometimes possible to make landings on 'Bad Island' (Ingmíkêrfíkajik), home to many Arctic plants and from where gyrfalcons have been spotted.

KUUMMIUT

Kuummiut is on the east side of the Ammassalik Fjord, 40km northeast of Tasiilaq and 34km north of Kulusuk. It is another hunting and fishing settlement but somewhat larger with a population of 250 people and perhaps twice as many sled dogs.

The settlement is tucked in against jagged mountains. Unusually, the harbour stays ice free during most winters which is why there is a small fish-processing factory. There is virtually no tourist infrastructure, just a school, a service house with public showers and a church with stained-glass windows. There is a Pilersuisoq supermarket (⏰ 09.00–16.00 Mon–Fri, 09.00–noon Sat) and on the edge of town is the heliport from where Air Greenland flies twice a week to Tasiilaq.

Arctic Dream (page 123) has a **cabin ($)** which can sleep up to eight in one bedroom. It also has a living room, kitchen and a composting toilet. As with the entire village, water has to be brought from the communal water tap, which is 100m away.

Most tourists visit as part of an excursion from Tasiilaq or Kulusuk. In summer there is some good hiking and fishing from the village, and in winter skiing is possible.

ITTOQQORTOORMIIT

Some 500km north of the Arctic Circle and sandwiched between the largest national park in the world and the largest fjord system in the world, this settlement is about as remote as it gets. The closest town is Tasiilaq 800km southwest. Walking along the rough gravel streets in town, you can spot seal, musk ox and polar bear skins drying on racks outside brightly painted houses. Just to stress how remote this is, it has its own time zone (GMT –1) and can only be reached by air from Iceland; there are no domestic flights to Ittoqqortoormiit.

The village of about 350 people is set at the mouth of the Scoresby Sound, named after Arctic explorer and whaler William Scoresby, who was the first person to map the area in 1822. In 1925, some 70 Inuit from Tasiilaq plus four families from west Greenland arrived by ship to establish the settlement. One of the first buildings was the small red wooden **church**, still in use today. The interior is entirely of wood, with circular lights over the aisle and blue roof beams. From one of the beams hangs a model of the ship that the settlers arrived in.

The small **local museum** (B-186; ☎991280; e kommuneqarfik@sermersooq.gl; ⏰ on demand) is managed by the school – drop in to get the key – and has many historic photos including those of the 80 brave first settlers. There are also local costumes, tools and stories of local people. Nanu Travel (page 130) runs a small **information centre** which also has a good gift shop; opening times vary. There is a Pilersuisoq **supermarket** (⏰ 09.00–17.00 Mon–Fri, 09.00–13.00 Sat) with a post office and phone shop inside it.

At the highest point of the village is the weather and telecom station, which releases a helium weather balloon twice a day to collect information for the Danish Meteorological Office. Internet and mobile phone service are both available in the settlement thanks to this station.

Do not venture out of Ittoqqortoormiit without a guide: there are hungry **polar bears** out there looking for lunch. There is a polar bear patrol for the village which goes out early every morning to check that there are no bears in town before the children walk to school, often in the dark. The patrol not only looks for bears but also endeavours to scare them away.

5

GETTING THERE AND AWAY Getting to Ittoqqortoormiit is a little complicated. Norlandair flies at least weekly from Akureyri in Iceland to the airport named Constable Point or Nerlerit Inaat (IATA code CNP). This is 40km from Ittoqqortoormiit across a fjord.

An Air Greenland helicopter is permanently stationed at Nerlerit Inaat airport to transport passengers to Ittoqqortoormiit heliport (IATA code OBY) which is located just 500m north of the town, just a 15-minute flight away. However, the helicopter's limited capacity means that passengers arriving from Iceland may have to wait their turn to be flown across the fjord to Ittoqqortoormiit.

If the helicopter cannot fly, then a snowmobile or dog-sled transfer may be arranged for you. It is a fun way to arrive but bear in mind that it is 50km, so wrap up warm.

TOUR OPERATORS

AdvenTours I/S Inutsaaip B-265; ☎494843; e adventours3980@gmail.com; w eastgreenland.com/providers/adventours-i-s. A small family business run by Naasor & Tsigaar. Their trips usually include staying as guests in their home, offering, as they say, a chance to live & partake in their culture, customs & traditions. Tsigaar's home cooking is a great way to get a real taste of local food & Naasor can take you dog-sledding for a few hours or a few days; you might even see polar bears. Also snowmobile tours, whale safaris & hiking in the area.

Guide to Greenland ☎582014; w guidetogreenland.com. This is a national agency with good links to the area & its small operators. They offer multi-day trips to Ittoqqortoormiit, including flights from Iceland if you desire. In summer their tours focus on hiking, boating & culture while in the winter you can dog sled & cross-country ski, as well as visit or stay in abandoned settlements.

Nanu Travel ☎991280; w nanutravel.dk. This is a locally owned company that has been running trips in this area since 1998 & is a specialist in Arctic travel, in winter & summer. All their guides were born in Ittoqqortoormiit or one of the now abandoned villages. Nanu has a wide range of trips which can be tailored to your individual needs & which can be packaged into a multi-day itinerary. They also provide comprehensive support for expeditions, from advice to logistics & provision of equipment & transport. Dog-sled trips run from Jan to mid-Jun & there are boat trips into the huge fjord system, as well as north along the coast of the national park from mid-Jul to Oct.

 WHERE TO STAY AND EAT

Ittoqqortoormiit Guesthouse (7 rooms) ☎581280; e ittguesthouse@outlook.com. This is the only accommodation in the village &, considering how remote this is, it is really quite comfortable. There are basic sgl & dbl rooms with shared bathrooms with flushing toilet & shower, a washing machine, 2 kitchens & lounge. The kitchens are well equipped, including a microwave, which is good as there is nowhere else to eat. You must bring in your own food or shop at the Pilersuisoq. It may be possible to eat with a local family, which is always an interesting experience. No Wi-Fi. **$$**

AROUND ITTOQQORTOORMIIT Ittoqqortoormiit is at the southern end of **Liverpool Land**, a land of frozen fjords, glaciers and remote mountains which was once thought to be an island. It was named by William Scoresby – he named the capes and sound along its 110km coastline after his friends from Liverpool, England. The whole area can now be explored on skis or by dog sled.

South of Liverpool Land is **Scoresby Sound,** a huge fjord system, probably the largest in the world, covering an area of over 38,000km². It extends inland for about 350km and is up to 1.5km deep. Ittoqqortoormiit sits in a bay on the northern side of the fjord mouth. As you travel along the fjord further inland, so the mountains rise higher and the land becomes wilder, particularly on the southern side where basalt walls rise 2km into the sky.

The whole system can be explored by boat, kayak, dog sled or snowmobile. Trips range from excursions of a few hours to longer multi-day trips visiting or staying in abandoned villages. Fishing is possible all year, fly fishing in summer for Arctic char or ice fishing in winter.

Just 9km southeast of Ittoqqortoormiit, **Uunarteq (Kap Tobin)** sits on a windswept promontory, a small abandoned village that is mainly used by locals as holiday and hunting cabins. Kap Tobin was once a village of 120, with a school and, from the 1940s to 1980s, a weather station. However, the population rapidly declined and the last permanent inhabitants left in 2004.

Opposite Uunarteq, 30km across the fjord mouth, is **Kap Brewster** on an equally windy promontory, and also abandoned. The cliffs here are some of the best bird cliffs in east Greenland and host an immense colony of **little auks**, home to millions of birds.

NORTHEAST GREENLAND NATIONAL PARK

Covering 972,000km², the Northeast Greenland National Park is the world's largest national park, with a land area larger than France and Germany combined. This vast wilderness accounts for nearly a quarter of the entire island of Greenland.

For thousands of years the Inuit lived and survived in this rugged environment, and along the coast many traces of former Inuit settlements have been found, including tent circles and tools. The 19th century brought whalers from Europe who sailed up the east coast but rarely landed. During the first half of the 20th century, hunters and trappers from Denmark and Norway travelled inland to hunt Arctic foxes and polar bears, sending the furs back to Europe. Some of these expedition and hunters' huts still remain today, and Inge Bisgaard, an architect from Nuuk, has worked in these remote locations taking great care to preserve some of the huts and restore them to their original state.

The national park was officially recognised in 1974 and then extended to its present size in 1988. The boundaries are basically straight lines drawn on a map. In 1977 the park was designated a UNESCO Biosphere Reserve and it is now overseen by the Greenland Department of Environment and Nature.

The interior of the park is covered by Greenland's ice sheet, a hostile world of ice and snow, but there are areas along the coast that are ice free in summer with mountains, rivers, fjords and lakes. Surprisingly, wildlife is abundant in the park – this pristine environment and isolated location creates a sanctuary for many plant and animal species.

It is difficult to count the number of polar bears in Greenland (though there are attempts at aerial counts), but it is widely agreed that the park is home to Greenland's largest bear population. It is estimated that between 10,000 and 15,000 musk oxen roam the park, nearly half the world's population; but only a handful of Arctic wolves remain – they were hunted to near extinction but are now protected, so their numbers may increase soon. Arctic hares and foxes thrive in these conditions, along with stoats and collared lemmings. All these animals have to survive periods of intense cold, with temperatures as low as –35°C (the record is –63°C).

Along the coast, there are healthy populations of walrus and harp, bearded and ringed seals; and beluga and narwhal whales can be spotted where sea ice has broken up. More than 60 species of birds nest around the cliffs, many migrating here for the summer breeding season. Common ravens and ptarmigan stay all year but,

5

THE SIRIUS DOG-SLED PATROL

During World War II, a small group of 15 men were selected by Eske Brun, the governor of Greenland, and tasked with patrolling the remote northeast coastline of the island. This 800km stretch of coast was thought to be a prime spot for a German landing. Most of the men were hunters, so they knew the area well, but patrolling this huge coastal area, where temperatures sometimes drop below –40°C, was a tough mission. Although they had a base consisting of a few huts, the men were frequently sent out to patrol the coastline. Each patrol consisted of just two men, each with a 12-dog sled and a rifle.

One of the patrols unexpectedly stumbled upon a secret German meteorological station on the remote island of Sabine. By predicting the incoming weather, this station was transmitting forecasts to the Germans, giving them accurate information for Atlantic crossings. Although the governor of Greenland and the US army were immediately notified about the existence of this weather station, nobody came to help. Instead a game of cat-and-mouse ensued over several months between the hunters, armed only with rifles, and the Germans, who were equipped with machine guns. The gripping story is recounted in *The Sledge Patrol* by David Howarth (Lyons, 2018). The Germans eventually were airlifted out and, miraculously, only one member of the patrol lost his life.

After the war, sled-dog teams still patrolled the northeast coastline and, in 1950, the patrol units were officially recognised by the Danish special forces and named The Sirius Dog Sled Patrol. They established their headquarters in Daneborg in what is now the Northeast Greenland National Park, and this remains their base still today. Now Sirius not only patrols the coastline and borders, but also enforces park regulations concerning the conservation of this pristine wilderness.

The vast area of the park is dotted with about 50 huts, some old hunter's huts, which the soldiers use. Supplies are brought in by boat or plane. At any one time there are six dog-sled teams patrolling, each with two men and up to 12 dogs. The selection process is rigorous and only the elite from the Danish army and navy are eligible. A course of duty lasts typically about two years and the challenges they face are numerous – extreme isolation, extreme cold, continual darkness, frostbite and polar bears are just a few. To cope with these challenges, each member of the team has to pass courses in a huge range of subjects from engine mechanics and sewing, to radio communications and first aid.

in summer, you may also spot barnacle geese, king eider, gyrfalcons, sanderlings, snow bunting and snowy owls. During the short summer, when the sun never sets, Arctic flowers briefly appear – yellow Arctic poppies, cotton grass, dwarf fireweed, pink moss campion, alpine gentians and many varieties of saxifrage. Dwarf birch and Arctic willow sometimes grow in sheltered spots.

Strangely, the northern tip of Greenland, a peninsula called **Peary Land**, is entirely ice free despite being only 700km from the north pole. The region is referred to as a 'polar desert' – precipitation levels are so low here and the air is so dry that it rarely snows – and scientists believe it has been like that for the last 8,000 years. The peninsula is named after Robert Peary, the first explorer to reach this remote spot in 1891.

Just south of Peary Land is an area of glaciers and ice caps that are not connected to the ice sheet. Most notable of these is the **Elephant Foot Glacier**, which has been created by ice pouring from high mountains on to a flat plain and forming a smooth, frozen, near-symmetrical pool measuring 5km across. Technically known as a Piedmont glacier, its striking shape has been photographed from space.

Nobody lives in the national park permanently. The Danish armed forces do maintain a surveillance unit called Sirius (see opposite) within the park boundaries, based in **Daneborg**, and usually have 12 to 14 soldiers stationed here year-round. One defence base, **Station Nord**, is located even further north in the park, on the Princess Ingebord Peninsula at more than 81° north. Established by the USA as a weather station in 1952, it proved to be almost impossible to support with supplies as there is no access by sea and, after 20 years of struggles, the station was closed, causing a great outcry from both researchers and military officers. In 1975, with a new airstrip, new buildings and new equipment, the base reopened. A permanent staff of five are stationed here for a 26-month period; in summer the base can house up to 14 scientists.

Weather stations along the coast and on the ice sheet are sometimes manned and in summer scientists stay at the research stations. The **Summit Station** (w summitcamp.org), a research and weather station, is located in the centre of the ice sheet at 3,200m; it has a webcam and its website also tells you current and past weather conditions.

GETTING THERE AND AWAY
The park is difficult to access, and no visitors are allowed into the park without permission from Greenland's Ministry of Nature and the Environment. Permission is most easily obtained through a local tour operator.

There is an airport, Nerlerit Inaat (Constable Point), which is located on Jameson Land, 40km from Ittoqqortoormiit, south of the park. The airport was built in 1985 by the US oil company ARCO who were looking for oil. In 1990, ARCO gave up their search and sold the airport to Greenland. There is always a helicopter based here for search and rescue cover, but which also provides a passenger service to and from Ittoqqortoormiit.

With no roads in the park, access is otherwise by dog sled or snowmobile. Nano Travel based in Ittoqqortoormiit specialises in Arctic travel and will provide logistical support for expeditions into the park. They offer dog-sled trips from a few days to several weeks covering areas travelled by famous explorers. They can provide sled outfits, boots, tents and sleeping bags.

5

6

Kangerlussuaq and the Arctic Circle Region

Rugged hills, tundra vegetation and abundant wildlife are all here in this untouched and wild landscape. The dramatic coastline is broken up by fjords that slash deep into the hinterland and small, mostly uninhabited, islands are scattered like jewels just offshore. Most of this area, where the Inuit have lived, hunted and fished for thousands of years, is north of the Arctic Circle, which cuts across at about 66°N; only the town of Maniitsoq lies to its south.

In 2018, a vast tract of this land was designated a UNESCO World Heritage Site. Covering more than 4,000km², this protected area is crossed by the 165km Arctic Circle Trail offering experienced walkers the challenge of hiking from the ice sheet at Kangerlussuaq to the sea at Sisimiut.

Kangerlussuaq is one of Greenland's few inland settlements, blessed with a more stable climate. Its location enables the easiest access to one of the country's true wonders: the ice sheet. Walking on the ice sheet or, even better, spending the night there, is an awe-inspiring and unforgettable experience. Reindeer and musk oxen are never far away. Sisimiut is Greenland's second largest city, but less than a third of the size of Nuuk, with fishing at its heart. With the sea on one side and the vast, wild backcountry on the other, it is an outdoor adventurer's paradise. Being just north of the Arctic Circle, this is the southernmost place for dog sledding.

The area is easy to access with international flights to Kangerlussuaq, and twice a week the coastal ferry sails along the coast. Travel around the region is relatively easy too, so there are plenty of opportunities to experience some of Greenland's greatest treasures.

KANGERLUSSUAQ

Kangerlussuaq (population 491) is 50km north of the Arctic Circle and sits at the head of a 170km-long fjord. The town is here because of the airport, its location chosen for the climate, with a claimed 300 days of clear skies every year. There is a danger that Kangerlussuaq is seen just as a necessary stopover, but it is actually one of the best places in Greenland to see wildlife – reindeer, musk ox, Arctic hare and ptarmigan – it's a good place in winter to see the northern lights and it certainly offers the easiest access to the ice sheet.

Kangerlussuaq is not a traditional Greenlandic town. Many of the buildings were originally part of the military air base and have now been repurposed as hostels, shops, housing and a museum. The town and airport occupy the flat land, much of which springs under your feet as you walk – that's the permafrost

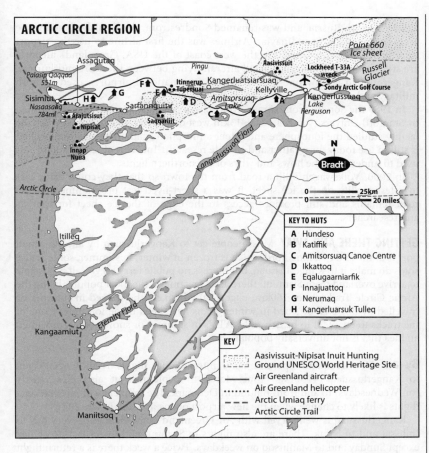

thawing beneath you. On either side of the fjord valley are rocky hills, snow-covered in winter and carpeted with mosses, lichen and low-growing bushes in summer.

A road winds out of town, south over the hills to Lake Ferguson (5km), the source of the town's water. A gravel road heads east up the valley to pass the Russell Glacier before reaching the ice sheet (37km); it is a road originally built by Volkswagen to test cars in cold climates. There is also a short road west to the small port (13km) on the fjord – this road is also the start of the Arctic Circle Trail to Sisimiut.

HISTORY The head of the Kangerlussuaq Fjord was a nomadic Inuit campsite for thousands of years. It was a great place for hunting and fishing, with easy access to the water and many herds of reindeer living in the hills. The first modern development occurred in 1941, when the US military decided that it was the ideal place to build an air base. One of their advisors had operated a meteorological station near Kangerlussuaq in the late 1920s and knew the area well.

The airfield was named Bluie West-8 and was one of a set of bases and airfields in Greenland that were used as staging posts for planes travelling between the USA and Europe. It also provided meteorological data for European weather forecasts. After World War II, the air base became important in the USA's

Cold War with Russia, and was renamed Sondrestrom, the Danish name for the area. In the 1950s, Scandinavian Airlines was the first airline to use the airport to refuel its flights to and from the west coast of the USA. Greenland's airports are still used as a stop-off for small aircraft flying between the USA and Europe. Kangerlussuaq is now one of Greenland's international airports, used by both military and civilian aircraft.

In 1983 the Sondrestrom Upper Atmospheric Research Facility was established by Stanford University at Kellyville, 13km west of Kangerlussuaq. For 35 years the facility studied the ionosphere and upper atmosphere, gathering information that is still in use today for weather and climate research. 'Incoherent scatter radar' was used to understand the hows and whys of the northern lights.

In 2000, Volkswagen built a road from the town so that they could drive cars to a test facility on the ice sheet. It was a short-lived test programme, but the road remains and still provides access to the edge of the ice sheet for tourists and researchers.

GETTING THERE AND AWAY Most people get to Kangerlussuaq by air. The small port is at the end of a long fjord which is frozen in winter; in summer, some cruise ships do make it to Kangerlussuaq, but there is no public ferry service. It is possible to arrive overland from Sisimiut: there are a few tracks, the most popular being the Arctic Circle Trail (about 160km; page 140) which can be walked in summer or travelled by dog sled or skied in winter. Plans have been made to improve one of the tracks to enable it to be driven by ATVs in summer or snowmobiles in winter, an idea that is not universally popular.

By air Air Greenland operates daily **international flights** from Copenhagen to Kangerlussuaq (4–5hrs). From March to September, it also flies weekly (on Wednesdays) to and from Billund in Denmark. The frequency of international flights is likely to change when the new airport opens in Nuuk in late 2024.

Kangerlussuaq is well served with Air Greenland **domestic flights** every day to Ilulissat and to Nuuk. There are also flights to Sisimiut and to Aasiaat every day except Sunday and to Maniitsoq on weekdays. Twice a week there is a return flight to Narsarsuaq in the south.

Kangerlussuaq Airport has a good cafeteria (page 139) and a proper restaurant; if you have time for a quiet drink, try the hotel bar upstairs (page 138). Baggage claim is, unusually, in the cellar and a lift transports you and your luggage back into the main hall. There is also a tourist information desk, run by Albatros Arctic Circle and Air Zafari (see opposite), where you can book accommodation and trips, even for the same day.

A duty-free shop can be found in the international departures lounge and, when that lounge gets busy, you'll find a quieter seating area upstairs. Passengers arriving from Denmark are not subject to any passport or customs checks.

GETTING AROUND Although Kangerlussuaq is a small place, it does stretch around both sides of the airport, so it can take a while to walk from one side of town to the other. There is a **bus** service (Apr–Sep 05.45–19.00 Mon–Sat, 05.45–14.00 Sun; 12kr). The buses start at the airport terminal at 15 and 43 minutes past the hour and take about 15 minutes to complete a loop east and then south around the end of the airport runway to the museum and back. The bus also does a 15-minute loop from the airport terminal west to Old Camp but only on the hour.

There is also a small **taxi** company (✆552323).

TOURIST INFORMATION AND TOUR OPERATORS There is no tourist office in Kangerlussuaq but all accommodation providers will be keen to put you in touch with their favourite tour operators.

Air Zafari In Kangerlussuaq Airport; \248554; w airzafari.com. Sightseeing from the air in comfortable planes with large windows & a sound system that blocks out the noise. It is great for photography, with views of the ice cap & wildlife,

& enables you to reach truly isolated locations. If you have time between flights in Kangerlussuaq, Air Zafari offers a 40min trip over the ice sheet & the glacier from the airport. This must be the best way to spend the transit time between flights.

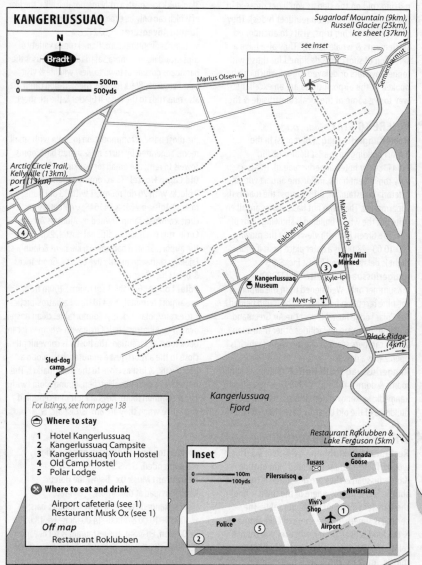

KANGERLUSSUAQ

Sugarloaf Mountain (9km),
Russell Glacier (25km),
ice sheet (37km)

see inset

Marius Olsen-ip

Arctic Circle Trail,
Kellyville (13km),
port (13km)

Balchen-ip

Marius Olsen-ip

Kang Mini Marked

3

Kangerlussuaq Museum

Kyle-ip

Myer-ip ✝

Black Ridge (4km)

Sled-dog camp

Kangerlussuaq Fjord

Restaurant Roklubben &
Lake Ferguson (5km)

For listings, see from page 138

🛏 **Where to stay**
1 Hotel Kangerlussuaq
2 Kangerlussuaq Campsite
3 Kangerlussuaq Youth Hostel
4 Old Camp Hostel
5 Polar Lodge

✖ **Where to eat and drink**
   Airport cafeteria (see 1)
   Restaurant Musk Ox (see 1)

Off map
   Restaurant Roklubben

Inset

Tusass ✉

Canada Goose

Pilersuisoq

Niviarsiaq

Vivi's Shop

Police

5

Airport

2

Albatros Arctic Circle ✎841648; **w** albatros-arctic-circle.com. This locally based company, with offices in the airport & Polar Lodge, organises a large and varied selection of tours including: walking on the ice cap & overnighting in a tent on the ice; driving over tundra to find musk oxen & reindeer; ice fishing on the frozen fjord; & dog-sledding trips lasting from 2hrs to 2 days, staying in hunting cabins (no chance of getting cold on the sled as you'll get dressed in full sealskin suits & sit on reindeer hides). They offer several hiking trips, visits to abandoned settlements & whale safaris. They also have a selection of short trips designed for those with longer layovers or delayed flights which can be booked at the airport; these are an excellent way to see some of the local countryside & the

wildlife. This is a well-organised and flexible tour operator who also own 2 hostels here.
Arctic Ice Tours ✎560102; **w** arcticicetours.com. Fancy a musk ox steak BBQ on a glacier? Friendly Arctic Ice Tours offers this together with a short hike at Russell Glacier. Or you can climb up Sugarloaf Mountain for great views & a good chance of spotting reindeer, Arctic hares & even musk oxen. For the energetic, Evald offers a winter hike on the 3km-thick ice sheet, a truly memorable hike, the like of which can only be experienced in Greenland.
Tundra Adventures ✎522122; **w** tundraadventures.com. Daniel runs a variety of trips including his Tundra Safari tour, which uses the backroads outside of town to view wildlife & visit Lake Ferguson, Black Ridge & the sled-dog camp. He also runs trips to the Russell Glacier & the ice sheet.

 ## WHERE TO STAY *Map, page 137*

Hotel Kangerlussuaq (70 rooms) In the airport building on the 1st floor – no lift; ✎841180; **w** hotelkangerlussuaq.gl. This is a very convenient hotel, inside the airport with a cafeteria & restaurant, & just across the road is the supermarket. The clean but basic rooms are all en suite but the whole building is showing signs of age. The Green Bar with views over the runway (🕐 10.00–23.00) is a quiet place to sit if your flight is delayed. Good b/fast inc. **$$$**
Kangerlussuaq Campsite ✎223399; 🕐 summer only. Well signed from the airport, the blue reception building can be found behind the Polar Lodge hostel & past the Air Greenland building. There are no facilities other than a tap for water; campers seem to use the airport which is open 24hrs a day. **$**
Kangerlussuaq Youth Hostel (Sleeps 75 in dbl rooms & dorms) Kyle-ip; ✎589897; **e** reception@ kangv.dk; **w** kangv.dk/en. This hostel is in the buildings of the old US army base's NCO club. It is

the most basic accommodation in town with small rooms separated by curtains & shared bathrooms. Towels to rent; use email for bookings. **$**
Old Camp Hostel (3 accommodation blocks, 2 blocks with 26 dbl rooms, 1 with 13 dbl bunk rooms) Aqisseq 266; ✎841648; **w** albatros-arctic-circle.com/old-camp. Owned by Albatros Arctic Circle, this is a good traditional hostel, 2km from the airport. Shared bathrooms, kitchens & lounges. Friendly staff who mostly live on site. Good prices & b/fast inc. **$**
Polar Lodge (13 dbl, 3 sgl rooms) 100m from the airport terminal; ✎841016; **w** albatros-arctic-circle.com/polar-lodge. A comfortable, clean hostel owned by Albatros Arctic Circle with whom you can book tours at reception. The hostel is conveniently close to the airport, just a minute's walk along a boardwalk, & just as close to the supermarket. The hostel has a communal kitchen, dining room (with TV) & common room. Keys are left in reception if you arrive when they are out. B/fast inc. **$**

✗ WHERE TO EAT AND DRINK *Map, page 137*

Restaurant Roklubben ✎841996; 🆕. This wonderful restaurant is located 5km outside Kangerlussuaq & they provide a free & frequent shuttle bus from anywhere in the town – book the transfer when you book your table. The setting is superb, on the shore of Lake Ferguson & the food is even better, whether you choose reindeer – 2 prime fillets – or the halibut or, maybe, musk ox. This truly is fine dining & a most

unexpected find. Vegetarian options. Highly recommended. **$$$$**
Restaurant Musk Ox Below the Hotel Kangerlussuaq at the airport; ✎841180; **w** hotelkangerlussuaq.gl/en/restaurants-bars; 🕐 06.30–10.00 & 11.00–14.00 Mon–Fri, 18.00– 22.00 Mon, Fri & Sat. The restaurant is set beyond the airport's cafeteria, below the hotel, & has its own small bar. Probably the best restaurant in the town

with a short but interesting menu. Depending on numbers, they may offer a buffet which is a great opportunity to sample some local Greenland food. 2- & 3-course menu, as well as à la carte. $$$
Airport cafeteria ⏰ 06.00–21.00 daily. In the airport & run by the Kangerlussuaq Hotel, this is a large cafeteria with a lot of seating & where everyone kills time between flights. Serving everything from pasta & pizzas to musk ox burgers, both the selection & the quality of dishes are surprisingly good. $

SHOPPING AND OTHER PRACTICALITIES There is nowhere to change money in Kangerlussuaq but there is one ATM in the airport.

There is a cluster of shops just outside the airport including two interesting gift and souvenir shops: **Vivi's Shop** (⏰ 09.00–12.30 Mon–Sat) and **Niviarsiaq** (⏰ 09.30–15.30 daily). Both sell Greenlandic souvenirs including many products made from warm but expensive musk ox wool & from sealskin. Across the street is **Canada Goose** (⏰ Mon–Fri, hours variable) which has a good selection of outdoor clothing and boots. Beyond this is the well-stocked **Pilersuisoq** supermarket (⏰ 09.00–17.00 Mon–Fri, 09.00–14.00 Sat) and the **Tusass** post office and phone shop (⏰ 09.00–11.00 & 13.00–15.00 Mon–Fri) where you can get a free pay-as-you-go SIM card for your phone and then load it with your initial payment, starting at 50kr.

On the other side of the airport is **Kang Mini Marked** supermarket (⏰ long opening hours but variable) with a selection of useful food items and take-away fast food.

If you plan to camp and need gas for your stove then this can be bought in the airport gift shop, in the Pilersuisoq and in Polar Lodge.

WHAT TO SEE AND DO The only interesting place to visit in town is the **Kangerlussuaq Museum** (⏰ summer 13.00–16.00 Mon, Wed, Fri & Sun, winter 10.00–13.00 Mon & Fri; 70kr, free under 12). Each room of this small museum, once a hotel for aircrew, is dedicated to a single aspect of the town's history – for example, the airport, dog sleds, Air Greenland, musk ox and reindeer.

Outside of the town, there is plenty of good **hiking** (w hiking.gl). The climbs to Sugarloaf Mountain (17km return) and Black Ridge (8km return) are both very popular and offer spectacular panoramic views. On a clear day, which is most days, you can see the ice sheet from either summit. For more extreme hiking there is, of course, the Arctic Circle Trail (page 140). Both Lake Ferguson and the fjord offer opportunities for **kayaking** and, in the fjord, you can also **fish** for Arctic char. In winter, the fjord is frozen and offers the opportunity to go **dog sledding** and ice fishing. You can even dog sled all the way to Sisimiut. If this all sounds too exhausting, then take a flight with Air Zafari to get a **bird's-eye view** of the whole area.

The road to the ice sheet The gravel road east from the town offers the easiest way to get into the Arctic tundra – the vegetation is primarily lichen and mosses with some stunted willow and birch and even miniature 'Labrador tea' rhododendron. As the road leaves the town, it passes a plantation of stunted pine trees, the remains of a 1974 experiment to test whether trees could grow in these climatic conditions. Less than 10% of the trees have survived.

The road follows the side of the glacial river which flows through several small meltwater lakes. On the river's plain is the **Sondy Arctic Golf Course**, originally established by American GIs of course, with flags marking the holes. Membership is now down to two, even though the annual fee is only 50kr. Players do, however, have to carry their own square of artificial turf with them from which to tee off.

Further towards the ice sheet, the road passes through a large area marked out with white posts. This was where the Americans detonated all their unexploded ammunition before they left in 1992. It was subsequently discovered that some ammunition had not exploded and the whole area is now cordoned off.

A little further along the track is the **wreck of a Lockheed T-33A** training aircraft. It is one of three that crashed in fog in 1968. Luckily, it was one of the first aircraft to be fitted with an ejector seat and all the pilots survived. The remains are remarkably well preserved and it is easy to identify the cockpit, engine and wings.

This far along the road sightings of musk oxen and reindeer are likely – the area is one of the best locations in Greenland to spot them. Both have a better sense of smell than eyesight, so if you are downwind, they are likely to ignore you. You may also see ptarmigan, Arctic fox and Arctic hare.

To visit the face of **Russell Glacier**, it is necessary to do a bit of off-road driving and then take a short walk. Unusually for an inland glacier, Russell has a 60m high face that calves in summer. The ice that falls then slowly melts and feeds the river. There is a second opportunity to see the glacier, a little higher up, at Reindeer Lake.

The road finally ends 37km from Kangerlussuaq at the ice sheet's terminal moraine, **Point 660**. This is a misleading name thought to result from a mistake: initially, it was thought that this point was 660m above sea level but has turned out to be only 525m. From here it is a short walk over the gravel of the moraine hills to reach the edge of the **ice sheet**. When the road was built in 2000, cars could drive off the end of the road and on to the ice sheet. Now, the ice sheet has retreated so much that you have to walk over the moraine to reach it.

Walking on to the edge of the ice sheet is tricky as there are underground rivers and holes under the snow; traps for the unwary. Good waterproof footwear, crampons and walking poles are needed and a guide is essential. It is an extraordinary place. As well as the snow sculptures, the wind-blown snow hills and the blue blue ice ponds, it is the profound silence and vast white expanse that hits you, no matter how long or short your walk on the ice sheet may be. If you walked for 1,700km north or 700km east you would still see nothing but snow and ice.

It is possible also to camp on the ice sheet with some tour operators, allowing you longer to experience this extreme environment, a world silent except for the sounds of the ice cracking and popping below you. Staying overnight also means you get to walk further, and even pull an ice sled laden with your overnight gear, treading in the footsteps of great explorers.

Every October, runners take part in the **Polar Circle Marathon** (w polar-circle-marathon.com), a race which claims to be the 'coolest marathon on earth'. The marathon and the half-marathon, which takes place the next day, both start on the ice sheet with a 3km loop (shoe spikes mandatory) before heading gently downhill across the silent tundra, passing meltwater lakes and glaciers and, no doubt, bemused reindeer and musk oxen. For the very fit, why not accept the Polar Bear Challenge and run both?

ARCTIC CIRCLE TRAIL

The Arctic Circle Trail is one of the world's great walks. The 165km trail links Kangerlussuaq on the edge of Greenland's ice sheet to Sisimiut on the west coast. It is an epic journey and most people choose to do it on foot, although it can be undertaken in winter by dog sled, in snowshoes or on skis. There is no fee, the nine huts are free to use and you can camp anywhere along the trail. All food has to be carried in except for fish, which you can catch along the way if you buy a fishing licence. Water sources are abundant and clean and, if you walk in the autumn, you can also collect Arctic blueberries and crowberries.

The trail route does not cross any glaciers and has a total ascent of 4,105m. The highest point on the main trail is a modest 450m above sea level, which feels quite low when you are surrounded by mountains that tower over 1,500m high. Walkers are guaranteed to see plenty of wildlife – reindeer, musk oxen, Arctic hares and foxes all frequent the area. A section of the trail is within the Aasivissuit–Nipisat Inuit hunting ground UNESCO World Heritage Site (page 150) and the government passed a law in 2018 to protect the area from development.

The trail attracts between 1,000 and 1,500 people a year. Most walkers start from Kangerlussuaq, making the crossing between June and September. Unfortunately, June to August is also mosquito season, so go prepared (page 39).

INFORMATION AND MAPS The best guidebook to the trail is Cicerone's guide by Paddy Dillon (page 205). The website w arcticcircletrail.gl is the best site for up-to-date information. You can also book a Personal Locator Beacon (PLB) on this site (500kr for 14 days), which you can pick up and return in either Kangerlussuaq or Sisimiut. A second website, w polarrouten.net, also provides some useful information, although it can be rather out of date. There is a very active Facebook group (◼ Arctic Circle Trail) – which is good for up-to-date information, both from locals and from people who have just completed the trail.

Greenland Tourism Trekking (w compukort.dk/Compukort/Grnlandskort. html) produces three detailed maps covering the trail at 1:100,000: 8-Kangerlussuaq, 9-Pingu and 10-Sisimiut. These give a lot of detail including 25m contours, recommended trails, camping places and hostels, and the maps' grids give UTM co-ordinates plus latitude in steps of 5' and longitude in 10'. The maps are available on waterproof and tear-resistant paper, and can also be downloaded to smartphones and tablets – do remember that there is nowhere on the trail to recharge your device.

Sagamaps (w sagamaps.dk) also produces maps but they are less detailed. Their Red Series map 8 Sisimiut, Holsteinsborg, Kangerlussuaq and Sondre Stromfjord covers that entire trail at 1:250,000 and is available in a choice of finishes – flat or folded, plain paper or laminated.

Only Nuuk has reliable map and bookshops (page 81) so, if you are not passing through Nuuk, you would be wise to buy your maps before you leave home.

EQUIPMENT The Arctic Circle Trail is very remote and requires complete self-sufficiency. There is no phone coverage and there are no settlements. It is vital that you carry a personal locator beacon (PLB) and have appropriate travel insurance which will cover your medical evacuation if needed.

The satellite SOS feature that may be on your phone, for example iPhone 14 and above, does not currently work in Greenland. The advertised service limit is 62°N and Kangerlussuaq is around 67°N, as is Sisimiut; and Greenland and Denmark are not in Apple's list of countries that support the service.

All experienced hikers have their own kit list, but there are a few extras that are worth considering for this trail.

- Insect repellent and head net, even if you are not walking in the peak mosquito season of June to mid-August
- Emergency repair duct tape and cable ties
- Extra zip-top bags for your rubbish – you are required to take out everything you take in, which means all your rubbish including used toilet paper
- Lip balm and moisturising cream as the air is very dry

6

THE TEN STAGES There are nine huts, two of which are close together, breaking the trail into stages. The huts vary in size and are very basic shelters, sleeping from just six to more than 20. You should carry a tent and not rely on the huts providing you with shelter as they often get full in the summer.

Where to start is your first decision – there are four options. The trail proper might be said to start as far west as Kellyville where the road ends, 13km west of Kangerlussuaq, or, more obviously, in Kangerlussuaq itself. Neither of these start points, however, enables you to walk from the ice sheet to the sea. The two options described in Stage 1 enable you to start on the ice sheet. The trail is described from east to west as this is the way most people walk it.

Stage 1: The ice sheet to Kangerlussuaq (25 or 37km) There are two possible starting points for this stage: the Russell Glacier, a finger of the ice sheet and 25km east of Kangerlussuaq; or Point 660, which is the real edge of the ice sheet, 37km east of the town.

At Point 660 you can pick your way up over the stony moraine for a few hundred yards on to the ice sheet proper. The route back to Kangerlussuaq is a dirt road, built by Volkswagen in 2000 to use as a test track for cars and trucks. Point 660 is at over 550m high, so the walk back is predominantly downhill, passing after 12km the Russell Glacier, and just above the very long Aajuitsup Tasia lake.

There is no accommodation on this stage though wild camping is an option. Your accommodation in Kangerlussuaq will be able to organise an early transfer to your chosen start point to enable you to walk back to town in daylight with just a light day pack.

Stage 2: Kangerlussuaq to Hundeso (20km) The first 13km of this section is a road running alongside the tidal fjord to reach the harbour, or Umiarsualivik. Here, the trail turns right, away from the fjord, to climb to the hamlet of Kellyville, also known as Tikilluarit, which was once a research site. Some walkers choose to begin their journey here. Soon the trail reaches Hundeso, where the 'hut' is a ragged collection of interconnected sheds and an old caravan.

Stage 3: Hundeso to Katiffik (20km) From Hundeso you need to navigate and watch for marked cairns. The whole section wanders gently up and down small hills around lakes, some with islands. At around 13km you'll ford your first stream, although this is hardly noticeable in dry periods. At the end of the walk is a gentle descent to the small Katiffik hut with its lake view.

Stage 4: Katiffik to Amitsorsuaq Canoe Centre (20km) There may be canoes in the rack at Katiffik; if so, you can choose to do this section by paddling along the Amitsorsuaq Lake. Otherwise, this is an easily navigated section along the lakeshore. The Amitsorsuaq Canoe Centre hut sits on the lake's beach and is the largest on the whole trail, with dormitories and a common room/kitchen. On a good day, there is also solar power here, the only chance on the whole trail to recharge electronic devices.

Stage 5: Canoe Centre to Ikkattoq (23km) A short 3km section brings you to the lake's outflow. The trail more or less follows the stream gently downhill to reach the next lake, Kangerluatsiarsuaq. Pingu Mountain dominates the northern skyline across the lake; this is a beautiful location and, if you have a tent, camping on the beach looks like a fine idea. Otherwise, the only way is, unfortunately, up as

you climb from 25m to 350m; the views on the way are stunning. Ikkattoq hut is another small one; make sure that you don't miss it and walk past.

Stage 6: Ikkattoq to Eqalugaarniarfik (11km) The climb is not over at Ikkattoq, but within 1km you do reach the summit at 448m. The view in every direction is breathtaking with mountains, lakes and ice all around. Some careful navigation is needed as you descend to cross Ole's Lakseelv and reach the trail's most challenging river crossing. Most walkers will be able to ford the river but there is now a footbridge 2.5km west of the ford if you prefer. Finally, there is a gentle climb to the Eqalugaarniarfik hut – this hut is not large, but the view from it is surely one of the best on the trail.

Stage 7: Eqalugaarniarfik to Innajuattoq (19km) The day starts with a gradual climb on to the east, and then north, slopes of Iluliumanersuup Portornga, from where the views are exceptional – lakes, mountains and, often, patches of snow. For the remainder of the day the trail stays high, skirting lakes until reaching the huts at Innajuattoq. The higher hut is a rather small one, tied down to ensure it does not break loose, but there is a hut twice the size down by the lake.

Stage 8: Innajuattoq to Nerumaq (17km) After walking along the lakeshore, there is a gentle climb before the trail traverses a scenic valley. Eventually the trail starts a gradual descent before rounding a bend and the final ford of the day and Nerumaq hut come into view. It's another small one but the upside is the river is full of fish for dinner.

Stage 9: Nerumaq to Kangerluarsuk Tulleq (17km) This is the lowest day of the trail's entire length and can be challenging in poor weather. Sections of the path can be boggy and there are three or four rivers to ford, depending on how wet it has been. There are sections where boulder-hopping is an option, but do take care as these boulders can be slippery. After following the shore of a lake, there is a choice of paths. If you keep right to follow the stream that is the outflow of the lake, you will reach the larger of the two huts, perhaps the better one too, set at the head of the fjord. If, however, you keep ahead on the trail proper, you will reach the higher of the two huts, rather small and less inviting.

Stage 10: Kangerluarsuk Tulleq to Sisimiut (20km) The final day's walk soon leaves the side of the tidal fjord to climb to a high valley, Qeeeortusup Majoriaa, which is followed for about 3km before a gentle descent to a stream ford. From here the trail climbs to pass across the saddle between Nasaasaaq to the south and Alanngorsuaq to the north. Soon you can see the ski lift on the side of Alanngorsuaq and the outskirts of Sisimiut ahead. The trail rounds the end of a lake to reach a track which then becomes a road that leads all the way into Sisimiut.

SISIMIUT

The heart of every Greenlandic town is its harbour and Sisimiut is no exception. It is a working port with fishing boats, large and small, and a twice-weekly visit by the coastal ferry. Brightly coloured houses cling to the steep hills around the port, and rising immediately behind the town are the imposing mountains of Palasip Qaqqaa (551m) and Nasaasaaq (784m), both snow-covered for much of the year.

Sisimiut is just 40km north of the Arctic Circle and, with a population of 5,436, is Greenland's second largest town. Fishing is the primary occupation and the big blue fish factory on the harbourside is the biggest in Greenland. It processes shrimp, cod and, in its new processing area built in 2021, snow crab.

Behind the port is Sisimiut's old quarter, at the centre of which is a very interesting museum housed in several 18th-century buildings. Above them, perched on a rock, is the prominent red Zion's Church. Further inland the town straggles along the main road with a range of useful facilities.

Sisimiut is a magnet for outdoor adventures at any time of year. It is a gateway to the easily accessible backcountry, where you can hike, bike, ski and dog sled through the stunning mountain landscapes and wide valleys. Many boat trips will take you out into the bay to spot whales, to fish or to visit settlements, some of which are now abandoned ruins.

HISTORY Inuit settled in Sisimiut as early as 2500BC. When the airport was expanded between 1988 and 2000 in the Asummiut area just north of Sisimiut, graves of both Saqqaq and Dorset cultures were found. A total of 14 graves were

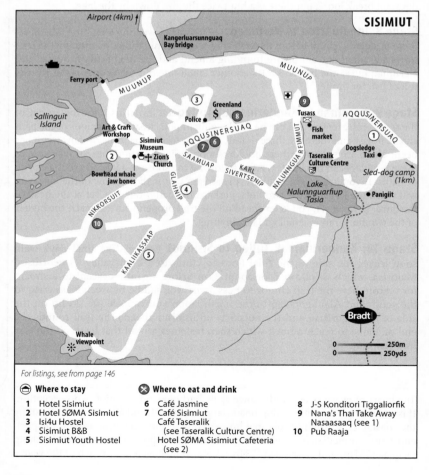

For listings, see from page 146

🛏 **Where to stay**
1 Hotel Sisimiut
2 Hotel SØMA Sisimiut
3 Isi4u Hostel
4 Sisimiut B&B
5 Sisimiut Youth Hostel

✖ **Where to eat and drink**
6 Café Jasmine
7 Café Sisimiut
    Café Taseralik
    (see Taseralik Culture Centre)
    Hotel SØMA Sisimiut Cafeteria
    (see 2)

8 J-S Konditori Tiggaliorfik
9 Nana's Thai Take Away
    Nasaasaaq (see 1)
10 Pub Raaja

identified as well as other evidence that showed that the area was occupied for over 4,000 years.

The first European full-time settlers were Dutch whalers in the 17th century who, when their trade was challenged by Danish Hans Egede in the 1720s, attacked his trading post and burned it down. The next Danish administrator, Jacob Severin, had the backing of the Danish navy and, after a series of battles in the late 1730s, the Dutch were chased out of the area. In 1764, Severin's company established Sisimiut as the trading hub for whale and reindeer skins, but the colonial settlement remained small. Like most settlements where whalers visited, they were repeatedly hit by waves of infectious disease; a smallpox epidemic in 1800 killed over 80% of the population.

In the early 1900s, there were only about 50 houses and 270 people in the town and most of the houses had stone and peat walls and peat-covered roofs. For those who lived here, hunting was already becoming difficult, with the near extinction of local reindeer and a shortage of seals. The whaling industry was also in decline. Hunters turned their skills to fishing, catching cod, halibut, catfish and even shark. The whaling company swiftly built a factory to produce salted fish and, in 1924, the first fish-canning factory opened here.

Hunters and fishermen were encouraged to invest in motorised fishing boats, and slowly fishing and shrimping became the town's main occupations, as they are today. This encouraged more people into the town, and by 1950 the population had grown to nearly 1,000 people. The population increased further from the mid-1950s when hunters from small settlements were resettled to Sisimiut; many of these men ended up working in the fish- and shrimp-processing factory.

Sisimiut continues to be the area's administrative centre and is home to one of Greenland's four high schools.

GETTING THERE AND AWAY Air Greenland flies most days between Sisimiut and Nuuk and every day except Sunday to Kangerlussuaq. The tiny airport is about 5km northwest of the town, across the Kangerluarsunnguaq Bay bridge, and the single-room building houses the check-in desks, two vending machines and a toilet. Most accommodation offers transfers to and from the airport.

From the second half of March until early January, the Arctic Umiaq passenger ferry (page 47) visits Sisimiut twice a week. On Saturday at 17.00, the ferry arrives having travelled overnight from Nuuk. It then leaves 2 hours later, heading north up the coast. On its return journey, the ferry arrives on Mondays at 09.30, staying in port for 90 minutes before it continues its journey south to Nuuk and then on down the coast as far as Qaqortoq. There are seasonal variations to the ferry schedule, so check their website for the dates you plan to travel.

Disko Line (w diskoline.gl) runs a weekly small boat service to and from the small settlements of Itilleq and Sarfannguit.

GETTING AROUND Sisimiut has a **bus** service (Apr–Sep 06.20–22.00 Mon–Fri, 09.00–21.00 Sat–Sun; 12kr) around town, but not to the airport. The buses run every 20 minutes following a clockwise loop around the town that takes about 40 minutes to complete. Don't be confused by them being numbered route 1 or 2, it is the same route, just run at different times of day.

There are many **taxis** and all use the same phone number (✆865533). The taxis also have an app for your phone, Sisimiut Taxa. It is in Danish but easy enough to understand. The app works out your location then dispatches a taxi; you tell the driver where you want to go.

TOUR OPERATORS

Boat Safari 📞525690; **w** boatsafari.gl. One local man, Jan Banemann, & his boat are all you need to get the best out of a boat tour from Sisimiut. Jan is a Sisimiut local who knows these waters intimately. Whether it is whale watching (he found us humpbacks very early in the season), fishing (4 cod caught in 15mins – you can also try fishing for snow crab or Arctic char) or visiting the abandoned settlements (his wife was one of the last to be born in now-abandoned Assaqutaq), Jan has the knowledge & skill to make your trip memorable. It's an open boat, so wrap up warm.

Dogsledge Taxi Kunuuteralaap 19; 📞539494; **e** dogsledgetaxi@outlook.dk; **f**. Based in Sisimiut, this local company offers dog-sledding trips of varying durations. They have a 3-day winter tour that takes you from Sisimiut to Kangerlussuaq or vice versa, staying in huts along the way. A chance to meet & learn more about Greenlandic dogs.

Greenland Dog Adventure **f**. Booked through Hotel Sisimiut, Greenland Dog Adventure not only runs dog-sled trips – eventually hoped to be year-round – but also lets you meet their friendly dogs. There is something quite special about meeting such a powerful, working dog, feeling their deep fur coat & learning how they are cared for.

Greenland Extreme 📞554500; **w** greenlandextreme.com. A highly specialised adventure company offering heli-skiing, sea or river fishing to catch Arctic trout, salmon or Greenland shark

Hotel Sisimiut & Tours Aqqusinersuaq 86; 📞864840; **w** hotelsisimiutandtours.com. Hotel

Sisimiut offers a comprehensive range of tours which are also offered as multi-day packages. In summer, tours include hiking, sea safaris, a cruise to visit the UNESCO Inuit hunting grounds & a popular catch-&-cook fishing trip which ends with a BBQ. In winter, you can dog sled, snowmobile, ski or snowshoe. A little less energetic, a tracked all-terrain vehicle will take you out, winter or summer, into the backcountry &, in winter, to see the northern lights. There are also bikes, snowshoes & skis to borrow, free for hotel residents. The hotel reception has a selection of free walking leaflets.

Hotel SØMA Sisimiut Tours Frederik D 1X's Plads 5; 📞864150; **w** hotelsoma.gl. The hotel offers packaged summer & winter trips of 2–10 days, combining the best activities in the area, including snowmobiles, dog sleds & whale watching.

Travel by Heart 📞550905; **w** travelbyheart.gl. Founded by Greenland travel expert Elise Bruun, Travel by Heart offer package tours of 3–7 days to the Sisimiut area & all tours can be tailor-made just for you.

West Greenland Wildlife 📞551134; **w** westgreenlandwildlife.com. A locally based tour operator specialising in fishing. Activities are centred around a wilderness camp, 2hrs by boat south of Sisimiut. This is an excellent hiking & fishing area & a great place to experience the life of the hunter or fisherman. They run an 8-day trip in Jul & Aug when you can go fly fishing for Arctic char or sea fishing for halibut, Arctic wolffish, salmon or cod.

 WHERE TO STAY *Map, page 144*

There are a number of houses available for holiday rental in Sisimiut; they are good value if you are travelling as a small group or a family. Prices range from **$$** to **$$$$** depending on size, quality and location. Also, check out Airbnb or Booking.com.

Hotel Sisimiut (40 rooms, 7 apts) Aqqusinersuaq 86; 📞864840; **w** hotelsisimiut. com. Locally owned Hotel Sisimiut is located 20mins' walk out of town but right at the start of many trails used in both summer & winter. The rooms are tastefully furnished in soft browns & creams, some with animal skins & murals of the local area, which adds to the feeling of being out of the town & on the edge of the backcountry. The superior rooms are larger with kettles & rather

fine boot driers & there are also a few family rooms which comfortably sleep up to 4. There is a small spa on a terrace with 2 hot tubs & a sauna. At a different location, the hotel has 7 apartments with lounges & kitchens (min stay 7 days). **$$–$$$**

Hotel SØMA Sisimiut (38 rooms) Frederik D 1X's Plads 5; 📞864150; **w** hotelsoma.gl. Part of the friendly Soma chain of hotels (page 68) and just 5mins' walk from the harbour & the museum, this is a centrally located place to stay. All rooms are en suite; the 'superior' rooms are larger & include a kettle. There is a small fitness centre with an outdoor hot tub. **$$–$$$**

Isi4u Hostel (5 dbl rooms) Berthelsenip 39; ☎528333; 🅕. Usefully located up the hill behind the police station & 2 large supermarkets, the hostel has great views from many rooms; great for sunsets. Shared bathroom, living room, terrace & kitchen. Free use of washing machine. **$**

Sisimiut B&B (4 dbl rooms) Glahnip 9; ☎552320; e reception@sisv.dk; w sissnow.dk;

🕑 Jul–Sep. A large blue house perched on a rock 5mins' walk from town with the same owners as the Sisimiut Youth Hostel. The rooms all share the bathroom, lounge & kitchen. Great views & good value for couples. Washing machine to rent; book via email. **$**

Sisimiut Youth Hostel (11 bunk rooms) Kaalikassap 25; ☎522514; e reception@sisv.dk; w sisv.dk/en; 🕑 Jul–Sep. A basic hostel in a quiet residential area, it is a 10min walk into town. The 2- & 4-person bunk rooms share a kitchen, bathroom & lounge with TV. Washing machines to rent; book via email. **$**

✖ WHERE TO EAT AND DRINK *Map, page 144*

Probably the nicest bar in town, **Pub Raaja** (Nikkorsuit 4; ☎865526; 🅕; 🕑 20.00–midnight Mon–Thu, 20.00–04.00 Fri–Sat) has live music most weekends. You may pay a modest entry fee if there is live music by someone special; check their Facebook page.

Nasaasaaq Restaurant In Hotel Sisimiut; ☎864700; w hotelsisimiut.com/nasaasaaq; 🕑 07.00–09.30, noon–17.00 & 18.00–21.00 daily. With a warm & friendly ambience, this offers probably the best dining in town. The antlers & skins on the walls & seating echo the backcountry feel of the place. The menu is extensive & includes international as well as local food; the Greenlandic buffet (🕑 17.00 Sat, 18.00 Sun) offers a wide range of local food including whale soup & musk ox roast (& it is timed to allow you to get back to the ferry before it leaves). We recommend the Nasaasaaq Special, which includes delicious snow crab. **$$$**

Café Jasmine Guutaaq 2; ☎866611; 🅕; 🕑 11.30–19.00 daily. Pleasant little café inside the sports complex serving, in their words, 'Thai food & miscellaneous food'. Eat in or take away. **$**

Café Sisimiut Aqqusinersuaq 16; ☎524455; 🅕; 🕑 11.00–21.00 Mon–Sat, noon–20.00 Sun. Basic but cheap fast-food café with a few Thai dishes. Eat in or take away. **$**

Café Taseralik In the Taseralik Culture Centre, Fahlip, Holsteinborg; ☎862808; w taseralik.gl/cafe-taseralik; 🕑 11.30–19.30 Sun–Fri,

11.30–21.30 Sat; also open for performances. Small café in the foyer of the cultural centre overlooking a lovely lake. It serves a selection of drinks, paninis, pizzas & other light snacks. **$**

Hotel SØMA Sisimiut Cafeteria Frederik D 1X's Plads 5; ☎864150; w hotelsoma.gl; 🕑 07.00–22.00 daily. As with most Hotel SØMAs, this is more a posh cafeteria than a restaurant but none the worse for that. The food, especially the dish of the day, is good value & the service is friendly. Good cappuccino too. **$**

J-S Konditori Tiggaliorfik Qaassuup 2; ☎865353; 🅕; 🕑 07.00–17.00 Mon–Fri, 07.00–16.00 Sat–Sun. In a lime-green building, set back from the main road, you will find a bakers & a small café. A huge selection of breads & cakes, as well as filled French sticks. Very popular with locals, to eat in or take away. **$**

Nana's Thai Take Away Aqqusinersuaq 67; ☎246800; 🅕; 🕑 10.00–17.30 Mon–Fri, 11.00–14.00 Sat, 11.00–15.00 Sun. Good selection of tasty Thai curries, noodle dishes & stir fries. There is a small area to eat inside & on the terrace if you only want to take your food that far. Good value; try the pad thai with shrimp. **$**

SHOPPING There are a few supermarkets around town including two just next to the Greenland Bank and the police station. Most shops are located along the main Aqqusinersuaq road including two outdoor clothing and equipment shops, one as the road rises up from the harbour and the other near Tusass.

The two larger hotels and the museum all have small gift shops. There are also two craft workshops. **Panigiit** (Jaakunnguup 19; ☉ 16.00–18.00 daily) is owned by a local couple and is a treasure house of local craftwork. The range varies but usually includes clothing made of musk ox, minerals and glassware, as well as jewellery. The second is the **Art and Craft Workshop** by the harbour, which is open most days. Climb upstairs to find many craftsmen and women carving reindeer bones and antlers. There is a good selection of jewellery, tupilaks and other carvings sold by the people who made them.

The **fish market** (☉ 10.00–17.30 Mon–Fri, 11.00–14.00 Sat–Sun) sells fish and meat brought in by the hunters. We've seen everything from minke whale and narwhal to cod, halibut and roe here; all fresh but not to everyone's taste.

OTHER PRACTICALITIES There is a branch of the Greenland Bank (☉ 09.30–15.30 Mon–Thu, 09.30–15.00 Fri) at Kaaleeqqap 4 and a Tusass post office and phone shop (☉ 10.00–17.00 Mon–Fri, 10.00–13.00 Sat) at Aqqusinersuaq 48.

The emergency numbers in Sisimiut are ☏701322 for the police, ☏113 for the fire service, ☏801112 for an ambulance and ☏868880 for a dentist.

WHAT TO SEE AND DO

In town Above the harbour at the entrance to the old quarter stand the **jaws of a bowhead whale**, symbolic of Sisimiut's past. The story goes that they were found floating in the water near the old whaling station, but they were so big that 2m had to be cut off before they could be transported back. Today the whale jaws are the unofficial emblem of Sisimiut.

Sisimiut Museum (☏ 862550; w sisimiut.museum.gl; ☉ Oct–May 10.00–16.00 Mon, Wed & Fri, Jun–Sep 10.00–16.00 Thu–Tue; 70kr, under 12 free) is set in the heart of the old quarter above the harbour. There are seven houses to visit plus more exhibits in the grounds. The ticket office and museum shop are in Sisimiut's first general store built in 1825, a fine example of the type of housing being shipped to Greenland from Denmark at that time.

The largest house is the old Colonial Manager's house, built in 1846; it was later used as the Trade Master's house and then as a telegraph office. The telegraph operator was Jorgen Olsen, whose statue is now in the museum's square. He later became a politician and was one of the first to call for home rule. The house now contains its own mini-museum of hunting and fishing, including a rather scary harpoon and instructions on how to attach your dogs to the sled.

The oldest house was built in 1756 but, like many houses in Greenland, it was moved, being rebuilt here in 1762 by a whaling captain. It houses a collection related to the Aasivissuit–Nipisat UNESCO World Heritage Site. The blue Bethel church was built in 1775 and was the first church in Greenland paid for by the congregation – they collected barrels of valuable whale blubber and these were shipped to Copenhagen to pay for the building. The church now houses interesting interactive exhibits which allow one to understand more about *angakkuq* (shamans) and how the Lutheran priests worked with the Inuit to confront their traditional beliefs.

The old smithy is now the museum workshop. Next door is the halfway house, a warehouse set halfway between the port and the town, which houses a collection of ships that once used the harbour. The final building is a reconstruction of a peat house as it would have been in the early 20th century. A hundred years ago more than two-thirds of the houses in Sisimiut were made of stone and peat. In the grounds near the peat house you'll see a selection of sleds; there is an explanation of the sled styles in the Colonial Manager's house.

Above the museum buildings is the red **Zion's Church** which is, unfortunately, usually locked, except when they are holding services. The interior is impressive with wood panelling and sealskin artwork.

At the other end of town and set on the edge of Lake Nalunnguarfiup Tasia, the **Taseralik Culture Centre** (**w** taseralik.gl) is a striking modern building, home to a theatre, cinema, an exhibition space and a small café. This is the focal point for the arts in Sisimiut. Check their website for what is on while you are in town. Sisimiut's five-day annual music festival **Arctic Sounds** (**w** arcticsounds.gl; 450kr), held around Easter in various venues including the cultural centre, hosts original artists from Greenland and Nordic countries.

In the backcountry The area around Sisimiut has a good choice of **day hikes**. Hotel Sisimiut has free walking leaflets and **w** hiking.gl has both route information and downloadable gpx files to use with your phone mapping app. An interesting short walk (3km return) to the southwest of town leads to a headland from where you can spot whales.

There is an interesting walk around **Sallinguit Island** (about 4km), reached by a bridge to the west of Sisimiut town. The island is largely undeveloped and full of historical interest, and the walk takes you through 4,500 years of human activity on the island visiting old graves, ruined houses, including three peat houses, and a beacon station. Pick up a free walk description leaflet at the museum.

If you wish to get further into the backcountry, how about renting an all-terrain vehicle (ATV)? Self-drive tours take place summer and winter, led by an experienced guide. In winter snowmobiles and ultra-terrain vehicle safaris (UTVs; the next stage up in 'ruggedness') will get you to places that are otherwise inaccessible. It is also a way to get out into the dark and have the best possible chance of seeing the northern lights.

Dog sleds are a quieter way to travel in winter: just you, the musher and the dogs. There is nothing quite like gliding across the snow and ice pulled by a dozen eager sled dogs, expertly controlled by the brief commands of their musher.

For more energetic winter travel in the backcountry, skiing and snowshoeing are good options. There are cross-country skiing trails at the east end of town, south of Lake Nalunnguarfiup Tasia. You can borrow or rent all the equipment needed – ask at your accommodation. You can even ski the whole way to Kangerlussuaq, 160km away.

Arctic Circle Race (**w** acr.gl; **f**) The 160km Arctic Circle Race takes place in March. It claims to be the world's toughest cross-country ski race and attracts international skiers from all over the world. The race is skied over three days with competitors staying overnight in tents along the way, contending with air temperatures that drop to −30°C. The route passes through magnificent, varied and sometimes harsh terrain. Obviously, entrants have to be very fit and all competitors have to carry at least 5kg of safety equipment, including a thermal blanket. Arctic tents are provided for skiers and meals are provided in a large, heated, tent; the skiers are escorted by dog sled and snowmobiles where possible. At the end of the race, a party is held for everyone involved. There is a shorter 100km race and mini-race for children.

On the water Boat operators and tour organisers offer a range of boat trips from the harbour and it is usually possible to mix more than one activity into a trip. Some whales can be seen year-round, but many species are seasonal and May to

The **'Aasivissuit–Nipisat: Inuit Hunting Ground between Ice and Sea'** UNESCO World Heritage Site covers a huge 4,180km² which runs from the coast just south of Sisimiut to the ice sheet north of Kangerlussuaq. Over this area the Inuit hunted, fished and foraged, built houses, buried their dead and developed technologies that enabled them to survive in this hostile environment for over 4,200 years. In 2018, the Greenland government protected the site to prevent mining and to control all other development, including tourism, the building of summer houses and trophy hunting.

The area is vast and there are seven major sites of archaeological interest from the Saqqaq, Dorset and Thule Inuit cultures.

NIPISAT ISLAND Nipisat Island is off Greenland's west coast, 15km southeast of Sisimiut. The ruins of the long communal houses can still be seen and, during excavations in 1989–94, more than 1,000 artefacts of the Saqqaq culture were found, including over 300 tools.

ARAJUTSISUT Arajutsisut is between Nipisat and Sisimiut and was used by the Thule people as a winter settlement in the 17th and 18th centuries. The ruins of ten houses can still be seen, including five communal houses which would have each housed four or five families, separated by partitions made from animal skins. It is possible to take a boat tour to Nipisat and Arajutsisut from Sisimiut.

INNAP NUUA Another Thule winter settlement is Innap Nuua. This one is also situated on the coast but 10km further south than Nipisat. Here there are the remains of three communal houses, as well as a number of graves.

SARFANNGUIT Almost a century old, Sarfannguit, located 36km east of Sisimiut, is still a fjord fishing village and, with a population of 101, is the only inhabited settlement in the whole site. In 2010, Greenland's first wind turbine was installed here. Sarfannguit can be visited on boat tours from Sisimiut.

SAQQARLIIT Saqqarliit was a fishing village 55km east of Sisimiut up the fjord. It was established around 1850 but abandoned in 1961 when the population were resettled in Sisimiut. The village still has many ruins, including the church.

ITINNERUP TUPERSUAI Itinnerup Tupersuai was another Inuit summer camp in the 18th and 19th centuries, probably for reindeer hunting. It is on the very north of the site, some 60km east of Sisimiut and 70km west of Kangerlussuaq.

AASIVISSUIT The most easterly of the archaeological sites, just 16km northwest of Kangerlussuaq, Aasivissuit was a Thule summer settlement and was used for perhaps 400 years. The remains are extensive and include many tent sites, meat stores and graves. Archaeologists have also found many Thule tools at the site, including ulu knives and axes. The site can be visited on foot from Kangerlussuaq with a guide or with a good map and a GPS device; the trail is not marked.

VISIT greenland

WHERE NATURE NARRATES A STORY
LOCALS TRANSLATE IT

SCAN
ME

LET LOCAL KNOWLEDGE BE YOUR GUIDE

world of greenland

Discover Greenland's Incredible Lodges with World of Greenland!

Eqi Lodge
- a unique experience with a view of the Eqi Glacier.

Embark on a memorable journey to Eqi Lodge, where you'll wake up to breathtaking views of the Eqi Glacier. Be enchanted by the ice's impressive power and beauty, just outside your window. Welcome to Eqi Lodge by World of Greenland.

Ilimanaq Lodge
– heavenly views and gastronomic delights

Take an unforgettable journey to Ilimanaq Lodge. Immerse yourself in a world of stunning natural beauty and dine in our cosy restaurant, where unique culinary masterpieces will tantalise your taste buds. Welcome to Ilimanaq Lodge by World of Greenland.

Igloo Lodge
– the ultimate igloo adventure

Open the door to an authentic adventure and create unforgettable memories with an overnight stay in an igloo, in spectacular surroundings near Ilulissat.
Welcome to Igloo Lodge by World of Greenland.

World of Greenland is your gateway to extraordinary adventures and exceptional natural beauty around Ilulissat. Let us take you on a wonderful journey to experience Greenland's rich treasures. Book your experience today at www.worldofgreenland.com to start your adventure!

Experience the magic in our

AURORA CABINS

Mittarfimmut Aqq. 1 // 3952 Ilulissat // Greenland
Tel. +299 94 41 53 // booking@hotel-arctic.gl // www.hotelarctic.com

Experience your own unique firsts

NUUK
visitnuuk.com

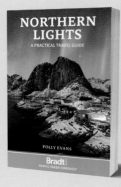

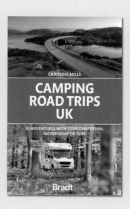
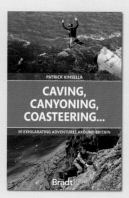

September is the main period to go whale watching, particularly for humpbacks. Fishing is also possible all year and it is fun to finish your boat trip by catching some cod for dinner.

Boat trips can be used to visit three archaeological areas within the UNESCSO World Heritage Site. **Sarfannguit** is 4 hours away and is also a working fishing village. **Nipisat Island** and **Arajutsisut** are closer and can be visited in a single trip (see opposite).

The abandoned settlement of **Assaqutaq**, known as the ghost village, sits at the base of the Nasaasaaq mountain on an island 13km east of Sisimiut – about 2 hours away. The last inhabitants left in 1969 and the village is accessible only by boat or on foot. There is a pretty church and cemetery and many ruined houses. Locals come here to fish for ammassat (capelin), a local delicacy. Taking the boat there and walking back is a very popular trip; there is a good chance of seeing whales in the fjord. The walk is well marked but does require a little scrambling over rocks (w hiking.gl).

MANIITSOQ

Maniitsoq is a small settlement on a remote, 14km by 10km rocky island of the same name, midway between Nuuk and Sisimiut. It is the gateway to some of the wildest scenery on the west coast, jagged peaks, deep narrow fjords, numerous glaciers and rivers teeming with fish. Tourism is in its infancy, even though Maniitsoq is only a 40-minute flight from Nuuk and is called at twice a week by the ferry; most visitors come from occasional visiting cruise ships.

The settlement was established in 1782 by the Dutch and soon became a trading post for reindeer hides. The town still relies on fishing and hunting. Until recently the population has been in decline; it is now fairly stable at around 2,500.

Owing to the hilly terrain on which the town is built, many houses are linked by wooden staircases, the longest of which leads up to the communications tower, known as the 'Eiffel tower'. All boardwalks and staircases are public; as a visitor it can seem strange to walk up the steps to, and past, someone's house to get somewhere.

GETTING THERE AND AWAY Maniitsoq Airport is about 2km west of the town. Air Greenland flies on most days from Maniitsoq to Kangerlussuaq and to Nuuk.

From the second half of March until early January, the Arctic Umiaq passenger ferry (page 47) visits Maniitsoq twice a week. On Saturday at 06.00, the ferry arrives having travelled overnight from Nuuk. It then leaves at 06.30 heading north up the coast. On its return journey, the ferry arrives on Mondays at 21.30, staying in port for 30 minutes once again. It then continues its journey south to Nuuk and then on down the coast as far as Qaqortoq. The ferry docks on a small island that is linked to the main town by a bridge. The ferry timetable does change with the seasons, so check timings before you travel.

There is a weekly small boat service run by Disko Line (w diskoline.gl) to and from Napasoq and Atammik. You'll actually travel in a boat from Maniitsoq Tour Boats (page 152). They also run their own boat service to and from Nuuk (⊕ Apr–Nov; 4hrs) – a useful alternative to the plane.

GETTING AROUND Maniitsoq has a **bus** service (Apr–Sep 06.30–21.00 Mon–Fri, 09.30–18.00 Sat–Sun; 12kr). The buses run every 30 minutes on a clockwise loop around the town which takes about 30 minutes to complete.

There are also plenty of **taxis** (✆520844).

MANIITSOQ

'Eiffel tower' (1km),
Flower Valley (2km)

PAVIA PETERSEN-IP

Maniitsoq
Museum

Police

Heliport

TUNOQQUSAAQ

TIKAASAQ

ATAQQAP

PETERSEN-IP

KUUTTARTOQ

ORTOOQQAP

Medical
centre

Airport (2km)

Brugseni

1

IVISSUAATERALAA

JENSERALAAP

LANGESKOVIP

Pisiffik

Greenland

Tusass

AJOQINNGUUP

Main
church

2

AALISARTUT

N

Bradt

0   200m
0   200yds

PUULUKILVIK

Ferry
terminal

For listings, see below

Where to stay
1   Hotel Heilmann Lyberth
2   Hotel Maniitsoq
      Hotel Toppen (see 2)

TOUR OPERATORS

Maniitsoq Adventure Tours 222508; e mat-3912@hotmail.com; . A small local company run by Ole Zeeb Skifte offering a wide range of trips using kayaks & boats from May to Sep. You can put together hiking, fishing – both fly & sea fishing – whale watching, staying in cabins or tents. Book by email with Ole or through Arctic Excursions (page 75).

Maniitsoq Tour Boats 520296; w mtb.gl. MTB have 3 large Targa boats all taking up to 12 passengers. They run the local ferry services which can be used as mini cruises. The boats can also be chartered for tours. Owned by the same family as the Hotel Heilmann Lyberth.

 WHERE TO STAY AND EAT   *Map, above*

Hotel Maniitsoq (21 rooms) Ajoqinnguup; 813035; w hotelmaniitsoq.gl. This hotel, set on top of a hill, has a good location in the centre of town. The rooms are modern, all en suite & most with the view over the harbour & fjord – watch for whales! The large, rather good,

restaurant (**$$$**) serves local & international food & shares that great view. **$$$$**

Hotel Heilmann Lyberth (20 rooms, 1 apt) Ivissuit 3; 813535; w hhl.gl. Small hotel on the edge of the town centre. All rooms are en suite

with TV. There is also a hotel café (🕓 11.30–17.00 daily; $$). B/fast inc. $$$
Hotel Toppen (9 rooms) Ajoqinnguup. This is really a wing of the Hotel Maniitsoq with 9 sgl rooms, all with en-suite shower & TV. It's a good option for single travellers. Reception & b/fast buffet are in the main hotel. $

OTHER PRACTICALITIES If you wish to buy food, there are two large supermarkets, Pisiffik and Brugseni in the centre of town and two smaller branches in the northeastern suburbs. There is a branch of the Greenland Bank (🕓 09.30–15.30 Mon–Thu, 09.30–15.00 Fri) at Langeskovip 4 and the Tusass post office and phone shop (🕓 09.00–15.00 Mon–Thu, 09.00–17.00 Fri) at Langeskovip 2.

WHAT TO SEE AND DO With a local history focus, **Maniitsoq Museum** (Illunnguit 11; 🕿 813100; w maniitsoq.museum.gl; 🕓 11.00–16.00 Tue–Thu also 13.00–16.00 Sat in Jul–Aug; free) is spread across four buildings from the 19th century. The large black building has some splendid carvings on display, all by local artists, and on the first floor there are works by more local artists and by Danish painter Aage Gitz-Johansen. There are also two collections of artefacts from Maniitsoq's old trading post and its old church. The second black building contains exhibitions on hunting and Inuit culture, focused on angakkuq (shaman) practices. The white building, once a carpenter's workshop, has a beautiful west Greenlandic national costume on display. The final, pink, building, the cooper's workshop, is usually closed.

Above the centre of town sits Maniitsoq's main **church**, a large, white building. The interior is modern, almost Scandinavian, but the altar is covered in sealskin and the font decorated with fish motifs. Above the congregation is a splendid organ.

There are three locations close to town that are good for whale and bird watching, **viewpoints** known as Nasiffik. One is next to the 'Eiffel tower' communications tower, reached beyond the museum up a lot of steps on a good boardwalk; another is off Tikaasaq at the seldom-used heliport and the third on the top of the small hill at the eastern end of Annertusoq – look for the boardwalk on your right and the whale jawbone arch. There are even picnic tables and a telescope. From April to November, you are likely to see humpback whales swimming close to shore.

An interesting **day hike** from Maniitsoq takes you into the hills and valleys northwest of the town into an area known to locals as Flower Valley. The walk can be started near the airport or from the 'Eiffel tower'. The trails can be walked in different combinations from 3km to 9km. There is a detailed description on w hiking.gl, together with gpx files to download. Be aware that the longest route, the red loop, is quite rocky.

There are a variety of **boat trips** available from Maniitsoq for whale watching and fishing but perhaps the most interesting and spectacular is into **Eternity Fjord** (Sermilinnguaq), which is situated just south of the small island settlement of Kangaamiut (population 291). This fjord is ice free from April and boats can travel up the more than 100km-long fjord, passing jagged 2,000m-tall mountains and many hanging glaciers on the way. At the end there is a calving marine glacier that blocks the fjord's southern arm. While most people visit on a day trip, you can stay overnight here on a boat and this opens up the area for exploration on skis.

7

Ilulissat and Disko Bay

In Disko Bay, you can lie in bed and listen to the thunderous rumble of a glacier calving, watch gargantuan icebergs float past your window and stand on a beach to hear the whoosh of air as a humpback whale breaches, its mighty tail raised high above the water.

Disko Bay is the largest open bay in western Greenland, measuring 150km across at its widest point. In the middle sits Disko Island, Greenland's largest island. This area has attracted people for thousands of years, the nutrient-rich waters full of whales, seals and fish, providing a good living for hunters and fishermen throughout the ages. Many of the settlements that they created still exist, their traditional communities of colourful wooden houses scattered around a harbour full of boats.

Today, the bay is dotted with settlements, from tiny Kangerluk (population 12), to busy Ilulissat, the centre of tourism in the area. Boats, ferries and helicopters connect settlements – in a single trip it is possible to visit the black-sand beaches on Disko Island, kayak around the waterways of Aasiaat, experience the fabulous living museum in Qasigiannguit and still have time to visit the UNESCO World Heritage-listed Ilulissat Icefjord. From the end of May until the middle of July, you can enjoy kayaking around the icebergs under the midnight sun and, in the winter, you can take a dog sled across the frozen fjord when the dark nights are perfect for viewing the northern lights.

ILULISSAT

Icebergs – huge natural sculptures like nowhere else on earth – are the backdrop to this bustling town. Blue, white or cream, huge or small, tall as a skyscraper or flat as a pancake – they are what you came here to see, and they never fail to captivate. Indeed, even local people can be seen just standing and watching them. In Ilulissat you don't need to get in a boat or plane to see them, you just look out to sea, and as the town is built on a hill, icebergs are always in view. Here, they are often stationary because they ground on the seabed, even though the water is up to 1.5km deep. When they break free, they float out to sea on the current, often freeing more icebergs that were jammed behind them. They all then, surprisingly, head north up the coast before the current carries them away from Greenland, across Baffin Bay to start their journey south down the east coast of Canada.

The town sits on a rocky promontory, pointing north into Disko Bay. It is a hilly, scraggly sort of place with one main street that heads south, uphill, from the centre of town. This is where you will find most of the interesting shops and tour operators. Heading east from the centre takes you across the high bridge behind the port, and beyond to the airport. In the opposite direction, if you take the dusty road downhill, you'll find the museum and the picturesque Zion's Church.

Ilulissat is Greenland's third largest town with a population of nearly 5,000 and it is ever expanding; there is building work everywhere. There are only 17km of roads and many just peter out into dusty tracks to nowhere. In midsummer (June, July and August) the town is very busy – the hotels are full and there are cruise ships in the bay. While everywhere may seem full, it is also the time when every trip is running. Outside of this period, the town can be remarkably quiet and it is easy to get a better-value room even though the choice of trips may be slightly more

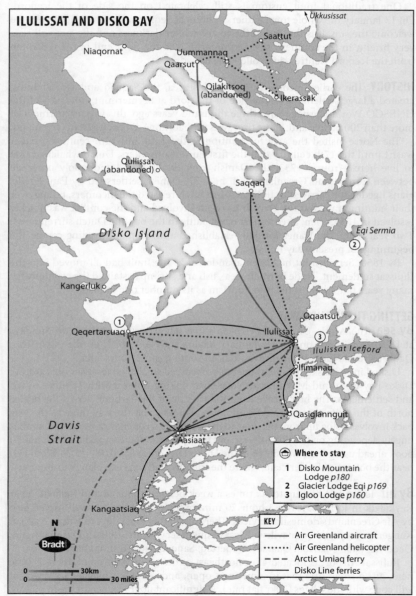

ILULISSAT AND DISKO BAY

Ukkusissat
Niaqornat
Saattut
Uummannaq
Qaarsut
Qilakitsoq (abandoned)
Ikerassak
Qullissat (abandoned)
Saqqaq
Disko Island
Eqi Sermia (2)
Kangerluk
Oqaatsut
Qeqertarsuaq (1)
Ilulissat (3)
Ilulissat Icefjord
Ilimanaq
Davis Strait
Qasiglannguit
Aasiaat

Where to stay
1 Disko Mountain Lodge p180
2 Glacier Lodge Eqi p169
3 Igloo Lodge p160

Kangaatsiaq

N
Bradt
0   30km
0   30 miles

KEY
——— Air Greenland aircraft
········ Air Greenland helicopter
— — — Arctic Umiaq ferry
——— Disko Line ferries

limited. As winter draws in, so the dog sleds and snowmobiles come out and the icebergs become lodged in the sea ice until spring. Winter skies are often clear and the northern lights really can light up the sky.

Just south of town is the Ilulissat Icefjord, one of Greenland's four UNESCO World Heritage Sites, and which encompasses the Sermeq Kujalleq glacier (Jakobshavn in Danish). Icebergs from the glacier fill the 55km-long icefjord as they slowly float out to sea. The site also has the most impressive visitor centre in the country.

One traditional Inuit custom is still celebrated on the side of the icefjord. On 13 January the whole town gathers at noon at Seqinniarfik, 'the place where we welcome the sun'. It is the end of the town's winter darkness and the sun will rise, very briefly, in the southern sky. Seqinniarfik is at the fjord end of the red route from the Icefjord Centre – just follow the crowds.

HISTORY The earliest people to live in this area, the Saqqaq and Dorset Inuit, created a large settlement on the side of the fjord at Sermermiut, now part of the UNESCO World Heritage Site. Three thousand years ago, this was a settlement of more than 200 people and, at the time, was probably one of the largest in Greenland.

The Norse visited the area for hunting in the 13th and 14th centuries, but it wasn't until the 17th century that the first European settlers, Dutch whalers, came to live here. Around 1733, the Danish king established a monopoly on trade between Europe and Greenland and, in 1737, Danish settlers led by Paul Egede, Hans Egede's son, arrived in Ilulissat. The Dutch resisted the incomers, taking over their hunting trade but the Danish navy got involved and the conflict was quickly resolved in 1739 when, after a short naval battle in the bay, the Dutch surrendered. Two years later, the Danes formally established a mission and trading centre, the beginnings of present-day Ilulissat.

By 1850, Sermermiut had been abandoned as the Inuit had all moved into the Ilulissat settlement. Trade in whale, seal, fish and shrimp sustained the economy for many years but, today, it relies on tourism as its number one industry.

GETTING THERE AND AWAY
By sea The Arctic Umiaq ferry (page 47; w aul.gl) usually arrives on Sundays at 15.30 from April until early January having travelled north up the coast from Qaqortoq and Nuuk. It then leaves to head south again 2 hours later.

Disko Line (w diskoline.gl/en) operates scheduled small boat ferry services around Disko Bay from mid-May to mid-November, linking Ilulissat with 11 other towns and settlements. The boats leave from the far side of the harbour, across the bridge north of the town centre; it's a 15-minute walk, easier on the way there as the way back involves a slog up from the quay to the road. The frequency of the services varies hugely depending on the time of year and how busy the route is; and it is essential to book ahead using their website or at the Disko Line office (⊕ 10.00–15.30 Mon–Fri) near the bottom of Fredericiaip, where the friendly staff can help plan your itinerary.

By air Icelandair flies up to six times a week between Ilulissat and Keflavik, near Reykjavik in Iceland; it is a 3 hour 20 minute flight. The town is well served also by Air Greenland's domestic services. There are flights most days to Nuuk, Aasiaat, Kangerlussuaq and Upernavik with less frequent services to Iliminaq, Qasigiannguit, Qeqertarsuaq, Qaanaaq, Qaarsut, Qeqertaq, Saqqaq and Uummannaq.

Ilulissat Airport is located 4km northeast of the town. At present, there is little here, just a small café that is sometimes open, and some left-luggage lockers that will cope with most bags (20kr flat rate). A significant upgrade, occurring in phases,

ILULISSAT

For listings, see from page 159

Where to stay
1 Hotel Hvide Falk
2 Hotel Ilulissat
3 Ilulissat Guesthouses
4 Paa & Jannik

Off map
Blue Trail Guesthouse
Hotel Arctic
Hotel Iceford
Hotel SØMA

Where to eat and drink
5 Brasserie Icecap
6 Café Iluliaq
7 Café Nuka
    Glacier Shop (see Glacier Shop)
8 Hong Kong Café
    Hvide Falk (see 1)
9 Inuit Café
10 Naleraq
    Rooftop (see 3)

Off map
Brasserie Ulo
Restaurant Iceford

Hotel Arctic & Brasserie Ulo (1km),
Hotel SØMA (1km), airport (4km)

Disko Line ferry port

Arctic Umiaq ferry port

Police

Inuit artists' workshop

Ilulissat Adventure

Ilulissat Art Museum (Kunstmuseum)

Disko Line Explorer

Greenland

World of Greenland

Fish & sea

maamut market

Glacier Shop

Air Zafari

Disko Line

Knud Rasmussen Museum

Albatros Arctic Circle

Zion's Church

Tusass

AARO MATHIESENIP

MITTARFIMMUT

KUSSANGAJAANGUAQ

EDVAR SIVERTSENIP

NUISARIA NNGUAQ

QUPALORAARSUK

MATHIA STORCHIP

ALANNGUKASIK

ELISABETH THOMSENIP

Ilulissat Icefjord Centre (1km)

Hotel & Restaurant Iceford (200m)

Blue Trail Guesthouse (1km)

0   200m
0   200yds

N

Bradt

AN INFAMOUS ICEBERG

In Ilulissat Icefjord in 1909, it is likely that a very large iceberg calved from the face of the Sermeq Kujalleq glacier. It may have been over 1.5km long and contained 1 billion tonnes of water, some of it snow that had fallen more than 15,000 years earlier.

For the next two years, it slowly drifted north up Greenland's western coast and then south on the cold Labrador Current along the east coast of Canada. It was not alone: this large iceberg travelled in a group of at least 18 other icebergs dotted across a few square kilometres of sea. The iceberg had become smaller over those two years and, by the time it came to be off Newfoundland, the iceberg was only 100m long and perhaps 25m high. That is, of course, the top 10%; the rest of the iceberg remained invisible below the water.

On 12 April 1912, the iceberg was seen by Captain Wood of the SS *Etonian*; he was sufficiently impressed by this particular iceberg that he took a photograph and entered the sighting in the ship's log. It was just one of around 300 icebergs that made it into the Atlantic shipping lanes that year. The next sighting was at about 23.30 two days later.

A lookout on the SS *Titanic* saw the iceberg appear out of the mist, dead ahead. He rang the warning bell and called the bridge, and, with its engines in reverse, the ship turned sharply. Rather than making a head-on impact, the vessel slid along the side the iceberg, shards of ice falling on the decks as the iceberg ripped a hole in the ship's side. Within 3 hours, the SS *Titanic* had sunk; more than 1,500 lives were lost. Within 14 days of the sinking, the iceberg, now in the Gulf Stream, would have finally melted.

As a result of the *Titanic* disaster, the International Ice Patrol was established. Using ships, planes and satellites, the movements of icebergs are monitored and the information is then relayed to all vessels in the area. In 2002 the Safety of Lives at Sea (SOLAS) convention required that all vessels transiting the region of icebergs must subscribe to the Ice Patrol service.

is planned between 2025 and 2027; it is likely that this will attract more long-haul flights to Ilulissat. The upgrade includes the extension of the runway from 845m to 2,200m, and a new control tower with new equipment installed to assist with landing in bad weather. Other airport infrastructure is also planned, including a much-needed new terminal building to include a café, shop and an ATM or two.

GETTING AROUND The centre of Ilulissat is quite small, but some hotels and the Icefjord Centre are a little way out of town. Most hotels will provide transfers to and from the airport, otherwise a taxi (499499) is the best solution. There is also a taxi app, Ilulissat Taxa, which makes it easy to request a ride. It is in Danish but easy to understand. There is a bus service, route 2, which runs every 30 minutes from 07.00 to 21.30 in a loop around the town. It does pass the harbour and goes to the Hotel Arctic but not the airport.

TOURIST INFORMATION AND TOUR OPERATORS There is a tourist information office (⏲ 13.00–16.00 Mon–Fri but only in season) in the centre of town.

Air Zafari Kussangajaannguaq 18; 584068; w airzafari.com; ⏲ Mar–Nov 09.00–17.00 daily. Air Zafari offers a 1hr flight over Ilulissat Icefjord and Sermeq Kujalleq. It really is even more spectacular from the air & you may see whales too. Max 4 people & everyone gets a window seat (25min flight; from 1,500kr pp).

Albatros Arctic Circle Edvard Sivertseniq 18; ☎ 295195; w albatros-arctic-circle.com; ⏰ 09.00–15.30 daily. This tour company runs trips in Ilulissat and Kangerlussuaq. Their summer activities (May–Sep) include whale watching, kayaking, boat trips to the Eqi Sermia Glacier & several guided hiking trips. In the winter (Nov–Apr), they offer dog sledding with a musher, ice fishing, self-drive snowmobiling, ice fjord boat trips & snowshoe hiking trips to view the northern lights. Some activities are half price for children under 11 years.

Disko Line Explorer Kussangajaannguaq 7; ☎ 946380; w diskolineexplorer.com; ⏰ 09.00–16.00 Mon–Thu, 10.00–16.00 Fri. Sister company to Disko Line & often using their boats. A wide selection of boat trips around Disko Bay all starting in Ilulissat, including a whale safari, a day trip to Eqi Sermia Glacier (the calving glacier), a fishing trip and a chance to view the northern lights from the sea while enjoying hot chocolate & marshmallows. There are half-price tickets for children under 11 years.

Greenland Travel ☎ 701107; w greenland-travel.com. Probably the largest tour company in Greenland with package tours & tailor-made trips from 2 to 14 days. Trips to Ilulissat can be combined with visiting other towns around Disko Bay. They offer an excellent personal service.

Ilulissat Adventure Kussangajaannguaq 3; ☎ 294171; w ilulissatadventure.com. This adventure company runs an extensive selection of trips which can be bought individually or as a multi-day package. Their comprehensive 8-day winter adventure is action packed: a city tour, a

snowshoe walk to watch the northern lights, a cruise among the icebergs in Disko Bay, hiking in the Eqip Sermia Fjord, snowmobile drives to & from the tiny settlement of Oqaatsut, a dog-sled ride, a further snowmobile ride into the wilderness to spend the night in an igloo & some optional ice fishing. Each activity can also be experienced on its own, along with kayaking, paddleboarding, whale watching & hiking – try the hike to stay in their wilderness cabin just north of Ilulissat. Experienced & knowledgeable guides who are flexible when weather conditions require a change of plan. Suitable clothing & equipment is available for all their activities.

Ilulissat Tours ☎ 549748; w ilulissattours.com. Ilulissat Tours use open boats to offer ice fjord cruises among the icebergs, a whale safari, a cruise under the midnight sun & a boat trip to the Eqi Sermia Glacier where you can watch it calve. They also offer day trips to the small settlements of Iliminaq or Oqaatsut. Children under 11 years are half price; a minimum of 5 adults is required for most trips.

Nalerak Sea Safari ☎ 544310; w nalerakseasafari.gl. A small local company offering boat tours of Ilulissat Icefjord including midnight sailings, whale safaris, fishing trips to the island of Oqaatsut & trips to the Eqi Sermia Glacier.

World of Greenland Fredericiaip 4; ☎ 944300; w worldofgreenland.com; ⏰ 11.00–14.00 Mon–Fri. This well-organised & 100% Greenlandic company offers the usual summer & winter tours, but for a special experience you can fly by helicopter or small plane over the icebergs to the Sermeq Kujalleq glacier, which is only accessible by air, then land on the Greenland ice sheet & enjoy a glass of champagne. World of Greenland also owns 3 remote lodges: Igloo, Glacier & Iliminaq.

 WHERE TO STAY *Map, page 157, unless otherwise stated*
Ilulissat is the town most visited by tourists to Greenland. The hotels are aware of how busy the town is, so at peak times rates soar; at other times there are bargains to be had. Our grading reflects average prices in high season.

In Ilulissat
Hotel Arctic (93 rooms & suites) Mittarfimmut; ☎ 944153; w hotelarctic.com. Claims to be the most northerly 4-star hotel in the world, this large hotel set high on a cliff is 25mins' walk out of town on the road to the airport; the No 2 bus passes the door & there is a free airport shuttle.

The rooms have some interesting murals & are all en suite; many rooms have a great view of the icebergs in the bay. There are also 7 glass-roofed 'igloo' cabins at the end of the peninsula, from which you can watch the northern lights while lying in your warm bed. The hotel also has a small gym. **$$$$**

Hotel Icefiord (36 rooms, 3 apts) Jorgen Sverdrupip 10; ☏ 944480; w hotelicefiord.com. This hotel is part of the Topas group that also includes Disko Line. It is set right on the icefjord, a 15min walk out of town, which means nearly all the rooms have an iceberg view; all have private bathroom, TV & kettle. The deluxe explorer rooms have a balcony & large skylight windows while the apartments have kitchens. Free airport shuttle. **$$$$**

Hotel Hvide Falk (37 rooms, 9 apts) Edvard Sivertsenip 18; ☏ 943343; w hotelhvidefalk.gl. A fine hotel in an excellent position overlooking Disko Bay & the icebergs & close to the centre of town. The hotel has undergone a lot of renovation in recent years. All rooms have private facilities, TV & kettle, as well as access to the shared balcony that runs around the building. Half the rooms have the view. There is no lift. The apartments, each with their own kitchen & private facilities, sleep 2–5 & are situated on the shore below the hotel. **$$$**, apartments **$$$$**

Hotel SØMA (21 rooms, 1 penthouse apt) Ilulissat Nuussuattaap 2; ☏ 944002; w hotelsoma. gl. This friendly hotel has all en-suite rooms, simply furnished & with either a kettle or a kitchenette; some front rooms have good views of the icebergs in the bay. There is a small b/fast room off reception. The penthouse apartment has 2 bedrooms, a full kitchen & can sleep up to 6. It is a 20min walk to town but the No 2 bus passes the front door. This is one of a chain of non-profit-making hotels also found in Sisimiut, Aasiaat and Nuuk. Any extra funds are used to support their charitable outreach work in the community (page 68). Good value. **$$$**, penthouse **$$$$**

Hotel Ilulissat (78 rooms) Kaaleeraq Poulsenip 6; ☏ 588600; w hotel-ilulissat.gl. Set on top of the hill in the centre of town, this is not the most attractive building, but all the rooms have views, particularly those on the 5th floor which face the fjord. There is a range of room standards but all are bright & spacious with a private bathroom, TV & kettle. Cheaper rooms face the city, more expensive rooms face the fjord. There's also a small fitness room & a children's playroom. **$$–$$$$**

Blue Trail Guesthouse [map, page 166] (22 rooms) Qoororsuup B 2053; ☏ 248777; w bluetrailguesthouse.com. This is really a hostel, with 16 sgl & 6 dbl basic but comfortable rooms all with private bathrooms. There is a pleasant shared

lounge & terrace & a kitchen with microwaves & a couple of cooker rings. It is a 20min walk out of town at the start of the blue trail to the icefjord; the No 2 bus passes nearby. Being on the edge of town, you can just sit on the terrace & watch the northern lights. In winter, the guesthouse is on the side of the main snow trail out of town, so you can watch hunters on dog sleds & snowmobiles returning from the hunt. Min 2-night stay. **$$**

Ilulissat Guesthouses (5 houses each sleeping 6); ☏ 278980; w ilulissatguesthouse.com. Run by Ilulissat Adventure, these houses are scattered in an area to the west of the town centre. Every house has a full kitchen, bathroom, laundry, lounge/dining room (no TV), outdoor terrace &, of course, views of those icebergs. Some can only be booked as a complete house, others can be booked by the room. A really good deal for families & small groups; min 3 nights. **$$**

Paa & Jannik (3 rooms, 3 apts) Alliit 4c; ☏ 545486; w bb.gl; ⊕ Jun–Sep. Set in a residential area a few minutes' walk from the town centre, the main house has 3 dbl bedrooms with a shared bathroom, kitchen & lounge with TV. There are also 3 apartments (for 3, 4 or 5 people) each with its own lounge, kitchen & bathroom. Everyone gets the views, of course. B/fast is available if ordered in advance. Rooms **$**, apartment **$$**

Around Ilulissat

Igloo Lodge [map, page 155] (5 igloos) Fredericiaip 4; ☏ 944300; w worldofgreenland. com/igloo-lodge; ⊕ 11.00–14.00 Mon–Fri. This is your opportunity to sleep in a real igloo in a remote location but only 15km inland from Ilulissat. The accommodation is sold as a 1-night trip that includes all meals & transport to & from the igloos in either a piste machine or on a snowmobile. Your igloo includes reindeer skins, winter sleeping bags & candles, which will keep the temperature up to around zero. Meals & drinks are served in a heated wooden cabin near the igloos, where there is also a dry toilet. While at the igloos, you can go on a snowshoe hike to a lookout from where you can see the icefjord. **$$$$**

Kiattua Camp [not mapped] (max 10 people) ☏ 529539; w nomadgreenland.com; ⊕ Jun–Sep. After working for over 26 years in Greenland, Jon & Anika Krogh have created a luxurious but sustainable camp in the wilderness. About 2hrs south of Ilulissat by open boat or 25mins by helicopter, Kiattua Camp is located in a remote & undisclosed location, 2 days' walk away from any other habitation. Accommodation is in tipi-like tents with heated beds & hot showers. There is a separate restaurant tent where you can watch your gourmet meal being prepared from local ingredients. You might also like to picnic under the northern lights. Your personalised guided tours can include fishing, whale & iceberg viewing, snorkelling, mussel or berry picking & walks visiting mountains & glaciers. Kiattua Camp is only offered as a fully inclusive package including transfers from the airport, private accommodation & tours while you are at the camp. **$$$$**

✖ WHERE TO EAT AND DRINK *Map, page 157*

Brasserie Ulo In Hotel Arctic; 944153; w hotelarctic.com/en/brasserie-ulo-2; 06.00–10.00, noon–15.00, 18.00–21.30 daily. Ground-floor restaurant, smart but with a relaxed atmosphere; there is a bar, a terrace & those great views again. International cuisine plus a number of Greenlandic dishes. Every Mon, their Greenlandic buffet offers a large choice of local dishes for you to sample &, every Sat, there is a BBQ on the terrace. Extensive wine list. **$$$$**

Brasserie Icecap Fredericiap 5; 942242; e info@ict.gl; ; Summer 18.00–01.00 Wed–Sun, 10.00–13.00 Sat–Sun, limited hours in winter. A modern, elegant restaurant with sealskins on the walls, right in the centre of town. It is part of the brewery, so fine beers on tap. An interesting menu of fish & local meat dishes – how about reindeer salad, musk ox burger & chocolate fondant for dessert? **$$$**

Hvide Falk Restaurant Edvard Sivertsenip 18; 943343; w hotelhvidefalk.gl/restaurant; 06.00–22.00 daily. Fine dining on the ground floor of the hotel with views of the icebergs. Local specialities include halibut from the bay, reindeer & lamb from south Greenland. On Thu there is usually a Greenlandic buffet with more than 20 different local specialities; reservation recommended. They also serve Greenlandic coffee. **$$$**

Restaurant Icefiord In Hotel Icefiord; 944480; w hotelicefiord.com/restaurant; 18.00–20.00 daily. One of the best set restaurants in town, on top of a small cliff overlooking the icefjord & passing icebergs. There are great views from the windows & a terrace where you can eat & drink on summer days. The menu is short & the food is excellent, using local produce in interesting ways: perhaps redfish from the bay & a dessert of Greenlandic blackberries with lemon & marzipan. **$$$**

Rooftop Restaurant In Hotel Ilulissat; 588600; w hotel-ilulissat.gl/dining-and-events; 06.00–midnight daily. Amazing views from this 6th-floor rooftop restaurant. The short menu includes fish & vegetarian dishes. The terrace is a pleasant place for a coffee too with magnificent views of the icefjord & the sea. Open to non-residents but booking recommended. **$$$**

Café Iluliaq Fredericiap 5; 942242; ; 11.00–21.00 daily. Friendly & good-value café in the centre of town. Lots of choice including Greenlandic musk ox pizza, yellow halibut curry, reindeer kebab & musk ox burger. It is an ideal lunch stop. Local beers are on tap &, if you ask, you may be able to visit the Immiaq Brewery in the same building. **$$**

Inuit Café Kussangajaannguaq 22; 944888; Mar–Nov 11.30–15.00 & 17.00–20.30 Wed–Mon. Octagonal café set back off the main road. Definitely one of the better cafés in town with a menu ranging from pasta to whale, musk ox & reindeer steaks to delicious snow crab & a good range of local beers. Their ice creams are popular too. **$$**

Café Nuka Kussangajaannguaq 17; 942525; 11.00–20.00 daily. This small café feels somewhere between a Chinese/Thai take-away & an American diner. Their no-frills dishes from all over the world are very reasonably priced. Brunch is served 11.00–14.00. **$**

Hong Kong Café Nuisarianguaq 9; 293338; ; 11.00–20.00 daily. Just 7 small tables in this cheap, basic Thai/Chinese café. Eat in or take away. **$**

Naleraq Kussangajaannguaq 23; 944040; food: 11.30–20.00 daily, bar: 20.00–midnight Sun–Thu, 20.00–04.00 Fri–Sat. The town's number one bar serves food early in the evening & has live music every weekend. **$**

Glacier Shop Pop-up coffee shop outside one of the best stores in town (page 162).

SHOPPING The main road up the hill, Kussangajaannguaq, is where most of the interesting shopping can be found. There is a supermarket there, too, and several others dotted around town. On the corner of the crossroads of Kussangajaannguaq and Fredericiap in the centre of town is a small fish and sea mammal market (⊕ 10.00–14.00 Mon-Fri but only when there is catch to sell).

Glacier Shop Kussangajaannguaq 14; ✆545735; w glaciershop.gl; ⊕ 09.00–17.00 Mon–Fri, 10.00–13.00 Sat. In the street of many souvenir shops, this might be the one with the nicest & most authentic gifts & clothing. The shop stocks a wide range of Great Greenland clothing & footwear, as well as hand carvings in soapstone & bone. There is also an interesting range of books, including a guide to local trails. In the summer they have a pop-up outdoor café serving coffee, beer & wine along with our personal favourite, hazelnut & apple pie.

Inuit artists' workshop ⊕ 08.00–17.00 daily. This little red house is hidden at the very bottom of Kussangajaannguaq, opposite the bank. Here, 10 craftsmen & women in a dusty workshop make tupilaks, ulu knives & carved figures, as well as jewellery. They are very happy to explain how each piece was made; it is a chance to buy direct from the artist.

OTHER PRACTICALITIES There is a branch of the Greenland Bank (⊕ 09.30–15.00 Mon, Wed & Fri, 09.30–12.00 Tue & Thu) at Kussangajaannguaq 4 with full banking facilities and an ATM (⊕ 02.00–23.00). You will also find cash machines in the larger supermarkets. There is a Tusass post office and phone shop (⊕ 09.00–16.00 Mon–Fri) at Illumiut 11, B-887.

In emergency, the ambulance phone number is ✆947859, the police are on ✆703211 and the firefighters are on ✆947859, although the nationwide 113 will work just as well. If you need a doctor (⊕ 08.30–10.15 Mon–Fri), call ✆801117.

WHAT TO SEE AND DO
Around town In town, you will not miss photogenic **Zion's Church.** Set on the water's edge on Oqaluffiup, the church's black form is striking, silhouetted against the huge blue-white icebergs floating behind it. It is one of the oldest churches in Greenland, built in 1779 and was, at the time, also the largest building in Greenland. In front of the church is the sculpture of a fisherman, celebrating 100 years of the halibut industry. The kayak club is also here and you may spot their rack of drying kayaks, modern versions of the traditional Inuit kayak.

Just inland from the church is the **Knud Rasmussen Museum** (Nuisariannguaq 9; ⊕ noon–16.00 Tue–Sun; 100kr), also called the Ilulissat Museum. The house was the childhood home of explorer Knud Rasmussen and part of the museum is packed full of artefacts and displays relating to his life (page 164). The museum also has a room with displays and photographs telling the history of Ilulissat. The top floor is dedicated to the kayak, and a great film (in English) shows how these were traditionally made and used when hunting. The entry ticket also gives you access to the **Ilulissat Art Museum** or **Kunstmuseum** (Aron Mathiesenip 7; ⊕ noon–16.00 Sat, Tue & Thu, 10.00–16.00 Sun), which is housed in one of the town's oldest buildings. Built in 1923, it was the home of many colony managers. The exhibition on the ground floor changes every two months, usually showing the work of one or more local artists. When we visited, we were mesmerised by the amazing 3D display of finely crocheted Greenlandic native plants. Part of the top floor houses a collection of contemporary Greenlandic art. The rest of this floor contains a large collection of paintings of Greenland by Emanuel Petersen, a Dane who visited Greenland 12 times between 1923 and 1946. This was a private collection that was given to the town. Today Petersen's depiction of Greenland is questioned.

The Ilulissat Icefjord and Sermeq Kujalleq glacier offer a unique and unforgettable natural spectacle, and in 2004, a huge area of land and sea – 4,000km² including the fjord and the glacier – was designated a UNESCO World Heritage Site.

Ilulissat has always provided scientists and visitors easy access for a close view of the front of a calving glacier that cascades down from the ice sheet and into the ice-choked fjord. This easy access means that it has been studied and measured for more than 250 years. Having records going back so far is extremely valuable to scientists studying climate change today.

Sermeq Kujalleq is huge at over 6km wide and 45km long, and it is one of the world's fastest-moving glaciers travelling 40m per day. It annually calves over 46km³ of ice, more than any other glacier outside Antarctica. This calved ice becomes huge icebergs in the fjord, icebergs so big that they are still actively eroding the fjord bed. The icebergs move very slowly down the fjord, frequently grounding and getting frozen in every winter when the sea ice returns; it is a journey that may take two years. Once free, the largest icebergs will not have melted until they reach the same latitude as New York City.

If you spot rough and jagged icebergs, then these are recently calved and have yet to be smoothed by wind, water and even grinding against the fjord's gravel bed. Whatever their shape or size, the icebergs are one of the most awesome sites in Greenland; spotting tiny birds perched on them is one of the few ways of appreciating how gigantic these monsters are.

The works of art are thoughtfully displayed and the accompanying texts help in understanding the works and pose interesting questions – why do none of the Inuit in Petersen's works have faces? Are the figures repeated in multiple paintings to tell a story or was it just easier to paint the same figures? There is also a small shop selling interesting local prints.

Ilulissat Icefjord Centre (555588; w isfjordscentret.gl; ⏺ summer 10.00–17.00 daily, winter 11.00–16.00 Sat–Sun, closed Jan; entry 150kr, grounds & walks free)

A 20-minute walk south from town up Kuunnguarsuk and Sermermiut streets brings you to the Ilulissat Icefjord Centre. (The walk takes you past a sled dog camp where there are many chained-up Greenlandic dogs which should not be approached.)

The Icefjord Centre is a stunning piece of modern architecture, a swirling shape of wood, steel and glass that looks even better when seen from the fjord. Opened in 2021, it has been designed to allow visitors to walk on the roof and enjoy panoramic views of the whole ice fjord area. The 'Tale of Ice' exhibition inside the centre covers the development of Inuit culture, including archaeological finds that have been 'frozen' in blocks of glass that look like ice. The exhibition also explains how Greenland's ice sheet was created and the challenge that climate change poses. The centre also houses guest art exhibits, and in the reception area is a book and gift store where you can pick up the free walking map for the area. The small café serves very good coffee.

Walking Three walks start near the Icefjord Centre, all giving fantastic views of the fjord and its gigantic icebergs. See the map on page 166.

The World Heritage Trail is the shortest (just 1.3km and wheelchair friendly) and takes you down a boardwalk to a point close to the icefjord's shore. The trail also runs past the archaeological remains of the Inuit settlement of Sermermiut but, today, there is not much to see. It is, however, impressive that Inuit were living and prospering here over 4,000 years ago – excavations by archaeologists have found that the permafrost has preserved the graves and artefacts of these people very well. At first glance, this may seem a bleak place to set up home, but the site is well sheltered by the low hills and the beach gives easy access to the sea and, therefore, seal and fish to eat. It is not known how long the Inuit lived here. They were nomadic, but we do know that the Thule Inuit were here around 1100 and that, in 1737, when Paul Egede arrived, this was thought to be the largest Inuit village in Greenland. To preserve the flora, you are asked not to stray off the boardwalk and you should not approach the beaches anywhere along the fjord. The signs inform you of the danger of death or serious injury from sudden tsunami waves caused by carving or rolling icebergs. This is a real risk, as 10m-high waves can suddenly appear.

KNUD RASMUSSEN

Explorer and anthropologist Knud Rasmussen is a folk hero in both Greenland and Denmark; streets, schools, glaciers and museums are named after him. Born in Ilulissat in 1879, his father was a Danish missionary and his mother a Greenlander of Danish and Inuit ancestry. From an early age Rasmussen was immersed in Inuit culture. He grew up with the local children, learning their language and traditions, and at the age of eight, his father gave him a rifle and dog sled. This was not unusual; even today in Greenland anyone over the age of 12 can buy a rifle. There were always hunters and fishermen around to teach him their skills and excite his imagination with stories of hunting. He soon acquired the skills needed to survive in the Arctic.

It must have been quite a culture shock when, at the age of 12, his parents moved to Copenhagen. He studied at school and university and then drifted into an unsuccessful career as an actor and opera singer. In 1900, he took a job as a journalist working for a Danish newspaper. This opened up many new doors and he wrote his first book about a trip to Lapland.

On a working trip to Iceland Rasmussen met Ludvig Mylius-Erichsen, a Danish explorer. They became good friends, and soon they were planning a trip to Greenland together – an expedition to travel to the remote lands of northwest Greenland where they would study Inuit culture. For over two years, they lived among the Inuit community collecting legends, myths and stories. Rasmussen acted as interpreter, recording many folk tales that had never been written down before. Following this expedition he wrote *The People of the Polar North*, published in 1908.

About this time he married Dagmar Anderson, the daughter of a Danish businessman living in Uummannaq. Dagmar could speak Greenlandic, which meant she was a great help translating her husband's findings into Danish and English.

Rasmussen's book was a success and it wasn't long before he was planning another expedition. In 1910, with the help of his friend Peter Freuchen, he established the Thule Fur Trading Station at Cape York (now Qaanaaq). The profits from the trading station helped fund Rasmussen's next seven expeditions. In 1912,

From the Icefjord Centre, the moderate **yellow trail** (2.7km) takes you west to pass the old cemetery and over a high bluff with great views. The trail then turns north to follow the coast to Ilulissat, passing the point where, underwater, there is a moraine bar that catches the icebergs and stops them from going out to sea. It is an even better walk in the opposite direction; to find the start, head out of town southwest towards the tall, blue power station chimney on the Minnerup road.

Our favourite trail is the more challenging **blue trail** (7km) which starts at the end of the boardwalk and then follows the side of the fjord east before curving north to bring you back into Ilulissat. We prefer to walk this, too, in the opposite direction, starting just in front of the Blue Trail Guesthouse and ending at the Icefjord Centre. All the trails can be walked all year, but in winter the coloured trail markers may be covered with snow, so take walking poles and a good map.

Other activities Although the icebergs in the fjord can be seen from all over town, the number one thing to do in Ilulissat is to get up close to these monsters. There are three ways that this can be done and the simplest is a **daytime boat trip**.

Rasmussen and Freuchen set off to test Robert Peary's claim that a channel divided Peary Land in the far north from the rest of Greenland. They proved Peary was wrong and, in doing so, they covered 1,000km over ice and nearly lost their lives.

Undeterred, in 1916 Rasmussen led a team of seven men mapping a little-known area of Greenland's north coast. This time two of his team died. He documented the journey in *Greenland and the Polar Sea*, published in 1921. He loved his life as an explorer and continued for several years collecting Inuit folk tales. His long-suffering wife spent long periods on her own looking after their three children.

In 1921, Rasmussen planned his most ambitious expedition. The aim was to discover the origin of the Inuit race and to prove they had migrated eastwards from Siberia to Greenland. To achieve this, he travelled for three years across the polar ice, crossing Canada and North America to Alaska; Rasmussen was the first European to cross the Northwest Passage by dog sled. His journey ended when he failed to get permission to enter Russia. Staying with Inuit families and communities along the way, he collected and recorded a vast number of stories and legends that had only ever been spoken. It became clear that stories told in Alaska were also told in many other communities across the Arctic and they had travelled by word of mouth, as far as Greenland. This was strong evidence to support his theory that the Greenland Inuit had migrated from the west.

Rasmussen's account of this mammoth trip is recorded in his 1927 book *Across Arctic America*. A film was also made, in 2006, about this expedition: *The Journals of Knud Rasmussen*. Rasmussen documented the stories told to him, publishing *Eskimo Folk Tales*. The original collection of stories in the Carlsberg Foundation in Denmark has never been published but, an edited and translated version by W Worster is now in paperback (page 206).

In 1933, during his last expedition, Rasmussen contracted food poisoning after eating pickled auks. A short while later, he died of pneumonia in Copenhagen aged 54. Over his lifetime Rasmussen had made a significant contribution to the understanding of the Inuit culture. His life is documented in the book *White Eskimo* by Stephen Bown (page 205).

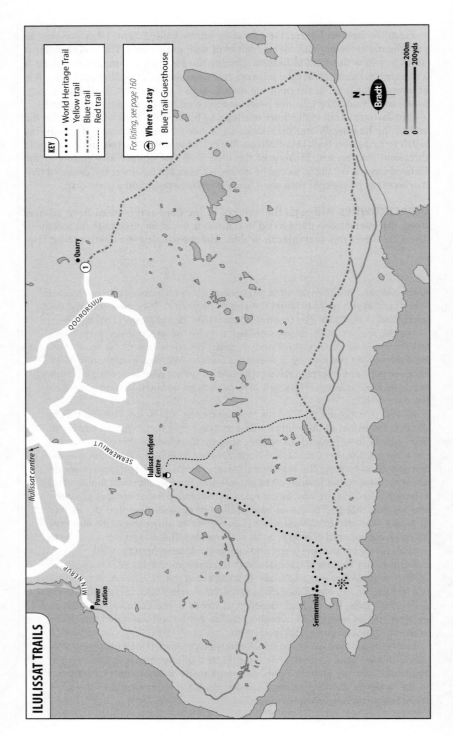

ILULISSAT TRAILS

KEY

- •••••• World Heritage Trail
- ——— Yellow trail
- – – – Blue trail
- ········· Red trail

For listing, see page 160

Where to stay

1 Blue Trail Guesthouse

Bradt

N

| 0 | 200m |
| 0 | 200yds |

Quarry

1

QOORORSUUP

Ilulissat centre

SERMERMIUT

Ilulissat Icefjord Centre

NINERUP

Power station

Sermermiut

This gives you the best opportunity for photography and is likely to get you closest to the actual glacier – check when you book how close they plan to go. The second is a **night cruise** around the icebergs. In June and July the sun doesn't really set this far north and, with the sun low on the horizon the icebergs are coloured in shades of pink, red and orange. The third is to take a **kayak trip**. Nearly all these trips are guided to ensure safety and this is the best way to feel the wildness of your encounter. On any trip, you may also see seabirds, whales and seals.

Some boat trips specifically set out to see **whales**, particularly humpbacks. Obviously, you will see icebergs on these trips but the route will be planned to maximise your time with the whales. As well as humpbacks, you may also see fin, bowhead, blue and minke whales. These trips often head further out to sea. When close to the whales, the boat's engine is cut so that the whales are not disturbed and to offer you the best opportunity to take photographs.

In winter it is also possible to take trips by **snowmobile**, **dog sled** or **snowshoe**. The routes are varied, depending on snow conditions and what you want to see and do. Snowmobile trips are either self-drive, with a guide, or you sit as pillion passenger. Dog sleds are always driven by a musher and you get to sit on the sled on reindeer skins, often, clad in a sealskin suit. It is the traditional way to travel and speeding across the snow does feel like going back in time. However you travel, you may be able to try ice fishing and you are almost certain to catch fish. The further away you get from the town's lights, the greater your chances of seeing the northern lights.

AROUND ILULISSAT

Ilulissat is an ideal base for touring the whole area with good boat and air connections to many smaller settlements, glaciers and remote accommodation.

OQAATSUT The Danes called this settlement Rodebay. For a long time this was thought to be derived from Red Bay because, as a whaling bay, the water was often red with whale blood. However, recent research has questioned this. It is likely that Rodebay is actually derived from the Dutch whalers' name for the bay which meant 'calm bay', which Oqaatsut Bay almost invariably is.

Today Oqaatsut – meaning 'cormorants' – is a tiny fishing village with a population of only 48 where time means nothing. People live in tune with nature and work when the light, tide and weather are best. There are no cars – there are no roads – but walking is unlimited. The lack of mechanical noise is extremely noticeable here and allows other sounds to be heard – the howl of sled dogs, the creek of icebergs and the blowing of whales out at sea.

There is one small church, which doubles as the school, a couple of places to stay and a scattering of houses. The settlement has just one small shop and accommodation is very limited. We would recommend that you book ahead – in summer you may otherwise find accommodation is fully booked and, in winter, everywhere may be closed unless they are aware you are coming.

On the shore are the villagers' most important possessions: fishing boats. Getting involved with the fishermen and their families bringing the catch in is interesting, fun and gives an appreciation of how hard life is in Greenland's small settlements. You will see fish drying around the village – Greenland halibut, Atlantic wolffish and codfish – and, no doubt, get the opportunity to eat them.

Getting there and away There is a popular 20km hike between Ilulissat and Oqaatsut, waymarked in orange. It can be walked in summer or in winter travelled by snowshoe, ski, snowmobile or dog sled. Most people arrive by boat, however, organised with one of the Ilulissat tour operators (page 158) or, if you are staying here at Hotel Nordlys or H8, they can organise the 20-minute boat transfer for you.

A popular day trip is to take a boat from Ilulissat to Oqaatsut and then walk back.

🏠 **Where to stay and eat** There are three places to stay, two with restaurants. You can also wild camp anywhere outside of the settlement and locals may also offer you their spare room – expect this type of accommodation to be very basic. The village has a communal service house that offers showers, toilets and laundry facilities to villagers and visitors. There is a small **Pilersuisoq** store (⏰ 10.00–15.00 Mon–Fri, 09.00–noon Sat) that stocks essentials; but don't rely on it having exactly what you need.

Bed & Breakfast (1 sgl, 2 dbls) 📞582820; e info@hotel-nordlys.com; w hotel-nordlys.com/en/bedbreakfast. This is not a B&B but a small house with 3 bedrooms, a kitchen, a living room with TV & a shared chemical toilet (you use the service house, 150m away, for showers & laundry). You can take b/fast at the neighbouring Hotel Nordlys 100m away, which has the same owner. **$**

H8 Guesthouse (6-bed mixed dorm) Mittarfimmut Aqqutaa B62; w h8-guesthouse-oqaatsut.booked.net; ⏰ Mar–Sep. This guesthouse, owned by Albatros Arctic Circle, dates back to the 1800s. B/fast is optional & there are also shared kitchen facilities, as well as a TV lounge & a shared 'bag toilet'. Again, the service house is used for showers & laundry. Wi-Fi costs extra. In the same building is the **Restaurant H8 Explorer** (⏰ noon–21.00 Mar–Sep; **$$$**), a small restaurant serving lunch & dinner. Many excursions to Oqaatsut stop here for a meal & it has a good reputation for serving excellent Greenlandic food including musk ox, reindeer or halibut. **$**

Hotel Nordlys (4 dbl rooms) 📞582820; e info@hotel-nordlys.com; w hotel-nordlys.com. The location of this hotel is wonderful with views over Disko Bay from the terrace & staying here will give you a real experience of life in a small Greenlandic settlement. It is a basic hotel with a bathroom, a chemical toilet & a limited water supply. As with all houses in the village, there is no piped water so it is all brought to the hotel in tanks. There is a **restaurant** (**$$–$$$**) open to non-residents; booking is advised. Ole offers transfers as well as trips to see whales, & maybe some fishing. In winter, transfers & tours may be by dog sled or snowmobile. **$**

ILIMANAQ Ilimanaq is a tiny settlement with just one hotel, one restaurant and one shop, but it is a lovely little place just to walk around and enjoy, as many of the buildings are old and well looked after. Today the population is only 51, but it is easy to see that this settlement was once much larger, with a population of around 250. In 2018 the village won a European award for the preservation of its cultural heritage.

There is a Pilersuisoq supermarket (⏰ 09.00–noon & 13.00–15.00 Mon–Fri, 10.00–noon Sat) on the waterfront, just south of Ilimanaq Lodge. As with all small settlement stores, it does provide a surprisingly wide selection of food, but it is unwise to rely on the store having precisely what you want.

Getting there and away Disko Line (w diskoline.gl/en) operates ferry services around Disko Bay, with services from Ilimanaq directly linking the town to Ilulissat, Qasigiannguit, Ikamiut, Akunnaaq, Aasiaat and Qeqertarsuaq. The frequency of services varies hugely depending on the time of year and how busy the route is – it is essential to book ahead via the website.

Air Greenland operates helicopter flights two or three times a week to Ilulissat and once a week to Qasigiannguit. The heliport is 300m east of town. In winter it is possible to travel to and from Qasigiannguit in the south by snowmobile or dog sled.

 Where to stay One of World of Greenland's wilderness lodges, **Ilimanaq Lodge** (15 cabins; ☏944300; e ilimanaq@wog.gl; w worldofgreenland.com/en/ilimanaq-lodge; **$$$$**) is an expensive and luxurious place to stay. Each waterside bungalow sleeps two with a private terrace and full bathroom. Some cabins have a better view than others; in the 'de luxe' cabins you will see icebergs from your bed and, maybe, whales. Bookings include meals, a guided walk and the boat transfer from Ilulissat, which takes about an hour dodging the icebergs on the way.

What to see and do If you are staying in Ilimanaq Lodge, then a comprehensive and complimentary **guided walk** is included in your stay. One restored building you'll see is the missionary's house, constructed in the 1750s in Copenhagen and brought to Ilimanaq as a flatpack to be reassembled. It was the home of the missionary Paul Egede and his family and was also used as the church until 1908, when today's church was built. The house is now the lodge's restaurant, the Egede. Another restored building is the old Royal Greenland Trading Company's shop and warehouse. Originally built in 1778, it is now the reception for the lodge.

Ilimanaq Lodge also runs an excursion from June to September to the **Ilimanaq Glacier**. This 7-hour trip begins with a boat trip to Itillip Ilua, followed by an off-road vehicle trip across the tundra to the Tasiusaq Fjord. Here a second boat weaves between icebergs up the fjord and lunch is taken beside one of the two glaciers – there is also a view of the ice sheet. It is quite an adventure into one of the remotest parts of the Disko Bay coast.

Hiking options are limitless, and you may see musk ox, Arctic hare and Arctic fox. Heading north along the coast, the icefjord is about 6km away or you can walk inland and up to Nordre Huse, a viewpoint overlooking the icefjord. About 5km south, you'll find a bay with a kilometre-long beach which is likely to be yours alone – probably a bit too cold for sunbathing. If you fancy a longer hike, then Qasigiannguit is about three days' walk south (40km). We'd recommend using Greenland Hiking Maps 17 – Qasigiannguit (1:100,000).

EQI SERMIA GLACIER Eqi Sermia Glacier is also known as the calving glacier because icebergs fall from the 4km-wide, 200m-high glacier face more than 100 times a day. Sitting in a boat in front of this beautiful yet menacing sight is unforgettable, as is the sight and sound of a pillar of ice calving. First you see it fall, then you hear the almighty crack and then the boat rocks as the shockwaves pass across the fjord.

Eqi is 70km north of Ilulissat, a 3-hour boat trip. It can be visited as a rather long day trip or you can stay at the lodge which overlooks the fjord. The boat trip is, in itself, a good way to see icebergs and, potentially, whales as you sail up the coast. There has never been a settlement here but Poul-Emile Victor, a famous Danish explorer, had his cabin 'the French hut' here as a base for his explorations of the ice sheet from 1948 to 1953.

 Where to stay *Map, page 155*
Glacier Lodge Eqi (15 cabins & tents) Fredericiaip 4; ☏944300; w worldofgreenland. com/en/glacier-lodge-eqi; ⊕ Jun–Sep.

These 2-person cabins & tents sit on a hillside overlooking the fjord and the Eqi Sermia Glacier. They are booked as a trip, so you get

2 boat transfers that last over 3hrs & FB. It is a steep climb up to the accommodation, so pack light. To get the most out of your trip, stay for 2 nights & take a guided hike. Various hikes are possible while you are at Eqi, including 1 on to the ice sheet. There are also marked trails if you prefer to walk unguided. On their final day, everyone gets an optional hike to the moraine for an up-close view of the glacier.

There are 4 levels of accommodation. Both glamping (in a fixed tent) & standard cabin options have neither water nor electricity, & toilet & shower facilities are at the café where meals are served. Comfort and deluxe cabins have private toilets & showers & solar electricity. All the accommodation is so close to the glacier that you will hear it calving while you lie in your bed. No mobile signal, no Wi-Fi, pure escapism. **$$$$**

QASIGIANNGUIT

Just 45km south of busy Ilulissat, Qasigiannguit is utterly unspoilt by tourism. The settlement has a few nice places to stay, as well as one of the country's most interesting museums. Boat trips run from the harbour and there are some well-marked trails into the backcountry.

Like many settlements around Disko Bay, Qasigiannguit was established by the Saqqaq people 4,500 years ago, although today's Inuit are most likely descendants of the later Thule culture. The modern town was established in 1734 as a trading and naval post. Today, it is a small town of just over 1,000 people that is focused on fishing for shrimp and halibut.

Qasigiannguit has a few shops including the usual Pilersuisoq (Christianshab; ⊕ 07.30–18.00 Mon–Fri, 07.30–15.00 Sat, 09.00–13.00 Sun) and a Tusass post office and phone shop (Poul Hansensvej 5; ⊕ 09.00–15.00 Mon–Fri).

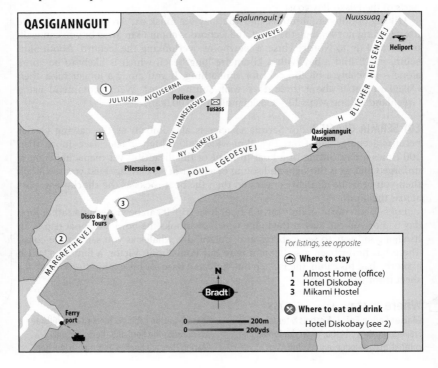

GETTING THERE AND AWAY Disko Line (wdiskoline.gl/en) operates ferry services around Disko Bay. Services from Qasigiannguit directly link the town to ten other towns and settlements. The frequency of services varies hugely depending on the time of year and how busy the route is. It is essential to book ahead using their website.

Air Greenland flies helicopters between Qasigiannguit and Aasiaat, Ilulissat and Ilimanaq. The heliport is about 400m east of town.

There is a trail (40km) from Ilimanaq if you would like to hike in or out. It takes two or three days – take a map. We'd recommend using Greenland Hiking Maps 17 – Qasigiannguit (1:100,000).

TOUR OPERATORS
Disko Bay Tours Margrethevej B665; ☏266038; w diskobay-tours.com. A group of very experienced local guides offer day tours & adventures lasting several days with nights in cosy cabins & tents. Dog-sled trips last from 2hrs to 3 days, & there is also a chance to walk on the Saqqarleq Glacier or take a boat trip to the nesting site of Arctic terns & razorbills. A large selection of guided hikes is available including Qasigiannguit to Ilimanaq (2 days), Paradise Bay (3hrs) and a cultural town walk (2hrs).

Guide to Greenland Inspektorbakken 8, Nuuk; w guidetogreenland.com. Guide to Greenland offers a small selection of private open or closed boat charters, ideal for a family or a small group. As well as spotting whales & icebergs, you can fish for Greenlandic halibut, Arctic cod, Atlantic redfish & Arctic char. Visits can be made to the abandoned settlement of Akullit, a ghostly place of ruins & memories, or to a seldom-visited Saqqaq archaeological site.

 WHERE TO STAY AND EAT *Map, opposite*

Hotel Diskobay (15 rooms) Margrethevej 34; ☏911081; w hoteldiskobay.com. A small hotel located high on a promontory near the harbour which gives it unrivalled views. In summer, humpback & fin whales can often be spotted from many rooms. All rooms are en suite. On the floor below the rooms is the **restaurant** (**$$–$$$**), open to non-residents, which serves local food including halibut, salmon, reindeer & musk ox. Everything is sourced locally – even the chef has been known to go out fishing, hunting & foraging. The restaurant & its terrace overlook the water, a great chance to spot whales over dinner. **$$$$**
Almost Home Juliusip 2; ☏588699; e kontor@ mintank.gl; **f**. Mariane & her husband have 3 houses dotted around the town. The largest

house has 3 dbl bedrooms, with TVs, which share 2 bathrooms, dining room, living room & kitchen. Their second house is similar but with just 2 bedrooms. Our favourite has just 1 dbl bedroom plus all the same facilities – it is your own private house. All 3 houses have a washing machine. **$$**
Mikami Hostel (12 rooms) Margrethevej 29; ☏250166; w mikamihostel.dk. A few converted old buildings – one was once a prison – offer a range of accommodation in sgl, dbl & bunk rooms. All the houses have shared kitchens, dining rooms, living rooms with TV, bathrooms, washing machines & terraces. Mikami also offers, in season, the ability to rent a tent (compete with sleeping mats & bags, & cooking utensils) & a cottage, a 20min boat ride outside the village. **$–$$**

WHAT TO SEE AND DO Despite being quite small, Qasigiannguit offers the chance to experience local culture at the same time as enjoying activities in the easily accessible backcountry.

Qasigiannguit Museum (☏914647; w qasigiannguit.museum.gl; ⊕ 13.00–16.00 Mon, Wed–Fri & Sun & 19.00–21.00 Tue; 30kr) The museum is housed in a little group of old buildings that date back to the 1700s. Indeed, the main building may be the oldest European building in Greenland, dating from 1734. The museum's collection is focused on the 2500bc Saqqaq culture and contains some incredibly old artefacts found in the local permafrost, including a blubber lamp, boots and knives.

Another part of the museum traces hunting and fishing from Saqqaq times to the present day and displays early hunting equipment – skin-tents, ice-fishing equipment and tools for hunters to make their own ammunition. The museum also has a team of volunteers who re-enact life here at the time of the late Thule culture. Dressed in traditional clothing, they demonstrate how their ancestors lived in peat huts, how fish were hunted and cooked on the huts' stoves, and how kayaks and umiaks were built and paddled. The volunteers also train others from around Greenland in traditional ways to work with skins and wood, as well as passing on traditional songs and stories. In the ticket kiosk is a small shop selling crafts, books and gifts.

Walking and other activities Greenland Hiking Maps 17 – Qasigiannguit (1:100,000) shows many **trails** and a number of routes are marked with yellow-, blue- or green-painted stones and can be walked independently or with a guide from a local tour operator. There is also a free map that you can pick up in the town or download (w diskobay.gl). The route along the Nuussuaq Peninsula (7km return, 2hrs) is popular. It starts on the right just past the heliport and takes you on to a long peninsula that almost crosses Tasersuaq Lake. Another walk goes to Eqalunnguit (10km, 3hrs), taking you along the west side of the lake to where the river flows from the lake into the sea. The walk starts at the very far end of Skivevej to the north of the town.

If you follow the shore to the left at Eqalunnguit you immediately reach Kangerluluk (Paradise Bay) beach. Back at Eqalunnguit, you can often cross the river by hopping from stone to stone and thus continue on to Salliup Tasia (18km, 6hrs) where there is an impressive waterfall. If you turn left immediately after crossing the river at Eqalunnguit then there is a trail along the shore that leads to Ilimanaq (2 or 3 days).

In summer, **boat trips** can take you whale and seal watching – Qasigiannguit means small spotted seals – or to visit offshore islands like Kitsissunnguit, many of which are home to hundreds of seabirds including Arctic terns and razorbills. You can also visit abandoned settlements including Akulliit.

In winter, Qasigiannguit is a great place for **dog sledding** and, however you go into the backcountry, there is a lot of wildlife including musk oxen, Arctic hares and Arctic foxes.

AASIAAT

Aasiaat is a small island (7.5km by 3.5km), at the northern end of an archipelago that stretches 100km down the west coast of Greenland from the southern edge of Disko Bay. The town has the best deep and sheltered harbour in the area. Aasiaat Island is what the Inuit call flat but which we might call a little hilly, making it ideal for hiking, snowshoeing and cross-country skiing. The islands around it create a network of sheltered waterways perfect for kayaking and loved by whales.

Aasiaat town is the fifth largest in Greenland but, with a population of under 3,000, it is small place. The town is still reasonably untouched by tourism, which is surprising given the good boat connection to other towns in the bay and the breadth of activities available, in both summer and winter. It is possible to rent equipment, such as kayaks and bikes, and self-guided hiking and skiing trails make this a great location for independent travellers.

Aasiaat is small enough to walk around but there is a local taxi company if you need one (✆894040).

HISTORY Niels Egede, Hans Egede's second son, established the town Egedesminde here in 1763, choosing this location because of the harbour and the fishing. There

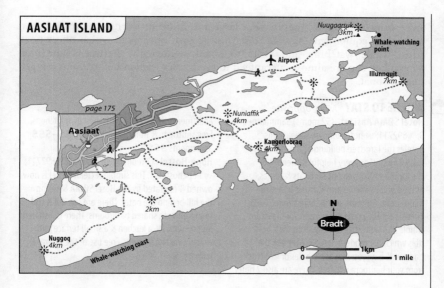

were already semi-nomadic Inuit living in the area; their name for the town was always Aasiaat. Most of the settlers who arrived with Egede were working in the whaling industry and they brought with them disease, particularly smallpox, which killed many of the indigenous Inuit. At one stage the town's population dropped to 21.

Aasiaat is still a fishing and hunting town. When whaling declined, cod became the main catch and a factory salted the fish to preserve it for onward shipment. Since the 1980s, the main catches have been shrimp, halibut and crab, and Aasiaat has also established itself as the regional centre for ship repairs.

The town was the first in northern Greenland to have a high school for girls, opened in 1932, and today it has one of Greenland's four high schools. Children come from the far north to study here, most students boarding in Aasiaat for the entire school year.

GETTING THERE AND AWAY The Arctic Umiaq **ferry** (page 47; w aul.gl) arrives most weeks from April until early January on Sundays at 06.00, heading north up the coast and going on to Qeqertarsuaq and Ilulissat. Later the same day the ferry calls again at 22.00 on its way south once more. Disko Line (w diskoline.gl/en) operates ferry services around Disko Bay. Services from Aasiaat directly link to 13 towns and settlements including Ilulissat, Qasigiannguit and Qeqertarsuaq. The frequency of services varies hugely depending on the time of year and how busy the route is. It is essential to book ahead using their website.

There are **flights** on most days to Ilulissat and Kangerlussuaq. There are also less frequent flights to Qasigiannguit, Qeqertarsuaq, Akunnaaq, Attu, Kangaatsiaq, Iginniarfik, Ikamiut, Kitsissuarsuit and Niaqornaarsuk. The airport is about 4km east of town and has a small terminal building but few facilities. Most accommodation will provide a transfer.

TOUR OPERATOR Aasiaat Tours (✆ 892711; w visitaasiaat.com) is part of the Hotel SØMA, where the dedicated staff offer a wide range of activities winter and summer, as well as hiring out kayaks, paddleboards, cross-country skis,

7

snowshoes and bikes. They have a large wardrobe of warm, waterproof gear and safety equipment. Aasiaat Tours has its own open boat which offers boat trips, whale watching and visits to small settlements. Between June and September you are almost guaranteed to see whales – often before you even get into the boat.

WHERE TO STAY *Map, opposite*

Hotel SØMA Aasiaat (52 rooms) Sammiarneq 9; 892711; w hotelsoma.gl/aasiaat. This hotel is the large red building at the end of the quay. The staff are very helpful & friendly, & the location is convenient for boats & ferries, as well as for walking into town. It is also the main centre for tours and activities (page 176). There is a huge range of rooms in 2 wings from simple sgls with shared facilities to their best dbls which are modern, large & overlook the harbour & bay; you may see whales or icebergs from your bedroom window. There are also 2 hotel apartments that sleep 4 with their own kitchens. Free shuttle to & from the airport inc. **$$–$$$**, apartments **$$$$**

Hope-Hostel (7 rooms) Killerpaat 32; 892711; w hopehostel.gl. This simple & clean hostel is now owned & operated by the Hotel SØMA & sits on the hill behind the hotel. There are sgl, dbl & trpl rooms all with shared bathrooms. There is a shared lounge with TV, a kitchen & a small terrace with a view over the harbour. Free use of the freezer & laundry. **$**

WHERE TO EAT AND DRINK *Map, opposite*

There are two bars in Aasiaat that you might want to check out if you are in need of a drink and, perhaps, some live music. At the back of town is the **Tulugaq** (Qaqqap Tunua 36; ⊕ 21.00–midnight Wed–Thu, 21.00–03.00 Fri–Sat) and, out to the east near the sports field, there is a pop-up bar that starts serving at around midnight at the weekends. Remember, at midnight it may still be light!

Café 3 Sissakkooriaq 22; 891704; ⊕ 11.00–21.00 Tue–Sat, 10.00–13.00 Sun. The blue café on the harbourside, from where you can watch the shrimp boats set sail, is very popular with locals, particularly for ice creams even when it is freezing cold outside. The café sells the usual range of food including hot & cold drinks, smoothies, pizza, pasta, sandwiches &, of course, ice cream. **$**

Café Puisi Pottersvej 12; 891112; ⊕ 11.00–20.00 daily. Located up the hill behind the large black church, the café looks a little scruffy from the outside, but it is popular & worth seeking out. The food is good value & a mixture of Greenlandic, Chinese and Thai, so not too spicy. Take away or eat in. **$**

Northstar Restaurant Sannerut 22; 527332; ⊕ 11.00–21.00. Trust the map, this little red restaurant is easier to find than you think. It may be just another red Greenlandic house on the outside, but it is a smart restaurant inside with friendly service. They serve the best pizza in town & a range of burgers. The restaurant is also a good place for an espresso or cappuccino. **$**

Somandshjemmet In Hotel SØMA; 892711; w hotelsoma.gl/aasiaat. This is more smart canteen than restaurant but the food is good, ranging from open sandwiches topped with smoked salmon & prawns to cakes. The à la carte menu includes fish & chips & pizzas plus a children's menu. For lunch & dinner, there is a very popular, good-value, hot dish of the day. The hotel also has a new, upmarket pop-up summer restaurant (w hotelsoma.gl/summer-restaurant-aasiaat; ⊕ Jun–Aug 18.00–21.00). Check their website for details. **$**

SHOPPING AND OTHER PRACTICALITIES There are two **supermarkets** in the town centre, Pisiffik (Fr. Lyngesvej 23; ⊕ 08.00–20.00 Mon–Sat, 10.00–20.00 Sun) and Pilersuisoq (Niels Egedesvej 1; ⊕ 07.00–20.00 Mon–Fri, 08.00–16.00 Sat–Sun). Both have ATM cash machines just inside the front door. It is unusual for there to be a state-run Pilersuisoq in a town which has a private Pisiffik store.

The Pilersuisoq is here only because Aasiaat is the port at which their large ships arrive and from where goods are transported to the Pilersuisoq stores in the small settlements. Theoretically the large ship arrives weekly in summer and every two weeks in winter but sea ice can stop ships for up to three months.

The Kalaalimineerniarfik **fish market** is on the harbourside and sells whatever is brought in by fishermen and hunters. This is likely to include fish and seal and, on occasion, whale.

There is a branch of the Greenland Bank (Edvard Johansenip 2; ⊕ 09.30–15.30 Mon–Thu, 09.30–15.00 Fri) just behind the harbour and a Tusass post office (Niels Egede's Plads 1; ⊕ 09.30–14.30 Mon–Fri) behind the Aasiaat Museum.

WHAT TO SEE AND DO The small but good **Aasiaat Museum** (✆894761; ⊕ 13.00–16.00 Mon–Sat; 15kr) is well worth a visit with a range of local artefacts including a complete traditional kayak with all its hunting gear and a really interesting explanation of how all the tools and equipment were used. There are also fascinating pictures and photos of the town dating back to its founding. A turf house is located above the museum and is fitted out inside as it would have been 100 years ago. You'll need to ask at the museum for the key. The cannons outside the museum are still fired on ceremonial occasions.

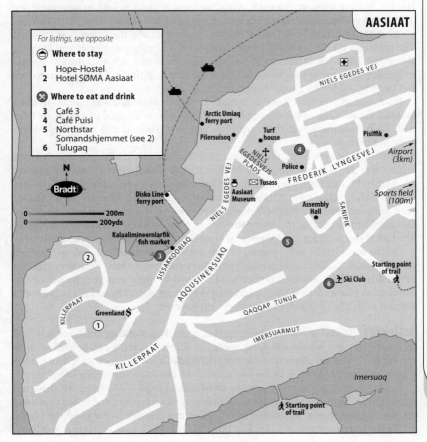

A young girl, Malina, was disturbed by a man who came to her bed in the night. Suspecting it might happen again, and wanting to know who it was, Malina put soot on her face. The next time the man came to her, he got soot on his face too. Malina lit her lamp and followed him to the communal house where she discovered that the man with soot on his face was her brother, Anningaaq. She was devastated by this and ran from him, holding her lamp to see the way. The brother ran after her but his lamp went out. They both ran so far and fast that they took off into the sky and that is why we still see Malina, the sun goddess, being chased by Anningaaq, the god of the moon, travelling across the sky.

Starting at the museum, the **Art 'n' Walk Tour** is a good way to see the town and also see the 24 murals, paintings and sculptures dotted around; you can pick up the leaflet from your accommodation or download it from w diskobay.gl/destinations/aasiaat. The third artwork on the trail is a sculpture of three heads of the Danish Royal family – the previous monarch, Queen Margrethe II, her husband Prince Henrik and the present monarch, King Frederik X –and is said to symbolise the links between Denmark and Greenland. It sits outside Aasiaat's large black **church,** a rather intimidating building but worth entering to see the impressive interior. The paintings on the back wall depict traditional and religious stories and hanging above the aisle are three model votive ships including a rather lovely umiak. In Danish, the nave of the church is called 'the ship' and the roof of the church does feel like the inside of a gigantic upturned boat.

Further along the trail there are a number of murals on housing blocks, all done by local artists. One of these (number 8 on the trail) is a mural based on an Inuit fable (see above) of which there are a few versions. There is also a painting of this fable in the church.

Exhibit 21 is a set of paintings inside the assembly hall, which is usually open during the day. The paintings are by **Per Kirkeby** and were all painted around 1969 when he was teaching at the local high school; they are inspired by Disko Bay and the local geology. Per Kirkeby donated the paintings to the people of Aasiaat with the condition that they will never be removed. He went on to become one of Denmark's most famous modern painters and these works are now worth millions. The hall is still used for civic meetings, bingo nights and wedding receptions.

On the outskirts of town you may come across **Greenlandic sled dogs**, chained and each with its own small house. These dogs are now, rather controversially, not allowed to be kept in town as they tend to howl at night and, if approached too closely, can bite to defend their pack. Sled dogs have always been kept outside and will not willingly go inside even in the worst weather.

Activities Behind the town there are many marked **walking trails**, which lead to viewpoints and **whale-watching spots**. In winter the trails can be walked with snowshoes. There are also **cross-country ski routes** most of which start near the Ski Club – the easiest skiing is in the snowmobile tracks or on the frozen lakes.

In winter, Aasiaat Tours can arrange **snowmobile trips** – which are self-drive but with a guide – and **dog-sled rides** with an experienced musher and a sled that takes up to three passengers. In the depths of winter, it is possible to travel off the island, across the frozen waterways to explore other islands. Ice-fishing trips are also offered.

In summer (May to September) you can rent **kayaks** and **paddleboards** to go on guided trips or, if you have a relevant qualification, to go out and explore on your own. For the less energetic, **sea safaris** are available with an incredibly high chance of seeing humpback, fin or minke whales. Taking a boat trip can also enable you to visit one of the local settlements like **Akunnaaq** where you will see fishing families at work and get a real sense of the true Greenland. Each settlement has to be self-contained with its own shop, church and electricity generator. In winter, ice conditions can prevent supplies arriving for many months.

Every June the community comes together to celebrate the midnight sun with the **Aasiaat Midnight Sun Marathon** (). Around 300 runners from all over the world take part in this race; it is also possible to run shorter distances. Running along the shore you may spot whales breaching out at sea.

KANGAATSIAQ

Kangaatsiaq sits on a flat headland that juts out into the Davis Straight, surrounded by other low-lying islands and interconnected landmasses that extend 50km north to Aasiaat. With just over 500 people, Kangaatsiaq is one of the smallest towns in Greenland with a degree of self-sufficiency; a new school was recently built and the heliport, just 200m outside of the town, enables transport in winter and spring when boat access can be restricted. This is a truly unspoilt community with seal hunting and fishing as the main sources of income; the narrow waterways teem with fish, seals and even whales. On land, reindeer and musk oxen roam together with Arctic foxes and hares and a wide variety of birdlife.

Disko Line (wdiskoline.gl/en) operates ferry services around Disko Bay and directly connects Kangaatsiaq with eight other towns including Ilulissat, Aasiaat and Qasigiannguit. Seasonal Air Greenland helicopter flights connect to Aasiaat, Ikerasaarsuk and Niaqornaarsuk.

The only tourist infrastructure is a self-catering hotel, the **Polar Cab Inn** (2 sgls, 2 dbls; Mittafeqarfiit; 522923; e polarcab@outlook.com; ; **$$**). Jens Filemonsen's little inn, which is open year-round, has four rooms which share the bathroom (with a flushing toilet and shower), kitchen and lounge with television and free Wi-Fi. There are no cafés or restaurants in town, but there is, of course, a Pilersuisoq supermarket (⊕ 14.00–20.00 Mon–Fri, 10.00–15.00 Sat–Sun). Jens can introduce visitors to local hunters, fishermen, guides and dog-sled mushers for the most authentic Greenlandic experiences.

East of the town, the 150km-long fjord with countless side fjords provides limitless kayaking opportunities. On land, hiking to view wildlife is easy and popular and, in winter, can be done with snowshoes or dog sled. The lack of light pollution means that there is a stunning display of the northern lights throughout the winter.

DISKO ISLAND

Disko Island is unique in Greenland, formed from volcanic activity, with over 2,000 hot springs, several waterfalls and a wide variety of relatively lush vegetation. The hot springs extend the growing season and at least 500 varieties of plant thrive here. The island, Greenland's biggest and more than 120km across, sits about 100km west of Ilulissat on the north side of Disko Bay, and 65km north of Aasiaat. To its northeast, the Sullorsuaq, or Vaigat, Strait, only a narrow channel, separates the island from the mainland.

The island is sparsely populated and much of it is difficult to access due to several glaciers and high mountains towering to nearly 2,000m which remain covered in snow and ice all year. There are only two settlements: Qeqertarsuaq (population less than 900) in the south and tiny Kangerluk, an hour's boat trip northwest. A third settlement, Qullissat, was abandoned in 1972.

Although a few cruise ships stop briefly, the island sees few tourists, which is a shame as hiking trails abound with amazing vistas and views over iceberg-studded Disko Bay.

QEQERTARSUAQ Erik the Red visited Disko Island around AD983 looking for new hunting grounds but he didn't settle here. From artefacts discovered, it is evident that Inuit lived in this area for several thousand years before Erik arrived. In the 18th century whalers came to the island and in 1773 the whaler Svend Sandgreen officially founded the settlement of Godhavn, now called Qeqertarsuaq. The town has been used as a base for hunting and fishing ever since.

The randomly scattered buildings sit on a peninsula that climbs gently from the harbour, with red-tinged mountains rising steeply behind the town. Among the mountains is the Lyngmark Glacier, just north of Qeqertarsuaq, which can be explored all year. Just west of the town, along the coast, is one of the best black-sand beaches, often dotted with stranded blocks of white ice. In Greenland, only Disko Island has black beaches, a reminder of its volcanic origins.

The University of Copenhagen's **Arctic Station** (w arktiskstation.ku.dk/english) was founded in Qeqertarsuaq by Danish botanist Morten Pedersen Porsild in 1906. It is still a year-round environmental research station, focusing on the function and development of entire ecosystems, monitoring, for example, weather, plants and wildlife. The buildings and facilities have been radically modernised in the last 20 years and can house up to 40 scientists and technicians. Outside their busy period (June to August) when the base is full of visiting scientists, it may be possible for a group to visit on a guided tour. Contact details are on their website.

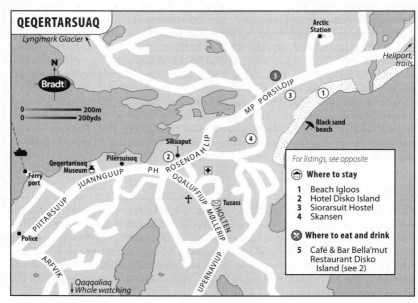

Getting there and away The Arctic Umiaq ferry (w aul.gl) from Ilulissat arrives most weeks between April and early January on Sundays at 10.00 on its way south via Aasiaat (page 47). Disko Line (wdiskoline.gl/en) operates ferry services that directly connect Qeqertarsuaq with six other towns including Ilulissat, Aasiaat and Qasigiannguit, but many services are seasonal.

There are scheduled helicopter flights to Aasiaat and Ilulissat. The heliport is about 1km east of the town.

Tour operators

Hotel Disko Island Ph. Rosendahlip 7; ☏921628; w hoteldiskoisland.com. A collection of guided tours & trips is organised by the hotel including a walk around the town &, for a longer trip, a 2-day hike to Lyngmark Glacier, spending a night in their wilderness lodge. Mountain biking & kayaking in the bay & around the island are also offered, as is ice swimming from the only black-sand beach in Greenland, quickly followed by a sauna!

Qeqertarsuaq Tours ☏562707; w qeqertarsuaqtours.gl. Small tour operator offering dog-sled & snowmobile trips in the winter & fishing & sailing trips in the summer. There is also a chance to do some rappelling at Red River & visit the village of Kangerluk. They also have 2 interesting beach igloos (see below).

Sikuaput MP Porsildip 3; ☏267799; w sikuaput.gl. This small tour operator offers a variety of dog-sled trips between Feb & Apr, sometimes including some ice fishing. The beautiful winter landscape can also be enjoyed from a snowmobile. In summer, guided hikes take you to hot springs, a whale lookout, waterfalls & mountain tops. There is a chance to dine with a local family & sample some home-cooked food.

 Where to stay and eat *Map, opposite, unless otherwise stated*

There are a few Airbnb properties which offer good value accommodation for families and small groups. As ever, you can free camp anywhere beyond the edges of the settlement.

In Qeqertarsuaq

Beach Igloos ☏562707; q qeqertarsuaqtours.gl/beach-iglos. Qeqertarsuaq Tours rents out 2 beach igloos set right on the black-sand beach. Each glass-&-wood hemisphere has a ground-floor lounge with a kitchen to the side & a bathroom. Upstairs, the bed is on a mezzanine floor with a skylight through which you can watch the northern lights. **$$$$**

Hotel Disko Island (31 rooms) P H Rosendahlip 7; ☏921628; w hoteldiskoisland.com. This is the settlement's largest hotel, right in the centre of things & overlooking the harbour. The hotel is spread over 6 buildings & the reception, the restaurant & 24 en-suite rooms are clustered together; the 7 rooms with shared facilities are in the Panorama building a short walk away. B/fast & transfers are included but Wi-Fi is extra. The hotel restaurant, open to non-residents, serves b/fast, lunch (**$**) & dinner (**$$**) Jun–Sep & meals in other months by prior arrangement. There are great views over the water to the mountains & a large terrace. **$$$$**

Skansen (2 houses) Siorarsuit B350; ☏583645; w skansen.gl. Skansen have 2 houses, one with 2 dbl bedrooms & the second with just 1. Both also have a sofa bed in the living room, as well as shared kitchen, bathroom & washing machine. Both houses are newly renovated & a third will soon be available. There is also a gift shop & guests can join the owners for dinner if they wish. **$$$**

Siorarsuit Hostel (8 rooms) ☏921628; w hoteldiskoisland.com/accommodation/hostel; ⏰ Jun–Sep. This small single-storey hostel, with the same owners as the hotel, is on the outskirts of town near the black-sand beach. The bunk bed rooms all share bathrooms & kitchens. Transfers are free, Wi-Fi costs extra. **$**

Café & Bar Bella'mut M P Porsildip 17; ☏260021; f; ⏰ 07.00–22.00 Mon–Wed, 14.00–midnight Thu–Sun. This blue-&-white building without a sign is actually a popular local café serving nachos & smoothies & a rather unpredictable range of light meals. Live music sometimes at w/ends. **$**

Around Qeqertarsuaq

Disko Mountain Lodge [map, page 155] (12 people) ☏921628; **w** hoteldiskoisland.com/ accommodation/disko-mountain-lodge. Owned by Hotel Disko Island, this basic hut is at the foot of the Lyngmark Glacier at 900m above sea level. It is a demanding 4hr hike to reach the hut, but the views of the glacier & Disko Bay are breathtaking. The hut has a kitchen & bathroom & the cost includes a guide, a lunch pack for the way up & then dinner & b/fast at the lodge. **$$$$**

Other practicalities There is a Pilersuisoq supermarket (P H Rosendahlip; ⏱ 07.30–18.00 Mon–Fri, 09.00–14.00 Sat–Sun) and a Tusass post office and phone shop (Holten Møllerip Aqquserna 3; ⏱ 09.00–15.00 Mon–Fri).

What to see and do Qeqertarsuaq Museum (☏921153; **w** museum.gl; ⏱ Jun–Sep 10.00–14.00 daily, Oct–May 11.00–14.00 daily) is housed in the old bailiff's home, built around 1840 and used until 1990 by north Greenland's most important government official. On the museum's ground floor are displayed an eclectic mix of local archaeological artefacts and the possessions of some of the families who lived in the house, particularly Phillip and Agnes Rosendahl. They arrived here in 1924 and lived in the house for over 15 years. The recorded voice of Agnes and the photographs of that time are particularly fascinating. In another room Otto Sandgreen is remembered. As well as being a religious teacher and priest, Otto is a great literary figure in Greenland. He founded a language society and a publishing house and wrote 44 books, mainly about Greenland's hunting culture. The room that once was the house's living room is now home to travelling exhibitions as well as cultural events. On the first floor of the museum are several exhibition rooms displaying paintings by Jakob Danielsen, Emanuel Petersen and Troels Brandt, as well as tools for building barrels and boats and a collection of photos, drawings and documents recording the history of the Arctic Station and the church. In a second building, the dog sled of the most important government official in north Greenland can be inspected.

Qeqertarsuaq has a beautiful red wooden **church**. Nicknamed 'God's ink pot' because of the building's shape, the church is rather jewel-like and closer inspection reveals more and more detail in the craftsmanship, both inside and out. The church has a service every Sunday and the rector wears traditional Greenlandic costume with some adaptions, including a white clerical collar.

Hiking and other activities There are plenty of opportunities for easily accessible, superb wilderness **hiking** in Qeqertarsuaq, with or without a guide. There is a good downloadable map on **w** diskobay.gl/destinations/qeqertarsuaq. The most popular walk is to the Lyngmark Glacier (12km return) on the mountain of the same name and this is best done with a guide, who can get you on to the glacier safely; there is also the option of staying in the wilderness lodge run by Hotel Disko Island (see above).

More walks start from the picnic site and river bridge to the east of the town. The one trail that heads inland from the picnic area soon splits but both trails join again after about 2km at Ajuaasaq, which has a good viewpoint at around 640m. On the far side of the bridge, a trail (1.3km) leads up the side of the river to where the river has cut deep into the land and the Qorlortorsuaq waterfall drops into a small lagoon. Partway up this trail, another forks off right to the viewpoint at Sanningsoq (2.9km), more or less following the Kuussuaq River all the way.

There are also a few trails west from the bridge, one of which follows the coast to Kuannit Qorlortorsuaq (3km). Kuannit is Greenlandic for angelica and the plant was traditionally picked here for use in cooking or just eaten as a snack, but the main draw here is an impressive outcrop of basalt columns.

In a totally different direction, it is possible to walk southwest to the very end of the peninsula at Qaqqaliaq, about 2km from the centre of Qeqertarsuaq and the southernmost tip of the whole island. It is the best **whale-spotting** site – there is even a little red-and-white hut so you can sit and watch for bowheads and humpbacks sheltered from the wind and weather. The frame of the hut is made from whale jawbones and has been chained to this rock for centuries. When a whale was spotted, a cannon was fired to alert the whaling boats.

Whales can, of course, also be seen on **whale-watching boat trips** which can be combined with fishing and a visit to the small village of **Kangerluk**. Other activities are possible, with both kayaks and mountain bikes for hire, and in the winter the snowmobiles and dog sleds come out and become the primary form of transport.

KANGERLUK Kangerluk is really remote and has a population of just 12, making it the second smallest settlement in Greenland. Astoundingly, there is a Pilersuisoq shop, open for just 2 hours every day, a church/school with four pupils and a small power station. For public gatherings, the carpenter's workshop is usually used. When the fjord is not frozen, a boat visits every two weeks from Qeqertarsuaq and some boat trips call in here.

QULLISSAT Qullissat coal mine was opened in 1924 in the hope that it would make Greenland self-sufficient in coal. Over the next 25 years, the mine and the town grew and it became the sixth largest town in the country. It was probably unique in Greenland's history in being a town based on an industry rather than hunting and fishing. Production peaked in the early 1950s but by 1966 it was making a loss, so the government, who owned the mine, decided to start to run it down. There was also a shortage of labour to work in cod factories, so about half the town's population were relocated to Qeqertarsuaq to undertake this work. The mine finally closed in October 1972 and the remaining population was relocated to Qeqertarsuaq.

Qullissat in now a ghost town, with building and machinery from the mining era slowly disintegrating. Some of the houses have been restored as holiday homes, both by their original inhabitants and by other Greenlanders. There are no facilities, and its remote location makes it difficult to visit.

UUMMANNAQ

Uummannaq is off Greenland's west coast 600km north of the Arctic Circle and it is the name of both the island and the town; indeed, it is also the name of the 1,175m-high, heart-shaped mountain that dominates the island. Uummannaq the island is just 12km², and Uummannaq the town sits on its southern tip with a population of 1,400. It is a small place, perhaps 1km across and 500m deep, its brightly coloured houses scattered on the rocky slopes that rise to the base of the steep gneiss and granite mountain. Beyond town, the few trails snake around huge rocks, outliers of the big Uummannaq mountain, whose bulk is ever-present above you.

The first permanent settlers were European whalers who arrived in the 18th century and established the present site in 1763. But for thousands of years the Inuit hunted and fished in this area; it was a tough life as this far north the sun remains below the horizon for two months of the year.

Today shrimp processing and fishing support the economy, though hunting remains an integral part of life. There are probably as many sled dogs on the island as people. Dog sleds are still an essential form of transport here. Travel, both between settlements and to go hunting and fishing, is by boat in summer and by dog sled in winter.

The seasons here are determined by the weather. It is considered to be summer when the fjord is no longer frozen and can be used by boats. That probably means June to September but it is totally dependent on climate conditions. Similarly, it is considered winter when the fjord is frozen and the sea ice is thick enough to take dog sleds and snowmobiles across it. This is generally February to April. In a good winter, it is actually easier to travel around on the ice than it is in summer on the water.

If you are looking to experience the vast uncompromising wilderness, the traditional Inuit way of life in an area untouched by tourism, you will find it here, along with experts who will take you out into the backcountry to meet other hunters and fishers and experience life in this remote corner of Greenland.

GETTING THERE AND AROUND It is a bit complicated. Air Greenland flies to the settlement of Qaarsut from Ilulissat at least once a week. From there Air Greenland's helicopter shuttles across the fjord to Uummannaq. Alternatively, it is possible to organise a private boat transfer (about 30mins) from Qaarsut to Uummannaq.

From Uummannaq heliport, about 700m northeast of the town, Air Greenland also flies helicopters to Ikerasak, Saattut, Ukkusissat and Niaqornat.

In town, there are **taxis** (✆582100; e 21taxavogn.gmail.com; ⬛) should you need one. In winter they have been known to take shortcuts across the sea ice.

TOUR OPERATORS

Siku Tours ✆262626; w sikutours.com. A local tour company offering a week-long adventure living like an Inuit – journey by dog sled, learn how to fish & hunt, & stay with a local family. In summer, you can spend a week camping in the wild & fly fishing for Arctic char. Lots of day trips including boat trips, dog sledding or ice fishing.

Uummannaq Seasafaris Qernertunnguamut B909; ✆560703; w uummannaqseasafaris.gl. A small local company owned by Paaluk & Svend, both experienced sailors with extensive local knowledge. In the winter they run a selection of dog-sledding trips including a 7-day expedition visiting small settlements, a chance to really get to know the area & your dogs. There are also opportunities to go ice fishing and, maybe, catch some Greenlandic halibut or local redfish. In the summer, they run a selection of boat trips including an intriguing trip to 'the desert', a strange landscape coloured by the sulphur & iron in the soil, & another to the old Inuit settlement of Qilakitsoq, where preserved mummies were found in 1972 (page 184).

 WHERE TO STAY AND EAT

Cafémma (5 rooms) Aqqusinersuaq B-799; ✆583300; w cafemma.gl. 3 of the rooms are over the café, right on the waterfront, with a sea, mountain & iceberg view. They share a kitchen, toilet & bathroom and come with free Wi-Fi & hot drinks. The other 2 rooms share a house in another part of town. Popular with locals, the **café** (**$$**) serves good coffee & meals indoors & out on the quayside. Hot dogs, burgers, chips & beer; occasional live music. **$$–$$$**

Avani (6 houses) Aqqusinertaaq B 665; ✆584200; w avani.gl. Avani rent out 6 houses which are dotted all over town, so check out where you want to be – their website has a clear map. 2 of the houses are quite small, for 1 or 2 people, another has 2 dbl bedrooms & the other 3 houses are large, sleeping 7/8 people. All the houses can be rented as a unit &, in the larger houses, you can rent just a room. All the houses have a kitchen, bathroom & lounge/dining room & most have a washing machine & Wi-Fi. **$**

OTHER PRACTICALITIES There is a Pilersuisoq supermarket (Aqqusinersuaq; ⏱ 09.00–22.00 daily) and a Tusass post office and phone shop (Pavia Leibhardtip Aqqutaa B-15; ⏱ noon–15.00 Mon–Fri). **Santa Claus** also has a gift shop on Trollep.

WHAT TO SEE AND DO Uummannaq's **museum** (Alfred Berthelsenip; ✆ 954556; e cjer@avannaata.gl), spread across several buildings, is a fascinating place to visit. The main, yellow, building, 'the Doctor's House', was once the island's hospital and dates from 1880. The exhibits are many and varied and there are some real gems including replicas of the clothes found on the Qilakitsoq Mummies and two motor sleds used by Alfred Wegener, a polar explorer and research pioneer. Wegener's lasting contribution to science is that he coined the term 'continental drift', bringing together his own and his predecessors' theories into a single concept. Other areas of the museum display many traditional tools and craftwork, as well as some boats. In one corner, you may also find a worker, busy replying to letters on behalf of Santa Claus. Another building was once used to store whale blubber but now contains a collection of local items. Outside, there are some turf houses, one of which was lived in until 1989. Their fitted-out interiors give a real insight into life in these basic dwellings.

Near the museum is the **church**, a striking stone building – the granite used in its construction came from the hills behind the town. The church's interior is quite plain with unplastered granite walls, a wooden beamed ceiling and a rather grand organ. Unfortunately, the church is only open for services.

Walking and hiking Hiking is limited on the island but there are a few interesting routes, some marked. In winter the marks may disappear but, with a map, the routes can still be walked, with snowshoes. Sagamaps Red Series map (1:250 000) No 12 Nuussuaq covers the area.

Santa Claus lives on the island of Uummannaq every summer. This is, of course, why you find his postbox next to the church. And Santa's cabin is about 2km north of the town, a traditional hut built of rocks and turf. It was built for a Danish Christmas television show *The Elf-Gang in Greenland*, which first aired in 1989 and has become a Christmas TV favourite. His cabin hasn't been changed since the show was filmed and is full of props and pictures. The hike to **Santa Claus's Cabin** (4km return) is very popular and follows a trail marked with red dots. It starts behind the housing to the west of the heliport and finishes at his turf hut overlooking the fjord.

Another short walk (2km return) is along the track north of the harbour to **Tasersuaq Qulleq**, the town's drinking-water lake. It is quite picturesque and, when you get there, you can scramble either way along the lake edge. Finally, the walk east along the coastal track, to Siaqqissoq (4km return), is interesting and offers good views of the icebergs and, potentially, whales. The walk takes you past the heliport, the football field, the cemetery and one of the town dumps before reaching a headland looking across the water to the neighbouring island of Storoen and the Inussugtalik mountain (1,418m).

Hiking is dependent on conditions underfoot but when the ground is snow covered you can change to snowshoes. In winter, you can also hike on the sea ice but only do this with an experienced local guide as sea ice in fjords is notoriously difficult to 'read'.

Other activities Fishing is possible year-round – in summer line fishing from the boat and in winter ice fishing through a hole in the ice.

In 1972, in the abandoned settlement of Qilakitsoq, an astounding discovery was made. Two brothers, Hans and Jokum, were out hunting for ptarmigan when under an overhanging rock they came across a large pile of stones. Being inquisitive young men, they removed a few stones to discover human remains. Covering up the bodies to prevent wild animals scavenging them, they returned home to tell their story.

At the time no-one appreciated the importance of this discovery. The Inuit frequently buried their dead under rocks, it being too difficult to dig in the rocky frozen ground. Once researchers arrived sometime later, the graves were opened up and, amazingly, eight mummies were uncovered – six women and two young boys, one only six months old – preserved by the cold, dry weather conditions and the protection from the overhanging cliff. The mummies were found laid on top of each other in two piles, 1m apart, and covered with sealskins, flat stones and turf. The bodies were fully clothed – each had two layers of clothing, the underlayer made from birds' feathers, the outer layer from reindeer and sealskins, including hats and boots. Next to them were spare clothes for life in the next world.

When scientists began testing, they were astonished to discover the bodies dated to around 1475, lying undiscovered for 500 years. The degree of preservation meant the scientists could learn a great deal about these people. Five of the six women were tattooed with lines on their foreheads and over their eyes, and two women had tattooed cheeks and lines beneath their chins. It is thought the woman who wasn't tattooed may have been unmarried. It was difficult for researchers to establish why they all died. One woman had an obvious tumour that may have caused her death and the older boy seemed to have a disability and evidence of disease. It is thought that the baby was buried alive – if a mother died leaving a baby under two years old and no-one could be found to nurse it, the Inuit custom at the time would be to bury the baby alive with its mother.

The four best-preserved mummies are on permanent display at the Greenland National Museum in Nuuk (page 82). Most people are shocked at how well preserved the mummies are. It is well worth a visit.

Qilakitsoq today can be visited by boat from Uummannaq. There is little to see but in this remote location, 450km north of the Arctic Circle, you can appreciate what a tough life these women had led. The eight mummies are now considered to be the oldest preserved human remains in Greenland.

Whale watching is popular in summer when fin, minke, humpback and pilot whales, along with many types of seal, may be seen. In winter, in the waters that are still free from ice it is possible to spot narwhal and white beluga whales, and seals may be seen resting on the sheets of sea ice.

AROUND UUMMANNAQ There are a few small settlements around Uummannaq that can be visited in summer by boat or, in winter, dog sled or snowmobile. Some of the settlements can be visited by helicopter but none has any tourist infrastructure. Camping is always permitted on the outskirts of settlements.

Qaarsut The settlement you are most likely to visit is Qaarsut, but probably only as far as the tiny airport, which does have a café. Set on Greenland's mainland on the Nuussuaq Peninsula, there is nothing else that is of particular note. There is a small Pilersuisoq shop and you may spot that the sign on the airport says Uummannaq, just to confuse you.

Niaqornat Niaqornat is really small with a population of around 34, which has more than halved over the last 25 years. On the western end of the Nuussuaq Peninsula, there is a shop and school with a chapel extension, a heliport and an electricity generator. In 2011, the fish factory was reopened by the community, having been closed down earlier in the year by the government.

Qilakitsoq Qilakitsoq was another settlement on the Nuussuaq Peninsula, almost opposite Uummannaq Island. It was abandoned by the Inuit around 1811 and nobody is sure why. It does, however, tie in with the time that Europeans were hunting seals in large numbers. It is likely that those living in the settlement where unable to catch enough seals, using traditional hunting methods, to feed themselves. The settlement is now best known for the mummies (see opposite) that were found on the outskirts of the village in 1972.

Ikerassak and Saattut Both of these towns sit on islands of the same name, and both are hunting and fishing communities where the sled dogs easily outnumber the human population. And both towns have a Pilersuisoq shop.

Ukkusissat In the far north of the area, Ukkusissat is another small community of around 150. Founded around 1794, it has always been a very small settlement but it does have all the usual facilities including a Pilersuisoq shop, which also acts as check-in for the helistop.

Illorsuit Until 2017, when it was hit by a tsunami caused by a magnitude 4.1 earthquake, Illorsuit had 67 people living in it. The earthquake also triggered a landslip into the Karrat Fjord, and such was the damage that the village was abandoned the following year.

8

The Far North

There are few people in the world that live this far north, and those isolated communities that do see few visitors, apart from occasional expedition ships and groups of scientific researchers or explorers. Despite the arrival of modern forms of communication, the traditional Inuit way of life here has hardly changed for decades. This is Greenland at its extreme.

In summer the sun does not set for four months; in winter the polar darkness lasts for over three months and the sea ice stretches out to sea 'further than a dog sled can travel in a day'. Living here is unlike anywhere else, even in Greenland, and staying here is a chance to experience life on the edge. Without the skills of the Inuit, learned over hundreds of years, survival would not be possible.

Starting in the south of this region at the Uummannaq Fjord, the west coast is a continuous string of offshore islands running for 450km, among which are

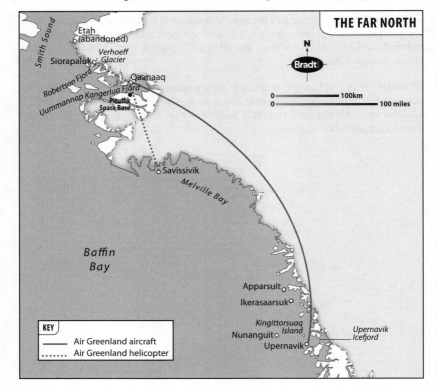

dotted 11 settlements. The largest is the town of Upernavik, while the smallest is Ikerasaarsuk with a permanent population of just one. North of this archipelago, the coast curves around Melville Bay and, for almost 400km, the ice sheet stretches to the sea, forming a barrier to both Inuit and migrating animals.

Just north of Melville Bay is Uummannaq Kangerlua Fjord, on whose shore is the small town of Qaanaaq, created in 1953 to make room for the US Space Base of Pituffik – controversial, incongruous and impossible to visit. Even further up the coast is Greenland's northernmost inhabited settlement, Siorapaluk. The North Pole is now much closer than Nuuk, and Arctic Canada is just 100km away across Smith Sound.

HISTORY

Inuit came to the Pituffik area from northern Canada across the narrow frozen straight as early as 2000BC, but the early Inuit settlers were displaced by later waves of migrants, the final one in around AD1100. Each wave of Inuit migration is named after where their remains were first found – this final wave was first identified in Thule and thus became known as the Thule Inuit.

In the early 19th century, the first contact between Europeans and the region's Inuit took place. In 1818 Sir John Ross, leading a British expedition, made contact and in 1849 James Saunders spent the winter here, his ship locked into the ice in North Star Bay. Robert Peary was the first foreigner to live on land here, using it as a base for his expeditions from 1892. Knud Rasmussen and Peter Freuchen named the location Thule when they established a missionary and trading post in 1910. It was Rasmussen who first noted that it would be an ideal location for an airstrip, an idea that he related to his friend US Colonel Balchen. In 1943 the US army established the Bluie East Six meteorological station at Pituffik, although the station was actually operated by Danes. It was one of many American 'Bluie' bases in Greenland, established during World War II to protect the island from German aggression and to provide weather reports to enable better planning by the Allies in Europe.

Once the war ended, rather than moving out, the US army enhanced the base with a gravel airstrip. Better housing, a power station and a radio station followed, establishing the US Armed Forces' most northerly base. Expansion meant that the Inuit who were living in Pituffik were relocated to the Thule Inuit settlement. However, in 1953, it was decided that even this settlement was too close to the US air base and the 130 inhabitants were moved again, this time to establish a new settlement at Qaanaaq, about 100km north. In 2003, the Danish Supreme Court ruled that this relocation was illegal and everyone affected was awarded damages.

During the Cold War, the USA needed the base at Thule for Strategic Air Command bombers and to detect and intercept incoming aircraft and missiles from the USSR. Over the years, there have been many projects based here, many quite bizarre. Project Iceworm planned to locate a network of 600 nuclear missile sites under the ice sheet in huge tunnels. Unstable ice conditions meant that the project collapsed before any missiles arrived. Operation Chrome Dome lasted from 1960 to 1968, an operation that ensured there was always at least one B-52 bomber armed with nuclear weapons in the air. The planes flew in circles around the USA and Canada, landing in Texas and at Thule. On 21 January 1968 one of them had a cabin fire and the crew had to abandon the aircraft, which then crashed in North Star Bay near Thule. The crash caused the conventional explosives on board to detonate and the area was contaminated with radiation. A massive clean-up operation took place, but part of one of the weapons was never found. Operation Chrome Dome was abandoned and controversy over the clean-up continues to this day.

Located on a small island, one of hundreds along the coast of Baffin Bay, Upernavik is the largest town in the far north, with a population of just over 1,000. The multi-coloured houses are spread across a south-facing hillside and, slightly strangely, the airstrip is on the top of the hill. Flying in, you are immediately struck by how many islands there are dotted along the coast and, everywhere, gigantic icebergs.

The settlement was founded here in 1772, but there is evidence that Norse explorers were in this area much earlier. On Kingittorsuaq Island, 20km further north, a Norse runestone was found, carefully positioned in a triangle made by three stone cairns and bearing the names of three Vikings. The stone has been dated to the 13th century and is now in the National Museum in Copenhagen.

In 1772, it was Danish whalers and sealers who set up the village though it seems to have been abandoned for long periods. It was only in 1826 that Danes established a permanent trading post and, seven years later, a mission. Hunting is still a part of everyday life here, but only licensed residents are allowed to hunt and they have strict annual quotas to adhere to. Narwhals, beluga whales, seals and polar bears are all stalked by local hunters. Fishing takes place all year round with cod, redfish and halibut common catches.

Owing to its airstrip – rather than a heliport – Upernavik is well connected to the rest of the country. There are services to Ilulissat every day except Sunday and to each of Qaanaaq, Kullorsuaq, Nuussuaq, Tasiusaq, Innaarsuit and Kangersuatsiaq two or three times a week.

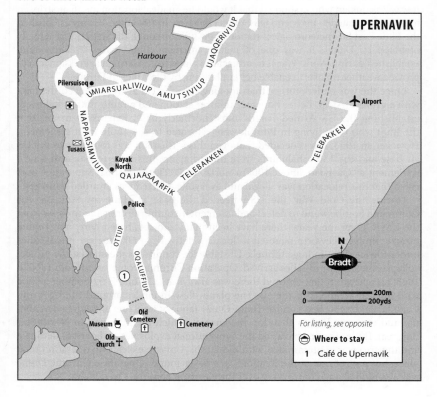

PITUFFIK SPACE BASE

In April 2023, the US Pituffik Space Base, or Space Base Delta One, came into being. The site, which had previously been named Thule and used as a US air base, is now a base for the USA's space surveillance, controlling sensors that enable the tracking of missiles and satellites; Pituffik is the original Inuit name for its location. There are up to 600 personnel on the base at any time – about two-thirds are Danish, a quarter American and 10% Greenlandic.

It is quite a place. There is an airport that handles more than 3,000 flights a year on a 3,000m runway – the longest in Greenland. The base itself has its own post office, chapel, hospital, police station, fire station, barbers, three restaurants, the Top of the World all-ranks club, a fitness centre, a library, a bakery, a dry cleaners, the North Star Inn hotel, a bowling alley and a combined cinema and theatre.

Unfortunately, you are unlikely to be able to visit any of these facilities as access for visitors requires a permit from the Danish Ministry of Foreign Affairs which is only issued if you have what they describe as a 'legitimate purpose'.

TOUR OPERATORS Zennifer and Nicolaj of **Kayak North** (Niuertup Ottup; ☎ 270820; w kayak-north.com) offer excellent guided kayak tours and can provide all the equipment that you need. Trips can last a couple of hours, a few days or even a couple of weeks. For overnight trips, they provide tents, sleeping bags, food and cooking equipment, and they are happy to include other activities, such as hiking.

 WHERE TO STAY AND EAT *Map, opposite*

Café de Upernavik (4 rooms) Niuertup Ottup; ☎ 270820; w kayak-north.com. This is currently not a café, although it may reopen during the lifetime of this guide. Rather there are 4 rooms sharing 2 bathrooms which can be rented. The owners run Kayak North. B/fast inc. **$$**

Upernavik Accommodations [not mapped] Aqqusinertaaq; ☎ 221312; e duda@upernavik.gl; w upernavik.gl. A selection of houses where you can either rent a whole house or just a room. All houses have kitchen, bathroom & lounge; running water is supplied from tanks. **$$**

OTHER PRACTICALITIES As you are likely to be cooking for yourself, you'll need the **Pilersuisoq** (⏰ 08.00–18.00 Mon–Fri, 09.00–14.00 Sat–Sun) at the northern end of town. A little further south, near the **hospital**, is the **Tusass** post office and phone shop (Napparsimaviup; ⏰ noon–15.00 Mon–Fri).

WHAT TO SEE AND DO At the very southern end of town, near the old harbour, you will find the museum, church and **old cemetery** (the current cemetery is further up the hill). Since the ground is permanently frozen, the graves are stone or concrete coffins, all above ground and arranged to face the sea so that the dead hunters can still keep watch. Among the graves is one to Navarana, the young Inuit wife of explorer Peter Freuchen (page 164) who died here of Spanish flu in 1921 when she was accompanying her husband on the fifth Thule expedition. She had not been baptised, so the priest refused to give her a Christian funeral, but Peter went ahead anyway with or without the priest's permission. The grave is marked with a curved metal plaque.

Upernavik is so far north that, from October to March, this is a great place to watch the **northern lights**.

Upernavik's **museum** (⏰ 10.00–noon & 13.00–15.00 Mon–Fri) is housed in six restored buildings, four of which are currently open, plus a peat house. The museum

The Far North UPERNAVIK

8

was founded in the early 1950s by Andreas Lund Drosvad and Helge Knudsen and may be the oldest museum in Greenland. Andreas moved to the country in 1925 as a teacher and, when he moved to Upernavik, became involved in improving the ways of fishing and hunting whales. He was an inveterate collector and accumulated most of the items now on show in the museum. Andreas also kept a daily diary, recording in great detail his life in Greenland, which he left to the Danish National Archive. The collection does, of course, have a lot of interesting fishing and hunting equipment including boats and sleds. There are also paintings by Gitz-Johansen, who visited Upernavik in the 1930s and 40s, and a whole collection of tupilaks carved by Otto Thomassen and his sons. The largest building, the administrator's residence, was originally erected in Imerissu around 1777, having been shipped out from Copenhagen. It was moved to Upernavik in 1832 and now houses the museum's office, shop and temporary exhibitions.

The **old church** was built in 1839 and from the 1950s was used for town council meetings. It is set up as it was in 1953 for one of these meetings, with all the furniture made by a local carpenter. There are also various archaeological finds including human skulls. The third building is the town's old shop, built in 1864 and displaying umiaks and kayaks, hunting tools and information about the animals that were hunted. The fourth building, the cooper's workshop, dates from 1848. The manufacture of barrels for the transport of seal and whale oil was critical to the town's economy. Latterly, the building was converted to being the town bakery before becoming part of the museum where it is now used as an artist's residence. The final two buildings are the old priest's residence, now the museum director's residence, and the old school, which has not yet been restored.

Around Upernavik, travel is by boat or kayak in summer and by snowmobile or dog sled in winter. It is interesting just to travel along the waterways and between the islands and giant icebergs. One of the most popular trips is up the **Upernavik Icefjord**, which is flanked by islands, to Upernavik Glacier. Birdwatchers can visit the **Nunanguit sea cliffs** just west of Upernavik to see a large common eider colony, or **Apparsuit**, further afield, where there is a large colony of guillemots. There are many small settlements, some abandoned, hidden among the islands and, weather permitting, it is possible to settlement-hop by boat or kayak.

QAANAAQ

The small town of Qaanaaq with just 630 people continues to attract explorers and adventurers, as it has done for more than 100 years. Explorers have lived with the Inuit and made use of their local knowledge and skills to survive in this unforgiving Arctic terrain. Both Knud Rasmussen and Robert Peary used Qaanaaq as a base from which to launch their expeditions.

Air Greenland flies more than once a week to and from Ilulissat, Upernavik, Pituffik and Siorapaluk. The airport is about 4km northwest of the town. In summer it may be possible to get a private boat transfer to Qaanaaq from settlements further south; in winter it may be possible to get a musher to bring you overland by dog sled.

TOUR OPERATORS

Guide to Greenland Inspektorbakken 8; w guidetogreenland.com. Between Jul & Sep, Guide to Greenland offers day trips from Qaanaaq, including an 8hr boat trip to Siorapaluk which heads towards the North Pole, & a 6hr trip sailing among the icebergs searching for wildlife, including narwhal. An 8-day trip with an Inuit hunter is also offered overnighting in tents & huts.

Nunataq Atsuk Travel 3971 Qaanaaq; ☎594366; e kristiansenaimads@gmail.com. This company is owned by Mads Ole Kristiansen, a trained Arctic guide who lives in Qaanaaq & has a wealth of local knowledge – he is also a musician & a sled & kayak builder. From Dec to Mar, dog-sled tours of 2–6 days are possible, sleeping in hunters' huts. From Jun to Aug, Mads Ole runs boat trips to watch walrus, narwhal, whales, seals & birds. He also offers hunting trips.

🏠 **WHERE TO STAY AND EAT** The **Hotel Qaanaaq** (✆ 971234; w hotelqaanaaq.dk; **$–$$**) is the only hotel and restaurant in town and is open all year. The hotel has terrific views across the bay and the lounge has a good selection of books about the area. The six double rooms share bathroom facilities. The restaurant (**$$**) serves three meals a day and is open to non-residents if you book in advance. Owner, Hans Jensen, can also help you organise trips, including dog sledding and hiking; between March and June, longer trips can include overnight stops sleeping in canvas tents erected over the sleds. You'll need a warm sleeping bag.

There is also a local bar, Tavfi (page 193).

OTHER PRACTICALITIES There is a Pilersuisoq shop (🕐 09.00–18.00 Mon–Fri, 10.00–13.00 Sat–Sun), which also houses the Tusass post office and phone shop (🕐 10.00–14.00 Mon–Thu, 06.00–17.00 Fri).

WHAT TO SEE AND DO The only visitors' site in town is the **museum**, housed in the former home of polar explorer Knud Rasmussen. It tells the story

---

LIFE IN QAANAAQ   *Edward Cooper*

Attractively situated on the shores of Inglefield Fjord and at the foot of an ice cap, Qaanaaq is Greenland's northernmost town. Vast icebergs grounded in the fjord dwarf its colourful houses in winter and summer. Qaanaaq is neighboured by two smaller settlements, Siorapaluk and Savissivik. The town itself is relatively new, built in 1953 to house the previously displaced inhabitants of Thule when the US military base there expanded during the Cold War.

The area around Qaanaaq is rich in history. Given its proximity to northern America, the surrounding area has been the gateway for Inuit migration to Greenland's shores for thousands of years. Its nearness to the North Pole and Northwest Passage has attracted Western explorers such as Peter Freuchen, Knud Rasmussen and Admiral Peary who were frequent visitors to the area. Peary made his North Pole attempt from the red cliffs of McCormick Bay which lies just around the corner.

The town is built on a hill and is split in two by a creek that runs from the glacier down to the fjord. There is a mix of original, wooden houses built for the displaced Thule Inuit and more modern housing to accommodate the expanding population. Despite its size it has all the amenities that you could hope for this far north: a well-sized supermarket, gymnasium, pub, hospital, church, museum and school. There is only one hotel, Hotel Qaanaaq, which is run by a charming elderly couple. The hotel is in the middle of town and boasts some of the best views across the bay. In the summer you can watch the hunters and local fishermen casting around in their boats and kayaks across the beautiful, iceberg-laden bay. In the winter, the bay turns to ice and visitors can watch a more traditional version of Greenland come to life. Down by the shore you will witness hunters dressed in fur clothing tending to their dogs and venturing out on sled journeys under vast, star-filled skies.

continued overleaf

SPRING AND THE RETURN OF THE SUN In February the sun, after four months of darkness, blesses the small town with its warming rays. It is a time for celebrations. The town gathers to wait for its return around the foot of the ice cap, with the more adventurous climbing to the hilltop to get an early sighting. A hush falls across the town as the first hints of light begin to appear as a burning orange glow. A roar erupts from the inhabitants as the sun pierces the top of the glacier to the south of Inglefield Bay. The dogs around town begin to howl as they sense the excitement. It is a cacophony of sound in a place where silence is a refreshing norm. It is only for an instant and then the sun is gone.

The day is marked by a dog-sled race out on the sea ice which is followed by kaffemiks hosted across town. These are a tradition, brought over by the Danes and the word literally means 'via coffee'. Hosts provide coffee, cake and other local delicacies. There is a palpable sense of relief after months of winter. The sun tells us that spring is just around the corner. For many this is the best time of year. A time when the days are becoming longer, the weather warmer and the ice still holds so that they can visit family and friends in the few towns that still remain in the northwest of Greenland.

LIFE OF FISHERMEN AND HUNTERS Sealing and whaling are traditional occupations in the area. With over 50% of the working population employed in public services, hunting is one of the few other options. Despite the many advancements in hunting technology employed commercially in other areas of the world, the hunters in Qaanaaq stick fiercely to traditional methods. The local Hunters' Union goes to great lengths to make sure that hunters adhere to these methods. Snowmobiles are banned and only dog sleds can be used in the winter. In the summer, speedboats are not allowed and hunters are required to use kayaks. The ban on sealskin imports to the EU in the 1970s had a dramatic effect on the hunting economy and there is still a lot of resentment over the implementation of this ban, the immediate impact of which, to the Inuit hunters, was an unintended and unforeseen consequence.

Halibut is now Greenland's largest export which has gone some way in replacing the lost income from seal. Strict quotas are in place for other animals such as narwhal, walrus and polar bear. Reindeer and musk oxen are also hunted locally. The animals' fur, meat and bones are used in clothing and for food. This is important given the town relies primarily on imports. Due to the high cost of air transport, when the sea ice freezes over in the winter, fresh vegetables and fruits are not available. The nutritional contribution of local, fresh meats is a key element in maintaining a nutritionally healthy diet for many of its inhabitants.

SOCIAL LIFE Kaffemiks are often held to mark special occasions such as birthdays, first days at school and confirmations. They are social gatherings where the host might prepare for days in advance to put on an array of foods along with the ever

of the area and of polar explorers, especially Rasmussen, Freuchen and Peary. The key to the museum can be collected from the school whenever it is open.

While the tourist infrastructure is not well developed here, the local people are very used to supporting visitors and explorers and will readily offer to help. They can accompany you on hikes or take you out in their boats, and you may be able present coffee. Homes become a revolving door for friends, family and colleagues who visit throughout the day. Tables are decked out in finery and laden with sweets such as apple tarts and marzipan cookies. Often larger meals are cooked, with reindeer, fish soup and musk ox all present.

Tavfi is the local bar, a small, wooden building on the eastern side of town at the top of the slope. The hospitality is welcoming and while there is no food on offer there is an array of alcohol available and a DJ who plays classic Western music late into the night. Over-indulgence is a risk, particularly in the winter months given the bar's situation at the top of an icy slope and the extremely cold temperatures.

Public celebrations are held in the school and the gymnasium where local bands and performers provide a range of entertainment from traditional choral singing and dancing to modern rock music.

Qaanaaq's main attraction is the museum on the eastern side of the town. The building itself was the original trading post built by Knud Rasmussen in 1910 and transported from Thule to Qaanaaq. It houses a number of interesting artefacts including traditional harpoons, clothing and a large chunk of meteorite which the area is known for.

COMMUNICATING WITH THE REST OF GREENLAND Qaanaaq is serviced by a giant satellite dish at the head of town which provides mobile phone reception and internet. A local SIM card can be purchased from a small shop at the base of the satellite dish for longer stays. Hotel Qaanaaq can provide internet access. Internet may be slower than in other parts of the world.

HOW LIFE IS CHANGING While the average age in Qaanaaq is on the rise, many of the younger inhabitants choose to stay in the area or indeed return after a period of studies or work abroad in Denmark. Despite being a difficult place to get to and with limited infrastructure in place, tourism is growing with many being lured to Qaanaaq by the hiking, sledding and wildlife-spotting opportunities available. USAID have recently announced a programme of English language education which can only make it more accessible and attractive to visitors by removing the current language barriers (Inuktitut, West Greenlandic and Danish are the most commonly taught and spoken languages in the area). Fishing is on the rise, as with the rest of Greenland, which should also provide a more sustainable source of income for hunters restricted by quotas on animals.

In 2014–15, modern-day explorer Edward Cooper lived for many months with the people of Qaanaaq and immersed himself in their way of life while preparing for his expedition to cross the sea ice from Greenland to the Canadian Nunavut islands. The story of this amazing journey is captured in his book The Inuit Way *(Journey Books, 2022). In the above text Edward describes his daily life with the Inuit.*

to try some long-line fishing. The waters off Qaanaaq are also where you are most likely to spot narwhal – they breed off the coast here.

In winter, the sea freezes and supply boats are unable to reach the community, and icebergs are frozen in where they stay until the spring thaw. A magical trip is to take a dog sled across this frozen wonderland, travelling between the icebergs and watching the northern lights appear in a dark winter sky.

SAVISSIVIK

Just off the northern coast of Melville Bay, the tiny island of Meteorite is inhabited by 50 people who live in its only settlement at Savissivik. Surrounded by giant icebergs, this is a challenging place to live, and the population has halved over the last 30 years. Savissivik in Greenlandic means 'the place where you find iron for knives'. It is believed that about 10,000 years ago a meteorite exploded in this area providing the Inuit with material to make ulu, Greenlandic knives (page 21). Numerous fragments from the meteorite – which it is believed weighed 100 tonnes before it exploded – have been found on the island.

CROSSING THE ICE SHEET

Until the 1800s there was no record of anyone having crossed the vast ice sheet that covers Greenland. Without planes to give an aerial view, it was impossible to assess the size and terrain of the ice sheet.

In 1888 a brave young Norwegian, Fridtjof Nansen, decided to attempt to cross from the east coast to the west coast. After his ship *Jason* became trapped in sea ice 56km offshore, Nansen and his five colleagues abandoned the vessel and headed west on the sea ice, pulling five sledges each laden with 90kg of gear. After several days, they eventually reached the ice sheet, only to be faced with a vertical cliff of ice and then a succession of steep ice ridges. Pulling sledges over the ridges was exhausting and dangerous; the crevasses between them so deep that they seemed bottomless.

Once through the crevasse zone, the ground was smoother and, for a while, progress improved. Strong winds and snow frequently caused white-out conditions and for days they were confined to their tent. Inside the tent, temperatures dropped to –40°C and they huddled three to a sleeping bag to keep warm. Slowly they dragged their sledges to the middle of the ice sheet, reaching an altitude of 2,500m and discovered that the ice sheet was not flat but domed. Good news, as the second half of their journey would be downhill. All was going well until they neared the western edge of the ice sheet when, again, they reached a zone of endless deep crevasses, ridge after ridge of ice and a series of parallel gaping holes. Finally, after two months, Nansen's team reached the west coast, thus completing the first ever crossing of Greenland.

In the spring of 1892, a young civil engineer from New York, Robert Peary, decided to cross from the west coast to the east by following the northern coast of Greenland with four men, sledges and dogs. On the route they encountered an Inuit settlement and befriended the people, who made them clothes out of animal skins for their onward journey. Conditions were difficult and slow and eventually they had to shoot all the dogs to provide food. On reaching the north coast, Peary described the view: '…deep valleys, mountains capped with cloud-shadowed domes of ice, stretched away in a wild panorama, upon which no human eyes had ever looked on before'. Retracing their steps, Peary and his companion were near to death when they eventually made it back to base camp after three months; they had travelled nearly 1,000km on the ice sheet. By reaching Independence Fjord they had achieved their goal, proving that Greenland was in fact an island.

American explorer Robert Peary was the first foreigner to see the meteorite remains in 1894 with the help of an Inuit guide. He then worked for three years to remove the largest single piece, which weighed 31 tonnes. He shipped it to the USA and sold it to the American Museum of Natural History in New York for $40,000 (equivalent to $1.3 million today). A slightly smaller fragment, weighing about 20 tonnes, can be seen in the Museum of the University of Copenhagen in Denmark.

Savissivik is not an easy location to reach. Air Greenland does operate a helicopter service to Qaanaaq via Pituffik Space Base weekly; and a few expedition and cruise ships call on their way to explore the Northwest Passage.

The next explorer to attempt a crossing was a young Greenlander, Knud Rasmussen. As a boy he was told by an old Greenlandic lady that people who lived in the north dressed in bearskins and ate raw meat; he had to find out if this was true. Fascinated by the Inuit culture, he lived with a northern Inuit community for eight months until he joined up with fellow explorer Peter Freuchen. With two Inuit companions, four sledges and 53 dogs, they followed a similar route to Peary, exploring even deeper along the north coast. The journey was tough but they did find time to draw maps, record plants and locate evidence of an ancient Inuit camp. They also succeeded in proving that one of Peary's claims was incorrect: Peary Land was not divided by a channel from the mainland of Greenland.

A young German, Alfred Wegener, heard about these expeditions. He believed that 'ice, seas and climate share a tangle of important links and Greenland is the key to understanding a much larger complex system'. In 1913, Wegener was joined by a Dane, John Peter Koch, to attempt another east–west crossing, this time across the widest part of the island. With four men, sleds and 13 horses, they embarked on a 1,050km journey. The following weeks and months were plagued with incidents. Wegener fell and broke his ribs, they lost some horses and supplies when a glacier suddenly calved; Koch fell into a crevasse and lost his theodolite. Progress was slow, they had to rest in their tents while injuries repaired and eventually they resorted to eating all their remaining horses. When they finally reached the west coast they had spent nearly a year on the ice.

Today you can hike across the ice sheet with modern equipment. Organisations like Adventure Consultants (w adventureconsultants.com), Greenland Adventures (w greenland.is), Jagged Globe (w jagged-globe.co.uk), Polar Explorers (w polarexplorers.com) and Sandgrouse Travel (w sandgrousetravel.com) will help you with logistics and provide back-up safety cover. The 600km crossing will take about 30 days; even with support, this is an extremely tough hike requiring a high level of fitness.

However, if you are reasonably fit, you can experience a trek in the Arctic wilderness; not across the ice sheet but still remote and following the Arctic Circle. The Arctic Circle Trail, 165km long, starts at Kangerlussuaq at the western edge of the ice sheet and finishes at the west-coast fishing town of Sisimiut. The route takes between one and two weeks and along the way there are huts you can stay in for free. More than 300 hikers complete the trail every year (page 140).

This small community does have a Pilersuisoq (◷ 09.00–15.00 Mon–Fri, 09.00–noon Sat), a church, a school and a heliport, but there is nowhere for a visitor to stay overnight.

SIORAPALUK

Siorapaluk is the northernmost settlement in Greenland at 78°N. The brightly coloured houses huddle together on the northern shore of the Robertson Fjord 50km north of Qaanaaq. At this latitude, the midnight sun lasts for 120 days and, in winter, for 108 days there is complete darkness. This is a close-knit self-sufficient community of only 41 people, and many of the inhabitants are descendants of the Inuit from the Canadian Arctic (Nunavut) who travelled across the Smith Sound in 1880 and settled here. Both Greenlandic and Inuktitut dialect are spoken.

Today to reach this isolated settlement you can take a helicopter three times a week from Qaanaaq 55km away. The heliport is only 250m north of town. In summer, a boat or, in winter, a dog sled will also transport you from Qaanaaq. The school and church are combined in one building as there are fewer than ten pupils. Unbelievably in this remote location there is a Pilersuisoq (◷ 09.00–15.00 Mon–Fri, 09.00–noon Sat). Because of the persistent sea ice, supply ships venture this far north only two to three times a year in midsummer.

Spending time in this community gives you a glimpse of their daily life. There is no tourist accommodation, but it is sometimes possible to stay and eat with a local family – contact Nunataq Atsuk in Qaanaaq (page 190). Even though there is now electricity, internet and satellite television, life is still tough and dependent on hunting and fishing and preserving the catch.

It is worth taking a boat trip along the **Robertson Fjord**, famous for the millions of little auks that arrive every May to breed in the mountains. At the head of the fjord you can see the **Verhoeff Glacier**. You might also see Arctic hares or foxes on the way.

Heading 78km northwest will take you to the abandoned settlement of **Etah**. It was once the most northerly populated settlement in the world, but in the 1980s the last Inuit relocated south in search of a less harsh climate and easier life. It is still a favourite spot, however, for polar bears. Today Etah is often used as a starting point for expeditions, including attempts to reach the North Pole. It looks across the Nares Strait to Ellesmere Island, an area usually frozen from October to July. This was the crossing point for Inuit for thousands of years, and still remains a crossing point for wildlife. Guide to Greenland (page 34) offers a day tour from Qaanaaq to Siorapaluk between July and September. This 6-hour trip gives you enough time to walk around the settlement and along the coast and visit the little auks' nesting site.

Appendix 1

LANGUAGE   *with Mirjam Johannesen*

There are three distinct dialects of Greenlandic: Kalaallisut, Inuktun and Tunumiit oraasia. All are Inuit languages and are closely related to the native languages of the north of North America and Siberia. Kalaallisut, or West Greenlandic, has been the official language of Greenland since 2009 and is the Greenland dialect used by 85% of the population. It is the language used in this section. Inuktun is the dialect of the Thule region and the Tunumiit oraasia dialect is used in east Greenland – both these dialects have only oral forms; they have no agreed written form. The three dialects are significantly different and people using one dialect are generally not understood by speakers from a different region. Most Inuit in Thule and east Greenland do also speak Kalaallisut and everything is written in Kalaallisut throughout the country.

Greenlandic is a language in which words are made by stringing together roots and suffixes. This allows the creation of long words which might be a whole sentence in most languages and look daunting to pronounce. However, if you just pronounce all the letters of the long word then you are likely to be understood as the written language is phonetic.

ALPHABET AND PRONUNCIATION There are only 18 letters in the Greenlandic alphabet – the letters B, C, D, H, W, X, Y and Z do not appear. If you see a word with any of these letters in it, then it is not Greenlandic and is probably Danish. Similarly, there are no accented letters, so if you come across é, æ, ø or å, then, again, it is probably a Danish word.

Most letters are pronounced in the same way as in English but there are, of course, a few exceptions. Doubled vowels – *aa*, *ii* and *uu* – are pronounced the same but held a little longer.

g	as *ch* in a Scottish *loch*
j	as *y* in *yes*
q	as *k* in *kite*
ai	as the English *eye*
gg	as *sh* in *shoe*
ll	as the double *ll* in Welsh or the *l* in *clue*
ng	as *ng* in *sing*
rn	as *ng* in *song*
rr	as *ch* in the German *ach*

VOCABULARY
Essentials

Good morning	*Ullaannguaq*
Hello	*Aluu*
Have a good afternoon	*Ulloq naalluariuk*

197

Have a good evening	*Unnuk naalluariuk*
See you	*Takuss*
Goodbye	*Baj*
My name is…	*…imik ateqarpunga.*
What is your name?	*Qanoq ateqarpit?*
I am from…	*…inngaaneerpunga.*
Pleased to meet you	*Nuanneq naapillutit*
Thank you	*Qujanaq*
Cheers!	*Kasuutta!*
Yes	*Aap*
No	*Naamik*
I don't understand	*Paasinngilara*
Please speak more slowly	*Arriitsumik oqalulaarit*
Do you understand?	*Paasiviuk?*

Questions

How?	*Qanoq?*
What?	*Suna?*
Where?	*Sumi?*
What is it?	*Sunaana?*
Which?	*Sorleq?*
When?	*Qaqugu?*
Why?	*Sooruna?*
Who?	*Kina?*
How much does it cost?	*Qanoq annikinngitsoq?*

Numbers

1	*ataaseq*	16	*arfersanillit/sajstanit*
2	*marluk*	17	*arfersaneq-marluk/sytteni*
3	*pingasut*	18	*arfersaneq-Pingasut/attenit*
4	*sisamat*	19	*arfersaneq-sisamat/nittanit*
5	*tallimat*	20	*marlunnik qulillit/tyvit*
6	*arfinillit*	30	*tredivit*
7	*arfineq marluk*	40	*fooru*
8	*arfineq pingasut*	50	*halvtredsit*
9	*qulingiluat*	60	*tressit*
10	*qulit*	70	*halvfjerdsit*
11	*aqqanillit*	80	*firs*
12	*aqqaneq marluk*	90	*halvfamsi*
13	*aqqaneq pingasut*	100	*hunnoruju-veq*
14	*aqqaneq sisamat*	1,000	*tusindit*
15	*aqqaneq tallimat/faamten*	many	*amerlasuut*

Time

What time is it?	*Qassinngorpa?*	today	*ullumikkut*
…o'clock	*…nngorpoq*	tonight	*unnugu*
morning	*ullaaq*	tomorrow	*aqagu*
afternoon	*ualeq*	yesterday	*ippassaq*
evening	*unnuk*		

Days

Monday	*Ataasinngorneq*	Friday	*Tallimanngorneq*
Tuesday	*Marlunngorneq*	Saturday	*Arfininngorneq*
Wednesday	*Pingasunngorneq*	Sunday	*Sapaat*
Thursday	*Sisamanngorneq*		

Months

January	*Januaari*	July	*Juuli*
February	*Februaari*	August	*Aggusti*
March	*Marsi*	September	*Septembari*
April	*Apriili*	October	*Oktobari*
May	*Maaji*	November	*Novembari*
June	*Juuni*	December	*Decembari*

Getting around on public transport

I would like a ticket	*Bilitsimik piserusuppunga...*
...one-way	*...siumuinnaq*
...return	*...siumut-utimut*
I want to go to...	*Angalarusuppunga...*
How much is it?	*qanoq akeqarpa?*
What time does it leave?	*qassinut aallassava?*
The ferry has been...	*Sinersortaat...*
...delayed	*...kinguarpoq*
...cancelled	*...taamaatsinneqarput*
here	*tamaani*
there	*tassani/taakani*
airport	*mittarfik*
arrival	*tikiffissaq*
boat	*angallat*
bus stop	*bussit unittarfiat*
bus	*bussit*
car	*biilit*
departure	*aallarfissaq*
dog sled	*qimussit*
dog	*qimmeq*
ferry	*umiarsuaq*
harbour	*umiarsualivik*
plane	*timmisartoq*
skis	*sisoraatit*
snowmobile	*qamuteralaat*
snowshoes	*apusiutit*
taxi	*taxa*
ticket office	*billetsilerivik*
timetable	*anguniagassatut pilersaarutiliaq*

Getting around on private transport

Is this the road to...?	*manna aqqusineruvoq...?*
Where is the service station?	*sumi garage-veq ippa?*
Please fill it up	*orsersinnaaviuk*
I'd like...litres	*literimut orserusuppara...*
diesel	*dieseli*

petrol	benziina
danger	navianartoq
no entry	Isertoqaqqusaanngilaq

Directions

Where is it?	sumiippa?	east	kangi
Go straight ahead	siumuinnaq	west	kitkimi
left	saamerleq	in front of	iffiorna
right	talerpik	near	qanittoq saniani
north	avani	opposite	akerleq
south	kujatimi		

Signs

entrance	isaariaq
exit	anisarfik
open	ammavoq
closed	matoqqavoq
toilets – men/women	perusuersartarfik angutit/arnat
information	paasissutissaq

Accommodation

Where is a cheap/good hotel?	Sumi akikitsumik unnuisarfeqarpa?
Could you write the address?	Najugaqarfik allassinnaavat?
Do you have any rooms available?	Inissaqarpa?
I'd like…	
…a single room	kisermaattariaqarusuppunga
…a double room	ini marluuttariaq
…a room with two beds	ini siniffiit marluk ilaginnikkusuppunga
…a room with a bathroom	ini uffarfimmik ineqarusuppunga
…to share a dorm	inersuaq sinittarfimmi siniffik
How much it is per night/person?	Qanoq akeqarpa unnummut/inummut ataatsimut?
Where is the bathroom?	Sumi perusuersartarfeqarpa?
Is there hot water?	Imeq kissartoqarpoq?
Is there electricity?	Sarfaqarpa?
Is breakfast included?	Ullaakkorsiutit ilaareerpat?
I am leaving today	Ullumikkut ingeqqissaanga

Eating out

Do you have a table for…people?	Inunnut…inissaqarpa?
I am a vegetarian/vegan	Naasuinnarnik/veganer nerisaliuvunga
Please bring me a…	…atorsinnaavunga
…fork/knife/spoon	ajassaammik/savimmik/alussaamik…
Please may I have the bill?	Akiligassaq tigusinnaavara?

Food

apples	iipilit	butter	punneq
bananas	bananit	carrots	musaq
beef	bøffi-veq	cheese	immussuaq
beer	immiaq	chicken	kukkukooq
bread	iffiaq	cod	saarullik
broccoli	broccolit	coffee	kaffi

dried meat	nikkut	potato	naatsiiaq
dried...	...panertoq	reindeer meat	tuttup neqaa
fish	aalisagaq	salt	taratsut
fruit juice	frugtjuice	seal meat	puisip neqaa
fruit	paarnaq	shrimp	raajat
greenland halibut	qaleralik	sugar	sukkut
lamb	sava	tea	tii
meat	neqi	vegetables	naatitat
milk	immuk	walrus meat	aarrup neqaa
oil	uulia	water	imeq
onion	uanitsoq	whale meat	arferup neqaa
pepper	qasilitsoq	wine	viinni
pork	puulukip neqaa		

Shopping

I'd like to buy...	Piserusuppunga
How much is it?	Ganoq akeqarpa?
I don't like it	Nuannarinngilara
It's too expensive	Akisuallaarpoq
I will buy it	Pisiariniarpara
Do you accept credit cards?	Akiliissutinik akuersuivutit?
more	annikinngitsoq
less/smaller	mikineq
bigger	angineq

Communications

I am looking for...	...sumiippa
...bank	Banki...
...post office	Allakkerivik...
...church	Oqaluffik...
...ATM	ATM...
...tourist office	Takornariaqarnermut allaffik...
...phone	Oqarasuaat...
I am looking for internet	Sumi Internet-eqarpa

Emergency

Help!	Ikiu
Call a doctor!	Nakorsamut sianerit
There's been a fatal accident	Ajunaarnerunikuuvoq
There's been a non-fatal accident	Ajutoortoqarpoq
I'm lost	Tammarpunga
Go away!	Peerit!
police	politiit
fire	qatserisartoqarfik
ambulance	ambulanci
thief	tillinniaq
hospital/clinic	napparsimmavik/nakorsiartarfik
I am ill	Pitsaanngilanga

Health

I am...

...asthmatic	*issanngusartuuvunga*
...epileptic	*noqartartuuvunga*
...diabetic	*sukkortuuvunga*
I'm allergic to...	*...sapigaqarpunga*
...penicillin	*penicillinimik...*
...nuts	*qaqqortarissanik...*
...bees	*igutsaat...*

antibiotics	*antibiotikummi-veq*
antiseptic	*antiseptisk*
condoms	*usuup puua*
contraceptive	*præventionsmiddel*
diarrhoea	*timminneq*
doctor	*nakorsaq*
midge net	*ippernaaqqut*
nausea	*meriannguneq*
paracetamol	*paracetamol*
pharmacy	*nakorsaataarniarfik*
sanitary pad	*nalequtaq*
sunscreen	*palersaat*
tampons	*tampongi-veq*

Travelling with children

baby changing room	*Nuunuaqqanut taarsiisarfeqarpa*
children's menu	*Meeqqanut nerisassaqarpa*
infant milk formula	*arnap immuanut taartaasoq*
nappies	*nangit*
potty	*qorfik*
highchair	*meeqqamut issiaveqarpa*
Are children allowed?	*Meeqqat iseqqusaappat?*

Other words

and/but	*aamma/kisianni*
this	*una/taanna*
beautiful	*kusanaq*
old/new	*pisoqaq/nutaaq*
early/late	*siusissoq/kingusittoq*
hot/cold	*kissartoq/nillertoq*
difficult/easy	*ajornartoq/oqittoq*

Appendix 2

GLOSSARY

ACT	Arctic Circle Trail (page 140).
angakkuq	an Inuit shaman; a spiritual and cultural leader who may also have been a traditional healer.
ATV	all-terrain vehicle; a typically lightweight vehicle having four-wheel drive and including quad bikes. ATVs can usually accommodate only one driver and a pillion passenger.
CITES	Convention on International Trade in Endangered Species of Wild Fauna and Flora; a multilateral treaty that endeavours to protect endangered flora and fauna from exploitation by international trade (page 58).
dry toilets	Flush toilets are often not possible in remote settlements. So-called dry toilets usually either use a bag, which is removed and sealed, or a bucket, which may contain some neutral material, wood ash or sawdust. There are also chemical toilets, which have a holding tank that is primed with a chemical to minimise odours.
glacier	a large mass of ice formed from fallen snow over many years and moving outwards from the ice sheet towards the coast.
GPS	Global Positioning System; a satellite system that allows devices to know their location by receiving messages from the satellites. GPS systems are found on most smartphones.
gpx files	text files that list a series of waypoints; they can be downloaded into GPS devices and smartphone mapping apps to show a route.
ice sheet	a mass of glacial ice that covers at least 50,000km². There are only two ice sheets in the world, the Greenlandic and the Antarctic.
kaffemik	a not-to-be-missed open house coffee and cake party (page 66).
kayak	a small, narrow closed boat, traditionally for one person and paddled with a double-ended oar. The name comes from the Inuit word *qajaq*.
nasiffik	a Greenlandic word meaning a lookout, particularly one used for whale watching.
piste machine	a tracked vehicle, usually with a snow blade at the front and a brush or roller at the rear. These machines are used to prepare tracks for snowmobiles and snowshoes and are also used as a means of transport.
piteraqs	the local name for a katabatic wind that blows down from the ice sheet at more than 180km/h, most commonly experienced on Greenland's east coast.

qajaq	see *kayak*; but also a brand of good beer.
qilaat	a drum that looks rather like a giant tambourine, played with a wooden stick or bone.
runestone	a standing stone, usually with a runic inscription and often dedicated to the deceased.
sermeq	glacier, in Greenlandic.
service house	a public building where villagers can wash, take a shower and do their washing. Service houses are most common in settlements where some houses are not connected to a water supply. The service house may also offer other facilities such as a communal workshop. Service houses may be used by visitors, usually for a small fee.
SUP	stand-up paddleboard; a floating board rather like a surfboard which is paddled by the rider who stands on the board, using a single long paddle.
tupilak	a spirit, but today this is used to mean a carved figure that represents a spirit (page 27).
ulu	a 'woman's knife' with a curved blade and T- or D-shaped handle. Ulu were used for many things, from cleaning skins to cutting hair, from trimming ice blocks to preparing food.
umiak	a 'woman's boat'; a large traditional skin-covered open boat used by women. Umiak are stable in the coastal waters and can also be dragged over sea ice.
UTM	Universal Transverse Mercator co-ordinate system; an international system of mapping co-ordinates used on some maps and by some GPS devices.
UTV	Utility or Ultra Terrain Vehicle; an off-road, four-wheel drive vehicle with at least two seats, side by side, and often two rows of seats. It is a larger type of ATV.
votive ship	displayed in many churches, and often constructed by sailors or shipbuilders, these ships are focal points for those making vows, offering prayers for those at sea or giving thanks for good fortune.

Appendix 3

FURTHER INFORMATION

BOOKS

Boertmann, David *Birds in Greenland* Ilinniusiorfik Education, 2003. The best English-language book for Greenland's birds; stocked by the Nuuk bookshop Atuagkat Bolghandel (page 81) if you can't find a copy locally.

Bown, Stephen *White Eskimo* Hachette Books, 2015. A very complete biography of Knud Rasmussen, capturing his childhood, his sense of adventure and his understanding of the Inuit culture.

Cooper, Edward *The Inuit Way* Journey Books 2022. Ed Cooper crosses 450km of the Arctic following in the footsteps of explorer David Haig-Thomas. This book also gives an insight into the traditions and customs of the Inuit people living in the far north of Greenland.

Dillon, Paddy *Trekking in Greenland: The Arctic Circle Trail* Cicerone, 2023. This is the best English-language guidebook to the Arctic Circle Trail and a must-read if you plan to do the trail. It does not, despite the title, cover any other trekking in Greenland except extra walks at the start and end of the trail.

Ehrich, Gretel *This Cold Heaven* Fourth Estate, 2003. Part history, part culture and part travelogue, Gretel Ehrich clearly loves Greenland. This book is not only a record of Inuit lives and cultures, both of which are changing remarkably fast, but also of her adventures over many years, criss-crossing Greenland.

Gertner, Jon *The Ice at the End of the World* Icon Books, 2020. A very readable book of an epic journey into Greenland's buried past and our perilous future.

Haig-Thomas, David *Tracks in the Snow* Hodder & Stoughton, 1939. David Haig-Thomas was an Olympian, a world traveller, an ornithologist and an explorer. In 1934, he worked under Shackleton on an expedition to Ellesmere Island and in 1937 led his own two-man expedition, himself and an Inuit guide, across northern Greenland. His record of this ground-breaking expedition forms most of this book; archaeological artefacts from the expedition are now in the British Museum. The book is out of print but available on Amazon Kindle.

Hall, Adrian *Follow that Musk Ox: Tales from Milne Land* Lulu, 2016. Kindle edition. An expedition to Milne Land, a remote island in the middle of the world's largest fjord in east Greenland.

Halliday, Geoffrey *A Flora of the East Greenland Central Fjord Region* Trollius Publications, 2019. The book gives accounts of individual species with modern taxonomy and includes information on altitudinal and latitudinal limits.

Hessell, Ingo *Inuit Art* British Museum Press, 1998. While being focused on the Canadian Inuit, this illustrated book gives a comprehensive introduction to Inuit Art irrespective of its geography.

Howarth, David *Sledge Patrol* Lyons, 2018. A gripping true story set in World War II about a group of men who patrolled the coast of northeast Greenland and encountered German soldiers setting up a meteorological station.

Jespersen, Kirsten & Olsen, Lissi *Greenland Plants for Body and Soul* Milik Publishing, 2022. An excellent guide to Greenland's plants and their use medicinally and in food and drink.

Kpomassie, Tété-Michel *Michel the Giant: An African in Greenland* Penguin Classic, 2022. The true story of one man's ten-year journey from a village in Togo, West Africa, to a new life in Greenland, where he had to adapt to the Greenlandic culture.

Nansen, Fridtjof *The First Crossing of Greenland* Frostbitten Tales, 2012. The story of Nansen's trek across the ice sheet, translated by Hubert Majendie Gepp and with all the original illustrations.

Rasmussen, Knud *Across Arctic America* University of Alaska Press, 1999. This is Rasmussen's own condensed account of his 32,000km journey by dog sled from Greenland to Siberia in 1921–24. Other books by Knud Rasmussen describing his expeditions in Greenland and the Arctic and still in print include *The People of the Polar North* (Andesite Press, 2015) and *Greenland by the Polar Sea* (Forgotten Books, 2018).

Rasmussen, Knud *Eskimo Folk-Tales* Create Space, 2015. Translated and edited by W Worster, this interesting little book is full of folk stories collected by Knud Rasmussen as he travelled through Greenland and other Inuit lands. The original book was illustrated with drawings by 'Eskimos' but the current version on sale is not illustrated.

Rix, Robert W *The Vanishing Settlers of Greenland* Cambridge University Press, 2023. Whatever happened to the Viking settlers who just seemed to disappear? Robert delves into one of Greenland's real mysteries.

Rune, Flemming *Wild Flowers of Greenland* Glydenlund, 2011. The definitive guidebook with every wildflower pictured and described in English and Danish.

Schmidt Mikkelsen, Peter *One Thousand Days with Sirius: The Greenland Sledge Patrol* Steading Workshop, 2005. Translated by David Matthews, himself once a geologist with the British Antarctic Survey, this tells the true story of the author's working life in the far northwest of Greenland between 1977 and 1980.

Sejersen, Frank *Rethinking Greenland and the Arctic in the Era of Climate Change* Routledge, 2016. An in-depth study of how the Inuit are dealing with the challenges of climate change.

Soper, Tony *Arctic: A guide to coastal wildlife* Bradt Guides, 2016. A detailed full-colour guide to plants, fish, animals and birds of the Arctic, with fine illustrations by wildlife artist Dan Powell.

WEBSITES The website w **greenlandic-english.vercel.app** is the only translator that handles English to West Greenlandic. It is not foolproof, but it is pretty good if you keep your sentence reasonably simple.

Government

w **dmi.dk** Denmark's Meteorological Institute provides good weather information for Greenland.

w **droneregler.dk/english** Laws regarding the use of drones in Denmark. The laws apply in Greenland too. Greenland also has a regulation that prohibits drones being used to film or pursue polar bears.

w **nyidanmark.dk** The Danish Immigration Service's website.

w **um.dk/en/about-us/organisation/find-us-abroad** The Foreign Ministry list of Danish embassies.

Hiking

w **avenza.com** Home of a mapping app, for Android and iPhones, which supports maps from many different suppliers including Greenland Tourism Trekking maps.

w **compukort.dk/Compukort/Grnlandskort.html** Greenland Tourism Trekking maps.

w **hiking.gl** Produced by Destination Arctic Circle, this site has some good walks in the Sisimiut, Kangerlussuaq and Maniitsoq areas.

w **magnetic-declination.com** Accurate and up-to-date information on magnetic declination. You need to understand this if you plan to use a map and compass in Greenland.

w **sagamaps.dk** Sagamaps homepage.

Jobs

w **workaway.info** A community of travellers and work opportunities across the world run by a not-for-profit organisation who charge a small membership fee.

w **workingtraveller.com** Another worldwide job opportunities service with a €10 membership fee, endeavouring to put travellers in touch with would-be employers.

Nature and the environment

w **aurorareach.com** Aurora Reach provides a forecast for the northern lights by city, taking into account cloud cover and visibility, solar wind and activity, and hours of darkness and of daylight.

w **g-e-m.dk** Greenland Ecosystem Monitoring, a long-term monitoring programme which has been running since 1995. It is probably the most comprehensive monitoring of Arctic climate.

w **greenlandtrees.org** Charity growing and planting trees. They used to import all the trees they planted but, since 2022, they have had their own greenhouse in Narsaq where they propagate native trees.

w **happywhale.com** A worldwide catalogue of whale sightings that you can contribute to. If you get a good photograph of a humpback's tail or the back and dorsal fin of most other whales, then this can contribute to their database. You may find out where the whale has been spotted before and get emails months or even years later telling you of new sightings of your whale.

w **natur.gl** Greenland's Institute of Natural Resources monitors the Arctic environment, including wildlife. Their population surveys of hunted mammals and birds are used as part of the hunting quota process.

w **summitcamp.org** The Summit Station is a research and weather station located in the centre of the ice sheet at 3,200m. It has a webcam plus graphs of weather. In midsummer it might be −18°C with a −24°C wind chill factor.

News

w **scitechdaily.com** Informed science and technology coverage and analysis every day.

w **sermitsiaq.ag** Greenland's newspaper online. It gives an excellent insight into daily life in Greenland.

Tourist information

w **destinationarcticcircle.com** Tourist information for the area from Sisimiut and Maniitsoq to Kangerlussuaq.

w **diskobay.gl** Disko Bay tourist information.

w **eastgreenland.com** East Greenland tourist information.

w **politi.gl/politistationer** The official map showing every police station in Greenland.

w **visitgreenland.com** Greenland's national tourist organisation's comprehensive site with a wealth of in-depth information.

w **visitnuuk.com** Nuuk's tourist information with a good events calendar.

w **visitsouthgreenland.com** South Greenland's wide-ranging tourist information website.

Index

Page numbers in **bold** indicate major entries; those in *italic* indicate maps.

INDEX OF ADVERTISERS

THE BRADT STORY

In the beginning
It all began in 1974 on an Amazon river barge. During an 18-month trip through South America, two adventurous young backpackers – Hilary Bradt and her then husband, George – decided to write about the hiking trails they had discovered through the Andes. *Backpacking Along Ancient Ways in Peru and Bolivia* included the very first descriptions of the Inca Trail. It was the start of a colourful journey to becoming one of the best-loved travel publishers in the world; you can read the full story on our website (**bradtguides. com/ourstory**).

Getting there first
Hilary quickly gained a reputation for being a true travel pioneer, and in the 1980s she started to focus on guides to places overlooked by other publishers. The Bradt Guides list became a roll call of guidebook 'firsts'. We published the first guide to Madagascar, followed by Mauritius, Czechoslovakia and Vietnam. The 1990s saw the beginning of our extensive coverage of Africa: Tanzania, Uganda, South Africa, and Eritrea. Later, post-conflict guides became a feature: Rwanda, Mozambique, Angola, and Sierra Leone, as well as the first standalone guides to the Baltic States following the fall of the Iron Curtain, and the first post-war guides to Bosnia, Kosovo and Albania.

Comprehensive – and with a conscience
Today, we are the world's largest independently owned travel publisher, with more than 200 titles. However, our ethos remains unchanged. Hilary is still keenly involved, and **we still get there first**: two-thirds of Bradt guides have no direct competition.

But we don't just get there first. Our guides are also known for being **more comprehensive** than any other series. We avoid templates and tick-lists. Each guide is a one-of-a-kind expression of an expert author's interests, knowledge and enthusiasm for telling it how it really is.

And a commitment to wildlife, conservation and respect for local communities has always been at the heart of our books. Bradt Guides was **championing sustainable travel** before any other guidebook publisher. We even have a series dedicated to Slow Travel in the UK, award-winning books that explore the country with a passion and depth you'll find nowhere else.

Thank you!
We can only do what we do because of the support of readers like you – people who value less-obvious experiences, less-visited places and a more thoughtful approach to travel. Those who, like us, take travel seriously.

Bradt GUIDES
TRAVEL TAKEN SERIOUSLY